STARMAKER

STARMAKER

David O. Selznick and the Production of Stars
in the Hollywood Studio System

Milan Hain

University Press of Mississippi / Jackson

The University Press of Mississippi is the scholarly publishing agency of the Mississippi Institutions of Higher Learning: Alcorn State University, Delta State University, Jackson State University, Mississippi State University, Mississippi University for Women, Mississippi Valley State University, University of Mississippi, and University of Southern Mississippi.

www.upress.state.ms.us

The University Press of Mississippi is a member of the Association of University Presses.

Research for this book was funded by a grant of the Czech Science Foundation (GA ČR), reg. no. 17-06451S, "Starmaker: David O. Selznick and the Hollywood Star System, 1935–1957."

Copyright © 2023 by Milan Hain
Translation © 2023 David Livingstone and Milan Hain
All rights reserved
Manufactured in the United States of America

First printing 2023

∞

Library of Congress Control Number: 2023008563
Hardback ISBN 1-4968-4605-1
Epub single ISBN 1-4968-4606-8
Epub institutional ISBN 1-4968-4607-5
PDF single ISBN 1-4968-4608-2
PDF institutional ISBN 1-4968-4609-9

British Library Cataloging-in-Publication Data available

CONTENTS

Acknowledgments vii

Prologue: *A Star Is Born* as the Quintessential Hollywood Myth ix

Introduction 3

1. The Construction of Naturalness: Ingrid Bergman and
   Intermezzo: A Love Story 19

2. Producing Prestige: Loan-Outs of Selznick's Female Stars
   in the First Half of the 1940s 51

3. While They Were Fighting: The Development of Male Stars
   during World War II 82

4. From Model Teenager to Teenage Mother: Shirley Temple
   as Selznick's Contract Star in the 1940s 112

5. Selznick (Goes) International: Selznick's Studio and
   International Stars after 1945 139

6. The Most Faithful of Them All: Jennifer Jones after
   The Song of Bernadette 166

Conclusion. The Selznick Brand: In the Tradition of
   Quality and Prestige 193

Appendix: Selznick's Star Stable in Numbers 209

Archive Collections Used 221

Notes 223

Bibliography 269

Index 279

ACKNOWLEDGMENTS

The origins of the project about David O. Selznick and his stars date back to January 2015 when I became a recipient of the Harry Ransom Center Fellowship and spent one month doing research in that wonderful facility in Austin, Texas. At that point I had no idea that a modest article about the US careers of Ingrid Bergman and Alida Valli would transform into a much more extensive and ambitious project detailing the star-making activities of one of classical Hollywood's luminaries. I am indebted to the Harry Ransom Center for this initial impulse and for providing me with first-rate service during my repeated visits (it was inevitable that I would return). Deservedly, it is one of the most respected archival institutions in the world. Specifically, I want to thank the film curator Steve Wilson, who helped me to navigate the vast and labyrinthine Selznick Collection; Bridget Gayle Ground, who administered my first stay in Austin more than eight years ago; and the ever-obliging and friendly staff of the HRC's reading room, especially Michael Gilmore and Kathryn Millan.

Other institutions and individuals were fundamental in bringing this book into existence. I was awarded a generous grant by The Czech Science Foundation (GA ČR) for the three-year period commencing in January 2017 that allowed me to fully focus on my research and preparation of the manuscript. I also highly value the research stipend that I received from the Bill Douglas Cinema Museum in Exeter, UK. In December 2018, I spent ten days looking through additional materials that significantly enriched my knowledge of Selznick's operations. I thank the museum curator Phil Wickham for his help and assistance. Other institutions that provided crucial materials for this book include the Margaret Herrick Library of the Academy of Motion Picture Arts and Sciences in Los Angeles; the Cinema Archives of Wesleyan University in Middletown, Connecticut; the Wisconsin Center for Film and Theater Research in Madison, Wisconsin; the Theatre and Performance Archive at the Victoria and Albert Museum; and the Reuben Library of the British Film Institute, the latter two located in London. For the permission to use selected reproductions from the Selznick Collection at the HRC, I extend my thanks to the producer's son, Daniel Selznick. I am also grateful to the staff of UCLA's Film and Television Archive for allowing me to watch Selznick's TV special *Light's Diamond Jubilee*, which seemed otherwise utterly unavailable. And, finally, I am certainly not the first nor the last person to acknowledge the activities of Eric Hoyt and his team at the Media History Digital Library. What would we do without it?

The conception of the book and its individual chapters benefited from my conversations with numerous colleagues and peers. Some of them may not even realize it but the opportunity to discuss Selznick and his stars meant a lot to me. Above all, I must express my gratitude to Jeanine Basinger, Helen Hanson, Thomas Schatz and, most importantly, Peter Krämer. I am also indebted to Jeanine Basinger for making it possible for me to access the holdings of Wesleyan University's Cinema Archives outside standard opening hours.

My project found essential support at my home Department of Theater and Film Studies at Palacký University in Olomouc. I thank the former Chair Jakub Korda for his generosity and for encouraging me at a crucial stage of the writing process by granting me a sabbatical leave to complete the manuscript. Students Kateřina Hejdučková, Eliška Charvátová, Anna Paulína Jelínková, Anna Kořenková, Jana Marková, Aneta Němcová, Eliška Sedláčková, and Lucie Zelená assisted me in locating and categorizing articles from trade journals. I also thank David Livingstone for translating a large part of the manuscript to English, and Václav Žák and Šárka Gmiterková for their insightful comments and words of encouragement. Martha Campbell and Larry and Susan Gilg were superb hosts during my two lengthy visits to Austin. Thank you for your hospitality.

I am very grateful that my book has found such an excellent publisher as the University Press of Mississippi. I am especially indebted to acquisitions editor Emily Bandy, who was very helpful throughout the book's development. I also thank the two anonymous reviewers for their encouraging responses as well as many useful comments that helped to improve the text substantially.

The largest amount of thanks, however, must go to my wife Ksenia, who was with me during the whole process of the book's development—not as a passive onlooker, but as a crucial collaborator. She assisted me during my research trips and visits to archives, spent numerous hours watching dozens of films of uneven quality, shared ideas and patiently provided feedback to every chapter. (As Robert Mapplethorpe used to say to Patti Smith: "Nothing is finished until *you* see it.") Her psychological and emotional support was also indispensable. With love and gratitude, I dedicate this book to her and to our other joint creations (obviously far more perfect than this text), sons Sebastian (born 2018) and Maxmilian (born 2020).

PROLOGUE

A *Star Is Born* as the Quintessential Hollywood Myth

Not all the stars of the screen crash into the headlines. Not all personalities most scintillating in the film world appear in major type in the programme. Among the credit titles, often inconspicuously placed, are names most vital to moving pictures. I refer, of course, to the producer. [...] It is not too much to compare these men [sic] to the suns of the film industry for, without their energy, it would cool and become moribund, and from the flame of their enthusiasm stars are born. [...] Stars are a necessity in the film firmament, but the suns, however few, have their place also.

—FROM AN ARTICLE ABOUT DAVID O. SELZNICK
IN THE MAGAZINE *PICTUREGOER*[1]

Those who employ the star will scarcely make an appearance. By diminishing the presence of audiences and owners, stars are made to seem more independent than they ever could be in real life.

—JIB FOWLES[2]

In 1937, *A Star Is Born*, now a Hollywood classic from independent producer David O. Selznick, premiered in US cinemas. The film tells the story of a young woman, Esther Victoria Blodgett (Janet Gaynor), who decides to leave her family farm in North Dakota to try her luck in Hollywood. After several rejections, she accidentally makes the acquaintance of the popular actor Norman Maine (Fredric March), who is enthralled by her and helps her get a screen test in the studio of the renowned producer Oliver Niles (Adolphe Menjou). Although she does not have any acting experience, she makes an impression due to her naturalness and directness and ends up receiving the desired contract. Everything goes incredibly smoothly from that point on: Norman's intervention ensures her a role in a film which receives a great deal of attention, she is embraced by the public, and, under the new name Vicki Lester, becomes an overnight sensation. Her rapid rise to stardom is crowned by being awarded an Oscar, the highest honor which an actor or actress can receive.

IX

Adolphe Menjou, Janet Gaynor, and Fredric March in a publicity still for *A Star Is Born*.

A Star Is Born represented an extremely personal undertaking for the thirty-five-year-old Selznick. He was the one who came up with the initial idea and consequently became involved in the writing of the screenplay, which shared a number of similarities with his earlier back-studio picture,[3] *What Price Hollywood?* (1932), produced during his time at RKO.[4] When Robert Carson and William Wellman (also the director of the film) received the Academy Award for Best Original Story in March 1938, the latter reportedly leaned over to Selznick and said: "You ought to get this—you wrote more of it than I did."[5] In a letter to his close associate Daniel (Dan) O'Shea, the producer did not hide the fact that he considered himself the main creative figure behind the film. "*A Star Is Born* is much more my story than Wellman's or Carson's. I refused to take credit on it simply as a matter of policy. [. . .] The actual original idea, the story line, and the vast majority of the story ideas of the scenes themselves are my own," he claimed when principal photography on the film ended in January 1937.[6] Selznick's influence is apparent, amongst other things, in the conception of the character of Oliver Niles,[7] the level-headed and sensitive head of the studio (extremely distant from the stereotype of the uneducated and loud tyrant), who holds a protective hand over his employees.

The picture was conceived by Selznick as a "true story of Hollywood." According to the official press release, it was supposed to "tell of the heartbreak as well as the happiness, the cruelty as well as the glamor, the bitter struggle as well as the radiant success. It should peer behind the scenes, probe deeply into the heart of the city."[8] The trailer for the film similarly prepared the moviegoers for the fact that this was not a typical "Cinderella story or a glorification of motion pictures."[9] The producer himself wrote that "ninety-five percent of the dialogue [. . .] was actually straight out of life and was straight 'reportage' so to speak."[10]

As with its predecessor *What Price Hollywood?*, *A Star Is Born* draws attention to the dark(er) side of the film industry, particularly by means of the male character: Norman Maine descends into dependence on alcohol, loses the support of his colleagues and the public, realizes that he has become a burden for those around him, and finally ends up committing suicide.[11] The trajectory of Maine's unstoppable professional and personal downfall (brought about more by a tendency for self-destruction than by the surrounding circumstances) is balanced in the structure of the picture by the rocket-like rise of his "discovery" and later life partner, Esther. Here the creators could also claim a certain level of authenticity that had been quite rare in previous films from the Hollywood environment. Several scenes, for example, reveal the process behind the development of stars: Esther receives the more acceptable artistic name Vicki Lester; we observe how the studio prepares her considerably embellished biography; she attends lessons in diction and posture; she sits through make-up sessions where veteran make-up artists experiment with the shape and placement of her eyebrows; and her contact with the public is mediated by the cold-blooded PR specialist Libby (Lionel Stander). Most of these episodes are, however, played for comic effect: the above-mentioned mechanisms are presented as absurd excesses, not as standard Hollywood practices that the audience should take seriously. The individual has to initially endure this, only to finally realize that his or her own "natural" persona is the most attractive. The role of the studio is therefore trivialized and marginalized; its heavy-handed mechanisms do not lead anywhere and instead represent more of an obstacle preventing a meaningful and genuine relationship between the actress and the public.[12] After all, even Oliver Niles recognizes that it is best to leave Esther unchanged, for "tastes are going back to the natural."

Despite its occasional glimpses behind the scenes, *A Star Is Born* tends to perpetuate rather than reject the individualist myth whereby basically anyone with charisma and a touch of talent can become a success if they remain honest and dedicated. According to Steven Cohan, while the film—in its promotional materials as well as several scenes—promises to demystify the film industry practices, it ends up reinforcing the mythical dimension of Hollywood as a place of make-believe and wish fulfillment.[13] It is enough for Esther to just be herself and wait patiently for the opportunity that will allow her "to be discovered." At one point, she is told by a casting clerk that only one aspirant out of a hundred thousand succeeds in Hollywood, but not even this mathematically negligible probability discourages her: on the contrary, she dreamily announces immediately after that that she might be the chosen one. As Richard Maltby states in his analysis, "at the same time as the movie announces that stardom is an impossible dream, it also asserts that any audience member with Esther's dedication can become a star."[14] Once she receives a contract at Niles's studio, everything proceeds seamlessly. A screen test is followed by a role in a movie and afterwards fame seems inevitable. The film leaves no one in doubt that Esther's eventual success is entirely due to her doing (and a stroke of good luck). The skills, expertise, and labor of dozens of film professionals, who usually contribute to the development of stars, are pushed aside and replaced by Esther's perseverance and good fortune at being at the right place at the right time.[15]

Selznick's film attempts to convince us that stars were born naturally and with ease in the Hollywood studio era; that they were wholly autonomous beings who could succeed due to their inherent qualities and despite the impersonal, business-like nature of the industry. The producer's own career, however, clearly demonstrates that stars were actually systematically created or manufactured: they were subject to sophisticated, long-refined industrial mechanisms, which could transform unknown individuals into attractive commodities designated for public consumption—whether they took the form of ethereal goddesses, hyper-masculine heroes, or more down-to-earth types with whom the audience could identify. In this book, I focus on this often-hidden process in the development and establishment of film stars and, particularly, on the way it was practiced by David O. Selznick—paradoxically, one of the Hollywood filmmakers most responsible for disseminating the misleading (but dramatically effective and widely appealing) individualist myth.

STARMAKER

INTRODUCTION

He was full of talents which were never fully recognized—much more than merely the
man who supervised productions of his films. [...] casting directors admit he was among
the best of them. [...] Publicity directors admit he was a genius in their field.
—MARCELLA RABWIN, LONG-TIME SECRETARY TO DAVID O. SELZNICK[1]

My function is to be responsible for everything.
—DAVID O. SELZNICK[2]

SELZNICK'S STAR STABLE

When Selznick was sixty years old and his career was definitively at an end, *Life* magazine contemplated publishing his profile which would recapitulate his numerous successes. A list of the film stars who the producer helped achieve fame was prepared upon this occasion. The four-page document contained twenty-three names in all, always supplemented by a short commentary. Specifically these consisted of the following individuals (in the order in which they appear in the document): Ingrid Bergman, Vivien Leigh, Joan Fontaine, Jennifer Jones, Dorothy McGuire, Gregory Peck, Joseph Cotten, Susan Hayward, Katharine Hepburn, Fred Astaire, Freddie Bartholomew, Tommy Kelly, William Powell, Kay Francis, Jean Arthur, Mickey Rooney, Louis Jourdan, Alida Valli, Rossano Brazzi, King Kong ("an animated star" for the film of the same name produced by Selznick, created by Merian C. Cooper in cooperation with the animation artist Willis O'Brien), Shirley Temple, Guy Madison, and Janet Gaynor.[3] Some of Selznick's discoveries dated to the time when he held management positions at Paramount (Jean Arthur, William Powell, Kay Francis), RKO (Fred Astaire, Katharine Hepburn), and MGM (Mickey Rooney, Freddie Bartholomew) in the first half of the 1930s. Most of them, however, are from the following period, when he ran his own film studio—first under the name Selznick International Pictures and subsequently, after its liquidation in 1940, as David O. Selznick Productions and Vanguard Films. The *Life* article apparently was not published, but the list, one of many thousands of items in the archive of Selznick's studio, serves as evidence of an important area of the producer's activities.

Selznick undoubtedly ranks among the legendary figures of the Hollywood studio era and his production activities are relatively well mapped out: his life and career are the subject of an extensive biography by David Thomson;[4] a richly illustrated publication by Ronald Haver, *David O. Selznick's Hollywood*, provides a basic overview of his work and contains detailed production histories of his most important films;[5] Thomas Schatz chose the functioning of Selznick's independent production company as one of the case studies for his groundbreaking publication on classical Hollywood entitled *Genius of the System*;[6] Leonard J. Leff described in detail the producer's exciting, but complicated, cooperation with the director Alfred Hitchcock;[7] and equally essential is the selection of Selznick's memos assembled by Rudy Behlmer.[8] An entire range of book publications and magazine articles deals with more specific themes (out of the most recent titles the monograph by Nathan Platte on music in Selznick's films stands out)[9] and particular pictures. The literature discussing Selznick's monumental *Gone with the Wind* (1939) alone consists of hundreds of items.

Very few, however, have analyzed in detail Selznick's activities linked with the development of stars: usually the authors make brief mention of this, but do not further analyze or evaluate these operations. The only book on this theme—*The Selznick Players* by Ronald Bowers, published more than forty years ago[10]—consists of career summaries of Selznick's contract actors and actresses, without attempting to provide a more nuanced historical analysis based upon the study of archive materials. The target group for the book (fans of classical Hollywood without an academic background) is similar to that for the numerous memoirs and literary biographies which map out the lives and careers of these popular actors and actresses associated with Selznick's studio, in particular Ingrid Bergman, Gregory Peck, Vivien Leigh, Jennifer Jones, and Shirley Temple. In contrast, there are only a handful of scholarly texts on this topic: the exceptions include in particular a study by Leonard J. Leff focused on the postwar career of Guy Madison;[11] an analysis of the short Hollywood career of Alida Valli by Stephen Gundle;[12] texts by David Smit on the star image of Ingrid Bergman;[13] and chapters in the book by Gaylyn Studlar, *Precocious Charms*, dedicated to Shirley Temple and Jennifer Jones.[14] The above-mentioned texts are concerned with the industry mechanisms which Selznick and his colleagues used in order to establish these actors and actresses as popular personalities against heavy competition, even when this was not always their main subject of interest.

INTRODUCTION

The literature that would treat Selznick not only as a producer of films, but also as a producer of stars, is therefore limited. My intention is to at least partially rectify this situation and shift the focus of attention from frequently discussed films such as *Gone with the Wind* and *Rebecca* (1940) to popular star identities shaped and launched under Selznick's supervision. The development of stars and the trade with them were not, in my view, merely a supplementary activity to the production of films. On the contrary, it was a significant domain which brought Selznick's company both major profits and the attention of the press, the public, and important players in the industry.

To illustrate this point: as of October 1941, in addition to directors Alfred Hitchcock and Robert Stevenson, Selznick's studio had the actors Alan Marshal and Gene Kelly and the actresses Ingrid Bergman, Joan Fontaine, Vivien Leigh, Dorothy McGuire, Phylis Walker (soon after renamed Jennifer Jones), and Martha MacVicar (later known as Martha Vickers) under contract. The producer could use their services not only in his own films but—as was the case more and more often—he could also provide them to other studios. The net profit from the loan-outs of these contract persons from the period from June 1940 to June 1941 amounted to almost \$250,000 and the overall value of their contracts (with an average length of around five years) was close to one million.[15] This was all at a time when Kelly, McGuire, Walker, and MacVicar had not had their film debuts, and Bergman was still awaiting her breakthrough role which would make her into a leading Hollywood star.[16] Only a few years later, Selznick regularly collected \$150,000 or more for a single transaction involving actors and actresses such as Gregory Peck, Joseph Cotten, Jennifer Jones, Ingrid Bergman, Joan Fontaine, and Shirley Temple. This makes it apparent how profitable investment in stars could be. Apart from the fact that they represented valuable capital, these popular personalities also formed the public image of Selznick's company, which was always eager to be linked with them by means of careful coordination of advertising and publicity.

DAVID O. SELZNICK, PRODUCER OF FILMS AND STARS

The development of stars became the predominant area of Selznick's activity in the late 1930s and early 1940s. The producer already had more than twenty years of experience in film behind him with numerous successes, which helped him establish a stable reputation and gain the respect of his colleagues as well as numerous contacts, without which it would have been impossible to do business with stars. I offer the following historical overview of Selznick's involvement in Hollywood so as to contextualize the case studies which make up the main part of the book.[17]

6 INTRODUCTION

David Selznick (born May 10, 1902, in Pittsburgh) became involved in film at an early age: while still a teenager, he and his older brother Myron[18] helped their father, a Jewish immigrant of Russian origin named Lewis J. Selznick, who from 1912 ran his own production company in New York. The firm, however, was ill-equipped to survive in the heavy competition and went bankrupt after ten years of existence. David was able to strike out on his own and soon demonstrated both invention and business acumen when, with a minimum of resources, he produced the short film *Rudolph Valentino and His 88 American Beauties* (1923). Shrewdly, he took advantage of the long-term absence of the idol of the day Rudolph Valentino on the big screen as a result of a controversy with his employer, the Famous Players-Lasky studio. The profits for the film ended up exceeding multiple times the modest budget. After this early success, Selznick, still in his early twenties, moved to California where he obtained a position in the screenwriting department at MGM. Although he made a name for himself and was appointed assistant to the producer Harry Rapf after several months, a conflict with other powerful men in the studio, Hunt Stromberg and Irving Thalberg, cost him his position. In January 1928, he began to work at Paramount as the assistant to the head of production B. P. Schulberg. He was responsible for the reorganization of the screenwriting department and made the acquaintance of the directors John Cromwell, William Wellman, and George Cukor. During Schulberg's half-year absence, he supervised the production of several dozen titles including a film dealing with gamblers, *Street of Chance* (1930), which he considered the first project he personally cared about.[19] The picture, directed by Cromwell, helped make William Powell into a leading Hollywood star. Jean Arthur and Kay Francis appeared in minor roles, and their careers also took an upward turn during Selznick's time at Paramount. Despite numerous hits, the studio was significantly impacted by the Wall Street crash and the subsequent economic depression. When Selznick was asked to accept a major cut in his salary in the middle of 1931, he announced his resignation.

His experience of working for two large Hollywood studios motivated him to establish his own company, which would focus on the production of a smaller number of carefully chosen titles, made under the producer's close supervision, as opposed to several dozen films churned out, factory-like, by the majors. The first attempt, for which he invited the directors and close friends Merian C. Cooper and Lewis Milestone, did not work out, however: simply put, Selznick did not obtain the capital necessary for such an endeavor. In October 1931, he therefore assumed the position of vice president in charge of production at the recently established RKO studio. Over the following fifteen months, he supervised the productions of the bold romantic drama *Bird of Paradise*, an adaptation of a popular play by Clemence Dane, *A Bill of Divorcement* (both 1932), and *King Kong* (1933), an adventure film involving revolution-

INTRODUCTION

ary special effects. He also authorized screen tests for both Fred Astaire and Katharine Hepburn, who soon became the main commercial draws for the studio (Hepburn debuted under the directorship of George Cukor in *A Bill of Divorcement*, Fred Astaire appeared for the first time in the small role of a dancer in the MGM film *Dancing Lady* [1933], which Selznick himself chose for him after his departure from RKO). Despite the commercial successes of a range of titles which Selznick greenlighted, and the cost-cutting measures which he introduced after assuming the position, RKO experienced difficulties coming to terms with the consequences of the Depression. In addition, the studio changed its management which led to limiting the producer's authority. At the beginning of 1933, Selznick made use of an offer from his father-in-law Louis B. Mayer and returned to MGM which provided him with his own production unit. In order to prevent accusations of nepotism, he invested a great deal of energy into ensuring that his first film would be a definite triumph. The all-star *Dinner at Eight* (1933) cost the studio $400,000, made $3 million, and brought Selznick the longed-for respect of his industry peers. This was followed by popular and critically successful titles such as the biopic *Viva Villa!* with Wallace Beery, *Manhattan Melodrama* (both 1934), starring William Powell and Clark Gable, and high-budget, brilliantly crafted adaptations of popular literary classics, including *Anna Karenina, David Copperfield*, and *A Tale of Two Cities* (all 1935).

Over the course of 1935, Selznick once and for all decided to abandon the ranks of Hollywood majors and resigned from his post at MGM. Thanks to the generous investment of the millionaire and film magnate John Hay Whitney[20] and smaller amounts from his brother Myron and the Thalbergs (Irving, with whom he made peace after erstwhile conflicts at MGM, and his wife Norma Shearer), he established his own independent production company, Selznick International Pictures, through which he wanted to finally translate into practice his long-contemplated philosophy, according to which "great films, successful films, are made in their every detail according to the vision of one man."[21] In his well-equipped studio in Culver City—only a few blocks from MGM—he wanted to restore the luster of the family name and produce "artistic pictures that are commercial successes."[22] From the very beginning, Selznick focused on a small number of films which met the highest standards, from the meticulous literary preparation to the carefully chosen cast up to the tasteful but effective promotion. In order to do this, he depended on a close circle of colleagues, to whom he delegated important duties (without, however, losing the right of the final word); these included his secretary and later vice president of Selznick International, Daniel O'Shea; Katharine "Kay" Brown, head of the New York office until 1942, who was responsible for seeking out new talent and suitable literary material; the head of the marketing department Russell Birdwell; the

Poster for Selznick's all-star production of *Dinner at Eight*.

production manager Ray Klune; and Val Lewton, who ran the screenwriting department. As Rudy Behlmer commented, "Selznick's idea of collaboration was to hire first-rate talent, extract certain attributes from that talent, and mold them to suit his vision."[23]

The first film in the company's portfolio became the adaptation of the children's classic by Frances Hodgson Burnett, *Little Lord Fauntleroy* (1936), with Freddie Bartholomew (fresh from the success of *David Copperfield*) in the main role. This was followed by the Technicolor romance *The Garden of Allah* (1936), with Marlene Dietrich and Charles Boyer; *A Star Is Born* with Janet Gaynor and Fredric March; another adaptation of a literary classic, *The Prisoner of Zenda*, with Ronald Colman; the screwball comedy *Nothing Sacred* (all 1937), with Fredric March and Carole Lombard; the adaptation of Mark Twain's classic *The Adventures of Tom Sawyer*; the comedy *The Young in Heart* (both 1938), with the appealing trio Janet Gaynor, Paulette Goddard, and Douglas Fairbanks Jr.; and the romantic drama *Made for Each Other* (1939), with Carole Lombard and James Stewart. In all of these films, with the exception of *The Adventures of Tom Sawyer*, where the leading actor Tommy Kelly was chosen on the basis of a nationwide talent search, freelance actors and actresses or, less frequently, those loaned out from other studios were used. In the early years of his company's existence, Selznick did not manifest great interest in the development of new stars and instead depended on already established individuals, who had the potential to increase interest of moviegoers in his productions. Emily Carman aptly described the symbiotic relationship that could develop between freelance stars such as Janet Gaynor, Carole Lombard, Fredric March, and Ronald Colman and independent producers headed by Selznick: "Stars could broker a lucrative salary for one film at a time, bargain for more creative discretion over their performance, and/or participate in the film's box-office gross in what was referred to as a 'percentage deal.' Likewise, independent producers did not maintain a large star roster of contract talent (as the major studios did) because they made only a few films per year."[24] This approach suited Selznick for a while, but starting in 1939, he shifted to a different model, which involved engaging unknown or lesser known faces, whose (presumed) success would make them valuable commodities that could be utilized in his own productions or in loan-outs to other producers.[25]

The first star whom Selznick employed, developed and introduced in his own film was Ingrid Bergman. Her debut in the romantic drama *Intermezzo: A Love Story* (1939) was followed by a series of loan-outs, which made her over a period of several years into one of the most sought out actresses in Hollywood. Selznick made other exciting discoveries in the late 1930s and early 1940s. Vivien Leigh, brought over from England, became an instant star when Selznick gave her the much sought-after role in the spectacular adaptation of Margaret Mitchell's epic novel *Gone with the Wind*, which was in the making for more than three years. Similarly, a single role—that of the unnamed young bride in *Rebecca*—was enough to make the formerly inconspicuous Joan Fontaine into a leading Hollywood lady. Selznick's star stable grew over the following years with the additions of Joseph Cotten, Gregory Peck, Jennifer Jones, Dorothy McGuire, and Shirley Temple. It was precisely the trade with stars that became the main area of his activity after 1940, when he was already functioning under the umbrella of the new company, David O. Selznick Productions (the original company was liquidated for tax purposes—after the colossal commercial success of *Gone with the Wind*, Selznick had the opportunity to make considerable profits and avoid massive taxation). With some simplification, it can be argued that the producer made use of the symbolic capital created thanks to the high-profile films from the end of the 1930s to set off on a career of producing different—yet related—products: stars. Actors and actresses signed contracts with him with the hope of illustrious careers, while he profited from the cooperation with them in both financial and symbolic terms.

Star business was also advantageous in that it meant he no longer had to bother with the stress related to the preparation of demanding film projects. After the physically and mentally exhausting experience with *Gone with the Wind* and *Rebecca*, Selznick planned a production hiatus and handed over several planned titles, including *Claudia, The Keys of the Kingdom*, and *Jane Eyre*, to Twentieth Century-Fox. Instead, he watched over the careers of his contract stars and negotiated lucrative projects for them at other studios. He only returned to active production with the patriotic family drama about the home front *Since You Went Away* (1944), in which he combined a selection of his own stars (Jones, Cotten, Temple) with other popular figures (Claudette Colbert, Robert Walker, Monty Woolley). Selznick depended on his own supply of talent for additional projects which came about under his close supervision: Ingrid Bergman and Gregory Peck were cast as the main characters in *Spellbound* (1945), one of the three films that Alfred Hitchcock directed for the producer (the fourth, *Notorious* [1946] also with Bergman, was completed by Hitchcock at RKO); and *Duel in the Sun* (1946), a megalomaniac Western in lush Technicolor, combined Jennifer Jones with Gregory Peck and Joseph Cotten.

Over the ten-year period in the position of an independent producer, Selznick met with numerous successes: most of his films became hits with the audiences with revenues in the millions of dollars;[26] *Gone with the Wind* and *Rebecca* won back-to-back Oscars for the best film of the year; and high income and the equally important symbolic validation in the form of various awards were also generated by the contract actors and actresses (Vivien Leigh, Joan Fontaine, Jennifer Jones, and Ingrid Bergman were each awarded Oscars over

INTRODUCTION

the years 1940 to 1945). Selznick managed to create a strong and respected brand based on a consistent fulfillment of highest artistic and industry standards.

All of that changed after World War II. The gradual decline of the company had a number of mutually linked causes. The crisis within the entire industry contributed to this. After the record year 1946, audience attendance declined rapidly. Another serious blow was the 1948 decision by the Supreme Court, which, after many years of investigation, reached a verdict that the Hollywood studios had been guilty of violating US antitrust laws. This led to a massive reorganization of the industry. The decision seemingly only concerned the vertically integrated majors, such as MGM, Paramount, and Warner Bros., but it soon became apparent that it also severely impacted other players who were dependent on large production and distribution companies. The whole industry was, in fact, a tightly woven microcosm.

The main reasons for the postwar decline were, however, of an internal nature. Firstly, Selznick's company, which employed dozens of people and oversaw large production facilities, consistently behaved in a wasteful way and the much-needed reorganization had been postponed repeatedly. Above all, overhead costs were extremely high and did not result in a corresponding productivity. After the war, Selznick produced one film per year maximum and although he tried to increase the volume of his production in various ways, he failed over the long-term. Dore Schary, hired back in November 1943 to produce several A-list films with a medium budget each year for Selznick's subsidiary company Vanguard Films, soon departed upon receiving an attractive offer from RKO. During his time at Vanguard, he managed to complete the successful drama *I'll Be Seeing You* (1944), with Ginger Rogers and Joseph Cotten in the main roles, but other films (*The Spiral Staircase* [1945], *Till the End of Time* [1946], *The Farmer's Daughter, The Bachelor and the Bobby-Soxer* [both 1947]) were finished at his new "home," where he became the head of production after the death of Charles Koerner.[27] The planned cooperation with Mark Hellinger and M. J. Siegel bore no fruits at all as both producers suddenly died (Hellinger in December 1947, Siegel in August 1948). As if this was not enough, in late 1946, Selznick established his own distribution company, Selznick Releasing Corporation (SRO), as a result of long-standing disagreements with his distributor United Artists over handling of his films. It worked at first: according to Thomas Schatz the move "enabled Selznick to cut his distribution costs by some 60 percent."[28] In time, however, the company became more of a burden than a competitive advantage without the ongoing supply of films. In January 1949, the *New York Times* announced that SRO will close "most of its branch offices in the United States, temporarily and perhaps permanently."[29]

While the lavish *Duel in the Sun* was a success with audiences (although not a particularly convincing one in light of the high costs), two other titles from Selznick's production company failed commercially: the star-laden *The Paradine Case* (1947) became the weakest result of the seven years of the professional alliance with Alfred Hitchcock, and *Portrait of Jennie* (1948) was an even more extravagant failure on Selznick's part, transforming a modest-sized romance into a costly fiasco (the long filming period, complicated postproduction, and the final spectacular sequence filmed in the revolutionary format Cyclorama all contributed to the $4 million loss). All this resulted in a debt of $12 million at the end of the 1940s. Selznick refused, however, to declare bankruptcy as his father had a quarter century earlier and instead began to sell projects under development and negotiate the exhibition of his older films abroad and on television, a medium which experienced a rapid rise after the war.[30] He also drew up co-production agreements with the British producer Alexander Korda and the Italian director Vittorio De Sica, although the only successful title was *The Third Man* (1949), directed by Carol Reed. Selznick astutely predicted the potential of foreign markets, but a success was hampered by his high demands, aggressive business character, and decreasing ability to delegate responsibilities to others.[31]

Not even in the field of star development was Selznick as effective as he had been in the early 1940s. Despite extensive efforts, he was unable to negotiate the renewal of contracts with Ingrid Bergman, Joan Fontaine, Dorothy McGuire, and Gregory Peck, and the new faces—Guy Madison, Rory Calhoun, Alida Valli, and Louis Jourdan—were unable to adequately replace them. In most cases, these failures were deeply rooted in the past: in 1942, Selznick's reliable talent scout Kay Brown, responsible for the discoveries of Bergman, McGuire, and Peck, left the company, and frequent changes in the key positions at the talent and advertising departments disrupted any attempts at forming consistent long-term strategies. Additionally, fewer and fewer films were made after 1945, while the costs for maintaining an ongoing stable of actors grew continuously.[32] As the company's debts increased, Selznick sought out the best ways to make money off of his stars, but this did not coincide often with his earlier careful implementation of the motto "in the tradition of quality."[33] While in the first half of the decade, the short-term and long-term goals of the studio were in harmony, a discrepancy began to gradually appear between them: Selznick, weighed down by financial difficulties and paralyzed by ever-present paperwork, began to have a preference for quick and easy profits at the expense of a carefully built-up company brand, and the business aspects of his activities were privileged over the creative ones. His actors and actresses, by way of loan-outs, repeatedly appeared in inferior pictures, which damaged their position in the market and decreased their economic and symbolic value.

Selznick finally met all his financial commitments, but it cost him a great deal of effort and his reputation. He decided on a final large project in the mid-

INTRODUCTION

1950s. The adaptation of Ernest Hemingway's war novel *A Farewell to Arms* (1957) was financed by Twentieth Century-Fox and starred Rock Hudson and Jennifer Jones, the latter being the only contract player who remained loyal to him (not surprisingly, since she had been married to him since 1949). As had become a custom, the making of the film was plagued by a number of disagreements between Selznick and both directors, John Huston and his successor, Charles Vidor. This might have also been one of the reasons why the picture ended in disappointment. The failure of *A Farewell to Arms* finally confirmed that Selznick's sensibility was largely incompatible with the industry trends of the postwar period.[34]

Despite the inglorious conclusion to his rich career, there can be no doubt that David O. Selznick was one of the formative personalities of the Hollywood studio era: as Thomas Schatz stated, as a filmmaker he was "both utterly unique and profoundly symptomatic" for this specific period.[35] He was a visionary who combined, perhaps better than anyone else prior to him or since, the creative, managerial, and business aspects of the film industry. My book attempts to demonstrate that this delicate balance was behind not only the production of his films, but also his treatment of stars.

FROM STARS TO THEIR MANUFACTURER(S)

In my research on Selznick and his star stable, I take a methodological cue from film scholar Paul McDonald, who views stars primarily as a phenomenon of production as opposed to a phenomenon of consumption.[36] This makes it possible to shift the interest from stars (as signifying systems, emblems of the time, social representations, or wholly autonomous individuals) to their producers.[37] A more thorough examination of the studio mechanisms and the input of individual agents (in the most general meaning of the term) is complicated, however, by the scarcity of the relevant materials which this kind of research necessarily depends upon. As Emily Carman reminds us, of the Big Five studios of the classical Hollywood era, only the corporate archive of Warner Bros. (currently under the administration of the University of Southern California in Los Angeles) is open to researchers.[38] Fortunately, in the case of David O. Selznick, there is no need to worry. The extensive archive of his company, documenting all the imaginable aspects of its activities, is available as part of the collection in the Harry Ransom Center in Austin, Texas. A project of this focus would have been unthinkable without access to these archive materials.

The aim of my book is to uncover the mechanisms which David O. Selznick and his colleagues used to discover, develop, and launch stars in the period from the late 1930s through the mid-1950s. As argued by Jeanine Basinger, a look back far into the past brings with it one major difficulty: in the beginnings of Ingrid Bergman, Jennifer Jones, or Gregory Peck, we often see "ready-made" stars and it is therefore extremely difficult to disengage from the knowledge of their later successful careers and the cumulative effect of their star images made up of dozens of roles, public appearances, etc.[39] By means of a wide range of period sources, I reconstruct the starting point, when it was not at all certain if the given individual would succeed, and describe the decision-making process of Selznick and his colleagues and their interaction with other important players in the US film industry. My text is therefore, among other things, an attempt at expanding the scope of academic star studies which has up until now only rarely looked at producers of stars and has instead focused on stars themselves or their audiences.[40]

I understand the production of stars as an organized, collective process, similar to the production of films, characterized by a division of labor: it involved the shared efforts and expertise of a number of individuals. In this case, however, there was one man, David O. Selznick, at the top of the hierarchy with the final authority in all important matters. He was the one who defined the goals of the company, delegated tasks to others (in accordance with their specializations), supervised their actions, and carried out the most important business and creative decisions. On the general level, I view Selznick as a rationally thinking agent who moved between various fields of activity and whose actions were both enabled and limited by the institutional base, the industry powers and processes, etc.[41] In this book, I argue that Selznick's decisions were motivated by an attempt to secure both economic and symbolic capital: he acted in order to ensure that his contract players were surrounded by attractive star identities, which would provide him with financial rewards (in the form of film revenues or profits from loan-outs) and enhance the good name of his organization inside the industry as well as in the eyes of the public. I specifically view the two-way transfer of symbolic capital into economic capital and back as the key to understanding his activities.[42]

From the outside, Selznick's company resembled the large Hollywood studios: it copied their organizational structure (although on a smaller scale) and was involved in production of films for the mass public with the aim of making a profit. Its position was, however, in many ways unique, and arguably, a fitting comparison in the historical context of the 1930s and 1940s can only be made with the company run by another Hollywood independent, Samuel Goldwyn. Selznick placed an emphasis on prestige and exclusivity and introduced a personal approach not only when producing films, but also in terms of managing his acting stable. Based on recommendations from his talent scouts, he chose candidates for stardom; decided who to sign a contract with; and controlled and molded the star identity of his actors and actresses

INTRODUCTION 15

in terms of what films they were cast in and what information was allowed to circulate. These behind-the-scenes negotiations, depending to the same extent on both official channels and informal contacts and ties,[43] remained mostly hidden from public view for success depended to a certain level on whether the public believed in the authenticity and autonomous nature of the stars they met on the big screen and in the pages of fan magazines. Selznick's role was not supposed to be completely invisible, but he was to be presented as more of a discoverer and mentor, gifted with an almost magical ability to recognize beauty and talent, as opposed to a greedy businessman and slick manipulator.

His control was not, of course, absolute. The producer frequently met with resistance from his actors and actresses, who tried to push forward their own notions concerning the direction of their careers, which were not necessarily in accordance with the business intentions of their employer. The entire process additionally depended on acceptance of the public, which ultimately decided, by means of their consumption behavior, success and failure. This reminds us that the film industry is essentially unpredictable as it depends on sudden changes and swings in taste and demand.[44] A system did exist, however, whose main aim was to minimize the risk of failure. Stars were specifically one of the most tested and proven means of economic control over the film industry and stabilization of audience interest. Speaking of stars as industrial products may seem inappropriate as people of flesh and blood are behind them. Hollywood was (and still is), however, an industry, and business with stars was a routine matter. This could take the direct form of loan-outs, which made possible the exchange of the actor's services for money, or it involved an indirect transaction when stars represented key elements of films used in advertising to gain an advantage in the market. Moviegoers could not purchase a given star, but their presence could convince the public to spend their money on a particular picture.[45] Using Selznick's example, my book should serve to demystify Hollywood stardom and present it as a result of complex industry strategies.

I finally attempt to bring more nuance into the understanding of business operations of David O. Selznick, who is too frequently described in popular as well as scholarly discourse as a disorganized meddler, an interfering autocrat or a cold-blooded businessman. Although encouraged to do so during his lifetime, Selznick did not publish his autobiography, and the books by Ronald Haver, Rudy Behlmer, and Thomas Schatz did not have such a resonance as the best-selling memoirs of Ingrid Bergman or Joan Fontaine,[46] which became the basis of several widely read biographies and frequently shown documentary films. Consequently, Selznick is often described as a "flesh peddler" in terms of his relations with his stars: greedy, merciless, arrogant, and often even chaotic and silly. Bergman, Fontaine, and other stars had legitimate reasons to disagree with their employer: being autonomous human beings in real life, they had their own longings and needs and often disputed Selznick's choice of roles for them or the distribution of profits from loan-outs. One should, however, realize two things: a) Hollywood was a place of constant negotiations, and quarrels and conflicts between employees and employers were a daily matter;[47] and b) information in the press and later accounts were often distorted to the advantage of the stars who could rely on the support and sympathy of representatives of the press and the wider public. In reality, Selznick's stars did not have it all that bad: apart from audience popularity and artistic recognition, they also received generous financial compensation, which made them some of the best rewarded personalities in the US film industry. Ingrid Bergman earned, for example, $750,000 over the years 1939 to 1946 (that is more than $100,000 a year), and although she only played in eleven films, she ranked among the best paid actresses in Hollywood.[48] Moreover, very few take into account the fact that the development of stars was an extremely costly activity with an uncertain result: screen tests, customized costumes, jewels and accessories, acting lessons, portrait photography, legal services, the operations of the advertising and PR department—all of this necessitated considerable financial resources.[49]

Memoirs involve a further problem: as they rely on the subjective memory of an individual, inaccuracies and mistakes can occur when describing situations that took place a long time ago, often dozens of years in the past. To a lesser degree, this may also apply to biographies, especially if they rely on the method of oral history. My research therefore mainly depends on the archive materials from Selznick's company, which came about alongside the events described in them and which served internal purposes. Of particular interest are memos (or memoranda) by means of which Selznick instructed his employees. They fulfilled several functions for their author, which he himself explained as follows: "(1) They help clarify my thoughts. (2) They serve as part of the record. (3) They clarify my instructions to the members of the company so that there is no doubt as to what I want. (4) They are in some way a catharsis for my own emotions. I give vent to what I've been planning, thinking, feeling."[50] Selznick's memos are fascinating materials documenting the creative process behind the production of films and the development of stars. As these do not involve recollections—which are necessarily skewed and incomplete—but records emerging "in the here and now," one can, while acknowledging their limits,[51] view them as more accurate and authoritative sources of information. I also made use of other types of materials, including legal documents (for example, contracts), financial records, various kinds of correspondence (telegrams, letters), and materials from the advertising and PR department. To achieve greater balance, I have not only consulted the rich archive of Selznick's company at the Harry Ransom Center in Austin, but also additional collections in the US and elsewhere (the Margaret Herrick Library in Los Angeles; the Cinema Archives at Wesleyan University in Middletown; the Wisconsin Center for Film and Theater Research in Madison; the British Film Institute, and the Victoria and Albert Museum in London). Finally, I have also made use of articles from the period press, which, apart from covering news from the film industry, provided responses to films in the form of reviews and informed regularly about their box-office performance. This data can also serve as an indicator of the success or failure of Selznick's star operations, along with audience research (Selznick was an avid proponent of empirical audience research and closely collaborated with George Gallup)[52] or the volume of fan correspondence. Although I worked predominantly with the US press, I also occasionally include commentaries from foreign periodicals, especially from the UK, which was the most important export market for Hollywood films during this period.

Besides the introduction and conclusion, the book is divided into six chapters, which cover approximately twenty years from the late 1930s to the late 1950s. My goal was not to provide a comprehensive overview of Selznick's activities in the field of star business, but to instead capture the main features and trends using case studies. The chapters are arranged in chronological order, and their topics were chosen with regard to representativeness: I include both male and female stars and discuss individuals originally from the US as well as those imported from abroad. Certain chapters in the second half of the book also emphasize Selznick's failures, which were not all that rare in such an uncertain business as star development.[53]

The first chapter is focused on the circumstances of the hiring of Ingrid Bergman and her presentation to the US public in a remake of her earlier Swedish film *Intermezzo*. Up until that time, Selznick focused on, or cooperated with, established actors and actresses when it came to the activities of his production company—most frequently those who worked freelance, making use of his familial bond to brother Myron who as an influential talent agent represented some of them, including Carole Lombard.[54] However, in 1938 and 1939 he reevaluated this strategy and began to build his own stable of stars in order to obtain a stronger position in the market, which the case of Ingrid Bergman serves to document. *Intermezzo* came about as one of Selznick's independent productions, but over the course of time the production of films made up an increasingly smaller part of his activities. The second chapter is focused on the challenges and opportunities linked to the decrease in film production in the early 1940s. Using the examples of Bergman, Dorothy McGuire, and Jennifer Jones, I demonstrate the strategies which Selznick used in order to negotiate lucrative roles for his contract actresses in pictures of other producers, thereby significantly increasing their economic and symbolic value. The following chapter is dedicated to male stars, on whose development the producer systematically focused during WWII as a consequence of shortages in the market due to a mass departure of young Hollywood actors to the armed forces. Although Selznick was able to associate his name with the successful careers of Joseph Cotten and Gregory Peck, he continued to be mainly viewed as a manufacturer of female stars.

The discussion of the renewed career of Shirley Temple, who underwent a transformation from a child star into an adolescent idol under Selznick's supervision, follows in the fourth chapter. As I demonstrate, though, by the mid-1940s, her career was impacted by her turbulent personal life (engagement, marriage, motherhood, divorce), which completely overshadowed all attempts to establish her as a serious actress. This is followed by an analysis of Selznick's efforts to expand his star portfolio with actors and actresses originally from Europe and thus to make a more substantial mark on the international market. Alida Valli, Louis Jourdan, and others, however, failed to resonate as powerfully with the public as their predecessors had. Although Selznick understood well the potential of the postwar internationalization, he was unable to profit from it in an adequate manner. In the final chapter, I am concerned with his professional association with Jennifer Jones, who as the most loyal member of Selznick's stable and his wife from the late 1940s, became the embodiment of many of the values and qualities which he had put into effect in his development of stars. Using the examples of two projects from the 1950s, I also demonstrate why he was unable to build upon the remarkable successes of the previous decade. In the conclusion, I return once again to the period of Selznick's creative apex (at least in terms of the production of stars) and summarize the specific version of stardom that became an important part of Selznick's corporate brand.

THE CONSTRUCTION OF NATURALNESS

Ingrid Bergman and *Intermezzo: A Love Story*

> Clearly, the "natural" is as much a construction as the "glamorous," the difference being that
> the latter foregrounds the notion of construction where the former suppresses it.
> —ROBIN WOOD[1]

It might seem that a chapter focused on Ingrid Bergman's beginnings in the United States cannot be particularly original as the actress represents a legendary icon of the Hollywood Golden Era who still meets with a remarkable interest of both the general and specialized public. Within the context of my book, however, a discussion of her arrival in the US film industry in the late 1930s is essential as it involved Selznick's first systematic attempt at turning an actress—completely unknown to the US public—into a full-fledged star. In addition, as Ora Gelley has pointed out, there has long been a gap in terms of serious theoretical and historical reflection of Bergman's stardom.[2] Journal articles and books about her are seldom informed by the methodological frameworks derived from star studies; on the contrary, they usually amount to popular texts of a biographical focus which do not make use of relevant theoretical concepts or original historiographical research. As a result, many of them only reproduce various myths, a number of which, as I will demonstrate, are connected with her beginnings in Hollywood. If the authors deal with the actress and her career in a more serious manner, they have mostly focused on her cooperation with Alfred Hitchcock[3] or on the circumstances and consequences of her scandalous relationship with Roberto Rossellini.[4] In contrast to Greta Garbo, Marlene Dietrich, or Rita Hayworth,[5] there is a lack of a multilayered analysis of her career. This is probably because the star identity of Bergman is, despite numerous contradictions, still perceived as straightforward and uncomplicated. One repeatedly comes across the view that the actress was more of "an anti-star," who did not succumb to the industry mechanisms of

20   CONSTRUCTION OF NATURALNESS

star development and who established herself despite the industry machinery, thanks to her natural appearance and unaffected demeanor.

This interpretation has its origins in the period of her arrival in Hollywood and her US debut *Intermezzo: A Love Story*. For example, in an interview in the popular magazine *Photoplay*, Bergman described her concerns about how Hollywood would treat her along with the unexpected reaction of her new employer David O. Selznick:

> I walked trembling into the studio the first day [. . .] and when the make-up man said, "Step this way, please," I almost fainted. I knew they were going to pluck my eyebrows, dye my hair, lift my chin and do all sorts of horrible things. I resolved to fight to the finish. Imagine my surprise when Mr. Selznick looked me over and said, "H-m-m-m-m-! You won't need any make-up." This couldn't be Hollywood![6]

Several years later, however, the actress depicted her first meeting with the celebrated producer in a strikingly different way. Her determination to resist "Hollywoodization" remained firm, but Selznick's reaction was far less positive:

> "Now what about make-up, because your eyebrows are too thick, and your teeth are no good, and there are lots of other things. . . . I'll take you to the make-up department in the morning and we'll see what they can do . . ."
>
> Now it was my turn to think. I said, "I think you've made a big mistake, Mr. Selznick. You shouldn't have bought the pig in the sack. I thought you saw me in the movie Intermezzo [the Swedish original—author's note], and liked me, and sent Kay Brown across to Sweden to get me. Now you've seen me, you want to change everything. So I'd rather not do the movie [the US version of *Intermezzo*—author's note]. We'll say no more about it. [. . .] I'll take the next train and go back home."
>
> [. . .] Suddenly he became very quiet. He looked at me very hard and said, "I've got an idea that's so simple and yet no one in Hollywood has ever tried it before. Nothing about you is going to be touched. Nothing altered. You remain yourself. You are going to be the first 'natural' actress."[7]

While the first version bears the marks of Selznick's marketing department and presents the entire situation to the advantage of his company, the second—originating from the actress's memoirs published in 1980—depicts the traditional conflict between an authentic artist and an arrogant producer, who only later discovers the truth which had to be apparent to others from the very beginning. Bergman here does not merely passively accept the verdict of someone else, but actively resists and forces the feared Selznick to reevaluate his original standpoint. Perhaps due to the general fondness for dramatic stories about strong-willed performers confronting the impersonal mechanisms of the film industry, the latter version eventually prevailed and entered popular discourse. For instance, Ethan Mordden, the author of a book on female stars in Hollywood, interpreted the relationship between Selznick and Ingrid Bergman at the beginning of her US career as follows:

> Into the strait maze of studio stardom came Ingrid Bergman, on a direct path, saying no. No, she would not change her name. No, she would not change her looks; she would not play the same character in every film. And no, she would not let her employer tell her how to run her personal affairs. This is the behaviour of an individual, not a star.[8]

A similar view can also be found in a number of academic publications. Film scholar Robin Blaetz, in the article "Ingrid Bergman: The Face of Authenticity in the Land of Illusion" from the collection *What Dreams Were Made Of: Movie Stars of the 1940s*, wrote that her intention is "to situate [Bergman] as an unclaimed iconic figure in the history of mid-twentieth-century feminism." Accordingly, she does not view Selznick as "the engine" of the actress's US career, but rather as its "caboose." Bergman, according to the author, "turned out to have been the person she said she was, which might be best conceptualized as *captured* rather than authored by the myriad of publicity that followed her career."[9]

In this chapter, I argue against this widely accepted position, according to which Ingrid Bergman represented a completely authentic actress resisting the mechanisms of the Hollywood star system. I will instead lean toward the views of Joseph Garncarz and David Smit (and, to a lesser degree, James Damico), who have examined the construction and control of her star identity over the course of the 1940s from the perspective of Selznick's company and his team of PR specialists.[10] In contrast to them, however, I will be focusing not on the end of the decade and the scandal which arose around her widely publicized adulterous relationship with Roberto Rossellini, which became a turning point in how the actress was perceived by the majority of American society, but instead on a period ten years earlier when she was first presented to the US public by means of the film *Intermezzo* and the elaborate PR campaign that accompanied its release.

Ingrid Bergman defied contemporary ideas of a typical Hollywood star of foreign origin. She was very remote from the wide-spread and often imitated type of a goddess-like, exotic woman surrounded by luxury and an aura of mystery, which was embodied by her ten-year-older countrywoman Greta

Garbo or other stars imported from Europe such as Marlene Dietrich and Hedy Lamarr.[11] In her book *A Woman's View: How Hollywood Spoke to Women, 1930–1960*, Jeanine Basinger calls this type "the unreal woman" by which she means a fantasy figure "whose beauty, elegance, and sexual appeal are somehow beyond the ordinary."[12] The image of Bergman, formed by films, advertising materials, and publicity, emphasized, in contrast, features such as her naturalness (manifested both in terms of her appearance and her behavior), health and stamina, innocence, naiveté, dedication to work, modesty, and an absence of star mannerisms. The naturalness and authenticity of the actress were directly related to the fact that there was supposedly a harmonic agreement between her private identity and her role in *Intermezzo*. As this was even more pronounced than with other stars, the spiritual quality which the actress was endowed with, according to this interpretation, could not be imitated; the only explanation for this had to be that it came from the inside and was a direct reflection of her inner beauty.

I'm not suggesting that Bergman was the first actress in Hollywood history to personify these qualities. Catherine Jurca pointed out that by the late 1930s Hollywood's conception of glamour was under fire, especially after "the Independent Theatre Owners Association (ITOA) accused the studios of extravagance and poor judgment for casting highly paid stars, 'whose dramatic ability is unquestioned but whose box office draw is nil,' in 'top bracket pictures.'"[13] The main targets of this campaign were precisely some of the most glamorous female stars including Greta Garbo, Marlene Dietrich, and Joan Crawford. Even before that, Myrna Loy and Sonia Henie were praised for their naturalness and simplicity, with press celebrating them for deposing the "Glamor Girl of yesterday."[14] We may also recall producer Oliver Niles from Selznick's 1937 production of *A Star Is Born* expressing the belief that "tastes are going back to the natural." It seems fair to say, then, that by the time Bergman was introduced to US audiences, the ideas around the "death of glamour" and the rise of naturalness had been circulating throughout the industry and the public for several years. My aim here is primarily to explore the sources of the actress's connection to these ideals and analyze the strategies of Selznick's firm, which, among all Hollywood studios, arguably championed the departure from traditional concepts of glamour most vigorously.

As this chapter demonstrates, attributing all agency to Bergman, as many sources have unequivocally done, and depicting Selznick (at least initially) as her opponent, is inaccurate or at least misleading. Even though her star image emphasized the qualities of naturalness, spontaneity and authenticity, this does not necessarily mean that the star identity of Ingrid Bergman was not a product of the Hollywood star machine. On the contrary, her presentation as Hollywood's first "natural" actress (as Selznick, in a clever—and deceptive—

marketing ploy, put it) depended on a complex process, which, apart from her own initiative, involved several levels of star development including strict requirements for the director and cameraman of her first film and painstaking coordination of promotion and publicity. In other words, Selznick mobilized various departments in his studio with the aim of creating an attractive product to gain an advantage in the market: by means of *Intermezzo* and the publicity which accompanied the picture, Bergman was to be formed as exactly the type which powerfully resonated with the changing tastes of the US public in the late 1930s. The naturalness of the actress was therefore only partially an issue of her essence. I am convinced that to a much greater extent this involved a specific presentation of her to the public by means of the film text, the advertising materials, and the press releases. It is more accurate to speak of "a construction of naturalness," thereby acknowledging the decisive role played by Selznick's studio in the overall process.

This perspective resonates with Jurca's description of the supposed incompatibility between glamour and naturalness:

> With a whole host of suggestions about how to accomplish the right look and feel of the thing, naturalness was, of course, as manufactured as glamour. Being natural, embracing genuineness more or less genuinely, was never as simple as just being yourself. And 1938's enthusiasm for the natural looked a lot like the praise for "a healthy, solid and substantial glamour" in 1935. The natural may have been another turn of glamour's many screws rather than a wholesale rejection of it. But the rhetoric of the time presented naturalness and glamour as different, indeed, utterly incompatible, ends.[15]

In Bergman's case, the myth of a purely natural and authentic actress, which has prevailed both in popular and partially in scholarly discourse, is only added evidence for how effective the strategy of Selznick's company was, as this was precisely the intention from the very beginning.

My conclusions are based on sources from the Selznick's archive in the Harry Ransom Center in Austin, although support can also be found in many newspaper and magazine articles and in a comparison of *Intermezzo* with the original Swedish version as well as with other films in which Bergman starred back home prior to her arrival in Hollywood. In the following text, I present the production history of her US debut with an emphasis on the acquisition of the material and the shaping of her role by means of cinematography and make-up. Further, I analyze the publicity and advertising which accompanied both the film and Selznick's new acting discovery. My primary aim is not necessarily to contribute to an understanding of Bergman's star image, but to direct attention to the strategies and procedures which Selznick's company used to transform an unknown actress into a sought-out star amongst both moviegoers and business partners. This chapter is therefore essential to establish how the company functioned, how it treated its contract actors and actresses, and how it got involved in the development of its own stars in the first place. Earlier, it primarily depended on cooperation with proven Hollywood personalities (in terms of female stars, especially Marlene Dietrich, Carole Lombard, and Janet Gaynor), while in two pictures which were developed in parallel fashion with *Intermezzo—Gone with the Wind* and *Rebecca*—the introduction of the stars (Vivien Leigh and Joan Fontaine, respectively) was more of an inevitable side effect of the costly and closely followed projects based on bestselling books.[16] The much more modest *Intermezzo* therefore seems to be a more appropriate case study for this type of historical analysis.

It is unavoidable that we currently view Ingrid Bergman as an acting legend and one of the biggest stars of classical Hollywood and we might be led to get the same impression from her early roles, which also display her talent and the roots of her future fame. The backward glance and knowledge about later developments can nevertheless lead to misconceptions where we easily miss or wrongly interpret important historical circumstances.

TWO SWEDISH ACQUISITIONS

In the middle of 1938, Selznick's gigantic project of adapting Margaret Mitchell's *Gone with the Wind* had been in a state of preparation for two years already— "for longer than any other film [he] had produced, and he had yet to shoot a single frame of film."[17] At approximately the same time, the producer had also purchased the rights to another current bestseller that he was planning to transform into a costly and prestigious picture: *Rebecca* by Daphne du Maurier. As Steve Wilson states, "[t]o keep his company afloat, he concentrated on making black-and-white films employing simpler stories and smaller casts while maintaining high production values."[18] The comedy *The Young in Heart* was filmed from May to June with Janet Gaynor, Douglas Fairbanks Jr., Roland Young, and Billie Burke in the main roles of professional fraudsters, accompanied in the cast by Paulette Goddard, who was one of the candidates for the role of Scarlett O'Hara at that time. The picture premiered in October 1938 when Selznick was already in the middle of filming another picture, a marital drama with comedic touches called *Made for Each Other*, starring James Stewart and Carole Lombard. In order to expand the number of these moderately budgeted pictures, Selznick told his employees in his New York office "to keep on the lookout for foreign pictures which we might purchase for either remake by ourselves, or as an investment for resale for remake purposes."[19] In a later memorandum, he explained that "one of the principal reasons for buying foreign pictures to remake is that when they are good they save a very large part of the agonies of creative preparation and a large part of the cost as well," as they make it possible to duplicate the camera positions and angles or the editing decisions.[20]

This was how Selznick learned about the Swedish film *Intermezzo* (1936), which was made by director Gustaf Molander for the company Svensk Filmindustri. Thanks to its domestic success, the picture was exported overseas, something which only occurred with a small number of Swedish titles at that time.[21] In the US, it was shown in selected art cinemas, particularly in central New York. The positive response in the press drew the attention of Kay Brown and her assistant Elsa Neuberger, who forwarded the message to Selznick in Los Angeles.[22] As it turned out, the subject of their interest was not only the attractive story of a love affair between a married violinist and a young female pianist, but also the young woman in the role, the twenty-three-year old Ingrid Bergman, whose performance met with acclaim in the US press, with a number of periodicals even predicting that her future would be linked with Hollywood.[23] Selznick instructed Kay Brown and his London representative Jenia Reissar to launch negotiations concerning the transfer of the rights for a Hollywood remake of *Intermezzo* and the possibility of engaging the actress who made such a favorable impression.

At first the picture and Bergman represented two independent transactions which did not necessarily have to be combined. As already indicated, the motivation to purchase the rights to *Intermezzo* (for $17,500[24]) was initially of a purely financial character and the commercial success of the remake was supposed to depend, among other things, on a quality cast, assuming the use of established stars—as with *The Young in Heart, Made for Each Other*, and most of the other films that Selznick International had filmed up until then. The male role of the concert violinist Holger Brandt was therefore offered to Ronald Colman, William Powell, and Charles Boyer, while Merle Oberon, Paulette Goddard, Hedy Lamarr, and Loretta Young were considered for the part of his lover Anita Hoffman, with Young being closest to gaining the role.[25] In light of the absence of other sure-fire attractions, such as a popular literary source or Technicolor, the casting of proven stars was the best guarantee of success with the audiences.

Bergman could have been introduced to the US public in another project. Selznick was undoubtedly fascinated by the actress. He later explained that he had "never seen a quality such as hers, a quality of spirituality and nobility and purity, plus a sensitive and restrained talent."[26] However, at the time of *Intermezzo*'s preproduction, he had never met her in person, had not seen the results of her screen tests, and could not judge the level of her English, which was essential to work in Hollywood. His hesitation therefore had a rational basis. There were also other complications involving the actress. She had been a leading female star in Sweden in the late 1930s (with ten films already under her belt and having been voted amongst the most popular film personalities of 1937 by Swedish fans),[27] but her fame was primarily of a local character. She was on her way to establishing herself in Germany (she was half-German on her mother's side) when she made the comedy *Die vier Gesellen* (*The Four Companions*, 1938) for the UFA studio. Her further career in this country was cut short, however, by political developments. This was ultimately fortunate for Bergman, because as it soon became apparent, more extensive cooperation with the film industry under Nazi rule would have been an obstacle not only for Selznick, but for any other head of a Hollywood studio.[28] The immediate move to the US and her participation in screen tests was further complicated by having to care for her daughter Pia, who was born to the actress and her husband Petter Lindström on September 20, 1938.

In the meantime, however, the casting of *Intermezzo* was not going as smoothly as Selznick had hoped:

> The difficulties of casting "INTERMEZZO" in an important showmanship way become more apparent daily; and there is seemingly no way of casting it properly, apart from showmanship, that would warrant the cost of the picture. I am commencing to feel that the way to handle this subject is to wait for Bergmand [*sic*], ballyhooing her debut in it.[29]

Selznick thereby reevaluated his original position, according to which the film was supposed to rely upon an already established domestic star and instead decided to conceive it as a vehicle for introducing a new personality imported from abroad. This decision particularly suited Bergman as she would be acting in a film which she already knew well from the earlier treatment, making it easier for her to adjust to a new environment.

The contract from February 14, 1939, which was negotiated and signed on behalf of Selznick International by Kay Brown in Stockholm, gave Selznick's studio the exclusive right to make use of the actress's services in the English language. For eight weeks of work on *Intermezzo*, Bergman was supposed to receive a weekly fee of $2,500. The contract further granted the producer option rights for one or two films yearly over the following five years. It was up to him whether these were to be films in his own production or loan-outs to other renowned producers. On the other hand, Bergman was free to do as many films in other languages than English as she pleased.[30] This gave her the opportunity to return to Sweden and continue her successful career there in case of her own dissatisfaction or negative reactions from the US public. Ingrid Bergman arrived in New York by boat on April 20, accompanied by the indispensable Kay Brown. Two weeks later, she reported to Selznick's studio in Culver City, where among the first to greet her was the British actor Leslie Howard, who had been confirmed in March as the leading man in the film.

CONSTRUCTION OF NATURAL BEAUTY
(FILMING *INTERMEZZO*)

Immediately upon her arrival in Hollywood, Bergman underwent extensive screen tests. The logic behind this series of experiments and evaluations was to come to a decision on the most appropriate way of filming her in *Intermezzo*. What kind of make-up would suit her best under the lighting equipment? Which camera angles were most appropriate? What kind of hairstyle would be most fitting for her figure in combination with her costumes? Although the answers to these questions were still being determined during the filming, the key decision was made in the early phase that Bergman would be presented to the public as a simple young woman endowed with an aura of naturalness and authenticity.[31]

Leslie Howard, the male star of the film and also its associate producer, after seeing the results of the screen tests, communicated the view of most of the crew that "without make-up [Bergman] looks much more natural and much more attractive and much less Hollywood. Her skin has a natural sheen and apparently she has a perfect complexion. Also the lips, instead of looking absolutely fakey and made up, seem to be very natural and attractive in the test without grease paint."[32] Although Howard's report stated that Bergman did not have any make-up on, in reality the presence of a camera and studio lights always required a certain level of greasepaint.[33] The actress was therefore treated by make-up artists, but the qualities of her complexion made it possible to reduce the amount of cosmetics to an absolute minimum.[34] A similar approach was chosen for her eyebrows, which were not to be plucked or drawn in. It was also decided that the hairdresser would leave her hair long so that her hairstyle would look well-kept but not at all artificial. All of this not only simplified the actress's preparation for the filming, but also created a great starting point for her publicity as it served to distinguish her from most Hollywood actresses, who could not appear in front of the camera without make-up and a painstakingly modeled hairstyle.

Other aspects of the production connected with the presentation of Bergman were also closely monitored. The costumes from the celebrated Irene (born as Irene Maud Lentz), who in the past had designed gowns for Ginger Rogers, Constance Bennett, and Jean Arthur, were supposed to mask the actress's wide shoulders and were not to reveal her legs, which the director Gregory Ratoff said the public should never see.[35] Some of the pieces of furniture were adapted so as to minimize the height difference between Bergman and Edna Best, who played Holger's wife, Margit.[36] And the dialogue instructor Ruth Roberts worked intensively on improving the actress's English and eliminating her foreign accent.

The greatest challenge, however, involved "the correct" lighting and filming of Bergman. As David Smit states, "Selznick was almost fanatical about what he considered the 'natural' beauty of Bergman's face, but he also thought her naturalness needed to be made up and photographed a certain way in order for the camera to capture it adequately."[37] He therefore carefully coordinated and supervised his employees, in particular the director and cameraman, and when they failed to achieve the desired results, he did not hesitate to replace them.

The experienced William Wyler, whose most recent success had been the adaptation of Emily Brontë's *Wuthering Heights* (1939, Samuel Goldwyn/United Artists), was chosen to direct *Intermezzo*.[38] After only a few days of filming, however, he was removed—or stepped down on his own (the views on this vary)—and, on June 5, he was replaced by Gregory Ratoff. Wyler, in his own words, worked on the picture for approximately six weeks, consulting on the script and the choice of music and supervising screen tests. He soon found himself, however, in conflict with Selznick, the reason possibly being his slow work tempo, an unwillingness to faithfully follow the original Swedish version, or the producer's dissatisfaction with the way he filmed Ingrid Bergman.[39] His replacement Ratoff, primarily an actor until recently, was supposed to work more efficiently and in greater cooperation with Selznick.

As director of photography, Harry Stradling initially worked on the picture, but it again became clear after several days that the producer was not fully satisfied with his work. In the case of Wyler, the surviving materials do not allow us to determine the exact reason for his disagreement with Selznick, but there is no doubt when it comes to Stradling: as the strongly worded memorandum from June 9, 1939, clearly shows, it specifically involved the poor quality of the photographic material with Bergman. In the report, Selznick repeatedly pointed out the importance of this aspect for the success of the entire film: "the difference in [the] photography [of Bergman] is the difference between great beauty and a complete lack of beauty. And unless we can bring off our photography so that she really looks divine, the whole picture can fall apart from a standpoint of audience effectiveness." The producer felt that the flat, conventional lighting, which did not suit the actress, was amongst the main problems, as it emphasized her flaws (Selznick mentioned her "unattractive lower lip") and made her look too ordinary and uninteresting. Stradling was to instead make use of all the available "lighting effects—whether it be shadows across part of her face, or unique angles, or rim lighting." According to Selznick, this was what made "the difference between a successful picture and an unsuccessful picture; the difference between a new star and a girl who will never make another picture here. [. . .] It would be infinitely preferable for the picture to be photographed in the most conventional and ordinary manner, and have gorgeous photography of Miss Bergman, than the reverse." The results thus far, however, lagged even behind the original Swedish version of *Intermezzo*, which was utterly inexcusable considering the higher quality of technical equipment as well as Stradling's twenty years of experience in Hollywood and Europe:[40] "The curious charm that she had in the Swedish version of *Intermezzo*—the combination of exciting beauty and fresh purity—certainly ought to be within our abilities to capture."[41]

Harry Stradling never had the opportunity to repair things: his services on the film were terminated only a few days after Selznick's criticism and he was replaced by Gregg Toland, who was lent by Samuel Goldwyn. Not even his reputation as one of the most reliable and innovative Hollywood directors of photography[42]—confirmed by two recent Oscar nominations (for *Les Misérables* [1935, 20th Century Pictures] and *Dead End* [1937, Samuel Goldwyn]) and his current artistic triumph in *Wuthering Heights*—protected Toland, however, from strict supervision and a constant flood of suggestions concerning his work. Selznick continued to monitor the material shot with Bergman and sent detailed instructions to both Toland and Ratoff. In a frequently cited memorandum from June 22, the producer once again pointed out that "the difference between a great photographic beauty and an ordinary girl with Miss Bergman lies in the proper photography of her," and compiled a manual of sorts as to how to attain the required quality of shots with the actress. According to Selznick, the desired result depended on

> avoiding the bad side of her face; keeping her head down as much as possible; giving her the proper hairdress; giving her the proper mouth makeup; avoiding long shots so as not to make her look too big and, more importantly, but for the same reason, avoiding low camera on her, as well as being careful to build people who work with her, such as Leslie Howard and Edna Best (as well, of course, the children, beside whom she looks titanic if the camera work isn't carefully studied); but most important of all, on shading her face and in invariably going for effect lightings on her.[43]

While the logic behind most of the instructions was to mask what Selznick viewed as physical flaws of the actress (above-average height, wide shoulders, a "worse" side of her face), the last note is worthy of a short commentary.

Intermezzo: Cameraman

Mr. Gregory Rateff — cc: Mr. Gregg Toland

PHOTOGRAPHY ON MISS BERGMAN — "INTERMEZZO"

6/22/39

Dear Greg:

The Toland tests of Miss Bergman prove indubitably what we have been saying since before the picture started — that more than with any other girl that I know of in pictures, the difference between a great photographic beauty and an ordinary girl with Miss Bergman lies in proper photography of her — and that this in turn depends not simply on avoiding the bad side of her face; keeping her head down as much as possible; giving her the proper hairdress; giving her the proper mouth make-up; avoiding long shots, so as not to make her look too big, and even more importantly, but for the same reason, avoiding low cameras on her, as well as being careful to build people who work with her, such as Leslie Howard and Edna Best (as well, of course, as the children, beside whom she looks titanic if the camera work isn't carefully studied; but most important of all, in shading her face and in invariably going for effect lightings on her. This means that there should not be a single sequence of the picture that is not staged for real effect lighting — whether it be morning, afternoon or night. One might say with justice that almost any dramatic picture benefits from this sort of careful attention to lighting effects, but in the case of "INTERMEZZO" the mood of the picture is dependent upon it to an extent far greater than what is true of most pictures. Thus, in photographing Miss Bergman properly we will be benefiting the picture as a whole. And I consequently urge you to give Mr. Toland every assistance in going for the type of job which some large studios might consider arty, but which in the case of this particular picture I regard as equally important with the dialogue and with the performances if we are to get the artistic gem that we hope out of our simple little story.

The only word of caution I should like to speak in this regard is to avoid putting any sequences in so low a key that with bad projection the audiences will not be able to see the expressions on the players' faces. We must remember that a great many theatres are still equipped with poor projection and manned with poor projectionists, so that when the stuff is too dark in its entirety the audience is simply bewildered rather than admiring. But this limitation should in no way cause a hardship in going for what we expect will be the most beautiful effect photography of the year.

DOS

Memo from David O. Selznick with detailed instructions to cameraman Gregg Toland. Courtesy of Daniel Selznick.

According to Chris Cagle, "effect(s) lighting" in the period jargon "referred to lighting motivated by specific sources on screen (e.g., a fireplace) but encompassed more broadly a range of atmospheric and dramatic lighting effects."[44] As the memorandum addressed to the original cameraman of *Intermezzo*, Harry Stradling, showed, Selznick was primarily insistent on the use of untraditional shadowing, effectively modeling the face of the actress, and rim lighting, usually isolating the figure from the background and creating "a halo" around her face. The visual quality, which was supposed to be tailor-made for Selznick's acting discovery, was to make the film, in his words, into "an artistic gem" and thereby secure for it both attention and recognition of the press and the public.[45]

The enhanced focus on the photographic quality of the scenes with Bergman was most apparent in her introduction in the film. The producer's interest in the actress's first appearance was understandable as it involved a scene through which she was to be presented to the US public for the first time. When the first take did not turn out as expected, Toland was instructed to repeat the scene and when Selznick was not satisfied for the second time, he insisted on a third version. As Patrick Keating noted in his study on the cooperation between David O. Selznick and his cameramen, the producer did not have sufficient technical knowledge to suggest specific lamps or lenses to Toland, but he used "the combined power of the memo and the retake to push the lighting in a very specific direction."[46] The completed film dedicates two wordless shots to introducing Bergman, in which her Anita enters Holger's house to the sounds of a central string melody. In the first shot, lasting five seconds, we see almost all of her figure, dressed in a dark coat, as she slowly walks through the corridor and approaches the camera. After a cut to Holger and his daughter, a more tightly framed shot follows, this time approximately three seconds long, in which Anita takes off her coat, while her face is modeled by means of light, with her eyes and forehead partially covered by shadow and another sharper shadow cast on her nose. The untraditional lighting, seemingly unmotivated by any visible source on the screen, but also not exclusively anti-realistic, provides the scene with a unique quality which signals the arrival of an important character and, at the same time, a new acting star. The presentation of the other characters in the film is not treated with as much importance. Selznick also paid attention to details such as the position of the collar on the actress's dress, whose white color, contrasting with the rest of her costume, also helps draw the audience to her face, which becomes the only possible focus of our attention.[47]

Apart from the opening scene, increased attention was also paid to the close-ups of Bergman, which were supposed to occur in the film as frequently as possible. Selznick once again urged Toland to choose camera angles and lighting patterns that would make the actress look as attractive as possible so that the public would have no other choice but to accept her as a new star: "Every beautiful shot we get of her is a great deal of money added to the returns on the picture."[48] The editor Hal Kern was even tasked with studying the film's rough cut and suggesting spots where additional close-ups of the actress's face could be placed without disturbing the flow of the narrative. The close-ups were

Bergman's introductory shots in *Intermezzo: A Love Story*.

Bergman's close-ups in *Intermezzo: A Love Story*.

amongst the main reasons why the retakes took up fifteen days, an unusually long period when one considers that the principal photography only lasted a little over a month.[49]

Selznick was satisfied with the laboriously achieved result: in a memorandum from September 29, he praised Toland's work and made mention of his chances of receiving an Oscar.[50] The visual qualities of *Intermezzo* are truly remarkable and, in accordance with Selznick's intentions, are primarily related to the presentation of Ingrid Bergman. The final effect was aptly described by David Smit:

> [. . .] in most of the crucial scenes between Anita Hoffman (Bergman) and her lover Holler Brand [*sic*, Holger Brandt] (Leslie Howard), Bergman is photographed with a high-angle shot of the left side of her face, usually with a great deal of high contrast that puts part of her face in shadow and gives her eyes her signature dewy look. [. . .] What we might call the "Selznick shot" of Bergman is [. . .] a major reason for her image as wholesome and spiritual. The shot literally highlights Bergman's beauty: the soft focus bathes her in light and shadow and captures the light in her eyes. Her look of longing and devotion, her posture of submission, all suggest something beyond the mere physical, something similar to the scenes of saints in medieval painting and in the work of El Greco.[51]

One could object that the previous lines, based on a study of archive materials and the finished film, overestimate the role of Selznick's studio; that Bergman, in line with her own interpretation in her memoirs, already possessed those qualities upon her arrival in the US and that Selznick only decided to replicate them by means of the technological film apparatus. I would argue against this reading. It is true that Bergman had drawn attention to herself in the Swedish version of *Intermezzo* through a combination of an unusual visage, a captivating smile, charm, and acting talent, as others along with Selznick never failed to emphasize. However, there was not as much photographic care paid to her in the original film (or in the other films she had made in her homeland, for that matter), and her persona was not consistently surrounded with an aura of authenticity and naturally attractive appearance as during her beginnings in Hollywood. In the majority of her Swedish films, Bergman had a marked layer of make-up, including eyeshadow and lipstick; her eyebrows were carefully shaped in an arched link, which gradually narrowed from the root of the nose to the temples; her hair was most often cut short and styled into regular waves; and in films such as *Valborgsmässoafton* (*Walpurgis Night*), *Swedenhielms* (both 1935), *På Solsidan* (*On the Sunny Side*, 1936), *Dollar* (1938), and *En enda natt* (*Only One Night*, 1939, all Svensk Filmindustri), she wore dresses and accessories which helped to define her as more of an icon of glamour than its antithesis.[52] The filmmakers usually chose flat lighting without the use of effects which Selznick later defined as the basic strategy for photographing the actress, and not much attention was paid to the choice of costumes which often unflatteringly emphasized her above-average height and wide shoulders. The introductory scene in the original version of *Intermezzo* could lead to the impression that in this case the actress would be depicted differently, as a simply dressed young woman without a weakness for luxury. Even here, however, a stylization prevails based on lavish costumes (the most pronounced being the glittering ball dress) and prominent make-up (her eye shadow, lipstick, and eyebrows modeled in the shape of a triangle are apparent in several scenes), which is further accented by a number of glamorizing close-ups. If the overall narrative trajectory and treatment of the isolated scenes remained the same in the remake as in the original Swedish version, this was not the case for Bergman's visual presentation.

It was thus only under Selznick's supervision, following extensive tests and experiments, that a specific and consistent visual identity was created for the actress based on naturalness and lack of artifice. A clear paradox is apparent at the core of these maneuvers: all the technical means and the specialized skills of the dozens of employees and collaborators which Selznick had at his disposal, in particular the leading Hollywood cameraman of this period, Gregg Toland, were used to construct an image which was not supposed to reveal any signs of manipulation or intervention. Another paradox is the fact that Bergman underwent this process in Hollywood, which had a reputation as a glamour factory.[53]

The extraordinary care paid to the presentation of Ingrid Bergman, which resulted in extensive screen tests, the replacement of the original cameraman, and numerous days of retakes, also had an impact on the final costs for *Intermezzo*: instead of the original estimation of $700,000 (still almost double the average cost of a Hollywood movie in the late 1930s),[54] the picture cost over $1 million, and this despite the fact that the actress herself received a fairly modest payment.[55] From a simple film, which was intended to primarily fill the cashbox of the studio, which had already invested great sums in the demanding productions of *Gone with the Wind* (in postproduction at that time) and *Rebecca* (with the beginning of principal photography set for September 1939), it became a costly project, whose main aim was not to bring instant profits, but to introduce a new personality to the public and representatives of the film industry.

Bergman in her Swedish films: *Walpurgis Night* and *Swedenhielms*.

Bergman in her Swedish films: *Only One Night* and the original version of *Intermezzo*.

NOT ANOTHER GARBO
(PROMOTION AND PUBLICITY)

The advertising campaign associated with *Intermezzo* and coordinated in cooperation with the distribution company United Artists, along with the publicity specifically linked to Ingrid Bergman, was supposed to cultivate and develop those attributes which were identified as desirable. The actress was not meant to be presented in the promotional materials, press releases, and interviews as sexy, enigmatic, or inapproachable. Her image was instead to be based on naturalness, spontaneity, openness, devotion to her profession, and a character still untouched by the Hollywood glitz. This constructed identity, rid of any sign of mystery and foreign threat, and in contrast involving directness, simplicity, and familiarity, was primarily aimed at the female audiences who were supposed to identify with Bergman as a talented, but modest artist, a faithful wife, and a model mother. The construction of the desired image was conditioned not only by carefully channeling information which reached the public by means of the press, but also by suppressing all aspects of the actress's persona that were not compatible with this objective. Both activities were the responsibility of the talent and advertising departments, whose tasks included disguising the actress's recent link with the German film industry as well as her partial German heritage, limiting her involvement in photoshoots and advertisements for cosmetics and other commercial products, and supervising her interviews with journalists. All of this was due to, amongst other things, the fact that Bergman had the reputation of being outspoken and having an unreliable taste in dressing and make-up.[56]

Two independent phases can be identified in Selznick's publicity campaign, separated by the premiere of *Intermezzo* in September 1939. There was not supposed to be any excessive commotion around Bergman from the moment she first stepped on US soil to the release of the picture in cinemas. Selznick was convinced that "the best thing to do would be to import her quietly into the studio [and] go about our business of making the picture with only such publicity attendant upon her casting as would be the case with any unimportant leading woman."[57] Bergman was therefore supposed to travel incognito or under her husband's name, as Mrs. Petter Lindström, avoid most interviews and photo sessions, and, in general, behave inconspicuously so that "press [doesn't] get hold of her."[58] There were several advantages to this tactic: Selznick minimized the possibility of potential resistance on the part of the public against another actress from abroad—resistance which was evoked several months earlier by the announcement of the casting of Vivien Leigh in the role of Scarlett O'Hara in *Gone with the Wind* and which had its origins in the earlier fiascos connected with the ostentatious (but ultimately unsuccessful) attempts by the producer Samuel Goldwyn to make stars out of Anna Sten and Sigrid Gurie.[59] In contrast, the strategy was to provide the public and the press with the opportunity to discover the actress more or less on their own, only on the basis of her performance and attractive presentation in the film. The absence of the usual ballyhoo also corresponded with the desired image of Bergman as a simple and modest young woman. Finally, Selznick's studio maintained the possibility to intervene in the entire process and, if necessary, carry out changes, which would have been extremely difficult if there had been a loud publicity campaign.[60]

The first correction had to be made immediately after the first interview which the actress provided to Harry Friedman from the *Los Angeles Examiner*. In an article entitled "Meet New Star from Sweden," some unfortunate information came out, including, for example, that the studio considered her "sexy," that she was unusually tall and "you wonder how she will look opposite the none-too-tall Leslie Howard," and that her husband is a Stockholm dentist, which was indeed true, but the public did not need to know about it.[61] This inconsistency when working with the press can be attributed to the fact that developing stars was still a fairly unexplored area for Selznick's PR department. To avoid another mistake like this, Selznick agreed with William Hebert, his head of publicity at the time, that the actress would avoid further interviews during the filming of *Intermezzo* (despite the fact that voices were heard in the studio that this tactic could harm her).[62] The situation concerning photoshoots had a similar result. Bergman was originally supposed to be photographed for *Vogue* and *Harper's Bazaar*, but Selznick canceled both as he did not view this as advantageous for the emerging image of the actress who was not supposed to be connected with glamour associated with fashion magazines.[63]

A sign of a crisis became apparent in September 1939, shortly prior to the premiere of the film. Three weeks after the invasion of Poland by the German armies and the declaration of war on the part of the United Kingdom and France, the *Los Angeles Examiner* informed its readers that "Ingrid Bergman is said to have gone straight back to Germany from here to make a picture for Goebbels. He is in charge of all German movies so she must have his approval."[64] Selznick responded by confirming with the actress, who was in Sweden at that time with her husband and daughter, that her earlier commitment to the UFA studio had been terminated and that her contacts in Germany were limited to relatives from her mother's side and by no means extended to highly placed political figures.[65] The damaging information was fortunately not taken up by other influential periodicals and the imminent scandal was successfully averted.[66]

The meticulous campaign for *Intermezzo* was ready to launch at the premiere with the aim of ensuring both the film and the actress a positive reception. The concept is illustrated well in the pressbook for the film, according to which Bergman—alongside her experienced film partner Leslie Howard and the mysterious, evocative title (which was supplemented with the subtitle *A Love Story* to specify the genre and ensure a more effective appeal to the female audience)—was one of the three attractions which the promo strategy was to focus on. The material, primarily directed at exhibitors, contained the following lines:

> A gorgeous new star to enchant them . . . Fresh, lovely and unaffected as her native seas and skies and winds . . . playing with a forthright simplicity and directness that brush aside all artifice . . . Beautiful of feature, lithe and springlike of figure . . . and with a dramatic power to feel and portray the profoundest passions . . . Ingrid Bergman will mean to your audiences a new, exciting departure in cinema heroines, and to your box-office the vitality that comes of a new, glamorous screen discovery with clear intimations of greatness![67]

The exhibitors were encouraged to "sell the fresh, youthful appeal of Ingrid Bergman" who embodies a "completely new type of star:"

> She still bears the name she was born with. Her own complexion photographs so well that she uses no make-up before the cameras. [. . .] Ingrid's tastes are simple and reflected in her clothes. White is her favorite color and predominates in her wardrobe. Corn on the cob, unknown in Sweden, has become her favorite edible. She has never dieted and doubtless never will have to. She is taller than the average screen actress—she is five feet six and weighs 120 pounds.[68]

The document is a dexterous combination of fact and fiction, and its intention was to present Bergman in such a way that her identity would ideally correspond to the character of Anita, while at the same time differentiating her from dozens of other Hollywood actresses who were also vying for fan support. The emphasis on vitality and authenticity is omnipresent and involves her name,[69] her attractive but artificially unembellished appearance, and her fresh performance style. The actress's Swedish origin was not masked but was instead presented as the source of her radiant health and connection with nature. At the same time, however, it wasn't supposed to stand in the way of her smooth Americanization. This was the logic behind the reference to corn on the cob, which along with chewing gum, sandwiches, and ice cream sundaes,

Publicity still for *Intermezzo: A Love Story*, with Bergman and Leslie Howard.

was allegedly the actress's weakness.[70] Misleading or outright untrue was the reference about Bergman's complete lack of make-up and the figures detailing her height and weight: she was in fact almost 5 feet 9 inches tall and her weight usually fluctuated between 130 and 135 pounds.[71] The pressbook also offered exhibitors a selection of posters, lobby cards, and photos where Bergman was most frequently depicted with her left profile visible in a loving embrace with Howard. Even though it was apparent from some of the materials that the film deals with potentially delicate themes such as a love triangle and infidelity, the affable smile of Bergman, along with her submissive position (the placement of the figures suggests that she is more the receiver than the initiator of the embrace) and her modest attire, make it sufficiently clear that her character is not by any means a female vamp. Her presentation on posters and photographs was crucial, as these visual materials were for many moviegoers the first contact with a yet unknown actress.

Bergman was supposed to give the impression of being a pretty, attractive woman, with her charm, however, having a different source than with many previous female stars.[72] If Margaret Thorp in 1939 defined glamour as a combination of sex appeal, luxury, elegance, and romance,[73] then Selznick's Bergman completely lacked the second ingredient and her sex appeal and romance were transformed in such a way as to not have any sign of aggressiveness and exoticism. A comparison with another Swedish star, the ten-year-older Greta Garbo, who Selznick met personally during the work on *Anna Karenina* for MGM, is particularly telling. Their shared origin led reporters and gossip columnists to look for similarities and parallels, but this is exactly what the producer wanted to avoid. Firstly, this would create excessive expectations of Bergman on the part of the public and secondly, her famous colleague embodied a completely different screen type.[74] Garbo had the reputation of "the Swedish Sphinx," a divinely perfect being who seemed to not even share the same world with ordinary mortals. Through her roles of fallen women and historical figures, doomed for solitude or a tragic death (for example, *Grand Hotel* [1932], *Queen Christina* [1933], *Anna Karenina, Camille* [1936] and *Conquest* [1937, all MGM]), she was associated with eternal melancholy and sadness. Her photogenic, statuesque face and mysterious appearance evoked both seductiveness and inapproachability, passion, and restraint. The mystique of Garbo was also provoked by her frequent androgynous stylization, which made her come across as enigmatic and potentially dangerous for society.[75] This was all in sharp contrast to the desired image of Bergman, who was supposed to be perceived as "a pure and fresh beauty" and an unaggressive attractive personality.[76] Selznick therefore instructed his employees in the advertising department to avoid formulations in the press releases which would make reference to Bergman as "a new Garbo," and instead to contradict these kinds of comparisons in the press.

The contrast between the actresses was also valid off screen. While Garbo was perceived as an introvert, reclusive, and uncooperative, Bergman was supposed to come across as undemanding, direct, and affable. Selznick's studio circulated a number of press releases, whose aim was to make "her natural sweetness and consideration and conscientiousness [. . .] something of a legend."[77] Readers could learn, for example, that she had won over the entire crew of *Intermezzo* due to her openness and absence of pretense; that she wanted to repair on her own a costume which did not fit her and which was designated for being thrown away; that there were no limits to her working tempo and that she left the studio only when absolutely necessary and never protested against overtime; that she reacted with surprise to her stand-in as she was not used to using stand-ins in Sweden; that she was enthusiastic about her dressing room even though it was not one of the largest on the lot (the cast of *Gone with the Wind* had those in use); or that she was honestly upset about the replacement of the director of photography and would have preferred to spare Stradling's feelings even at the cost of lower picture quality.[78] Further, the studio rejected offers for tie-ins for consumer products (cosmetics, clothes, or jewels), as it would lend an undesirable mark of commercialization to her image.[79]

In summary, advertising and publicity aimed at presenting Bergman as an agreeable, open, and unspoiled professional in contrast to glamorous and pampered stars surrounded by luxury. In the words of Selznick, her image was to be "completely in keeping with the character she plays in the picture and [. . .] with the fresh and pure personality and appearance which caused me to sign her."[80] The PR department therefore based its approach on those features of the actress's personality which manifested themselves during the filming of *Intermezzo* and which were identified as desirable for her to make an impact in the market. Attributes that were not compatible with this strategy, including attractiveness based on open sexuality or exoticism arising from her foreign origin, were carefully avoided. The final impression of naturalness and authenticity was therefore paradoxically based on a controlled process of selection, masking, and fabrication.

Selznick had so much confidence in the appeal of this constructed identity that he decided to make changes to the promotional materials. While the name of Leslie Howard, the star of *Romeo and Juliet* (1936, MGM) and *Pygmalion* (1938, Pascal Film Productions/MGM) was originally supposed to dominate, the updated version was to have the name of Ingrid Bergman (with the word *introducing* before it) in the same size billing.[81] The potential success of the film was therefore to be closely linked with whether, and how effectively, the new personality would be sold to the public.

AN ANTI-STAR IS BORN
(REACTIONS AND COMMENTARIES)

Bergman underwent several rounds of internal evaluations from various departments at Selznick's company prior to and during the filming of *Intermezzo* but the final word always rested with the press and first and foremost the audiences. Without the paying public's validation, the process of star development could never be considered complete. The initial sign that the public would be willing to accept "the lexicon," which Selznick had chosen for the actress, came from the reactions to a series of previews.[82] The aim of the first preview in Huntington Park was to identify in the 100-minute-plus cut of the film expendable scenes and technically problematic shots, which had to be re-done. The following previews of the eighty-minute and the final seventy-minute versions of the film in Santa Barbara (August 17) and Pomona (August 31) were accompanied by detailed analyses of audience reactions, who recorded their impressions in structured questionnaires. Overall, the reception was positive—80 percent of the respondents referred to the film as "excellent" or "very good" (as expected, it received higher numbers with women). Out of the total of 545 participants, more than 86 percent stated that they liked Ingrid Bergman, and almost 58 percent declared that they would go to the cinema to her next film only to be able to see her once again on the big screen. With these positive numbers, which Selznick labeled as "particularly startling," the actress even surpassed Leslie Howard, who as an established star received the approval of 82 percent of the tested public (51.6 percent of the respondents stated that they would specifically go to the cinema to see his next film). The participants had the possibility to request a photograph of any of the film cast as a gesture of thanks for filling in the questionnaire: ninety-four of them (16.7 percent) did not take advantage of this offer, but those remaining usually preferred Bergman. Her portrait was distributed to 234 people (which amounts to 41.6 percent of the overall number of respondents), while Leslie Howard's photograph was requested by 138 people (24.6 percent).[83] A poll was also conducted amongst Selznick's employees: to the question "what interested you most in the picture?," ten out of fifteen mentioned the name of Bergman, with only two, in contrast, preferring Leslie Howard.[84] The results were seen as satisfactory and raised expectations for the response of critics and the paying public, with first reports arriving at the studio immediately after the film's premiere on September 22, 1939.

Intermezzo was highly commended for its sensitive and mature treatment of infidelity, the artful cinematography of Gregg Toland, the tasteful musical score, and the quality of performances of the leading trio. Ingrid Bergman as a new face received a great deal of attention. Selznick immediately declared "unprecedented critical enthusiasm for her"[85] but also stated that the unanimous positive reaction did not come as a surprise to him. He wrote in a telegram to John Hay Whitney: "YOU WILL RECALL I MADE WHAT SEEMED LIKE THE INSANE STATEMENT THAT I THOUGHT SHE MIGHT HAVE A BIGGER FUTURE FOR US EVEN THAN VIVIEN [LEIGH]. I PERSONALLY NEVER GET TIRED OF LOOKING AT HER AND EACH TIME I SAW THE PICTURE I BECAME MORE ENCHANTED BY HER LOVELINESS AND PERSONALITY."[86]

The assumption about the main target group proved correct. A study concerning the audiences in selected cinemas in Philadelphia and New York revealed that 60 to 85 percent were women and even though men reacted mostly positively to the story, their responses were not as enthusiastic compared to females.[87] Selznick was extremely satisfied with the results as "there is nothing better to make than a picture which women adore. We all know too well the disastrous result of any picture that men adore and women don't like."[88] For this reason, the producer made it a priority that female reviewers wrote about the picture, because they (rather than their male colleagues) would be more appreciative of the melodramatic plot and the unaggressive version of femininity personified by Bergman.

It soon became apparent, though, that men were also not immune to the charms of the actress. A review by the leading film critic of the time Frank S.

Nugent for the *New York Times* is typical in terms of its celebratory tone and is worth citing in a longer excerpt:

> Sweden's Ingrid Bergman is so *lovely* a person and so *gracious* an actress that we are rather glad David Selznick selected the quiet "Intermezzo, a Love Story," for her Hollywood debut instead of some more bravura drama which, while it might not have overwhelmed its star, might have overwhelmed us and made us less conscious of the *freshness, the simplicity and the natural dignity* that are Miss Bergman's pleasant gift to our screen. The reticent, gentle, frequently poignant qualities of the [. . .] new film are safely entrusted to Miss Bergman's hands—and to those of Leslie Howard and Edna Best, who have assisted at her debut. [. . .] Miss Bergman's share in it is, of course, the nicest part of it. She is *beautiful, and not at all pretty.* Her *acting* is surprisingly mature, yet singularly *free from the stylistic traits—the mannerisms, postures, precise inflections—* that become the stock in trade of the matured actress. Our impression of her Anita, who is pallid one moment, vivacious the next, yet always *consistent,* is that of a lamp whose wick burns bright or dull, but always burns. There is that *incandescence* about Miss Bergman, that *spiritual spark* which makes us believe that Selznick has found another great lady of the screen.[89]

The extent to which Nugent's reaction corresponds with the intentions of Selznick's studio is remarkable. His choice of words almost precisely reflects the presentation of Bergman as a star of a new type, based on a modest charm, acting skill, and authenticity (perceived as an uncomplicated blending of her role and private self). Worthy of mention is the observation concerning the appropriate choice of material: *Intermezzo*'s main draws were its simple story and performances, making it an ideal vehicle for the presentation of a fresh acting talent. Other periodicals also welcomed Bergman as an emerging star in their review columns. *Variety,* for example, mentioned the fact that the actress overshadowed Leslie Howard, despite his character being given more space, and further praised Bergman as "beautiful, talented and convincing, providing an arresting performance and a warm personality that introduces a new stellar asset to Hollywood. She has charm, sincerity and an infectious vivaciousness that will serve her well in both drama and comedy."[90]

Although the critical community praised *Intermezzo* as a quality production in all aspects, its members also agreed that it had only limited commercial potential. The material appealed to an educated, mostly female audience in large cities (as in the above-mentioned New York and Philadelphia), while it usually met with a cooler response from male and female viewers in smaller towns and from families with children.[91] The focus on a sophisticated adult audience, high production costs resulting from extensive retakes, and the unusually strong competition in cinemas (the year 1939 is often referred to as "Hollywood's greatest year")[92] meant that *Intermezzo* eventually failed to meet expectations at the box office. Although Selznick had difficulty hiding his disappointment in front of his employees,[93] he did his best to view the situation in a positive light. The film might not have made a profit during its initial run, but this was not as important in the end as the enthusiasm evoked by his new acting discovery and the promise (economic and symbolic) that it signaled for the future. The original motive behind *Intermezzo* was to make a medium-budget film with a minimal risk of commercial failure. After the casting of Bergman, however, this approach was reevaluated in order to present the new acting acquisition most effectively to the US and international public, regardless of the immediate profits.[94]

The unanimously positive acceptance of the actress was confirmed in the number of articles profiling the actress, which began to appear in accordance with Selznick's strategy after the premiere of the film. Many of them contained the same characteristics and comparisons as in the publicity generated by Selznick's studio, which further solidified the consistency of her newly formed public identity.

The authors often praised the unusual tactics of avoiding publicity, including interviews and public appearances, until *Intermezzo* finally hit the cinemas. The British magazine *Picturegoer* praised the fact that Selznick "has purposely avoided the usual fanfares as well as the 'ostentatious mystery' build-up that led us to expect too much of some of Mr. Goldwyn's Young Ladies." While Goldwyn's foreign discoveries Anna Sten (originally from Ukraine) and Sigrid Gurie (of Norwegian origin, although born in the US) were accompanied by a "million-dollar ballyhoo campaign," Bergman was brought to Hollywood in silence, which gave a truly special level of control to the public to decide to either accept her or not, purely upon the basis of her performance in *Intermezzo*.[95] An article by Dora Albert for *Screenland* expressed it clearly: "You made her a star! You, and you, and you created her. You're responsible."[96] Bergman was in other words presented as a personality created by fans as opposed to an artificially evoked fuss.

The absence of an excessive hoopla campaign also chimed in with the presentation of Bergman as an authentic young woman, (seemingly) untouched by the usual mechanisms of star development. The praise for this was attributed to her own determination not to allow herself to be changed as well as to the "wily, astute" foresight of her Hollywood discoverer, David O. Selznick: "[H]e realized that the quality that had made her a great star in Sweden was her naturalness. So he didn't spoil that quality by making her wear her hair in

Medusa ringlets, with every hair glittering with artificiality; he didn't change her mouth; he didn't ask make-up artists to turn her into another Hollywood glamour girl. He just let her be."[97] (As I have written in the introduction to the chapter, the interpretation later turned against Selznick, with the primary initiative being ascribed to Bergman.)

Trade journals, general interest magazines, and newspapers all took over the rhetoric of Selznick's studio in other areas as well. Just as the producer had hoped, they built up a legend around the actress's modesty and lack of pretense. For example, Jack Stinnett wrote in the *New York World Telegram*: "as unspoiled as a fresh Swedish snowfall, as naïve as a country lass approaching her first smorgasbord, this twenty-four-year-old apple-cheeked Stockholm matron is in the unique position of being a Hollywood star (see 'Intermezzo: A Love Story') without having the slightest conception of what the Hollywood furore [*sic*] is all about."[98] Apart from the obligatory information on the absence of make-up, Stinnett made mention of the fact that Bergman did not need a hairdresser, since her simple hairstyle did not require it; to maintain her appearance and health, she did not need to do anything else than regular exercise (skiing, swimming) and spend time in the outdoors, as commanded by her Scandinavian nature;[99] and during the filming of *Intermezzo*, she insisted on wearing her own well-worn tweed coat in several scenes in her role of Anita. The author also emphasized her lack of interest in Hollywood glitz, which manifested itself in her preference for family—her husband and one-year-old daughter—over interviews and society events (Bergman supposedly refused two interviews and an important meeting because "it's the nurse's day off and I can't leave the baby"). The article, aptly subtitled "She fits exactly your idea of what a star isn't like," was complemented by a large photograph of the actress's smiling face, which helped to present her as the antithesis of exotic and unapproachable Hollywood stars.[100] As Robin Wood noticed within the context of the overall publicity of Ingrid Bergman, the emphasis on her dazzling smile (in contrast to the inscrutable, contemplative look or shots emphasizing bodies and expensive dresses with jewels and fashion accessories) implied "openness and generosity" and helped draw attention away from any sign of threat or "feminine mystique."[101]

An article by Harry Evans for the family magazine *Family Circle* presented Bergman also as the embodiment of "simplicity, integrity, and unaffected loveliness." The author documented these qualities with several examples, which were supposed to convince even the greatest skeptics that a new type of star had arrived in Hollywood: undemanding, discreet, hard-working, and utterly charming. He did not merely stop, for example, with the simple statement that Bergman did not need make-up to look attractive. To give increased credence to his words, he provided the readers with a direct testimony: "[a] friend of mine did not believe this, so she sneaked into Ingrid's bathroom one night. She found a toothbrush, some toothpaste, and a cake of soap. That was the works!"[102] The paean to the appearance and character of the actress had, however, a surprising conclusion. When Bergman, after several months of separation from her family, returned to Sweden, Evans made a powerful appeal concerning her return to Hollywood:

> You came to America a stranger. And you were with us but a little while. Yet you left with the love and affection of every person who came to know you well. So you remind us, at a time when the world needs so sorely to be reminded, of the close kinship of all the people of the world. And how senseless it is to hate anyone just because he [sic] lives in another part of the world and speaks another language. Thanks for knowing you, Ingrid Bergman—and please hurry back.[103]

Even though the actress maintained a strongly apolitical attitude and the only film which she had made in Hollywood thus far was an escapist romantic drama about a love triangle, her identity was also imbued from the very beginning with powerful ideological meanings. Her image, based on naturalness, openness, and immediacy, enabled her not only to embody the ideal of femininity but also become a symbol of humanism and solidarity at a difficult time when the Western society was profoundly tested by the reverberating economic crisis and the ongoing military conflict.

CONCLUSION

Intermezzo began as a modestly budgeted project designed to generate relatively easy profits. After the casting of Ingrid Bergman, however, the intentions of the studio changed. The material was now supposed to primarily introduce the fresh quality of Selznick's acting acquisition. His close supervision of both the film and the publicity made it possible to construct the actress's burgeoning identity in the required manner and present her as a simple and authentic young woman, powerfully resonating with public's contemporary preferences. Although the film did not become a hit (being too modest and too narrowly profiled in terms of its target audience in a particularly prolific year), the reactions by the public, journalists, and important players within the film industry all testify to the fact that the main task was accomplished. The carefully mounted campaign for Bergman generated interest and presented her as an acting discovery with bright prospects. After *Intermezzo*, she had not become a leading Hollywood star, but she certainly was on the right path. This process was completed in the following years.

Out of the ten films that the actress went on to make as part of her contract with Selznick, only one was personally produced by him: Alfred Hitchcock's *Spellbound*. In the remaining cases, they involved loan-outs to other studios, from 1941 onwards exclusively for their high-profile A-titles, which generated profits for Selznick in the hundreds of thousands.[104] *Intermezzo* eventually profited from this situation, too, as after the actress reached a position of a leading star, the picture returned repeatedly to the cinemas and thereby "caught up" in ticket sales what it had not achieved during its first release in the years 1939 and 1940. The decision to prioritize symbolic capital in the form of presenting an attractive acting personality instead of immediate profits thereby had a beneficial financial impact over the long-term.

Bergman's US launch was made possible by focusing on her aura of naturalness and authenticity. *Intermezzo* thereby established a benchmark for the actress for the coming years. As David Smit noticed, "Selznick's control over Bergman's photography may be the source of much of the associations of Bergman's beauty with innocence and spirituality."[105] The strategy of the studio was motivated from the beginning by an interest in creating a consistent image around her based on spontaneity and simplicity. In contrast, all those aspects which did not coincide with this intention, including intensity, passion, sexuality, and exoticism, were systematically suppressed in her initial roles and publicity.

Selznick's aim was not, however, to link the actress with one fixed type. The 1941 adaptation of Stevenson's *Dr. Jekyll and Mr. Hyde* (MGM) presented her in the role of a simple-minded and openly sexual London prostitute Ivy, while further roles provided her with other challenges. The initial impression created by *Intermezzo* was, however, so powerful that it was able to neutralize all those attributes which were not in harmony with it. The roles of prostitutes, promiscuous women, and *femmes fatales* (apart from *Dr. Jekyll and Mr. Hyde*, for example in *Casablanca* [Warner Bros., 1943], the adaptation of Edna Ferber's *Saratoga Trunk* [Warner Bros., 1945], and Hitchcock's *Notorious* [RKO]) were perceived as acting challenges, as opposed to projections of her actual personality. Bergman was supposedly cast in these roles against her natural type, and it was consequently only thanks to her skills and talent that the public accepted and believed in them.[106] The emphasis upon her acting versatility, which soon became another pillar of her professional image, made it possible to cast her in diverse roles without causing any fundamental rupture to her star identity depending upon naturalness, nobility, and spirituality. This also explains why her affair with Roberto Rossellini at the end of the decade met with such a negative reaction. People had been so convinced of the image which Selznick's studio had created around the actress, that the revelation of her extramarital relationship made them feel deceived. Selznick's company with its strategies and behind-the-scenes machinations contributed to a unified perception of Bergman as an authentic and approachable Nordic type without signs of mystery. Only with the weakening of the institutional control, after the dissolution of their cooperation, did irreconcilable contradictions begin to surface in Bergman's image.[107] As Selznick himself later confessed:

> I'm afraid I'm responsible for the public's image of her as Saint Ingrid. I hired a press agent who was an expert at shielding stars from the press, and we released only stories that emphasized her sterling character. We deliberately built her up as the normal, healthy, unneurotic career woman, devoid of scandal and with an idyllic home life. I guess that backfired later.[108]

The previous lines demonstrate that her presentation in *Intermezzo* and the attendant campaign played a key role in this process.

2

PRODUCING PRESTIGE

Loan-Outs of Selznick's Female Stars in the
First Half of the 1940s

> [David O. Selznick] is one of the movies' top producers—when he wants to be. When
> he doesn't, he prospers under his system of owning stars and renting them.
> —FROM THE ARTICLE "SELZNICK AND HIS GIRLS," *LOOK* MAGAZINE[1]

PROLOGUE: THE ACADEMY AWARDS CEREMONY, 1944

The sixteenth annual Oscars ceremony, organized by the Academy of Motion Picture Arts and Sciences, took place on Thursday, March 2, 1944. For the first time in history, it was not conceived as a mere banquet for the invited, but rather as a large public event, with a corresponding venue: the renowned Grauman's Chinese Theater on Hollywood Boulevard. Several hundred tickets were available for sale and the more than two thousand people attending included members of the US Army, who were admitted free of charge. The evening was hosted by the popular comedian Jack Benny and a live broadcast, for those who could not attend the ceremony, was provided by the Los Angeles radio station KFWB. As Oscar historians Robert Osborne and Tom O'Neil, respectively, said, "after fifteen years, the intimate little industry dinners became a thing of the past"[2] and "the Oscars, as they're widely known today, were born."[3]

The Academy Awards of 1944 represented an important moment for David Selznick, even though he did not have any of his films in competition. If he had, however, achieved his greatest success as a movie producer in 1940 and 1941, when he won twice in a row in the main category with *Gone with the Wind* and *Rebecca*, then the year 1944 was a clear triumph for Selznick as a producer of stars. Three representatives of his acting "stable" were nominated in the Best Actress in a Leading Role category: Ingrid Bergman for the role of

51

Maria in an adaptation of Hemingway's *For Whom the Bell Tolls* (Paramount); Joan Fontaine for the role of Tessa in the romantic drama *The Constant Nymph* (Warner Bros.); and Jennifer Jones for the title role in an adaptation of Franz Werfel's novel *The Song of Bernadette* (Twentieth Century-Fox).[4] (The five nominees further included Jean Arthur for her performance in the comedy *The More the Merrier* [Columbia] and Greer Garson for the title role in the biopic *Madame Curie* [MGM]).

Selznick was present at the ceremony, most of the time surrounded by his actresses, as evidenced in several archive pictures.[5] Although he predicted that the award for the lead actress would go to Ingrid Bergman,[6] the winner was eventually Jennifer Jones, who had received a Golden Globe (awarded for the first time in history) a month earlier. On the day of her Oscar triumph, the actress celebrated her twenty-fifth birthday and during her emotional speech, she did not neglect to emphasize the contribution of David Selznick, even though at first glance he did not have anything to do with *The Song of Bernadette* as it was produced by Twentieth Century-Fox.[7] The Hollywood insiders, however, knew very well that it was Selznick who provided Jones with the role in this prestigious film with high commercial and artistic potential. The same happened with his other two nominees, Ingrid Bergman and Joan Fontaine in *For Whom the Bell Tolls* and *The Constant Nymph*, respectively. As the following chapter demonstrates, the predominance of Selznick's contract actresses at the Oscars of 1944 symbolically proved the leading position of his company in the female stars' market that came about as a result of an elaborate business strategy.

THE MARKET WITH FEMALE STARS DURING WWII AND LOAN-OUTS OF SELZNICK'S CONTRACT ACTRESSES

It can be argued that Selznick provided two basic products for sale: films that he produced as an independent and offered to the public through his distributor; and talents, including actors and actresses as well as directors (Alfred Hitchcock, Robert Stevenson), with whom he had exclusive long-term contracts and who were offered to other film studios as loan-outs.[8] A look at the portfolio of the company clearly demonstrates that the first type of product predominated in the second half of the 1930s, when Selznick completed eleven films in rapid succession, while business with stars became his key activity during the prolonged production hiatus that began in 1940, after completing *Rebecca*.

Based on the successes of Ingrid Bergman in *Intermezzo: A Love Story*, Vivien Leigh in *Gone with the Wind* and Joan Fontaine in *Rebecca*, Selznick focused first and foremost on the development of female stars.[9] Jennifer Jones, Dorothy McGuire, and Shirley Temple were soon added to the above-mentioned trio and Selznick gained the reputation of an infallible assessor of acting talent and star potential in Hollywood. In January 1944, *Look* magazine published an article "Selznick and His Girls," which informed its readers that "behind six Hollywood box-office beauties [Bergman, Leigh, Fontaine, Temple, Jones, and McGuire] is a shrewd maestro—David Selznick."[10] While Bergman, Leigh, and Fontaine achieved fame and recognition in his own productions and Temple came to him as a (former) child star, Jones and McGuire were introduced to the public in films of other studios.[11] The planned production inactivity on the part of Selznick's company could have initially been seen as an obstacle for introducing new and developing existing stars. The studio, however, was able to adjust effectively to the new terms and over the years 1940 to 1945 contract actresses were repeatedly provided with lucrative roles in prestigious films by large Hollywood companies, which resulted in considerable income, a range of awards and a leading position in the market for Selznick.[12]

If the promotion of films in Selznick's production was aimed at the movie-going public with the goal of obtaining the highest possible ticket sales (which eventually translated into company profits), the trade with stars required communication within the film industry, with other producers and studio management. The value of female stars increased significantly during the war. A front-page article in *Variety* published on March 8, 1944, mentioned an escalation of loan-out fees for popular actresses to twice the amount in contrast to the situation a few years earlier. According to the magazine, a number of studios focused to such an extent on the development of new male personalities, as a consequence of the departure of young actors to the armed forces, that they neglected female stars. The situation was critical for many of them: "Few of the film companies have more than a single outstanding dramatic femme star while some of the studios have none."[13] The problem was intensified by the increasing number of actresses preferring to work on a freelance basis, giving them the freedom to choose their own projects and have increased creative control.[14] In light of these developments, Selznick's rather small company was doing particularly well: "Selznick, operating independently, is in perhaps as strong a position as any major studio for femme dramatic talent, getting from $100,000 per picture and upwards for such of his contract stars as Jennifer Jones, Ingrid Bergman, Dorothy McGuire, and Joan Fontaine."[15]

Over a short period of time, Selznick with his female stars achieved a privileged position in the market. It might have even seemed that his company at this time was no longer functioning as a traditional film studio, whose primary goal was the production of films, and that it was more akin to a talent agency (like the one successfully led by David's brother Myron). While the first part of the above is merely a statement of the facts, the second needs a correction and specification. Selznick secured his contract actors and actresses roles in films of other studios, but they continued to be his employees. The essence of their relationship was therefore extremely distant to the professional dynamics between the star and his or her agent. Significantly, for instance, Selznick's financial benefits from these transactions greatly exceeded the standard 10 percent commission of Hollywood agents. While the talents continued to receive their weekly salary as specified in the contract, Selznick was paid several times this amount for providing their services (the loan-out contract was always drawn up between Selznick's company and the business partner and the given performer was usually not involved with any direct financial gain).

One should add, however, that the actors and actresses received a regular salary even during times of inactivity, that Selznick's company provided them with first-rate services, and that the development of stars itself was an extremely costly affair with an uncertain result. This side of the business with stars was usually hidden from the public, however, and Selznick gradually received the unflattering label of a flesh peddler who was paid astronomical sums without making a significant contribution to the success of his stars.[16] This view was explicitly present, for example, in a comment by Ed Raiden published in *Showmen's Trade Review* in January 1944, only a few weeks before the Oscars ceremony with the dominant representation of Selznick's actresses:

> This is the season for Academy Awards in Hollywood, and all the moviemakers are busy pressing the claims of their favorite candidates and pictures for Oscars. And while they press, D. O. Selznick stands by and grins. Or is that a snicker? Let the studios advance Ingrid Bergman for "Casablanca" and "For Whom the Bell Tolls," and Joan Fontaine for "The Constant Nymph," and Jennifer Jones for "The Song of Bernadette." Let them fight for the honor, and Selznick will stand by and pick up the marbles. Why? He holds the contracts of all three stars, as well as the contract of Dorothy McGuire, whose job in "Claudia" may rate her some award.[17]

It is my hope that the following will demonstrate that Selznick was not a mere passive observer, taking advantage of the success of the actresses who he was fortunate enough to have under contract. Instead, he was an active originator of their position and value in the market. Their involvement in prestigious films with in-demand roles, which provided them with recognition and star status, was a direct consequence of Selznick's focused activity behind the scenes.[18] I will specifically focus in this chapter on the loan-outs of Ingrid Bergman for *For Whom the Bell Tolls*, Dorothy McGuire for *Claudia*, and Jennifer Jones for *The Song of Bernadette*. I chose these three case studies to cover approximately the same period (from 1941 to early 1944), but also with the aim to explain various aspects of the negotiations concerning these loan-outs. Each case involved different challenges for the company. Ingrid Bergman had already completed four US films when Selznick lent her for *Casablanca* and *For Whom the Bell Tolls*, which finally catapulted her to the position of a top Hollywood star. For Dorothy McGuire, in contrast, *Claudia* became her film debut, and Jennifer Jones was in a similar position, having only been in two Republic Pictures B-movies several years before making *The Song of Bernadette*. One can therefore trace their transformation from completely unknown faces into valuable commodities after the release of both films.

My goal is to uncover the mechanisms which Selznick used to acquire desirable roles for his female talents in films of other studios, and while doing so, describe the requirements which these productions had to comply with. Furthermore, I reconstruct Selznick's communication with the companies which developed these projects and discuss strategies by which he ensured the engagement of his contract actresses. Finally, I trace the conditions which Selznick negotiated for these loan-outs and take notice of the consequences they had for his further operations.

HOW DO YOU SOLVE A PROBLEM LIKE MARIA?
INGRID BERGMAN IN *FOR WHOM THE BELL TOLLS*

Intermezzo was the means of presenting Ingrid Bergman to the public in 1939 as an exciting new personality of the screen. In comparison with *Gone with the Wind* and *Rebecca*, it was a much more modest project without guaranteed media attention which translated into limited revenues and audience impact. Bergman had to therefore wait for her chance to become one of the leading stars of Hollywood. Selznick, on the strength of unanimously positive responses to her US debut, hoped that he could place the actress in an important film from a major Hollywood studio, but the offers did not come. Under pressure, he finally agreed with her loan-outs for two films with medium-sized budgets, *Adam Had Four Sons* (1941, Columbia) and *Rage in Heaven* (1941, MGM). He had no illusions about their qualities,[19] but her participation in the latter caught the attention of MGM executives who offered Bergman a supporting role in their ambitious adaptation of *Dr. Jekyll and Mr. Hyde* with Spencer Tracy in the title (double) role. The association with a leading male star and the costly screen version of a respected literary work were promising. The following months were supposed to decide whether Bergman joined the ranks of the most valuable and sought-after Hollywood actresses or whether she remained, in terms of A productions, classified as merely a competent performer in supporting roles.

Dr. Jekyll and Mr. Hyde also encouraged Selznick to reevaluate his approach to the choice of roles for Bergman. He wrote in December 1940 that the film will present the actress as "a sexy bitch; and while a few months ago I'd have opposed Ingrid's doing anything but a divinely spiritual role [. . .] I think the important thing to do is to get her into a really fine and outstanding picture [. . .] and, further, to show her versatility. I have a hunch that she could come through with a sex quality that would startle everybody."[20] Selznick therefore decided to further promote Bergman as a universally skilled actress with an emphasis on her mastering the acting craft, thereby increasing her value in the market and making her available for a wide range of roles.

One of the projects selected to develop her career further was the adaptation of Ernest Hemingway's current novel *For Whom the Bell Tolls*. Immediately after its publication in October 1940, a bidding war broke out, with Paramount emerging victorious. The studio paid the record sum of $150,000, which was three times what Selznick had spent four years earlier on *Gone with the Wind*.[21] The high price seemed to be justified, however, as the novel immediately became a bestseller thanks to the author's reputation, the topical, socially provocative theme and the high praise in the press.[22] Paramount planned to approach the eagerly awaited adaptation in great style and turn it into one of the most expensive and spectacular films ever made.

Kay Brown from Selznick's New York office referred to *For Whom the Bell Tolls* as a possibility for Bergman as early as November 1940.[23] The actress was greatly interested in the role of Maria, the traumatized Spanish girl who joined the anti-fascist rebels during the Civil War, and pushed Selznick to obtain it for her. The producer maintained restraint, though, aware of the fact that Paramount had a number of their own actresses in mind, whose use would be more financially advantageous for the studio and whose participation in such a high-profile picture could lead to the establishment of a new star as had been the case with Selznick's own contract actresses in *Gone with the Wind* and *Rebecca*.[24]

The situation changed, however, in January of the following year. On the release of *For Whom the Bell Tolls*, *Life* magazine published a portrait of Ernest Hemingway accompanied by a series of documentary photographs from the Spanish Civil War. This was supposed to help the Paramount filmmakers with the visual conception of the film and therefore also with achieving the highest level of authenticity. The writer himself made use of this occasion and his own authority to express his views concerning the casting of the upcoming film adaptation. He wanted his friend Gary Cooper for the main role of the US volunteer Robert Jordan,[25] while considering Ingrid Bergman as the ideal actress for the character of Maria.[26] These views were registered by Selznick's studio and subsequently became the basis for its strategy to encourage Paramount to hire the actress.

Precisely a week after *Life* published the above-mentioned article, Selznick dictated a draft of a letter addressed to Paramount's management (president Frank Freeman and the newly appointed vice president Henry Ginsberg), in which he referred to the growing value of Bergman on the strength of projects already completed or under preparation (in particular *Dr. Jekyll and Mr. Hyde*) and the need to plan further steps in her career. If there would be interest on the part of Paramount, he would be willing to free her up for the role of Maria. On the other hand, he continued, "I feel it necessary that we make clear to Mr. Hemingway and to the readers of the book that if she does not play the role, it will not be because she is unavailable for it."[27] It is not apparent from the preserved materials whether the letter was sent in this exact wording (the company could have decided that Selznick's threat was formulated too aggressively and could harm the negotiations). In any case, the communication that took place over the coming weeks and months, mostly by means of Hollywood trade journals, was conducted in a similar spirit.

In late January, Selznick took advantage of the fact that his brother Myron's agency represented Hemingway in negotiations with Paramount concerning the sale of rights to *For Whom the Bell Tolls* and obtained access directly to the writer. He mentioned the results of their private conversation in a report to Kay Brown:

> I pinned Hemingway down [. . .] and he told me clearly and frankly that he would like to see [Bergman] play the part. He also said this to the press today. [. . .] I am also personally supervising a publicity campaign to try to jockey Paramount into a position where they will almost have to use her. You will be seeing these items from time to time. [. . .] If she doesn't get the part, it won't be because there hasn't been a systematic campaign to get it for her![28]

A key point in this concentrated campaign involved the arrangement of a personal meeting between Hemingway and Bergman, which took place on February 1, 1941, in Jack's Restaurant in San Francisco.[29] In order to ensure that the public and Paramount's executives (the actual addressees of this indirect communication) learned about it, Selznick invited journalists and photographers from *Life* magazine, where the original article about Hemingway and *For Whom the Bell Tolls* had appeared. Later in February, *Life* published a detailed report containing several photographs depicting Hemingway and Bergman having a friendly chat. During their conversation, Hemingway reportedly turned to the actress with the words, "If you don't act in the picture, Ingrid, I won't work on it," and when saying goodbye he gave her his novel with the dedication: "To Ingrid Bergman, who is the Maria of this book."[30] Although Selznick was behind the meeting, the public was supposed to be under the impression that it came about at Hemingway's instigation:[31] as was the usual custom in Hollywood, the effectiveness of the strategy depended to some extent on whether these machinations remained hidden from public view. Apart from *Life* magazine, other periodicals made mention of the meeting. The *Los Angeles Examiner*, for example, quoted a statement by Hemingway about Bergman that "[s]he looks exactly like the girl I had in mind when I wrote the book," and repeated his threat that he would not participate in the picture if she was not given the role.[32] Selznick gained additional allies in the persons of Gary Cooper, who was from the beginning the only candidate for playing Robert Jordan, Sam Wood, who became the director after Cecil B. DeMille declined, and their shared employer, the independent producer Samuel Goldwyn.

Selznick's intervention, leading to the personal involvement of Hemingway, represented an important move, which was supposed to impress the public and foremost the tens of thousands of readers of his book who viewed him as an authority. Paramount undoubtedly noticed the results of Selznick's campaign but remained unyielding. Instead of beginning official negotiations, as Selznick had hoped, they began to test their own contract actresses, including Paulette Goddard and Betty Field. Selznick was not discouraged by this, however. His publicity department regularly released reports that Bergman was the only possible choice for the role of Maria; that the author of the novel, Gary Cooper, and the public were on her side; that the requirements of his company were extremely modest in comparison with regular Hollywood custom; and that the only one who was holding up the deal was Paramount.[33] In this fashion, Selznick also created a positive image of his company, in accordance with his interest in informing the public about the "difference in our policy against the big studios policy of not lending their people—in contrast with our willingness to lend them for anything important if it will boost their careers."[34] As evidence of his generosity, he recalled the casting of the role of Rhett Butler in *Gone with the Wind*, when his studio—in an effort to heed the wishes of the moviegoing public—agreed to the excessive demands of MGM and gave up half of the film only to obtain Clark Gable. This was supposed to support the impression that a similar situation had occurred with *For Whom the Bell Tolls* and that its makers should listen to "the voice of the people," who would not accept anyone else in the role. The rhetoric was exaggerated, of course, as Bergman was by far not the public's only choice. It did, however, undoubtedly have an impact. In June 1941, several trade journals informed that Paramount had received thus far around 7,000 suggestions for the casting of the female lead with the highest percentage of votes for the foursome of Paulette Goddard, Betty Field (both of them with contracts to Paramount), Ingrid Bergman, and Vivien Leigh.[35] Since the information was provided by Paramount itself, and it was in their interest to publicize primarily their own actresses, it is highly probable that the support for Bergman (and Leigh, even though her casting was not even a remote possibility) had to have been considerable.

Due to demanding preparations and the postponement of principal photography because of the US entering World War II, the process of selecting the actress for Maria dragged on for a year and a half (from January 1941 to the middle of 1942), rivaling in length the casting of the role of Scarlett O'Hara in *Gone with the Wind*, which lasted only several months longer. Speculation by industry insiders and the general public led to articles with titles such as "Who Will Play Maria?"[36] that regularly appeared on the pages of the press and supplied Paramount with welcome publicity.[37] With the first day of filming scheduled for the beginning of July, however, there was a need to make the final decision. Despite the strong support for Bergman, the studio gave preference to their own contract actress Vera Zorina for the highly contested role. The financial aspects spoke in her favor, as the budget of *For Whom the Bell Tolls* had reached almost $2.5 million (more than five times the average cost at the time) and a considerable amount of it was designated for the salaries of Gary Cooper and Sam Wood, who were provided by Samuel Goldwyn.[38] Any savings were therefore welcome. Moreover, the actress and ballerina originally from Norway (actual name Eva Brigitta Hartwig) had been marked out by the studio as a future star and a potentially extremely valuable commodity.

The film crew moved to the Sierra Nevada where filming began on July 2. After two weeks, however, the work came to a stop and Zorina was removed from the project. According to the press, the actress could not get accustomed to the high altitude and her look was also compromised by the unflattering haircut which was chosen for the role.[39] These factors could have played a role, but I believe that the main reason for such a radical step was much more likely related to dissatisfaction with the performance of Zorina, who had until then only performed in musicals and comedies and did not have any experience with demanding dramatic roles. This is also confirmed by the words of Ernest Hemingway, according to whom Zorina was "so terrible in the rushes from the first shots [. . .] that they finally got rid of her."[40] The film's producer Buddy DeSylva, fully aware of the responsibility for this prestigious, high-budget film, therefore leaned toward the only solution possible in such a precarious situation: he addressed David Selznick with a request to borrow Ingrid Bergman.

At that point, Bergman had met with success in *Dr. Jekyll and Mr. Hyde*, was nearing completion of another high-profile film, *Casablanca*, at Warner Bros., and was already accepted by much of the public as Hemingway's Maria thanks to Selznick's campaign. Being a recognized dramatic actress on the rise, she also represented a much greater guarantee of success and safer protection of the large investment than Zorina, who had limited acting experience. Bergman underwent a screen test in early August and the results were referred to as "wonderful" by Paramount executives.[41] The only issue, which remained to be solved, was the financial conditions of the transaction. Earlier, Selznick was willing to sacrifice one or two films with Bergman to Paramount only to be able to obtain the role for her.[42] Now, however, there was no need for such a concession. Paramount was in serious trouble due to the removal of Zorina and the investment of several million dollars was up in the air. Selznick was therefore expecting an amount between $100,000 and $125,000.[43] (For comparison, the company received $34,000 for *Dr. Jekyll and Mr. Hyde* and $25,000 for *Casablanca.*)[44] In the end, a compromise was reached wherein Selznick billed Paramount $8,000 per week with a ten-week guarantee and a proportional sum when exceeding the contracted filming period.[45] The overall income therefore reached a sum of $90,666.[46] It was further agreed that Bergman would be billed in the credits (above the film's title) as well as on promotional materials in the same font size as Gary Cooper. She joined the crew on August 6, only a few days after her duties on *Casablanca* came to an end.

Selznick's campaign with the objective of securing a highly desirable role in a prestigious film for his contract actress—a campaign "as carefully worked out as plans for the invasion of Sicily" as *Look* magazine later remarked[47]—paid off in the end, even though the result eventually depended on factors beyond the producer's immediate control. In a certain sense, however, even the failure of Zorina could have been a consequence of pressure from the public and her close colleagues, the majority of whom preferred Bergman and did not make it a secret. Bergman was generally viewed as the ideal choice for Maria thanks to the mobilization of Hemingway, Cooper, and Wood, and Selznick's ingenious behind-the-scenes strategizing and the regular communication with the public by means of press releases. In contrast, the original decision by Paramount to entrust the role to Zorina was immediately viewed as the "worst casting error in years."[48]

It was in the commercial interest of Paramount to get on board with this rhetoric which is exactly what happened after the completion of the film. On the occasion of the Hollywood premiere, an advertisement, for example, was released with the following wording:

In 1941 Ernest Hemingway presented Ingrid Bergman with an autographed copy of his celebrated novel "FOR WHOM THE BELL TOLLS," bearing this inscription "For Ingrid Bergman, who is the Maria of this book."

In 1942 Paramount selected Ingrid Bergman to play Maria [. . .] in "FOR WHOM THE BELL TOLLS," one of the three greatest motion pictures ever made.

In 1943 Next Monday [August 16], Southern California will realize the full meaning of Hemingway's prophetic inscription, when it sees Ingrid Bergman as Maria in her superb emotional performance with Gary Cooper as Robert Jordan.[49]

Bergman was suddenly presented as the only possible actress for Maria, with the blessing of the novel's author himself, and the listing of three years in succession in the ad was designed to create the impression that her involvement in the film had been inevitable. In this manner, the studio tried to distract attention from the complicated and prolonged process of casting the female lead and most importantly to sweep under the rug the fiasco involving Zorina.

Particularly remarkable about the entire situation was the obvious paradox that an actress of a Swedish background and endowed with typical Nordic features—tall, majestic, light-haired, and blue-eyed—was not only promoted but widely accepted as the most suitable candidate for the role of the young Spanish woman, who Hemingway described in the novel as follows:

> Her teeth were white in her brown face and her skin and her eyes were the same golden tawny brown. She had high cheekbones, merry eyes and a straight mouth with full lips. Her hair was the golden brown of a grain field that has been burned dark in the sun but it was cut short all over her head so that it was but little longer than the fur on a beaver pelt.[50]

Maria in the book functions as an embodiment of Spain itself, traumatized by the Civil War and containing qualities which are often (perhaps stereotypically) associated with this country and its people (inner strength and determination, devotion, passion, but also innocence and a certain vulnerability). In contrast, the public image of Bergman up until that time, formed by her roles, interviews, profile articles in the press, and so on, depended on her presentation as the "Swedish dynamo," "Nordic natural," or "North Star."[51] Selznick, however, planned to launch the actress in Hollywood as a versatile performer, without a clearly defined type, and what better evidence could there be for her universality and versatility than a role which was in sharp contrast with what was perceived as her true self? The acceptance of Bergman was also made easier by the fact that she was viewed as the antithesis of the Hollywood conception of glamour. Her beauty did not depend upon a connection with exoticism and luxury, but instead on natural charm and simplicity. This was all very convenient for the role of Maria, a simple country girl living in inhospitable mountains, wearing men's trousers, and a tattered blouse.[52]

Almost three years had gone by from the purchase of the rights to Hemingway's novel when *For Whom the Bell Tolls* was finally released in cinemas in July 1943. The attention of both the media and the public was constantly focused on the film throughout the period and the expectations were extremely high. After seeing the film, a number of commentators criticized its three-hour running time, over-reliance on dialogue, and dulling of the political edges contained in the novel. But the public ended up receiving exactly what they

Gary Cooper and Ingrid Bergman in a publicity still for Paramount's *For Whom the Bell Tolls*.

had expected: a large-scale Technicolor spectacle with a love story taking place against the exciting backdrop of a war. The distribution patterns and advertising campaign corresponded to the importance of the picture. Paramount initially road-showed the film at a premium price, only to finally let it go into general release in 1945. It was a genuine film event in all respects, in all probability the greatest since Selznick's *Gone with the Wind*. The gross receipts exceeded $7 million, with only the patriotic revue musical *This Is the Army* (Warner Bros.) achieving better results out of the films premiered in 1943.[53]

Ingrid Bergman, who was universally lauded for her performance as Maria, played a significant part in the film's success. Lee Mortimer from the *Daily Mirror* stated, for example, that "every time [her] beautiful, fluid, expressive face flashed on the screen" he experienced "heart palpitation." For these reasons he did not hesitate to refer to her performance as "one of the outstanding cinema performances of all time."[54] Apart from an Oscar nomination, her involvement in *For Whom the Bell Tolls* brought additional awards, for example, a place amongst the five best female performances of the year according to *Film Daily*, where she in fact took two positions, the second for her performance of Ilsa Lund in *Casablanca*.[55] The Warner Bros. production, in which she appeared alongside Humphrey Bogart, also became a huge hit (ending up sixth in revenues for 1943 with $4.15 million[56]) and the surprising winner of the Academy Award for Best Picture, thus also greatly helping Bergman achieve her A-star status.

In September 1942, *Variety* informed that Bergman "was viewed as a risk to a great extent" and that her future would depend on how *For Whom the Bell Tolls* turns out.[57] Merely twelve months later, she was acknowledged as one of the most important actresses in Hollywood, with a value comparable, for example, with Bette Davis, Barbara Stanwyck, and Claudette Colbert. This also translated into her first-ever placement in the Quigley Top 25 of the greatest box-office draws for 1944 (with a shared 24th place).[58] According to an internal survey from February 1944, her so-called "marquee value" put her on seventh position among Hollywood actresses, ahead of Olivia de Havilland or Colbert.[59] Selznick from then on lent her out only for the most prestigious projects, gradually demanding up to a quarter million dollars for her services.[60] The financial value of Bergman thereby multiplied over a short period of time, and the actress, thanks to loan-outs to *Casablanca* and *For Whom the Bell Tolls*, became one of the most valuable articles on the Hollywood market.

FROM BROADWAY TO HOLLYWOOD:
DOROTHY McGUIRE IN *CLAUDIA*

Claudia represents a different case than the preceding *For Whom the Bell Tolls* and the following *The Song of Bernadette*, as it was initially a project developed and conceived for realization within Selznick's studio and only later sold off to Twentieth Century-Fox. Selznick made use of his position as the original owner of the film rights and stipulated that the title role had to go to his contract actress Dorothy McGuire, who had also portrayed the character in the successful Broadway play. McGuire was not, however, the only candidate. Selznick considered entrusting the part to his other fresh acquisition, Jennifer Jones, still known at that time under the name Phylis Walker. For this reason, *Claudia* and *The Song of Bernadette* are part of the same historical narrative.

The popular character of Claudia, a young bride who is suddenly confronted with the bitter truths of everyday existence, was created by the writer Rose Franken. Her stories were first published in the magazine *Redbook*; then, beginning in 1939, they came out in installments in book form, and subsequently were adapted for radio, theater, and finally film and television. The title heroine won over a faithful circle of followers, especially women, who awaited with anticipation the release of another novel or the broadcast of a radio play.[61] *Variety* aptly stated in the spring of 1941 that "*Claudia* becomes an industry."[62] Today, one would say that it represented a lucrative franchise which pervaded various media platforms and the synergy generated major profits for the author and her business partners.

Selznick knew of the material's existence at least since October 1939, but his business interest was only aroused by the play that opened on February 12, 1941, in the New York Booth Theatre. A day after the premiere, Kay Brown sent her boss a telegram in which she did not hide her enthusiasm and recommended he immediately begin negotiations:

> "CLAUDIA" BY ROSE FRANKEN OPENED LAST NIGHT WITH GIRL NAMED DOROTHY MACGUIRE [*sic*] THAT REALLY CAN ACT AND REALLY IS WORTH BREAKING YOUR NECK ABOUT. SHE IS PERSONAL CLIENT OF LELAND HAYWARD AND HE WILL HANDLE DEAL. LIKEWISE CLAUDIA IS A PLAY WORTH PAYING MONEY FOR.[63]

Selznick's contract director Robert Stevenson reacted with similar enthusiasm, also encouraging his employer to purchase the rights to *Claudia* and take over part of the acting ensemble headed by McGuire, who according to him was "SUPERBLY CAST IN AN INCREDIBLY DIFFICULT PART."[64] Selznick wanted to personally see the production, but the trip to New York would not only be expensive, but also time-consuming. He decided, as he had many times in the past, to trust the judgment of his close colleagues. In March, official negotiations got underway concerning the purchase of the film rights and the engagement of Dorothy McGuire.

Selznick was attracted to the material for at least four distinct reasons: first, the film adaptation represented what is often called a "pre-sold" property, as it had the interest of the public assured ahead of time thanks to the book bestsellers and the successful run on Broadway; second, it could be filmed cheaply as it was mostly a low-key conversation piece that took place in several interiors; third, it had the potential to become the basis for a successful film series and could be easily utilized in tie-ins for various commercial products; and fourth—since the title protagonist is a young woman—it could serve as a means to launch a new actress. MGM, Paramount, and Warner Bros. had the same motives for their interest in *Claudia*, though, and Selznick had to offer the enormous amount of $187,000 to beat the competition, thereby exceeding the recent record held by Paramount for *For Whom the Bell Tolls*. The transaction covered the entire body of materials by Franken including the novels and the magazine short stories, which suggests that Selznick's intention was to make *Claudia* into an ongoing film series. According to the contract, the first film was supposed to be released after the end of the Broadway production which was scheduled to run at least until the end of 1942. This gave Selznick and his talent department sufficient time to choose an ideal cast and, particularly, the actress for the title role.

In the audition for the theatrical production, Dorothy McGuire defeated more than 200 other aspirants and later met with great success as Claudia. Selznick signed a five-year contract with the talented actress in May 1941, but surprisingly did not insist that she had to necessarily appear in the film version of the play. The materials in the Selznick archive suggest that the producer viewed the purchase of *Claudia* and the acquisition of Dorothy McGuire as two independent transactions (as he had earlier done with Ingrid Bergman and *Intermezzo*) and contemplated instead entrusting the actress with the supporting role of Nora in the upcoming adaptation of A. J. Cronin's bestseller *The Keys of the Kingdom*.[65] At the same time, however, he did not want to deny her the opportunity to compete for the role with which she had made a name for herself on Broadway and which she wanted to play on the big screen. Therefore, he decided to have her undergo screen tests.

Under the supervision of the cameraman Harold Rosson (who had been the DOP on *The Garden of Allah* for Selznick), silent close-ups of McGuire were shot in New York along with several scenes from *Claudia* with the aim of judging her photographic qualities and acting skills.[66] Elsa Neuberger from the New York office mentioned in her report the actress's temperament and initial unwillingness to give in to what she perceived as "Hollywoodization," that is, adjusting her appearance to look better on camera. Otherwise, she evaluated her as an "excellent actress [who] fits somewhere in the difficult category between [Katharine] Hepburn and Margaret Sullavan."[67] After seeing the material, Selznick identified two problematic areas. Most importantly, the tests in his view showed that McGuire had acquired a number of mannerisms in the theater—gestures, facial expressions, voice inflections—that were not suitable for the screen. In addition, she turned out to be a rather difficult subject to film: "It is going to take an absolute master cameraman somewhere near as good as [Gregg] Toland to photograph her. This means extra money, but even this additional cost will be as nothing compared to the extra cost that we will have in shooting time on the girl because of the photographic problems of lighting, arranging action to avoid bad angles etc."[68] He nevertheless believed in her star potential, but only on the condition that "we will photograph her as we see fit, make her up as we see fit, and direct her as we see fit."[69] In other words, Selznick was convinced that McGuire could become a star only if willing to submit to the expertise and proven mechanisms of his company.

Arguments against Dorothy McGuire, based on her lack of photogenicity and acting technique incompatible with the film medium, became even more pronounced with the arrival of a new candidate for the part. Selznick made an acquaintance with the aspiring actress Phylis Isley Walker in July 1941 by means of Kay Brown. After an unsuccessful attempt to get the title role in the Chicago production of *Claudia*, Walker was interested in gaining the same part in the film version.[70] The twenty-two-year-old Walker, whose parents used to make their living as tent-show operators, was a fitting counterpart to McGuire: she was very photogenic, elegant and attractive, with a childlike innocent face and a delicate complexion, which perfectly reacted to light. According to certain voices in the studio, she was almost "too beautiful" for the role of Claudia, a simple, unremarkable young woman.[71] Along with Dorothy McGuire and Phyllis Thaxter, the new acting discovery of Rose Franken who was chosen for the Chicago production over Walker, she underwent a series of screen tests in New York, which, nevertheless, did not bring about any resolution. As Kay Brown stated, Thaxter did not have an attractive enough appearance for the film screen; Walker, in contrast, came across as "a French doll"; and McGuire was only attractive at times—"her face in repose I found piquant and enchanting, but her face in action annoyed me. [. . .] There's no use to get into a terrific hubbub over McGuire, [. . .] [she] is not the only answer to Claudia."[72]

Another round of screen tests took place in September and October, this time with the selection narrowed down to McGuire and Walker. The latter signed a long-term contract with Selznick at the end of July and became another member of his expanding acting roster. The question remained however, over which actress would be presented to the public in the highly anticipated role of Claudia and which would have to wait for another debut of a comparable importance. While the July tests seemed to slightly favor Walker, the situation changed in September. Since McGuire repeatedly refused to undergo tests in Hollywood, Selznick sent an experienced director of women's films, George Cukor, to New York. Cukor managed to get the actress to deliver a subdued but heartfelt performance, which overshadowed her photographic insufficiencies. Moreover, McGuire received decisive support in the person of Rose Franken, who directed her in several hundred Broadway performances and pushed for her as the best possible film Claudia. The opinion of the author, with a powerful protective relationship to her own literary creation, could not be ignored because she had approval rights over the casting in the film adaptation.

The final decision came about in November 1941 when Selznick announced that Claudia would be played by McGuire. The conviction that "[Dorothy] is a girl of enormous ability, and the possessor of an enchanting personality,"[73] her considerable experience with the role from Broadway, and Franken's consent all led to choosing her over the equally promising Phylis Walker. Doubts concerning her photogenicity did not go away, however. Selznick criticized both the actress and her agent Leland Hayward for refusing to take part in screen tests in Hollywood with a leading cameraman, such as, for example, Gregg Toland or George Barnes. His studio therefore could not fully evaluate her photographic qualities, carry out thorough experiments with the aim of determining the most flattering camera angles and lighting patterns, and try out various kinds of hairstyles and make-up. Now it was up to the talent department to create an identity for her, which would mask her lack of photogenicity or even transform it into an advantage. The strategy involved an emphasis on three qualities, which McGuire had at her disposal and which were supposed to distinguish her from the competition: "an extraordinary talent; a pixie kind of personality; and cute mannerisms—she is gay and buoyant, youthful and natural."[74]

Claudia was held on Broadway for more than two years,[75] and the shooting of the film version had to be postponed for the entire time—not only due to the unavailability of McGuire, but also to ensure that the film did not damage the theater box office. Before the cameras could finally start rolling, however, Selznick reevaluated his production plans and decided on an ambitious transaction. He announced on November 16, 1942, that Twentieth Century-Fox would acquire from him the rights to *Claudia* as well as to other projects then under development (*Jane Eyre, The Keys of the Kingdom*). The sale of *Claudia* included as a condition the casting of McGuire in the main role, even though the designated director, Edmund Goulding, had a preference for Joan Fontaine and the producer William Perlberg for Phylis Walker (known at that time already as Jennifer Jones). Selznick insisted, however, that the use of McGuire was binding and that "all rights to the property are negated and revert to us if she doesn't play it."[76] Selznick's immediate income for *Claudia* amounted to $275,000: $150,000 for the film rights and $125,000 for McGuire. He had to, however, also give up half of the contract with the actress, with the justification that if she became a star after *Claudia*, it would also be thanks to the work of Fox, and it was therefore reasonable that the studio benefited in a corresponding manner. Selznick and Fox thereby had alternating rights to make use of her services over the following period, each for a period of twenty-six weeks in a year.

Selznick's involvement did not come to an end with the sales of rights and the signing of the contract to loan out McGuire. In December 1942, he insisted that William Goetz, the head of production at Twentieth Century-Fox, plan "uncommon and exhaustive" screen tests with the aim of making up for what his own studio did not manage due to the actress's unavailability in Hollywood: "[A]t least two or three weeks, and preferably longer, should be allowed her for trying every conceivable type of arrangement with her hair, her eyebrows, her make-up, etc., leaving enough time for further changes should initial experiments prove wrong." His letter indicates that he had a clear idea concerning the result:

> She has got to be photographed attractively, and her face has to be studied and altered with make-up considerably, without in any way

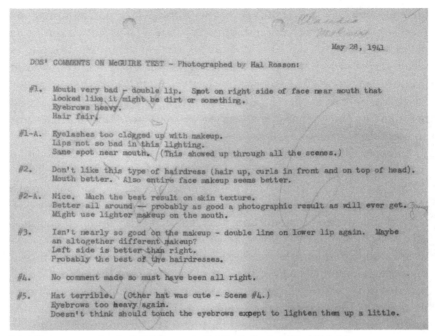

Selznick's comments on Dorothy McGuire's screen test for *Claudia*. Courtesy of Daniel Selznick.

glamorizing her to an extent that would defeat proper casting of the simple and unglamorous Claudia. [. . .] McGuire is probably the ideal personality in the world for this role; she has exactly the right qualities of personality and of basic appearance, if only the proper study is made as to how she can be presented to the best advantage.[77]

Sending detailed instructions to the producer or director, supervising screen tests, offering further consultations and control of the results were all part of the regular services provided by Selznick's studio when lending out contract actors and actresses. This was even more important in the case of McGuire because she was an inexperienced film actress, unknown to the moviegoing public, whose future depended on this one picture. If *Claudia* succeeded, she could become a star and sought-after commodity almost overnight. If the opposite occurred, she would become more of a burden for both companies. Through regular communication with Fox and strict supervision of the tests and the final film, Selznick was therefore reasonably protecting his interests and financial investment.[78]

The film, directed by the experienced Edmund Goulding, was shot from late April to mid-June 1943. The reliable Robert Young was lent by MGM for the role of Claudia's husband, David. The gala opening took place in August in Omaha, Nebraska, Dorothy McGuire's hometown. This choice sent a clear message that the actress was the main face of the film and was on her way to becoming a popular star. *Claudia* went into general release in September and met with great success: the domestic gross reached $2.5 million, placing it among Fox's Top 10 hits of the season.[79] It was assumed that most of the audience was women, who would have found in the story of Claudia many similarities with their own lives.

The press praised the intelligent dialogues and Goulding's sensitive direction, but the most positive reactions were focused on the acting skills of Dorothy McGuire. *Film Daily* wrote that she "bursts like a comet upon the consciousness of the film-going public," and labeled her performance as "one of the most aspicious [*sic*] film debuts ever." The reviewer further stated that McGuire was "no beauty of the Hollywood school, but she possesses an inner quality that exerts a fascination far more potent than mere pulchritude. [. . .] Her conception of Claudia has an uncanny accuracy. Not often has a player, young or old, played a character to such perfection."[80] Similar superlatives appeared in *Showmen's Trade Review*, whose critic announced after seeing the film that McGuire immediately ranked among "star[s] of the first magnitude. Her stage career is eclipsed by her screen performance and although comparisons are sometimes revolting, Miss McGuire offers screen fans a Margaret Sullavan–Katharine Hepburn quality combination in both looks and acting ability."[81] With her involvement in a single film, McGuire immediately obtained a position among the most keenly observed young actresses in Hollywood and was at the forefront of various surveys concerning the discovery of the year.[82]

As is apparent from this account, McGuire was not the only choice for Claudia. After signing a long-term contract with Selznick, she underwent a long process of testing and evaluation, only to be finally designated as the most suitable performer for the title role in the film adaptation. Selznick had originally intended to make the picture in his own production, but eventually included it in a package sold to Twentieth Century-Fox along with *Jane Eyre* and *The Keys of the Kingdom*. The agreement, however, included a clause that the main roles in all three films had to be given to his contract players; in addition to Dorothy McGuire, these were Joan Fontaine and Gregory Peck, respectively. Although Selznick lost control over the actual creation of these projects, he nevertheless ensured that the roles would go to his talents, with the success thereby helping to further their careers. Of course, Selznick was not motivated by selfless altruism; the success of Dorothy McGuire in *Claudia* generated considerable financial benefits for his studio. The actress immediately became a precious commodity with a value around $100,000 per film, which Selznick made use of in a series of additional loan-outs between 1944 and 1946 (*The*

Dorothy McGuire in a publicity still for *The Enchanted Cottage*.

Spiral Staircase, The Enchanted Cottage [1945, RKO] and *Till the End of Time*). McGuire provided parallel services to Twentieth Century-Fox, which, thanks to *Claudia*, took control over half of her contract and cast her in two films directed by the promising Elia Kazan, *A Tree Grows in Brooklyn* (1945) and *Gentleman's Agreement* (1947), as well as in the sequel to her triumphant debut, *Claudia and David* (1946). She continued to demonstrate her qualities and dedication to the acting profession in demanding dramatic roles and received her only Oscar nomination in 1948 for portraying the fiancée of the journalist investigating the pervasive anti-Semitism in US society in *Gentleman's Agreement*.

McGuire never starred in a film personally produced by Selznick[83] and never became one of his company's most prominent faces. During her involvement with the studio, she repeatedly complained about a lack of interest from her boss, who made use of her as a tool for easy profits after her success in *Claudia*.[84] The conflict usually involved disagreements over the choice of roles for the loan-outs, as in the case of Joan Fontaine who also often defied Selznick's authority, rejecting selected projects and demanding a greater share in the profits. For a significant part of her time with Selznick, McGuire was therefore on suspension: her contract was interrupted several times due to her "disobedience" and the actress went without pay.[85] Being a self-confident artist with a clear sense of the type of projects she wanted to be involved with, she pushed for a greater level of creative autonomy, which Selznick refused to provide. Their cooperation therefore came to an end prematurely in 1947, when all the attempts on the part of the producer to extend the contract were rejected. When McGuire returned to film after a three-year break in 1950, it was on a five-year non-exclusive contract with Twentieth Century-Fox, which provided her with much greater freedom when choosing projects and colleagues.[86] Her case clearly illustrates both the positive and negative aspects of star loan-outs. On the one hand, they could involve a means for placing actors and actresses in attractive roles, which they themselves were interested in. But they could also become a source of disputes, due to questions of creative autonomy (differing opinions concerning the quality of the given film, the suitability of the role, etc.) or distribution of the financial gains from these transactions, which one-sidedly favored the studio.

A FAKE DEBUT: JENNIFER JONES IN
THE SONG OF BERNADETTE

Selznick's collaboration with Phylis Walker developed in a different manner, although the starting position was practically identical as with Dorothy McGuire. Both actresses signed long-term contracts with the producer in the middle of 1941 (McGuire for five years and Walker for seven) and even though they were quite different in appearance and type, they were both tested for the film version of *Claudia*. As already described, after long considerations McGuire finally got the part, but this did not by any means lessen Selznick's faith in the star potential of the other actress. Moreover, it was soon apparent that his interest in Walker was not only professional, but also personal. Selznick found an ideal star in his lover and, since 1949, wife: faithful (according to some, even submissive), almost never defying his decisions, and always accepting his instructions and advice. The beginnings of this dynamic were apparent immediately upon the signing of the contract in the second half of 1941, when the producer began to transform the twenty-two-year-old Phylis Walker into a future Hollywood star, Jennifer Jones. The key role in this process was played by the loan-out to another prestigious production of the war years, *The Song of Bernadette*.

The adaptation of the eponymous novel by Franz Werfel was based on a true story of a fourteen-year-old French girl who repeatedly saw a vision of "a Beautiful Lady" (presumably the Virgin Mary) in the foothills of the Pyrenees in 1858. The project was developed by Twentieth Century-Fox, which purchased the rights for $125,000 from the original owner, the director William Dieterle.[87] The high-budget film was to be at the beginning of a "spiritual series" initiated and strongly supported by the new president of the studio, Spyros Skouras (other examples include *The Keys of the Kingdom* and *Come to the Stable* [1949]).[88] As soon as Selznick heard of Fox's plans to cast the title role, he mounted a systematic campaign, as had been the case with Ingrid Bergman and *For Whom the Bell Tolls*, which was aimed at convincing the leading representatives of the studio that his actress was the best and, in fact, the only possible choice for the part.

The success of the campaign depended to a large extent on whether excitement could be generated within the film industry about an unknown actress. The first step involved a change in her name. Selznick was convinced that neither Phylis Isley (maiden name) nor Phylis Walker (her married name) created suitable connotations and therefore announced a competition in the studio for a new name to solve the issue. Out of dozens of submissions, he chose the combination Jennifer Jones, which (with its alliteration and neat rhythm) associated nobility and grace, qualities which were to characterize the newly constructed artistic identity of the actress. The new name was also supposed to distract attention from the fact which Jones had long hidden from the studio and which came to light only after signing the contract: that she had appeared in two inferior films for Republic Pictures in 1939, a Western with John Wayne, *New Frontier*, and a fifteen-chapter crime serial, *Dick Tracy's G-Men*.[89] Selznick had intended to launch the actress as his own exciting discovery and her involvement in two low-budget projects at a second-rate studio could endanger this plan. If Jones had any advantage over the competition, apart from her youthful and attractive appearance, it was her freshness and novelty. The talent department therefore received the task of spreading a version of the Cinderella story presenting Jones as a simple girl from Oklahoma without any experience from Broadway or Hollywood. In similar fashion, information about her marriage to the actor Robert Walker and their two sons was supposed to be removed from the official studio biography, as this might endanger her chances of receiving the role of the virginal Bernadette. As Whitney Bolton, at the time the head of Selznick's PR department, stated in instructions to his subordinates: "Her name will be Jennifer Jones as though it were her actual name. We are to forget Phylis Walker or Phylis Isley. We are to forget her husband and children. She is Jennifer Jones of Tulsa, Oklahoma for our purposes and nothing else."[90] This strategy was finally not implemented all that strictly (Selznick himself said that if some of the "undesirable" information reaches the public, "it is not tragedy"),[91] but it nevertheless reveals many of the tactics which were to be used to launch Jones's career.

The casting of the role of Bernadette represented a major challenge for Fox. The successful candidate had to have a youthful look (the story begins when the girl is only fourteen), an aura of innocence and a hard to define spiritual quality. The novel by Franz Werfel was based to a great extent on historical documents and accounts from the descendants of the witnesses to the events that took place in the second half of the nineteenth century.[92] The filmmakers wanted to preserve this unsentimental, mostly realistic mode and the adequate casting of the title role was key so that the public would accept and believe the story.

Fox considered hundreds of actresses for the part, both established Hollywood figures and complete beginners. They initially investigated their own stable, where the leading contenders consisted of Linda Darnell and Anne Baxter. But the management was not against offers from outside either and these were coming from various sides, with the public also expressing their opinions: Fox recorded approximately 1,000 suggestions for the leading actress each week.[93] Selznick became involved in the negotiations with the aim of convincing all that his candidate was the most suitable. In his correspondence with William Goetz, the newly established head of production (covering for Darryl F. Zanuck who was serving in the army at that time), as well as the producer William Perlberg and the director Henry King, he mentioned his previous experience and unerring judgment in the development of female stars. He repeated these two basic arguments—the typological suitability of Jones and his own reputation as a starmaker—in a telegram from August 1942, in which he described the beginning of his negotiations with Goetz and Perlberg:

JUST AS PARAMOUNT FOOLED AROUND FOR A YEAR AND A HALF, AND FINALLY WOUND UP WITH WHAT I TOLD THEM AT THE OUTSET—THAT BERGMAN WOULD BE THE ONLY "POSSIBLE" [candidate for Maria in *For Whom the Bell Tolls*], SO I TELL THEM NOW THEY CAN LOOK ALL OVER THE WORLD AND THAT JENNIFER IS THE PERFECT PERSON IN QUALITY AS WELL AS ABILITY AND APPEARANCE FOR THEIR PICTURE.[94]

While in the case of *For Whom the Bell Tolls*, Selznick had used indirect pressure on Paramount by means of his close cooperation with the press and careful manipulation of public opinion, in the case of *The Song of Bernadette* he carried out negotiations directly with the heads of Fox. This was possible because of friendly professional relations (Selznick and Twentieth Century-Fox were frequent business partners, which was evident in the complex transaction

74 PRODUCING PRESTIGE

including *Claudia* already mentioned previously) as well as close family ties: William Goetz was Selznick's brother-in-law at this time (his wife was Edith Mayer, the sister of Selznick's first wife Irene), and he could therefore succumb to an informal pressure in contrast to his predecessor Darryl Zanuck.[95]

Selznick worked from the very beginning with the argument that *Bernadette* needed Jones more than Jones needed *Bernadette*. He tried to convince Goetz in a telegram from October 11, 1942, that

THE SUCCESS OF "BERNADETTE" IS GOING TO DEPEND IN LARGE MEASURE UPON THE SUCCESS OF THE CASTING OF THE PRINCIPAL ROLE; AND INDEED THE WHOLE DIFFERENCE BETWEEN SUCCESS AND FAILURE MAY WELL BE IN THIS ONE PIECE OF CASTING, ASSUMING A FINE PRODUCTION JOB BY PERLBERG AND KING.[96]

In other words, the film could not succeed without the actress, while she could be just as effectively introduced in another picture (in the same telegram, Selznick did not neglect to emphasize the interest of Warner Bros. connected with the romantic drama *The Constant Nymph*; the role later went to Joan Fontaine). According to Selznick, Jones had the perfect combination of talent, charm, and innocence, which guaranteed that the production would result in a triumph for the studio. The fact that Jennifer Jones was completely unknown to the public was presented amongst her main advantages:

I BELIEVE THAT IT IS GOING TO BE AWFULLY HARD TO SELL AUDIENCES THE SAINTHOOD OF SOMEBODY THEY HAVE SEEN PLAYING A CUTIE ON A DOUBLE BILL A WEEK BEFORE; AND THERE EVEN MAY BE SOMETHING INDECENT ABOUT IT.[97]

To protect her freshness and status of a novice (although, as I have stated earlier, this was a fiction to a certain extent), Selznick kept her inactive and very carefully guarded her interaction with the press. The only occasion when the public could see her since the signing of the contract with the studio was her week-long involvement in the stage production of William Saroyan's one-act play *Hello Out There!* in Santa Barbara in September 1941 when she still went by the name Phylis Walker. All other film and theater offers, along with requests for interviews and photoshoots, were categorically rejected.[98]

Goetz was undoubtedly impressed by the young, attractive, and talented actress but was not intending to cast her in the most prestigious female role of the year, make a star out of her, and observe how Selznick would profit from the exclusive contract over the coming years. As was the case with Dorothy

McGuire several weeks later, he demanded a share of her contract.[99] Even at this early stage, though, Selznick viewed Jones as a potentially very valuable commodity and did not want to give her up that easily. He told Goetz bluntly:

FORGET HOW MUCH I BENEFITED BY HAVING LEIGH AND FONTAINE EXCLUSIVELY AFTER "WIND" AND "REBECCA" RESPECTIVELY; AND BEAR IN MIND HOW MUCH THE PICTURES THEMSELVES WOULD HAVE SUFFERED HAD THEY NOT BEEN SO IDEALLY CAST.[100]

Goetz did not back down, however, and convinced Selznick to sacrifice to Fox at least one film per year if Jones received the role, which was still not a certainty.[101] An interesting comparison arises in this connection with the two cases described earlier. With Ingrid Bergman, Selznick initially considered giving up part of the contract to Paramount, just to obtain an important role for her. Eventually, this was not necessary, as the actress in the meanwhile had achieved sufficient star status and the studio had in addition found itself with unexpected problems due to the removal of Zorina and had no other option than to accept Selznick's conditions. In McGuire's case, the split of the contract into two halves was in contrast unavoidable, as her value in the market was minimal prior to the release of *Claudia* and Fox needed a guarantee that it would profit correspondingly from its success. The conditions for the loan-out of Jennifer Jones are closer to McGuire's case and reflect the fact that she was also yet an unproven actress. At the same time, though, it is important to point out the differences: the contract with McGuire was divided into two equal parts, with each of the companies having an identical right to the actress defined as a clearly designated time interval. In contrast, in the case of Jones, the agreement was only to provide Fox with one film per year which had to meet clearly defined criteria concerning its quality in terms of the budget, the director, etc. This makes it apparent that from the beginning, Selznick had greater interest in Jones's career, practicing stricter control over her in terms of the selection of her projects and colleagues, and expecting higher financial returns of his investment.

Although the conditions for the loan-out were prearranged back in October 1942, in order for them to be put down on paper and signed by both parties, Jones was still required to undergo screen tests and outperform her rivals. Selznick first caught the interest of the producer William Perlberg and director Henry King by showing them a reel with Jones's screen tests for *Claudia*.[102] Tests for *Bernadette* took place at Fox in late November and early December. The studio had previously considered dozens of candidates, including, for example, the newcomer Gene Tierney and, curiously, the very experienced, forty-nine-year-old Lillian Gish.[103] The selection was finally narrowed down to a group of six, which, along with Jennifer Jones, included Anne Baxter, Linda Darnell, Teresa Wright, Mary Anderson, and Beatrice Pearson. Under the supervision of Henry King and director of photography Leon Shamroy, each of the actresses performed selected scenes from the screenplay and in the final phase they were asked to present their own interpretation of Bernadette's vision of the Virgin Mary in the cave. This moment turned out to be decisive. According to King: "The other five did very well. But only Jennifer looked as if she saw a Vision."[104] The official materials from Fox later explained that only Jones "among all the young women tested, possessed that rare and indefinable quality which makes you feel, during every precious moment she is on the screen, the presence of something very great, very moving, very wonderful."[105]

That Fox assigned Jennifer Jones the title role in *The Song of Bernadette*, sidelining their own candidates Anne Baxter and Linda Darnell,[106] was a major victory for Selznick's studio, which heavily promoted the actress as the finest and most authentic choice for the part, arranged for her participation in the screen tests and created around her an identity based on innocence and a natural and fragile spiritual charm, which was required for the film. All the important trade journals and newspapers in the Los Angeles area referred to the casting of Jones. *Showmen's Trade Review* wrote on December 12, 1942, that the final decision concerning *Bernadette* "brought to an end a talent search in which thousands of hopefuls in the United States, Canada, Australia and England deluged [Twentieth Century]-Fox studios for the past six months with letters and photographs, and in which practically every available young star of established Hollywood screen reputation was tested."[107] The popular fan magazine *Photoplay* informed in a similar spirit that "the search is over, the actress found and the chapter on 'Find A Bernadette' closed. Jennifer Jones, a young woman under contract to David Selznick, who has had comparatively little professional experience, has been chosen and more hearts are left to ache in silence than ached over the Scarlet [*sic*] O'Hara role."[108]

Fox secured Jones's services for *The Song of Bernadette* for a mere $12,300, twice the amount of the salary which she was to receive during the eight-week shoot from Selznick. Another $2,000 was to be paid as compensation for the costs related to her preparation for the role.[109] The relatively low overall sum reflected the fact that Jones was still an unknown personality with uncertain audience appeal and thus a potential risk for this costly project. The immediate income was not of primary importance for Selznick's studio, however. The contract was signed in the belief that the actress's value would immediately rise after the film was released. During negotiations about the contractual conditions, Selznick appealed to his lawyers to "be careful not to give them [Fox] any more pictures than was agreed to in that exchange of wires"—that is, one film a year except for the second year, which was supposed to involve two films.[110] Additional instructions concerned advertising and publicity:

> I assume in all publicity being arranged by Twentieth Century it will be made clear that [Jones] is under contract to us, is my discovery, including the fact that it was I who suggested she play "Bernadette" and fought for the role for her, offering to give up a piece of her contract if they would give her the part. It should be made clear that we do not "share" the contract as this term is generally understood—they have one more picture this year, two next year and one a year thereafter.[111]

Selznick's brand was more and more dependent on business with stars, and therefore these kinds of protective steps were essential. Industry peers, representatives of the press, and the public were all supposed to know in no uncertain terms that Jennifer Jones was his exclusive discovery, and that Fox would profit from her without a large contribution of their own. If information appeared to the contrary, Selznick's people were supposed to rectify things and ensure that this would not be repeated. The title credits for *The Song of Bernadette* therefore explicitly stated that Jones was appearing in the film "by arrangement with David O. Selznick"[112] and this became established practice with most future loan-outs.

The principal photography on the $2 million film began in late March 1943 and the postproduction on the picture was completed at the end of the year just in time to meet the deadlines for the Oscars. The world premiere, which took place in the leading Los Angeles movie palace Carthay Circle Theatre, was conceived in grand style and clearly signaled that the production was intended as a candidate for the yearly prizes and high profits.[113] Although Jones dominated many posters and other advertising materials (an eighty-foot-high portrait of her in the role of Bernadette by Norman Rockwell was installed in front of the entrance to the Rivoli Theatre in New York), at Selznick's instructions she did not participate in the picture's opening or in other public events, in order not to disturb the fragile illusion of innocence, etherealness, and absolute blending with the part and possibly also, as the press speculated, to preserve her freshness for a role in what turned out to be Selznick's return to active production—the ambitious drama *Since You Went Away*.[114]

Most of the periodicals were enthusiastic about *The Song of Bernadette* and Jones's performance in particular. They were highly appreciative of the actress's suitability for and sensitive approach to the difficult role. They also commended the fact that the film proved that a picture could succeed without established stars. *Time* stated that "as Bernadette, newcomer Jennifer Jones makes one of the most impressive screen debuts in many years"[115] and the critic Delight Evans went

Jennifer Jones with the Oscar for *The Song of Bernadette*.

even further in her column for the magazine *Screenland* when she wrote that "nothing has ever equaled in movie history the inspired performance of Jennifer Jones as Bernadette. [. . .] Most appealing is her unshakeable faith in her visions of the 'Beautiful Lady' [. . .] and her dignified simplicity."[116] Jones received the first Golden Globe for Best Actress ever awarded in January 1944 and added an Academy Award in the same category in March, with the film receiving the total of four Oscars out of twelve nominations, thus becoming the most acclaimed title of the year.[117] The revenues were also remarkable, with the gross receipts of almost $5 million making *Bernadette* the fourth highest-grossing film of the year and the biggest hit in the history of Twentieth Century-Fox until that time.[118]

The Song of Bernadette represented a milestone for the professional career of Jennifer Jones. Selznick's studio decided to restart and effectively rewrite her previous career in film, and in cooperation with Fox presented her as a completely unknown and inexperienced personality who was catapulted to stardom thanks to her very first role.[119] The financial compensation for providing the actress was minimal, but of more importance was Jones's value in the market immediately after the completion and release of the film. Selznick treated the actress as an exclusive commodity and planned to use her in his own productions as well as in the most prestigious films made by other studios. As he stated in a report to his colleagues in December 1943: "I think our flat and definite policy on Jennifer from here on should be no loan-outs except for something so outstanding that we couldn't refuse it, making clear that even if we did approve something the price would be either a great star in exchange or $150,000—and not under $125,000."[120] Selznick expanded Jones's range and avoided the imminent threat of binding her with fragile, saintly types, by writing for her the part of a temperamental, adolescent girl in the contemporary drama *Since You Went Away* and announcing her casting in the romantic Western *Duel in the Sun*, which was supposed to demonstrate her sensuality and as yet little-displayed sex appeal. This strategy mirrored earlier casting decisions for Bergman in *Dr. Jekyll and Mr. Hyde* and *For Whom the Bell Tolls*. In the meantime, Jones was lent along with Joseph Cotten to Paramount for the romantic drama *Love Letters* (1945), where the overall financial compensation for his studio exceeded $300,000.[121] Over a period of only two years, Jones joined the ranks of the top female stars in Hollywood with a significant economic and symbolic value.

LOAN-OUTS AS A MEANS TO PROFIT AND PRESTIGE

This chapter has focused on three actresses with long-term contracts with David Selznick who all appeared in one year in high-profile pictures of other studios, met with recognition of both the industry and the public for their performances (two of them received Oscar nominations), and thereby joined the ranks of leading female stars. However, it would be a mistake to overestimate the importance of this one historical moment. The 1943–44 season was merely the culmination of the long-term aims of Selznick's company to establish itself in the market with (female) stars. Apart from Ingrid Bergman, Dorothy McGuire, and Jennifer Jones, who were the focus of my case studies, Vivien Leigh (until she returned to England), Joan Fontaine, and Shirley Temple ranked among the most valuable and sought-out commodities in the mid-1940s. These actresses jointly caused Selznick to be associated with a certain type of female stardom based on quality and prestige.[122]

The turn in the business strategies and public image of Selznick's company came about due to the producer's creative exhaustion after a series of pictures from the late 1930s, particularly his unprecedented blockbuster *Gone with the Wind*. Instead of continuing producing films, Selznick began in the early 1940s to increasingly focus on the development of stars whom he would offer for loan-outs to leading Hollywood studios. He ensured that his actresses only appeared in the most prominent Hollywood pictures, most frequently high-budget adaptations of respected literary classics or current bestsellers. Because each studio had its own stars or at the very least promising candidates for stardom, there was a need to first convince their management of the suitability of his candidates. Selznick presented his contract actresses in his negotiations as exclusive articles who would significantly contribute to the artistic quality and financial profitability of the given films. Since Selznick's company did not have the resources to provide enough films for its stars, and thus justify their long-term contracts and high weekly wages, it was essential to rely on the ties with companies such as Paramount, Twentieth Century-Fox, RKO, and Warner Bros. While these same studios would often carefully guard their contract players and primarily make use of them in their own productions, loan-outs became for Selznick an economic necessity and a standard part of his *modus operandi*.

Careful selection of projects for contract talent was of essence within the context of Selznick's production inactivity: the choice of first-class films helped protect his acting acquisitions and at the same time ensured that they would return to him as even more valuable commodities. The profits took various forms:

- immediate income from loan-outs, which depended on the current status of the actress, and which might range from $12,000 (Jennifer Jones in *The Song of Bernadette*) to $250,000 (later loan-outs of Ingrid Bergman);
- increased value of the star due to her participation in a successful film which meant that the price for the next loan-out could possibly be several times higher (after *The Song of Bernadette*, for example, the value of the services of Jennifer Jones increased ten times);
- the opportunity to reissue older pictures with an actress who was not a leading star at the time and did not possess such commercial potential (this happened repeatedly, for example, with *Intermezzo*, which returned to cinemas in 1944 and once again three years later);[123]
- enhancing the symbolic and commercial capital of the actress which could be used by Selznick when he finally decided to return to active production of his own pictures; the positive responses in the press or various awards played an important role here (Jennifer Jones, as an already established personality and Oscar winner, joined the all-star cast of *Since You Went Away* and further contributed to the project's attractiveness);
- increasing the prestige of Selznick's entire company, which was indirectly associated by means of its contract actresses with quality A-films produced by its competitors.

In this manner, Selznick generated financial returns for his company, while at the same time building up his own brand, which could be further monetized: symbolic capital consisting of prestigious roles, laudatory references in the press and various recognitions and awards were accumulated with the aim of sooner or later transforming them back into economic capital (further loan-outs, production of his own films, reissues of older titles).

The results achieved by Selznick over this short period of time are remarkable. Thanks to his excellent understanding of the market, extensive and well-developed professional and informal contacts with leading Hollywood executives, filmmakers, members of the press, and other important industry players, and the well-thought-out transformation of his company which redirected its focus on the discovery and development of female stars, Selznick's studio became in the mid-1940s a leading player in the business with actresses. Ingrid Bergman, Jennifer Jones, Dorothy McGuire, Joan Fontaine, Shirley Temple, and, to a lesser degree, Vivien Leigh appeared in prestigious, culturally valued and commercially successful pictures and between 1940 and 1948, they received a total of four Oscars and eight nominations, with three wins and five nominations coming from roles in films produced by other Hollywood companies.[124] This brought hundreds of thousands of dollars to their "home" studio, testifying to their being highly profitable and prestigious commodities.

3

WHILE THEY WERE FIGHTING

The Development of Male Stars during World War II

There never were too many men in the film colony at any time. And for the past year the shortage of leading men has been more acute than ever. Hollywood is seriously concerned as to what might happen in the next few months. Will films become predominantly more feminine? Will elaborate musicals stage a hurried comeback? Will the stages again be filled with daringly gowned and strikingly alluring choruses—with perhaps a single male member to indicate that the male isn't completely extinct?
—FROM THE ARTICLE "MAN SHORTAGE FORCES STARS TO HIRE ESCORTS!,"
BY CRAIG WHITE, *HOLLYWOOD* MAGAZINE, AUGUST 1942[1]

Between September 1939 and April 1940, David O. Selznick completed and released three films in which three new stars were introduced to the public: Ingrid Bergman in *Intermezzo: A Love Story*, Vivien Leigh in *Gone with the Wind*, and Joan Fontaine in *Rebecca*. Over the course of the following year, Selznick's company signed long-term contracts with Dorothy McGuire and Phylis Walker, later known as Jennifer Jones, who were also earmarked as potential stars based on extensive tests. All these actresses provided the studio with luster and prestige, significantly shaping its public image, and represented valuable assets to be sold for profit, particularly at a time when competition was short of attractive and talented female stars.[2]

In contrast, Selznick displayed little interest in the development of male stars until 1941. He regularly placed established figures who worked freelance or actors borrowed from other studios in the main roles in his films. These included Charles Boyer in *The Garden of Allah*, Fredric March in *A Star Is Born* and *Nothing Sacred*, Ronald Colman in *The Prisoner of Zenda*, James Stewart in *Made for Each Other*, Clark Gable in *Gone with the Wind*, and Laurence Olivier in *Rebecca*. By 1941, Alan Marshal was the only actor with a long-term contract in Selznick's company but in no way could he be considered a popular and sought-after star. The turning point in Selznick's strategies came with the changes in the film industry brought about by World War II.

The entering of the US into the war in Europe and the Pacific, which followed the Japanese attack on Pearl Harbor on December 7, 1941, resulted in a mass drainage of male personnel. Significantly, a fourth of the approximately 6,000 male employees who went to war from the film industry consisted of actors.[3] A number of popular screen personalities joined the armed forces with a great deal of media attention, among them James Stewart (in March 1941), Clark Gable, Henry Fonda, Robert Taylor, Robert Montgomery, Van Heflin, and Tyrone Power. A special group consisted of British actors working in Hollywood during the 1930s who returned across the ocean to join the military forces or otherwise get involved in the struggle against fascism after the war broke out in Europe. These included renowned names such as David Niven, Laurence Olivier, and Leslie Howard. Studios were weakened by these losses and therefore attempted to compensate for the situation with an increased emphasis on other attractions, including Technicolor spectacles, adaptations of bestselling books, and new types of protagonists. As noted by Thomas Schatz, "jokes [circulated within the film industry] about male stars being replaced by dogs (Lassie), horses (Flicka), kids (Margaret O'Brien, Baby Jean), and aging character actors (Charles Coburn and Barry Fitzgerald, both of whom won Oscars during the war)."[4]

It was apparent, however, that some prominent and consistently popular genres, such as romances and comedies, as well as patriotic war films, could not function without young men. Beginning in 1941, all studios therefore made discovering and introducing new male stars their priority. As remarked by Randy Roberts, "a leading man during the war needed a good profile and an adequate voice, but more importantly he had to be either over forty, married with two or more children, or 4-F."[5] Paramount, for example, used the services of the Welsh-born Ray Milland and Alan Ladd, the latter of whom had initially joined the Army Air Forces, but had been released several months later for health reasons. MGM perfected the boy-next-door type with Van Johnson, who had suffered an injury to his skull during the filming of *A Guy Named Joe* (1943), preventing him from entering the armed forces.[6] Due to paternal obligations, Dana Andrews was deferred from service, becoming a leading actor during the war for Twentieth Century-Fox. And Roy Rogers, a leading man at Republic Pictures, became increasingly popular in the Western genre.[7]

Just like his competitors at the Big Five studios as well as those at smaller production companies, David O. Selznick was aware of the situation. He therefore made the development of male leads one of the main goals of his company as soon as the first men left Hollywood for the war in the first half of 1941.

Selznick did not have any films in the making at the time, having interrupted his production activities after a series of particularly demanding projects in the late 1930s and early 1940s. Instead, he planned to complement his star portfolio exclusively made up of women and use these personalities as trade articles in relations with other studios and producers. Because the development of new stars is a costly, time-consuming endeavor, he initially decided to make a star out of his only contract actor at that time, Alan Marshal. In this chapter, in addition to Marshal, I focus on three other male acquisitions made by Selznick during the war years: Gene Kelly, Gregory Peck, and Joseph Cotten.

THE HUMAN FACTOR: ALAN MARSHAL

Marshal made his debut in 1936 in a supporting role in Selznick's *The Garden of Allah*. After completing the film, he signed a standard seven-year contract with the producer but did not appear in any more of Selznick's productions. He was instead loaned out regularly to other studios as a supporting player in their A-films, or, less often, as a lead in B-films. He played, among other things, in *After the Thin Man* (1936, MGM), the second installment in the popular murder mystery comedy series, in the historical drama *Conquest* with Greta Garbo, the biopic *Parnell* (1937, MGM), starring Clark Gable, the high-budget adaptation of Victor Hugo's *The Hunchback of Notre Dame* (1939, RKO), and in the low-budget romantic drama *Married and in Love* (1940, RKO). Marshal was on loan for fifteen films in all over the years 1937 to 1940, providing the studio with modest but steady income. While his market value remained constant, his weekly wage gradually increased, however. In the upcoming option period, he was supposed to get $1,000 a week and it began to be apparent to Selznick that the contract's terms would no longer be favorable for the company. He therefore instructed his employees in the middle of 1940 to launch a campaign which would make Marshal a popular leading man[8] and mentioned the upcoming RKO drama *Kitty Foyle: The Natural History of a Woman* (1940) as an example of an ideal project because "one picture with Ginger Rogers is worth about nine with [Anna] Neagle in the development of a leading man."[9] The vice president of Selznick International and Selznick's right hand Dan O'Shea was somewhat skeptical, however, about Marshal's potential: "When I say I don't think we can make him into a first-line featured player, I mean that we can't do it by loaning him out. Most of the studios have young men under contract to them and they are forcing their own players into their pictures at the present time."[10]

Selznick's production inactivity in the early 1940s turned out to be an obstacle for the development of Marshal's career. Ingrid Bergman, Vivien Leigh, and Joan Fontaine had become stars thanks to films personally produced by

Selznick, which were adjusted for (and in the case of *Intermezzo* even subordinated to) this purpose on the level of narration and style as well as promotion and publicity. In Marshal's case, however, Selznick—in contrast to established practice—hoped that this result would be achieved by means of loan-outs for films of other studios over which he had very little control.[11] Even so, he was not willing to consider terminating the contract. "I STILL HAVE FAITH IN HIM, THINK HE WILL GET BETTER AS THE YEARS GO ON, AND DO NOT WANT TO LOSE HIM," the producer stated in a telegram in August 1940.[12]

After failing to succeed in placing Marshal in *Kitty Foyle*, he at least secured him a role in another RKO film starring Ginger Rogers, *Tom, Dick and Harry* (1941). Marshal appeared in this entertaining comedy alongside George Murphy and Burgess Meredith as one of the suitors to the main heroine. His second film in 1941 was the romantic drama *Lydia*, produced by Alexander Korda, where Marshal was one of the four fatal men in the life of the title protagonist played by Merle Oberon. Although the actor received positive acclaim in the press for both films, his roles continued to be supporting ones and the impact on his professional status was therefore limited.

In August 1941, Selznick announced that he would personally take control of Marshal's career along the lines of his female stars (Dan O'Shea had been responsible for him previously): "I think that he is now at the point of his career where it is up to me to devote some time to it."[13] The situation with the actor at this time had become increasingly problematic. Marshal was paid $45,625 from August 1940 to December 1941, while the studio received only $29,416 for providing his services to RKO and Korda.[14] His weekly salary was once again raised to $1,250 and something had to change for the contract to remain lucrative for the studio.

His five years in Hollywood had resulted in Marshal being typecast as a supporting player. But how to create an aura of prestige around him and turn him into a more valuable commodity? The campaign to convince Hollywood of Alan Marshal's worth as a leading man was carried out in several steps and it was no coincidence that this took place at the same time when the US was about to enter the war. The departure of male stars from the film industry made it possible for Selznick to offer Marshal as a substitute for similar types, which included Clark Gable, who joined the Air Force in early 1942, and Laurence Olivier, who after a stint in Hollywood served the war efforts in his native England. Marshal, born in Sydney to an Australian mother and English father, was not an American citizen and therefore avoided active service.

Selznick first increased the price for Marshal's services to between $25,000 and $30,000 per film. He also released him to perform in the stage production of Shaw's *The Devil's Disciple* at the Lobero Theatre in Santa Barbara. This attempt to attract the attention of the media and the public and increase the actor's prestige in the film industry paid off, when, for example, Hedda Hopper in her regular column for the *Los Angeles Times* wrote of Marshal's performance with enthusiasm and added that "now David [Selznick] has himself a new star."[15] Agents, authorized by Selznick to negotiate with most of the studios of the Big Five and the Little Three, were assigned to obtain important roles for the actor.[16] Selznick even contemplated leaking out the information that Marshal was being considered for the role of Rochester in the upcoming adaptation of *Jane Eyre*, even though this was not the case. He justified his idea by the disappointment with the offers up to that point for Marshal and the insufficient publicity.[17] He finally abandoned the proposition, however, as it might have damaged negotiations with actors who were in fact auditioning for the role.[18]

In March 1942, Hedda Hopper designated Marshal as the actor with the greatest chance to make it big in the following year, thereby legitimizing the efforts of Selznick's company to turn him into a star.[19] The director Mervyn LeRoy, who was preparing the romantic drama *Random Harvest* (1942) for MGM, was one of the first to express interest in him. The much more popular Ronald Colman, however, received the role of the English soldier suffering from amnesia and was nominated for an Oscar for his performance. Negotiations with Warner Bros. concerning a role in the boxing biopic *Gentleman Jim* (1942) and with the independent production company of David Loew and Albert Lewin for a role in the melodrama *The Moon and Sixpence* (1942) also ended in failure. Selznick blamed Whitney Bolton, his director of advertising and publicity, for not bringing these and other negotiations to a successful end.[20] A final turning point occurred in the second half of 1942 when Selznick's secretary Virginia Olds was given the task of assembling a show reel of Marshal's finest moments in previous films and providing it to agents as a tool for further negotiations.[21] The first offers involved minor roles in the films *Saratoga Trunk*, *Lady in the Dark* (1944, Paramount) and *Frenchman's Creek* (1944, Paramount), which Selznick deemed inadequate. Finally, in February 1943, Marshal was confirmed as a leading man in MGM's romantic drama *The White Cliffs of Dover* (1944), in which Irene Dunne was cast as his partner. Selznick's studio received $25,000 for Marshal's services. The agreement included an option for another two films with the actor, which were to bring in an additional $35,000 and $50,000, respectively.[22]

The role in a prestigious film of a large studio, alongside a recognized female star, was exactly what Selznick had been working towards for over a year and a half. The success for this was attributed to the reel with Marshal's best scenes which had been presented to Louis B. Mayer and other top figures at MGM in a meeting. The same approach was supposed to be repeated at all of the remaining studios of the Big Five.[23] In a letter to Dan O'Shea, Selznick emphasized how important it was to build upon the role in *The White Cliffs of Dover*

Alan Marshal and Irene Dunne in a publicity still for *The White Cliffs of Dover*.

with additional prestigious assignments: "We fooled around seven years with Marshal and gambled a fortune to get to this very moment, so I do hope that you will make it the very first order of business."[24]

The role in the MGM film was also important for the future of the business relationship with Marshal. The actor had complained repeatedly in the past that he had not played in any of the films personally produced by Selznick, which was an objection which the producer had also heard from other contract players, both male and female. With the approaching end of the original seven-year contract, negotiations began about further cooperation and Selznick wanted to make use of the recent success to establish mutually acceptable conditions for the next term. He offered Marshal a further increase in salary in exchange for a new seven-year contract, which would ensure that the studio would receive back their investment. (Selznick's losses over the last three years due to Marshal's inactivity had amounted to several tens of thousands of dollars.) The result was a compromise in the form of a shorter, five-year contract which guaranteed the actor a gradual increase in pay from $2,250 to $3,000 per week.

While *The White Cliffs of Dover* was in production (it was shot from June 1 to September 17, 1943), efforts to obtain further prestigious and lucrative roles for Marshal continued. The desired results, however, did not come all that easily or quickly and Selznick repeatedly criticized the work of his advertising and talent departments: "Marshal has one of the most important parts of the year, in one of the biggest and best sponsored pictures of the year; yet we've managed to keep this a deep, dark secret."[25] Henry Willson, the head of the talent department, had to explain that Marshal was less than exciting as an actor and private person and therefore uninteresting for the press and the public. According to Willson, he was unable to relax during interviews and thereby provide the media with an attractive story.[26] The small number of articles about Marshal in fan magazines such as *Photoplay* and *Screenland* support Willson's point: they were mostly generic texts about how the actor lived a happy family life alongside his wife Mary and son Kit, supplemented with obviously staged photographs from his home.[27]

Dissatisfaction with the work of his own studio led Selznick to hire Helen Ferguson, an external agent and leading expert on public relations, whose task was to get more distinctive and noticeable references to Marshal in the press.[28] He also continued using the tried and tested promo tape when approaching leading Hollywood studios. For example, Selznick turned to Universal with an offer to lend Marshal for the next film with Deanna Durbin, though without the desired effect. Another hopeful project was a biographical drama about Frédéric Chopin, *A Song to Remember* (1945), planned as a Columbia production. The thirty-five-year-old Marshal did not, however, fit the role in terms of type and age, and it was finally secured for Cornel Wilde on loan from Twentieth Century-Fox. Selznick himself did not take the opportunity to entrust Marshal with the leading role in *Spellbound* and instead gave preference to Gregory Peck. His faith in Marshal's star potential remained firm, however: "I'll make the town [Hollywood—author's note] aware of Marshal as a great new leading man or die in the attempt!" he said, hyperbolically, in October 1943.[29]

Selznick's determination alone was not enough, however. The producer had initially decided to apply the same principle to Marshal which had proved effective with other contract actors and actresses: keeping him inactive rather than giving him less prestigious or completely subordinate assignments. The circumstances, however, forced him to change his position. When he was unable to place Marshal, after almost a year, into a film of the same stature as *The White Cliffs of Dover*, he agreed to provide him for a routine romantic comedy by RKO *Bride by Mistake* (1944). Dorothy McGuire, a recent acquisition of Selznick's and the fresh star of the adaptation of the theater hit *Claudia*, was also originally supposed to appear in the film. She refused the role, however, due to the low quality of the screenplay, and Selznick feared the same reaction from Marshal, who was also unimpressed with the material. Nevertheless, it was essential for the actor's career that he remain in the public eye: "Let's tell him [Marshal] right now that we don't think the picture is a great picture, but we think it has every chance of turning out to be a very outstanding picture and one which certainly cannot hurt him [. . .] this is the first time in our entire operation that we have forced an important player to do a part that they did not want to do, and [. . .] we are doing this out of consideration for the jam he is in."[30] Selznick was also interested in preserving good relations with RKO, since the studio planned to place Marshal in the leading role in the upcoming romantic drama *The Enchanted Cottage* and offered $75,000 for ten weeks of the actor's services.

Marshal's prospects improved in June 1944 when *The White Cliffs of Dover* finally made it into the cinemas. The story about an American woman working as a volunteer in the Red Cross during World War II and recollecting her marriage with her deceased British aristocrat husband resonated with both the American and international public and became one of the most successful films of the year with gross receipts of more than $6 million.[31] Its popularity is testified to by the fact that it was only the fifth picture in the history to remain on the screen of Radio City Music Hall, one of the largest movie theaters in the world, for more than six weeks in a row.[32] Critics compared it to hits of previous years, in particular *Mrs. Miniver* (1942, MGM) and *Random Harvest*, and valued not only the sensitively treated current theme, but also the performances of Irene Dunne and Marshal. Bosley Crowther from the *New York Times*, for example, stated that "Miss Dunne gives to her character a nice glow of American charm and Mr. Marshal makes Sir John Ashwood a thoroughly pleasant and graceful Britisher."[33]

Marshal's second film *Bride by Mistake* premiered two months later. Despite the modest expectations, it also received a positive response, although the ticket sales were limited due to the absence of elite stars (the female roles were played by Laraine Day and Marsha Hunt), lower production values, and modest advertising. The *Motion Picture Daily* referred to the film as a successful escapist comedy marked by "clever dialogue, excellent acting, and sequence after sequence of hilarity. [. . .] Laraine Day and Marsha Hunt [. . .] both give sterling performances, and Alan Marshal is splendid as the man in the middle."[34] *Showmen's Trade Review* expressed several objections to the story and its construction, but also the conviction that it would amount to a commercial success thanks to the attractive cast led by Marshal who "does exceptionally well in his role of the flyer, when one considers that he plays the role of a sappy heel with dialog to match."[35]

But Selznick's company did not get the opportunity to profit from these positive reactions in the press. Alan Marshal's contract was terminated for health reasons on July 28, 1944, the exact day when the trade press published the first reviews of *Bride by Mistake*. As it turned out, the actor suffered from an unspecified mental illness, which prevented him from continuing in his career. The breaking of the contract resulted in the termination of the agreements with MGM, which owned the option, after *The White Cliffs*, for two films with Marshal, and RKO, which had to replace Marshal in *The Enchanted Cottage* with Robert Young. Selznick's studio thus lost $160,000.

Marshal returned several times to the payroll of the studio, but each time it was a false alarm, so to speak. Selznick offered the actor several roles in an attempt to profit from the hard-earned and dearly paid-for success in *The White Cliffs* and *Bride by Mistake*, but all of his propositions were rejected. Marshal thereby missed out on roles in the comedy *She Went to the Races* (1945, MGM), the thriller *The Spiral Staircase*, the drama *Christabel Caine* (eventually made as *Born to Be Bad* in 1950 [RKO]), the crime picture *Ivy* (1947, Universal), the romantic film *Cass Timberlane* (1947, MGM), and another thriller, *The Unsuspected* (1947, Warner Bros.). As late as October 1947, Selznick still had hopes for Marshal's comeback: "Alan Marshal is now eager to go back to work, and I think would accept many of the roles he has turned down. [. . .] I think we should look for parts of importance for him immediately. [. . .] I still have great faith that Alan can be an enormous favourite. I put in a great many years of past effort on him and have always felt that this was not wasted and that one day he would come round."[36] This was only, however, one in a series of false hopes. In February 1948, the professional alliance between Marshal and Selznick came to a definitive end.

Marshal's buildup—the systematic process of making him into a prominent male star—made sense from a business point of view. The actor was under a long-term contract with Selznick's studio and had the reputation of being a competent professional with an attractive appearance. Hollywood had been experiencing a lack of leading actors starting in the second half of 1941, and with the absence of similar types such as Clark Gable, Laurence Olivier, and David Niven (and as a result of Ronald Colman being not particularly busy in this period), Marshal's potential increased significantly. The difficulty lay in the fact that Selznick did not use films in his own production for the advancement of his career, but instead relied on loan-outs to other studios. These were hesitant, however, to treat Marshal as an elite star. Another limitation was the actor's insufficient cooperation with the press. Marshal was described as a reclusive person by the employees of the studio; he was unable to relax during interviews and was reluctant to share details from his private life. This negatively impacted his relations with the public. The actor only rarely participated in activities of the marketing department, refused offers for novel and fresh publicity, and came across as forced and unexciting in his few interviews and profile articles.

Despite this, Selznick's studio succeeded in obtaining two leading roles for Marshal in the years 1943 and 1944, one of them being in a prestigious film at MGM that became a hit of the season. The costs, however, greatly exceeded Selznick's profits: since 1941, the actor was always paid more than $1,250 per week (and as much as $1,750 beginning in September 1943), while the studio during this time collected only $75,000. A conservative estimate at Selznick's losses for the period from January 1, 1942, to the termination of the contract in July 1944 would be between $70,000 and $80,000. The actor's illness, which could have limited him even earlier, for example in his contact with the media, prevented further development of his career and a more substantial return of Selznick's investment. Although there is ample evidence on the screen that Marshal had the prerequisites to become a popular star, with undisputed acting talent and an attractive appearance,[37] and despite receiving mostly positive responses in his roles as a charming, elegant, romantic type, his potential remained untapped to a great extent.[38]

TALENTS FROM BROADWAY: GENE KELLY AND GREGORY PECK

Selznick's company did not rely from the very beginning exclusively on Alan Marshal. The actor became the first candidate for stardom because he had already a long-term contract with Selznick, but efforts at discovering and developing other leading men were coordinated as of January 1941 in all the various departments of the studio. The key role in this was played by Selznick's talent scout Katharine (Kay) Brown, who was part of the New York office. Brown's job was to carefully monitor the situation in the entertainment industry on the East Coast and provide detailed reports about the most promising acting talents. The major focus was on Broadway theaters, where both male and female performers usually had sufficient talent and experience. This meant that their transition to film could take place without complications, which could otherwise arise for newcomers without any training.[39] There was also the added advantage of obtaining "free" publicity with those who had appeared in a successful Broadway hit. Most of the large studios also employed talent scouts who monitored the New York scene and as a result, fierce competitions were fought over the most desirable actors and actresses. These bidding wars often led to an escalation in weekly wages demanded by the performers and their agents.

Gene Kelly was one of the rising Broadway stars in the early 1940s. Kay Brown, along with many other observers, noticed him in his first main role, and shortly after the opening night wrote her boss a note: "I certainly think he is excellent in 'Pal Joey,' and a magnificent hoofer."[40] Selznick was captivated by the young and talented actor. While Alan Marshal, thanks to his origin and accent, took on British types and was suitable for roles of charming aristocrats or reserved gentlemen from higher society, Kelly corresponded more to the idea of a man of the street, being vital, energetic, and purely American. His engagement would therefore ideally complement Selznick's growing stable of contract players. The producer believed in his potential to such an extent that he was willing to sign a contract with him without ordering screen tests, an extremely rare practice in his case.

MGM, however, also had a great interest in Kelly. Arthur Freed, who supervised his own production unit since 1939, planned to use the actor and dancer in a series of musicals, a genre that the studio was increasingly identified with. The competition between the two companies was marked by a series of offers and counteroffers as well as several misunderstandings between Kelly and his agent, Leland Hayward. While Hayward preferred the stability of a large studio, Kelly was more inclined to the prospect of cooperating with Selznick, who had promised a more personal approach and exclusive participation in prestigious projects. In his effort to acquire the actor, Selznick was at least partly motivated by his ambition to beat his father-in-law and former boss Louis B. Mayer. He was therefore willing to offer extremely attractive financial conditions to Kelly, which proved to be decisive in the end.

Kelly signed a seven-year contract with Selznick's studio on July 17, 1941, which guaranteed him an increase in weekly salary from an initial $775 up to $2,250. The actor was supposed to abandon the production of *Pal Joey* and immediately report to Hollywood, although the contract allowed him to work on selected theater projects in the future.[41] Several options were considered for Kelly's film debut. A logical step was an effort to secure the actor the title role in the film version of *Pal Joey*, which he knew intimately from Broadway and which the public associated him with.[42] The film rights were owned, however, by Columbia, which had initially included the project in its production plans, only to postpone it indefinitely.[43]

The archive materials indicate that Selznick experienced difficulties in how to handle his new acquisition over the following months. There are repeated references to the possible casting of Kelly in the next picture by Alfred Hitchcock, in a contemplated anthology film with the working title *Tales of Passion and Romance* and in an unspecified film based on an original screenplay by Ben Hecht. The association between Kelly and Hitchcock seems from today's perspective especially provocative, but it primarily testifies to the fact that Selznick refused to treat Kelly as a mere musical actor. When the possibility of casting him in the adaptation of *Pal Joey* fell through, he was prepared to use him in various roles and genres based on his current needs.

Selznick decided to sell his next Hitchcock film to Universal in September 1941, which also meant the end of speculations concerning the casting of Kelly. The possibility of entrusting him with one of the roles in the upcoming adaptation of A. J. Cronin's novel *The Keys of the Kingdom* subsequently seemed most probable. The actor tested for the part of the doctor Willie Tulloch in January 1942 and along with Burgess Meredith, Joseph Cotten, Franchot Tone, Spencer Tracy, and Henry Fonda belonged to the wider circle of candidates for the much-desired leading role of Father Chisholm, a Scottish missionary working in China. The preparations dragged out, however, and the film finally met with the same fate as other Selznick projects from that time: it was sold in a package to Twentieth Century-Fox along with adaptations of *Claudia* and *Jane Eyre*.[44]

Selznick's production inactivity during the war years seemed to be an obstacle in furthering Kelly's career, just as it had been with Alan Marshal. Leland Hayward began to pressure his client and repeatedly presented him with the advantages of an engagement with a large studio, which produced dozens of films a year, and with whom there would not be a threat of extended idleness. Hayward finally convinced Selznick to sell the contract to MGM, which had been interested in the actor from the very beginning. The agreement was signed in February 1942 and the producer received generous financial compensation and priority rights for the actor's services for one film per year. Kelly was immediately cast in the musical war drama *For Me and My Gal* (1942), produced by Arthur Freed, and became the sensation of the season after the film was released in October.

Kelly's transfer to MGM illustrates in short some of the differences between an independent producer and a major Hollywood studio. While with Selznick, Kelly had to wait for the producer to negotiate a suitable acting opportunity, at MGM he was guaranteed a steady supply of roles. These were not always projects of the highest category (for example, the second film with Kelly, *Pilot #5* [1943], was more of a B-production for MGM and met with negative reactions in the press), but they nevertheless ensured that the actor remained in the public eye. The main reason for Kelly's ultimate success, however, was genre and personal compatibility with the studio. After it became clear that the film adaptation of *Pal Joey* was not an option, Selznick was willing to disregard Kelly's previous acting profile and planned to place him in dramatic, non-musical projects. MGM, in contrast (with only a few exceptions), made use of Kelly's dance talent and training from the beginning and quickly integrated him as an important member into Freed's production unit. Kelly had the opportunity to closely cooperate with the leading directors Busby Berkeley, George Sidney,

Gene Kelly and Kathryn Grayson in a publicity still for MGM's romantic comedy *Thousands Cheer*.

and Vincente Minnelli, the actresses Kathryn Grayson and Judy Garland, and the choreographer Charles Walters, who along with high production values ensured consistent quality of the studio's musical productions. Kelly managed to make another seven films, including the musical comedies *DuBarry Was a Lady* (1943, MGM), *Cover Girl* (1944, on loan-out for Columbia), and *Anchors Aweigh* (1945, MGM), by the end of the war, which helped make him into a leading Hollywood star.[45]

Selznick, in contrast, never got around to making his films with Kelly. The producer first planned to sell off his option to Twentieth Century-Fox, only to come into conflict with MGM's executives who, after the completion of *For Me and My Gal*, insisted on the maximum possible use of the actor at his new "home" studio. The further chain of events is not entirely clear from the archival materials, although it seems that Selznick refused to wait and decided to at least gain something from the situation: he therefore gave up his remaining share of Kelly's contract for $85,000.[46] Even though he first emerged victorious in a competition with MGM and signed Kelly to a long-term exclusive contract, he eventually released the actor to the same studio, thereby making possible the development of his career within the musical genre, which was his forte and with which he has been exclusively associated since.

The case of Gene Kelly and the circumstances surrounding his move to Hollywood have a lot in common with the beginnings of the film career of another actor originally based in theater: Gregory Peck. Kay Brown was again the first to recommend him to Selznick, when she learned about him ahead of the competition when he was still a student at the New York Neighborhood Playhouse School of Theatre in February 1941. Only a few days after the first report about Kelly, she wrote Selznick that she had "a very strong hunch" regarding this twenty-four-year-old man.[47] That very same day she sent Peck's photographs to Selznick's studio in Culver City with a more detailed commentary in which she compared his appearance to Gary Cooper and Abraham Lincoln and further stated: "My impression is that there will be no half-way about this boy. He will either be terrifically good or an absolute bust."[48] In this case, Selznick did not share the enthusiasm of his close collaborator, but nevertheless ordered screen tests in New York, with their direction entrusted to Robert Ross, Peck's acting coach from the Neighborhood Playhouse. Peck performed scenes taken over from the recently completed novel by Eric Knight *This Above All* and Selznick's earlier film *The Young in Heart*.

After viewing the tests, Selznick sent out a telegram where his reserved position was apparent: "GOOD, BUT HARD TO CAST—BAD EARS. TERRIBLE IN 'YOUNG IN HEART' SCENE. ROSS DIRECTION BAD."[49] He elaborated on his evaluation in a later letter:

> I am sorry to have to say that I don't see what we could do with Gregory Peck. Maybe a big studio could use him, but we would have great difficulty in either using him ourselves or in getting other studios to use him that didn't have him under contract. He photographs like Abe Lincoln, and if he has a great personality I don't think it comes through in these tests. He must be a fine legitimate actor, judging by your great interest in him, and while his performance in the scene from "This Above All" is satisfactory, considering how much work was done in one day, and considering the circumstances under which it was made, it is nothing to get excited about. As for his performance in [the scene from] "The Young in Heart," my respect for Doug Fairbanks, Jr., goes up after seeing Peck play this scene.[50]

After this, communication concerning Peck halted for more than a year and a half. The negotiations were terminated on account of the actor's lack of experience and the poor direction and insufficient technical level of the tests. This case serves to reveal the limits of Selznick's system for discovering potential stars from the East Coast. Evaluation of talent from a distance—based solely on reports from Kay Brown, photographs, and screen tests—could not replace

DAVID O. SELZNICK PRODUCTIONS, INC.

NEW YORK CITY

Inter-office Communication

TO Mr. Selznick; cc: Mr. O'Shea   DATE 2/5/41

FROM   Miss Brown   SUBJECT GREGORY PECK

Dear David:

I am attaching hereto pictures of Gregory Peck. He is the boy
that is studying at the Neighborhood Playhouse under Bob Ross. He is about
6'2", extremely lanky, 24 years of age. The pictures that unfortunately look
like Gary Cooper were taken on a model's job in New Jersey showing the happy
life of a General Electric worker. The Abe Lincoln dinner jacket shows you
exactly what he looks like. He wears his hair long, practically over his ears.
I think the reason for this is that the left ear has been smashed. However,
Mr. Gable's done all right with a pair of ears and I think this is something
that can be taken care of. My impression is that there will be no half-way
about this boy. He will either be terrifically good or an absolute bust.
He doesn't think he is ready to go to pictures because he has had no professional experience. He has four offers for summer stock. I persuaded him
that for the most part the directors in summer stock weren't worth anything and
it would be much better to go out to California and work under some really
good people.

He is tenacious about the theatre and the kind of deal we would
have to make at this time would be: Options for 2 periods of 6 months each,
starting June 1st this year, with a further option limited to 4 or 5 months
making him available for the theatre season of 1942; he to have six months off them,
our option to start upon termination of his play; three further 6 months options with
a return to the theatre for 6 months; then a straight picture contract for the re-
mainder of the seven years.

He has been working on all the scenes from Galsworthy's "Escape," and
Bob and I thought to use the opening scene on the Park Bench. Would you like to
see him in dinner jacket for close-up, and outdoor clothes looking toward
"Ox-Bow Incident?"

Please advise if you are willing to give the two periods off during the
term.

kb*ab—enc.

Memo from Kay Brown to David O. Selznick concerning the young Gregory Peck. Courtesy of Daniel Selznick.

personal contact and tests carried out in the professional facilities of a Hollywood studio. Selznick had incredible faith in Brown and often relied on
her judgment when making decisions (she was, after all, responsible for the
discoveries of Ingrid Bergman, Dorothy McGuire, and Jennifer Jones, among
others). If, however, there was evidence which contradicted her views, Selznick
needed to carefully weigh the pros and cons. The partially improvised screen
tests, which were carried out under semi-professional conditions and the supervision of which was entrusted to a person without film experience, worked

to Peck's disadvantage. Selznick subsequently failed to utilize his privileged position and priority rights to the actor's services, negotiated by Kay Brown, and allowed him to walk away.[51]

The importance of personal contact when judging the merits of potential stars became apparent to Selznick in October 1942 when Peck traveled from New York to California. The first meeting between the producer and the actor took place on October 29, and Selznick's reactions were sharply different from the evaluation of the screen tests eighteen months earlier. According to a report from the secretary Frances Inglis, Selznick said that Peck was "very interesting looking" and proclaimed him "the best bet as a leading man that had come along [in Hollywood] in a long, long time."[52]

However, Peck's position dramatically changed since March of the previous year. Due to a spine injury suffered during a movement exercise at the Neighborhood Playhouse, he was classified as 4-F and therefore unfit for military service, which allowed him to fully focus on the development of his acting skills.[53] He took part in a stage tour of Shaw's *Doctor's Dilemma* alongside Katharine Cornell in late 1941 and further appeared in several productions on Broadway where he received positive notices in the press. Most recent was his role in the staging of *The Morning Star* at the Morosco Theatre under the direction of Guthrie McClintic, Cornell's husband. The *New York World Telegram*, based on his impressive performance, wrote the following: "Especial praise must go to Gregory Peck, a remarkable young actor [. . .], sensitive, intelligent, expert and an uncommon type who promises to go far."[54] This and similar evaluations did not escape the notice of talent scouts from most Hollywood studios. The film industry at the end of 1942 was considerably impacted by the lack of male stars which meant that young actors like Peck became valuable commodities. It came as no surprise, then, that Selznick was not the only one interested in Peck's services.

The twenty-six-year-old actor was represented in negotiations with Hollywood studios by Maynard Morris from the influential talent agency operated by Leland Hayward. Morris strategically refused offers involving exclusive long-term contracts, which came from MGM and Warner Bros. as well as Selznick, and instead came up with a solution which was met with admiration by a number of people in the business. Peck signed contracts for a certain number of films with several companies at once, thereby ensuring at the end of a complicated process participation in prestigious projects of MGM, Twentieth Century-Fox, Selznick, and another independent producer, Casey Robinson. As *Time* magazine later wrote, "when the moguls were through shuffling around their pieces of Mr. Peck, he was the most owned and least available leading man in Hollywood, and one of the most valuable."[55] Peck's commitments were divided up as follows: Fox had the right to four films, Selznick and MGM to

Early studio portrait of Gregory Peck.

three, and Casey Robinson to two.[56] Of particular interest was that the details of all business transactions were finalized even before Peck's attractiveness could be confirmed or evaluated by the moviegoing public.

It did not therefore matter all that much that Peck's Hollywood debut, the war film *Days of Glory* (1944) produced by Casey Robinson and purchased for distribution by RKO, did not meet with much success amongst either moviegoers or critics. The story of a group of Russian partisans, fighting a lost battle against a superior German force, probably lost out due to staginess and too many declamations as opposed to action.[57] Even before it was released in June 1944, Peck succeeded in a competition among dozens of actors and gained the role of Father Chisholm in the high-budget drama *The Keys of the Kingdom* at Twentieth Century-Fox. David O. Selznick, who originally owned the project, was instrumental in making sure the desired role went to him. Although the material now belonged to his rival, the producer knew that its success would have a positive impact on Peck's popularity when his own project would finally come along. Peck himself attributed his gaining of the role to circumstances related to the war: "If it weren't for the shortage of leading men, a place like 20th Century-Fox wouldn't have been interested in me—think of it, they've lost Henry Fonda, Victor Mature, Tyrone Power, Richard Green, John Payne . . ."[58]

Despite the extensive advertising campaign, *The Keys of the Kingdom* lost money upon its initial release[59]—losing out in the competition with other "spiritual" films such as *A Guy Named Joe* and *Going My Way* (1944, Paramount) that were released during the same season. But the reactions in the press made it apparent that Peck had passed muster in the main role. *Look* magazine referred to him as the "screen-discovery-of-the-year" who completely dominated the more than two-hour-long adaptation of the bestseller.[60] The *New York World Telegram* was also enthusiastic: "There have been intimations of his forceful talents on the stage and screen. Nevertheless, there is an astonishment awaiting everyone who sees *The Keys of the Kingdom*, with this fledgling movie actor tossing in one of the soundest and most intelligently presented performances of the year."[61] The result was an Oscar nomination, which served to confirm Peck's status as a new Hollywood star.

After Casey Robinson and Twentieth Century-Fox, it was up to Selznick and MGM to come up with their pictures with Peck. Selznick placed the actor in another collaboration with Alfred Hitchcock, *Spellbound*, while MGM chose for him the adaptation of the Marcia Davenport's bestseller *The Valley of Decision* (1945). Both projects were costly and were accompanied by extensive advertising and publicity. Peck appeared in them for the first time alongside leading female stars: Ingrid Bergman in *Spellbound* and Greer Garson in *The Valley of Decision*. Both ranked among the biggest box-office attractions during the war and were also associated with an aura of prestige, caused, amongst other things, by their recent Academy Awards wins (Garson received an Oscar for the title role in *Mrs. Miniver*, Bergman was awarded for her performance in *Gaslight* [1944, MGM]). The association of Peck with these popular and recognized female stars served to confirm his own star status.

The shortage of leading men in Hollywood during the war led producers to treat Peck as a ready-made, established star from the very beginning. Peck did not have to undergo any "trial" period where he would have to take extensive screen tests and be cast in minor roles with the aim of determining and analyzing the public reaction. Without any film experience and entirely on the basis of positive responses from the theater (in productions which didn't have longer runs than thirty performances), he received main roles in a series of prestigious titles which did not give the public any other choice but to accept him as the successor to Henry Fonda, James Stewart, and Gary Cooper.[62] Dozens of articles celebrated his rapid rise to stardom by using similar statements such as the one by Thomas M. Pryor, who wrote for the *New York Times* that "[n]ot since

Clark Gable crashed upon the screen over a dozen years ago has the arrival of a new leading man created as much commotion as did that of Gregory Peck."[63] *Collier's* chimed in, saying that "[s]uccess so big and so speedy never happened to anybody anywhere, not even in Hollywood, not even to Garbo or Gable."[64]

If *Days of Glory* and *The Keys of the Kingdom* failed to meet with the expected commercial success, the opposite was the case for Peck's next films. *The Valley of Decision* earned more than $4.5 million in rentals and placed among the ten highest-grossing pictures of the year. Although *Spellbound's* release was postponed until November 1945, this did not seem to harm its box-office performance, as it grossed almost $5 million. The picture thus ranked third among the hits of 1945, behind *The Bells of St. Mary's* (Rainbow Productions/RKO) and *Leave Her to Heaven* (Twentieth Century-Fox).[65] By the end of the year, Peck was receiving more than 3,000 fan letters per week and found himself in a leading position in several surveys concerning the most popular new figure on the screen.[66] In 1946, he ended up fourth among male stars according to George Gallup's research and in 1947 he appeared for the first time in Quigley's Top 10.[67] His position was thus confirmed by both popularity among audiences and his box-office success.

It is not surprising that Selznick considered taking steps which would bind Peck tighter to his company. Over a mere two years, the actor became a valuable commodity and the price for his services reached the amount of $150,000 per film.[68] Peck was apparently satisfied under Selznick, but also did not have any reason for making changes to the way he managed his career. It was the specific arrangement of his commitments to several studios at once that ensured him a supply of prestigious projects, a variability of roles and genres, and a maximum workload during the key war and postwar years. The cooperation between Selznick and Peck thus continued along the lines of their 1943 agreement and the producer could only regret that he had missed out on the opportunity to obtain exclusive rights to Peck's services two years earlier.[69]

Selznick attempted to at least assert his limited influence by shaping the actor's star image. In Fox's *The Keys of the Kingdom*, Peck appeared as an honorable and hard-working Catholic missionary with unwavering moral integrity, and in MGM's *The Valley of Decision*, he played an enterprising son of a steel magnate pursuing reconciliation between the management of the company and its laborers. In contrast, Selznick emphasized Peck's disturbing characteristics in the choice of roles for him. *Spellbound* made use of the contrast between Peck's tall, robust body and his almost boyish, vulnerable face, and blended elements of the mystery thriller and romance. Another film personally supervised by Selznick was supposed to go even further. The producer planned "to capture the sex quality that I believe to be his appeal" in the epic Western *Duel in the Sun*.[70] He thus contributed to the fact that Peck, already at the beginning of his career, avoided typecasting and was instead recognized as a versatile actor capable to take on a wide spectrum of roles in various genres. In the words of the editor of *Time* magazine, Peck "is U.S. cinema's first male idol to resist typing: the first to devote himself successfully to the art of acting, rather than a stylized display of physique and personality."[71]

In conclusion, Selznick had only partial control over Peck at the end of the war but was nevertheless able to effectively make use of the situation for both his and the actor's benefit: he profited from Peck's success and the publicity that circulated around him, while the actor welcomed challenges in the form of rewarding roles which prevented him from being associated with a fixed screen type by the film industry and the public. When James Stewart (serving as a bomber pilot in the US Air Corps), Henry Fonda (employed in the US Navy), Tyrone Power (enlisted in the US Marine Corps), and others began to return from the armed forces in 1945, they had extremely strong competition in the person of Gregory Peck.

AN IMPROBABLE ROMANTIC HERO: JOSEPH COTTEN

Like Gene Kelly and Gregory Peck, Joseph Cotten had also experienced success in theater. Unlike them, he was only noticed by Selznick's company after he had appeared in the movies. He drew attention to himself through his long-term professional association with Orson Welles, which began in radio in the mid-1930s, continued with the Federal Theatre Project and the activities of Welles and Houseman's Mercury Theatre (the stagings of *Caesar*, *The Shoe-maker's Holiday*, and *Too Much Johnson* became legendary), and culminated with Cotten's film debut in *Citizen Kane* (1941, RKO). Cotten also starred in the Broadway production of *The Philadelphia Story*, in which he played the role of C. K. Dexter Haven (he was replaced by Cary Grant in the MGM film version), and was cast in the romantic film produced by Alexander Korda *Lydia*, in which he (along with Alan Marshal) appeared as one of the heroine's four suitors.

Selznick's interest in Cotten's services was caused by difficulties with the casting of the role of Father Chisholm in *The Keys of the Kingdom* when the film was still being prepared at his own studio. The candidates gradually dropped out or proved unavailable. The most serious prospect in March 1942 was Van Heflin, but Selznick, despite the actor's recent win of the Best Supporting Actor Oscar for his outstanding performance in *Johnny Eager* (1941, MGM), had doubts about his skills and compatibility with the role, and therefore considered other options. Cotten in *Citizen Kane*, *Lydia*, and in the recently completed *The Magnificent Ambersons* (1942, RKO) had convincingly played roles covering several decades (with the assistance of make-up artists) and the same requirement, to an even greater extent, was the case with Chisholm, whose story in *The Keys of the Kingdom* begins in 1878 and ends sixty years later. Only few Hollywood actors were able and willing to undergo such radical transformations in appearance. In addition, Cotten's non-exclusive contract with Alexander Korda was for up sale at that time for $50,000 and Selznick viewed it as an opportunity to expand his acting ensemble with another talented personality.[72]

Cotten underwent screen tests for the role in mid-April but was not satisfied with them and evaluated them quite harshly. He informed Selznick by means of a telegram that he "DOES NOT FEEL HE COULD PLAY IT" and "WOULD BE MISERABLE AS CHISHOLM."[73] The producer answered the actor that "HE UNDERESTIMATES HIS VERSATILITY AND ABILITY" but he respected his decision and pressed no further.[74] Cotten nevertheless ended up as one of Selznick's new acquisitions: in the middle of 1942—after Charles Koerner became the head of RKO—Welles's creative unit, which was responsible for the making of *Citizen Kane*, *The Magnificent Ambersons*, and most recently the low-budget thriller *Journey Into Fear* (released in 1943)[75] fell apart, and not even Cotten's second employer Alexander Korda, getting ready for his return to Britain, had a use for the actor. Selznick, convinced of his qualities and abilities, therefore quickly offered him an exclusive seven-year contract. After a discussion with his agent Leland Hayward, Cotten agreed. As with Gene Kelly earlier, Selznick promised him a more personal approach and more selective offerings of projects and roles than would be the case with any of the large Hollywood studios.[76]

When Cotten joined up with Selznick, he was thirty-seven years old, eleven years older than Gregory Peck, seven years older than Gene Kelly, and four years older than Alan Marshal. Because of his age, he was not obligated to join the armed forces, but Hollywood—under the influence of his earlier films, in which he played even older men—approached him as more of a character actor as opposed to a romantic type suitable for leading roles. Along these lines, Cotten's first part with his new employer was Uncle Charlie in the psychological thriller *Shadow of a Doubt* (1943), which Alfred Hitchcock, like Cotten on loan-out from Selznick's studio, directed for Universal. Although the film did not become a hit upon its first release (with rentals of approximately $1.2 million),[77] it was warmly received by the critics. Cotten met with complimentary reactions throughout the film industry and the press for his role of a cold-blooded murderer of lonesome widows. E. A. Cunningham wrote for *Motion Picture Herald* that "Joseph Cotten is excellent as the murderer, cool and malevolent,"[78] while Bosley Crowther in the *New York Times* stated that "[a]s the progressively less charming Uncle Charlie, Joseph Cotten plays with smooth, insinuating ease while injecting a harsh and bitter quality which nicely becomes villainy."[79]

Although the response to Cotten's performance in *Shadow of a Doubt* was positive, it also contained a potential threat that the actor would be typecast as a villain. Selznick did not want this to happen and declared his interest in finding positive, heroic roles for him. The motivation behind this was undoubtedly a financial one as Selznick was aware of the situation in the market, knowing that there was a lack of actors for playing romantic leads, who were much more valuable and scarcer than character actors. The talent department was therefore tasked with providing Cotten with a suitable project that would present him to the film industry and the public in a new light.

An offer arrived in Selznick's studio in August 1942, when Hitchcock's film was still being shot, for a role in Fritz Lang's dramatization of the events surrounding the assassination of the Reichsprotektor of Bohemia and Moravia Reinhard Heydrich, *Hangmen Also Die!* (1943, Arnold Pressburger Films/ United Artists). Although the role of the doctor and member of the resistance František Svoboda[80] met all the heroic parameters, Selznick was dissatisfied with the development of the romantic line: "The story gives no indication of the conclusion of the romantic angle. [. . .] in view of our desire to get Cotten into romantic roles so that he isn't limited or stamped as a character actor, we ought to insist that the love story be concluded with him instead of with the other character."[81] Selznick therefore pushed for a significant change in the screenplay with the aim of forming Cotten's image in a desirable manner. He also demanded the right to choose Cotten's female costar, with an interest in the trio of Valerie Hobson, K. T. Stevens, and Jennifer Jones. Although the film was eventually made without Cotten (Brian Donlevy received the part), Selznick's notes reveal a great deal about the plans which the studio had with the actor.

The producer Hunt Stromberg, who was working on an adaptation of a detective novel written by the infamous striptease dancer Gypsy Rose Lee under the title *The G-String Murders*, also expressed an interest in Cotten. The film would have been an opportunity to present Cotten alongside the star Barbara Stanwyck, but Selznick had objections to the material, being concerned about Cotten appearing in two films in a row about mass murderers, and therefore rejected the offer.[82] He instead discussed with Twentieth Century-Fox the option of the actor's loan-out for the upcoming Ernst Lubitsch project *Heaven Can Wait* (1943) and the adaptation of *Claudia*, in which he had earlier secured the title role for Dorothy McGuire. The producer addressed William Goetz, who in the absence of Darryl F. Zanuck had been entrusted with overseeing the production at the studio, and tried to convince him of Cotten's value:

The minute the Hitchcock picture, "A Shadow of a Doubt," [. . .] is released, Cotten's price will be exactly double what it is today. [. . .] Reports from the preview are that Cotten is an absolute sensation in the picture [. . .] and I think he will have considerable name value as soon as it is released. It is also obvious that he won't be sitting around waiting for parts, so out of my interest in seeing "Claudia" as good as possible, and having McGuire have the best possible "David" opposite her, I urge you to think seriously about Cotten.[83]

He sent word to Lubitsch along the same lines, informing him that '[Y]OU ARE GOING TO BE THE SORRIEST DIRECTOR IN HOLLYWOOD IF YOU HAVEN'T SELECTED COTTEN. HE IS ABSOLUTELY MAGNIFICENT IN [*Shadow of a Doubt*], AND PROVES HE CAN PLAY ANYTHING, AND WITH GREAT CHARM."[84]

Selznick's insistence, coupled with arguments based on the actor's versatility and bargain price at a time when his predicted triumph in *Shadow of a Doubt* had not yet been confirmed by the public reaction, did not have the desired effect, and the roles in *Heaven Can Wait* and *Claudia* went to Don Ameche and Robert Young, respectively. It wasn't until several weeks later that the studio could finally celebrate as they succeeded in negotiating the male lead in Universal's *Hers to Hold* (1943). The project met all the criteria set out by Selznick for Cotten's next film: it was an A-category romantic comedy in which the actor's costar would be Universal's top leading lady at the time, the sixteen-years younger Deanna Durbin. The film had the guaranteed attention of the media and the public as it was the third installment in the successful series consisting of *Three Smart Girls* (1936) and *Three Smart Girls Grow Up* (1939, both Universal).[85] Durbin repeated the role of Penelope Craig, an affable millionaire's daughter, with the difference from the previous installments that she was the subject of the romantic plot this time. The advertising materials and articles in the press emphasized this aspect and stated that the role for Durbin "completes her romantic coming-of-age."[86] Cotten could only benefit from this constellation as her new romantic partner. The character of the war pilot Bill Morley undergoes a transformation in the story from a carefree dandy to a mature man genuinely in love, allowing the actor to present himself to the public in a completely different light. The linking of Durbin in her first truly adult part and Cotten in his first leading role in a romantic film was a success. The film grossed $1.7 million and was amongst five films with highest rentals for Universal in 1943.[87]

In addition to suitable roles in terms of type, it was important to provide Cotten with corresponding publicity. But this proved to be a problem. Like Alan Marshal, Cotten had more of a reserved, intellectual personality. When he did speak with the press, he tended to make inappropriate comments, for example, at the expense of his age. In an interview for *Hollywood Citizen News*, he mentioned that it was lucky *Hers to Hold* was made at Universal, "where they're experts at horror make-up. [. . .] If they can make a young man look old, maybe they can do the reverse for me." Cotten openly admitted his age to the reporter (thirty-eight years), declaring that he looked even older on film and in photographs.[88] Selznick was upset about confessions of this type and concerned that this could both damage the actor's standing with the public and harm his position when negotiating for other loan-outs. In order to prevent further incidents, he told Cotten that "'frankness' about his age is uncalled for" and that at thirty-eight years of age "he is young enough to be Ronald Colman's son, and Colman is still playing romantic leads; and that he is a good deal younger than the two top romantic stars of the screen, Messrs. Clark Gable and Spencer Tracy."[89] Instead of focusing on Cotten's age, the publicity should concentrate on his acting and (still neglected) screenwriting talent (*Journey Into Fear*), his distinct sense of humor, and his impressive intelligence.[90]

Dan O'Shea expressed another type of concern, warning in connection with the offer of the part in Lang's *Hangmen Also Die!* that "it might be a mistake for Cotten to be playing a heroic character and not be in the armed services."[91] Selznick countered that James Cagney (in *Captains of the Clouds* [1942, Warner Bros.]), Errol Flynn, and "all the other male stars" were in the same position and the public did not seem to be concerned.[92] He further added that "I don't think it is going to be possible for <u>any</u> man in pictures not to play this sort of part in the next few years."[93] Selznick knew what he was talking about: after the loan-out to Universal for the role of the army pilot Bill Morley, he was planning to place Cotten in his own home front opus *Since You Went Away*, marking his return to active production after almost four years. The role of Tony Willett, a lieutenant in the US Navy, was written directly for Cotten with the aim of building upon his success in *Hers to Hold* and developing those attributes which Selznick viewed as desirable.[94] In order to rewrite the recollection of the public in connection with Uncle Charlie from *Shadow of a Doubt*, Selznick conceived Tony Willett as a kind and thoughtful friend to the Hilton family, consisting of the mother Anne (Claudette Colbert), daughters Jane (Jennifer Jones) and Brig (Shirley Temple), and the father Tim, in the US Army at the time. Tony exudes charm and is viewed as a desirable bachelor by the ladies, while being secretly in love with Anne. Tim's long absence from the family provides Tony with an opportunity to grow close to her and possibly even seduce her, but their relationship remains platonic, even at the cost of Tony never falling in love again.

Even though Selznick viewed the film as a star-studded ensemble drama, along the lines of his own *Dinner at Eight*, and that it focused on "the women's lot" during the war, Cotten filled a prominent place in both the narrative and the advertising and publicity. The fact that the film was being made as Selznick's own production meant that the studio could control much more effectively than in *Hers to Hold* the content of the press releases and the advertising materials and thereby influence the attitude of the public. In order to confirm

Joseph Cotten's portrait from the souvenir program for *Since You Went Away*.

Cotten's status as a new romantic lead and his popularity among the female audiences, Selznick had his portrait on some of the posters supplemented with the slogan "A New Role for Your Favorite Heart Throb!"[95] The texts in the commemorative program and articles in the press commented on Cotten's successful transformation from a character actor into a performer of romantic roles and gave credit to Selznick, who was allegedly the only one to discover the actor's hidden potential. For example, on the occasion of the completion of *Since You Went Away*, *Screenland* magazine published an article entitled "Joseph Cotten Turns to Romance," which was introduced with the words: "When Joe Cotten first came to Hollywood he played a character [in *Citizen Kane*] who spent most of his time in a gray wig and a wheel chair. Now the bold, blond and handsome guy comes into his own in romantic roles."[96] Texts like this, obviously modeled on materials provided by Selznick's talent department, created the impression that Cotten's previous career had been a mistake from the perspective of typecasting and that only now, thanks to carefully selected projects, had Cotten reached the position which naturally belonged to him.[97] Cotten's rise thus also enhanced Selznick's own aura of being an infallible discoverer and producer of Hollywood stars.

Cotten's next film in 1944 was *Gaslight* for MGM. Selznick had long-term friendly relations with the studio of his father-in-law, Louis B. Mayer, which he made use of when negotiating loan-outs for his contract stars. Cotten had not yet achieved star status by mid-1943, and the parts which MGM offered did not correspond to Selznick's requirements: "We would like to lend you Cotten, but you keep offering us these second-rate pictures. [. . .] He is available for one of your more important pictures, but I urge you to move fast, because you know as well as I do the terrific shortage of leading men, and that none of them is idle very long."[98] Cotten's casting in the important role in Selznick's production of *Since You Went Away*—his first film since *Gone with the Wind* and *Rebecca*—forced MGM's management to rethink their previous position and obtain the actor for the prestigious adaptation of the psychological drama by Patrick Hamilton, *Gaslight*, which was being made under the supervision of the producer Arthur Hornblow and direction of George Cukor. Cotten played the role of Brian Cameron, a Scotland Yard detective who suspects that the daughter-in-law of a murdered opera singer is imprisoned in her home by her psychopathic husband. The remaining two main parts were given to Ingrid Bergman, also loaned out by Selznick, and Charles Boyer.

Due to the involvement of his two stars, Selznick was naturally interested in the project, and when asked by Mayer and Hornblow to provide his opinion concerning the rough cut, he compiled a long report in which he commented on a range of aspects of the production. One of Selznick's criticisms concerned the burgeoning romance between Cotten's detective Cameron and the terrorized wife, Paula, played by Bergman: "I don't believe it, and there is no reason why I should believe it. [. . .] I don't understand why or when Cotten could possibly have fallen in love with the woman. And I certainly won't for a moment believe that she could have had the slightest opportunity or inclination to become interested in him."[99] Although Selznick wanted Cotten to have more romantic roles with the goal of definitively breaking through the label of a character actor, he did not want to achieve this at any price: "I'd like to see Cotten's very weak part become as important as possible; but in the final analysis, it is the picture which is important, and the better the picture, the more even Cotten will benefit."[100] Although Selznick had extremely specific views concerning the development of Cotten's screen identity, he thought it was of more benefit for him to have weaker roles in strong films (that is, A-films with high budgets, star casts, and high production values) than the opposite. Despite Selznick's insistence, the final scene in *Gaslight* contains a hint of the shared future for Cameron and Paula.[101] The producer's correspondence with MGM, however, reveals his priorities when dealing with the loan-outs of contract actors and actresses to other studios.

Gaslight and *Since You Went Away* were shown in cinemas alongside *The White Cliffs of Dover*, *Double Indemnity* (1944, Paramount), and the musical comedy *Bathing Beauty* (1944, MGM), and despite the strong competition, succeeded. Selznick's film, according to *Variety*, became the second highest-grossing film of the year, right after Paramount's *Going My Way*.[102] Cotten's career was therefore clearly on the rise. *Showmen's Trade Review* predicted in January 1944 that the following year would be a breakthrough for the actor.[103] Apart from *Gaslight* and *Since You Went Away*, this was supposed to be the result of his casting as the leading man in the upcoming Hitchcock-Selznick project with the working title *The House of Dr. Edwardes*. According to Leonard J. Leff, Cotten was Hitchcock's first choice because he "could project menace (as he had in *Shadow of a Doubt*) and romance (as he would with Jennifer Jones in *Love Letters*)"[104]—two qualities necessary for the character of a traumatized man pretending to be a respected psychiatrist.

The circumstances, however, forced Selznick to assign the role to Gregory Peck and Cotten was soon after made available to the producer Dore Schary, who was supervising the romance *I'll Be Seeing You* for Selznick's newly established company, Vanguard Films. The last of Cotten's films finished during the war—but released after its end—was another romantic drama, *Love Letters*. Both films, without significant modifications, followed the model presented in *Hers to Hold* and *Since You Went Away*, completing the actor's transformation from a character actor into a leading romantic idol. Under Selznick's management, Cotten specialized in roles of soldiers or war veterans, who despite psychological difficulties, long-term isolation from home, and other hardships maintained romantic relationships with similarly tested women (a prison sentence in *I'll Be Seeing You*, loss of memory in *Love Letters*). The producer also insisted that Cotten's partners in these films were popular Hollywood stars: after Deanna Durbin in *Hers to Hold*, Claudette Colbert in *Since You Went Away* and Ingrid Bergman in *Gaslight*, he was paired with Ginger Rogers and Jennifer Jones.

The careful choice of roles and female costars, the refusal of second-class projects even at the price of loss of immediate earnings, the creation of the role of Tony in the war epic *Since You Went Away*, and the thorough coordination of advertising and publicity—all of this contributed to the fact that by the end of the war Cotten ranked among the most valuable commodities and sought-out male stars in Hollywood. Over a short period of time, the price for his services rose from $2,000 per week (*Shadow of a Doubt*) to more than five times as much (*Love Letters*).[105] Public opinion polls, which Selznick commissioned, demonstrated that Cotten was a more popular personality than even Ingrid Bergman in mid-1945 and that his pairing with Jennifer Jones in *Love Letters* had "practically the same marquee value as the Ingrid Bergman–Gregory Peck combination in *Spellbound*."[106] All films Cotten made since joining Selznick became hits, which was also evident in the amount of fan letters: while the studio recorded 3,160 letters in 1943, it was ten times as much a year later and by 1945 the number had risen to more than 60,000, that is 5,000 per month.[107] Most of these came from girls and women,[108] which only testifies to the fact that the strategy to bet on Joseph Cotten as the next Hollywood romantic lead had been right. It wasn't until after the war that the actor started to depart from this type, most significantly in Selznick and Alexander Korda's *The Third Man*.

CONCLUSION: IN THE SHADOW OF WOMEN

Although Selznick's company paid a great deal of attention to the development of male actors during the war, they never met with comparable success to its female stars. The case studies in this chapter show why: the career of Alan Marshal was slowed down for a long time by his being labeled a mere supporting player. When it did seem as if he could break out from this category, mental problems prevented his further professional development. In the cases of Gene Kelly and Gregory Peck, both young actors of great promise with a theater background, Selznick didn't demonstrate his legendary judgment and failed to predict their star potential, which in the case of the former led to the complete termination of his contract and with the latter to cooperation limited to a small number of prestigious titles. Only Joseph Cotten attained star status and the position of a leading romantic hero through his exclusive connection with Selznick's studio. He was among the top twenty-five box-office draws in Hollywood in the last year of the war according to an exhibitor poll, taking the seventeenth position (eleventh among men). Peck reached the twenty-second position that same year, but in light of the fact that *Spellbound* at the time of the survey had only just been released, Selznick could claim only limited credit (the actor's reputation at the end of 1945 was based on the trio of earlier films: *Days of Glory, The Keys of the Kingdom,* and *The Valley of Decision*).[109] The producer nevertheless slyly made use of the acquired popularity of both and placed them in the roles of feuding brothers in his extravagant high-budget Western *Duel in the Sun,* where they played alongside Jennifer Jones.

During the war, Selznick's company tested and tried to establish other male actors, some of whom later met with solid success. One example would be Guy Madison, who Selznick placed in a minor role in *Since You Went Away*. His four-minute appearance in a navy uniform met with unexpected response

Joseph Cotten and Jennifer Jones in a publicity still for *Duel in the Sun*.

primarily from female fans who sent him an astonishing 115,000 letters to the address of the studio over two years (1945 and 1946).[110] As Leonard J. Leff later pointed out, however, this was only a short-term craze on the part of adolescent American girls (known as bobby-soxers due to their favorite type of socks) as opposed to stardom based upon a fully defined position in the film industry. After the war, the interest in the actor sharply fell. The industry, due to his remarkably good looks and limited skills, viewed him as "more model than actor"[111] and his engagements over the course of the 1940s, when he had an exclusive contract with Selznick, were limited to a range of B-movies.[112] Apart from *Since You Went Away*, the only other A-title in his early filmography was the drama *Till the End of Time*, where the second significant male role was played by Robert Mitchum. Selznick purchased part of Mitchum's contract from his home studio RKO in May 1944, and although he became, in contrast to Madison, a leading star over a short period of time, it would be a stretch to argue that the producer made a significant contribution to his rise to stardom. As the actor's biographer, Lee Server, states, their contacts were limited to short meetings and telephone calls and most of the work was carried out by the relevant departments at RKO.[113] Selznick tested additional actors during the war, including Gordon Oliver, Christopher Adams, Richard Kendrick, and Neil Hamilton. None of them, however, had much of an impact at that time, or any other, for that matter.

Apart from Joseph Cotten and to a certain extent Gregory Peck, then, Selznick did not produce any other male star during or immediately after the war who could compete with his triumphs with Ingrid Bergman, Joan Fontaine, or Jennifer Jones. The films made by his company were mostly conceived as star vehicles for female acquisitions and the loan-outs of his contract players also profiled him as an expert on female talent. Despite a logical attempt to succeed in the field of leading men during the war, Selznick's reputation continued to rest upon his connection with star actresses.

4

FROM MODEL TEENAGER TO TEENAGE MOTHER

Shirley Temple as Selznick's Contract Star in the 1940s

"Goldilocks Grows Up, But Definitely"
—TITLE OF AN ARTICLE FROM THE *NEW YORK TIMES MAGAZINE* ABOUT THE
SIXTEEN-YEAR-OLD SHIRLEY TEMPLE[1]

When David's goal had not been money, he had gotten Ingrid *Jekyll and Hyde* and *For Whom the Bell Tolls,*
and gotten Jennifer *The Song of Bernadette,* which made her a star. As his deals grew more outrageous,
I couldn't grasp what it was all about, particularly as the waste in the studio became monumental.
—IRENE MAYER SELZNICK ON HER HUSBAND'S BUSINESS EXCESSES[2]

As the previous chapters have demonstrated, David O. Selznick significantly limited his production activity during the war, but in contrast became extremely active in the field of star development. After his successes with Ingrid Bergman, Vivien Leigh, and Joan Fontaine and approximately at the same time when Jennifer Jones and Dorothy McGuire were making their first pictures as part of their commitments with Selznick, the producer signed a seven-year contract with the former child star Shirley Temple. Although the fifteen-year-old actress had a series of commercial flops behind her, her new employer was convinced that she still had unused potential, which could once again make her a valuable commodity. Considering her young age, she also represented a type which ideally supplemented Selznick's already existing female star stable: Joan Fontaine (eleven years her senior) and Jennifer Jones (nine years her senior) played much younger characters in certain roles (*The Constant Nymph* and *The Song of Bernadette,* in particular), but only with the arrival of Temple could Selznick think of creating a prototype of a teenage star adapted to the war period.

Thus far, I have mostly focused on moments of transformation of unknown or aspiring film actors and actresses into new stars. In this case, I draw attention to the treatment of a contract actress over a longer period covering the whole professional alliance between Selznick and Shirley Temple from 1943 to the end of the decade. Another specific feature of this case study is that Temple came to Selznick as a former child star known to the public throughout the world. Despite her young age, she had a career of more than ten years already behind her at the time she signed the contract, and her new employer was not interested in *creating* a star personality for her but rather in *transforming* it and *adapting* it to the new circumstances linked with the actress's maturation and the wider changes in the public's taste and the situation in the US film industry. However, the attempt to create an adolescent idol out of Shirley Temple, adjusted to the war and postwar years, ran into challenges related to her personal life—in particular her early marriage (at the age of seventeen) and motherhood (at the age of nineteen). The second set of factors, which influenced the treatment of Temple, had its roots inside Selznick's company. From the very beginning, the producer, in line with his frequently declared professional policy, was focused on the formation of a specific star image associating quality and prestige. When his company found itself in serious financial difficulties in the late 1940s, however, short-term financial profits became of primary importance and lending actresses to other producers, without any consideration of the quality of the projects or possible long-term damages to its reputation, was one of the ways out of the crisis. The comeback of Shirley Temple was therefore shaped, on the one hand, by the interests and needs of the studio and, on the other, by her eventful private life, which had become a constant subject of public interest due to her past as America's sweetheart.

A FADED CHILD STAR

The earliest materials in Selznick's archive labeled with the name Shirley Temple come from the end of 1939, when the producer considered making an adaptation of the children's bestseller *Pollyanna*. In a telegram addressed to the main investor in his company, John Hay Whitney, Selznick made reference to the possibility of obtaining Temple for the title role in this popular story.[3] Whitney responded, however, that the actress was no longer such a draw and that her films for Twentieth Century-Fox were unimpressive from a commercial perspective; gambling on the earlier box-office champion in this phase of her career would therefore represent a significant risk.[4] The following months, in which the last of the actress's films made as part of her contract with Fox were released, revealed Whitney to have been in the right. Selznick informed

Shirley Temple at the height of her popularity (ca. 1935).

his close colleagues in September 1940 that "Temple is absolute poison" and definitively abandoned the plans to film *Pollyanna*.[5]

Shirley Temple was at the height of popularity between 1935 and 1938, when she found herself four times in a row at the top of the exhibitor's list of the most lucrative Hollywood stars. Her films represented an important source of income for Twentieth Century-Fox (Fox Film Corporation until 1935), which employed her throughout all this time. The consistent profits were also made possible by low production costs of around $300,000 per picture.[6] For millions of people all over the world, Temple as a child star represented a much-needed symbol of determination, optimism, and hope for a better tomorrow during the most difficult years of the Depression. As many commentators point out, her characters, often orphans or otherwise troubled children of a prepubescent age, served as a means of smoothing out otherwise insurmountable social (class, generational, gender, and racial) conflicts and thereby fulfilled an important ideological function.[7] Through songs, dance, charm, indefatigable dedication, and selfless affection, she provided moviegoers with a utopian escape from the grim, joyless world. According to Peter Lev, in the context of the late 1930s she represented "a magical figure because everything she touches turns out right."[8] Kathryn Fuller-Seeley provided a similar interpretation when she wrote that "Shirley's appeal in the Depression was that she offered pure, selfless, healing love to sad, lonely people."[9]

The public's interest in the up-to-that-point immensely adored actress dramatically decreased, however, at the end of the decade. *Susannah of the Mounties* (Twentieth Century-Fox), released in June 1939, served as the first warning that something was not right. But it was primarily two films from the following year, the sentimental family fantasy *The Blue Bird* (Twentieth Century-Fox), clearly modeled on *The Wizard of Oz* (1939, MGM), and the old-fashioned story of a family of vaudeville artists *Young People* (Twentieth Century-Fox), that conclusively confirmed that Temple was no longer a guarantee of success. The maturing actress gradually lost the cuteness (a chubby child's body, dimples in her cheeks, hair arranged in the iconic curls, baby talk) that, to a great extent, had defined her. In addition, with the transformation of the economic and social situation in the US, she lost her importance as a product endowed with a symbolic value. In the words of Kathryn Fuller-Seeley, "[u]ltimately [. . .] Shirley Temple's talent could not stop the march of time, nor Fox's production trends, nor cultural shifts in the later 1930s."[10] While she was still in the fifth position in the exhibitor poll of 1939, she dropped from the top 25 in the following year and never returned there again. After her film failures from 1940, the actress's parents and legal guardians, Gertrude and George Temple, bought her out from her contract with Fox (which was still valid for another year) for $250,000.[11] After several months spent on "a study break," Temple attempted a comeback in a derivative romance *Kathleen* (1941, MGM) and a comedy about class differences, *Miss Annie Rooney* (1942, Edward Small Productions). Both moviegoers and critics unanimously rejected them and many predicted that this was the end for the fourteen-year-old actress.

In early 1943, David O. Selznick began working on a screenplay for the drama *Since You Went Away*, adapted from a series of letters which Margaret Buell Wilder, a working mother of two adolescent daughters, wrote her husband serving in the US Army.[12] Selznick conceived his return to active production as an open celebration of the home front and a tribute to women during the war. He also wanted to make it an ensemble project in the style of his ten-year-older triumph *Dinner at Eight*.[13] For the role of Brig, the younger daughter in the family of Anne and Tim Hilton, he had chosen—perhaps surprisingly—Shirley Temple. This time, the producer was not discouraged by her recent failures. On the contrary, he may have viewed her struggling career as a challenge to succeed where his competitors had failed. In addition, Temple in the meantime had overcome what the press had labeled her "awkward age," that is, the time of early adolescence situated "between the paper-doll and sweater-girl period" (which was usually considered unproductive in terms of interesting acting opportunities).[14] Another positive factor was the fact that the commercial fiasco of her most recent films and several months of absence from the screen had reduced her price from the earlier $9,000 per week to "less than we would pay for just the ordinary featured player."[15]

Selznick received encouraging news in March that Shirley Temple was not currently contractually bound to any production company and that the role of her agent had been taken on by her father George.[16] The subsequent negotiations between the studio and the Temples ended successfully and on May 10 the actress was announced to the public as the first major name in the cast of the upcoming picture. Soon after, she signed a seven-year contract which gave Selznick's newly established company Vanguard Films the exclusive rights for the commercial use of her name and image. Despite Temple being out of favor among film audiences, at least based on the results of her latest films, as an established star she was able to negotiate numerous advantages that would have been unthinkable for a complete newcomer. Her weekly salary started at $2,250 and was to increase to a final $5,000, with each additional option period. Selznick had the right to loan out the actress for films of other "major producers," but their number could not exceed three per year; moreover, he was obligated to set aside 10 percent of the profits from all such transactions for her. If the producer required Temple's presence outside a radius of twenty-five miles from his studio in Culver City, he had to provide first class transport and adequate accommodation not only for her but also for her mother and an additional escort.[17] After the signing of the contract, Gertrude Temple declared, in both her own and her daughter's name, that "[w]e were delighted [. . .] because we knew from the fine things Mr. Selznick has always done that Shirley would always have the most tasteful care and consideration possible."[18] The role of Brig in *Since You Went Away* was intended to repair the damage caused by her most recent films, present her in a new light as a likable teenager and by means of a high-budget, star-packed picture associate her persona with quality and prestige, values essential for all of Selznick's acting acquisitions.

A TEENAGE IDOL: INTRODUCTION OF THE
TYPE IN *SINCE YOU WENT AWAY*

With Temple, Selznick returned to a strategy which had worked successfully in the past with, for example, Ingrid Bergman and Joan Fontaine. This involved initially presenting the actress in a film produced by his company, triggering the interest of the industry and film audiences, waiting for a positive reaction from the press and the public (as was typical for him, he would not admit that it might turn out any differently), and only then, when her price rose, offering her to other studios. In June 1943, he therefore resolutely rejected an offer from MGM of a role in a picture which they would have managed to finish prior to the beginning of the work on *Since You Went Away*.[19] For the same reason, he refused to free her up for a theater engagement on Broadway or elsewhere, even though his studio would have profited financially.[20] It was apparent that Selznick was not interested at this point in short-term financial profits generated by the remains of the actress's popularity from her time at Fox. Instead, he wanted to create a more lasting value.

Selznick wrote the screenplay for *Since You Went Away* himself which, considering the concentration of his contract stars in leading roles (Temple, Jennifer Jones, and Joseph Cotten), allowed him to effectively manipulate with the space designated for their characters, their visual attributes and personal characteristics, and the narrative trajectories surrounding them. Margaret Buell Wilder's letters served the producer only as a starting point, which he used to construct storylines in accordance with his dramatic and business intentions. While the fourteen-year-old Brig is only generally outlined in Wilder's material, she receives increased space and clearer contours in Selznick's screenplay.

Earlier, prior to becoming Selznick's contract player, the basic ingredients of Shirley Temple's popularity consisted of her cuteness (curls, child talk), talent (dancing, singing), evocation of parental love, unselfishness, and determination to meet difficult situations head on. It was not in the interest of Selznick's studio to disrupt all continuity with her successful childhood career, but some of these qualities were unsustainable for an adolescent actress. Therefore, her star identity needed to be redefined. Newly, it was supposed to be based on three main pillars: her maturation, patriotism in the context of World War II, and the aura of prestige. All three were to be nurtured on the pages of various periodicals by the coordinated efforts of the studio's publicity and talent departments.

As Brig, Shirley Temple was supposed to become a universally acceptable representative of the teenage generation: healthy, energetic, always in a good mood, but at the same time inexperienced and sexually inactive. The desired type can be characterized best by a comparison with the character of Brig's older sister Jane, who in *Since You Went Away*—in her second role for Selznick after *The Song of Bernadette*—was played by Jennifer Jones. Jane undergoes a turbulent development. She gets to know the bitter reality of war after being placed in a military hospital for wounded soldiers. She also begins to experience romantic feelings, which are initially platonically directed at a family friend Tony (Cotten) and later toward someone closer to her own age, the young corporal Bill (Robert Walker), with whom she plans a shared future. After receiving news of Bill's tragic death, Jane becomes a completely different person: the events force her to reevaluate her priorities and push her into genuine adulthood. Brig, in contrast, is more of a static figure. She is not associated with such an eventful storyline and at the end of the picture she is more or less the same

Shirley Temple and Jennifer Jones in a publicity still for *Since You Went Away*.

person as at the beginning. Brig does her part in support of the US military, but her involvement through the sale of war stamps and collecting of waste does not entail witnessing the consequences of bloodshed on the battlefields. In contrast to Jane, she has no interest in boys and all her love for the opposite sex is limited to her father, whose absence from home is particularly difficult for her. Brig is quite practical, suggesting, for example, that the family accept a lodger to increase their modest income. Otherwise, however, she comes across as still a child. She uses teenage slang and spends her free time either with her shy friend Gladys or caring for the family pets. Her position in the family and the community is further illustrated by her name (nobody calls her by her full name Bridget) and her typical clothing, the latter displaying her still limited interest in her own appearance. The slogans on the posters for *Since You Went Away* announced that "America's Sweetheart is Grown Up Now!"[21]—grown-up perhaps, but not fully mature, one might add.

Surprisingly, Selznick soon identified a threat in constructing Temple's new identity of an innocent and still inexperienced young lady. This surfaced when analyzing the attitude of the public towards his fresh acquisition. "Officially," women, children and, as of recently, maturing girls of an early adolescent age made up the target audience for Temple. An analysis of fan letters which Selznick had commissioned at the end of 1943 demonstrated, however, that she also had an unexpected major fan base amongst young men including members of the armed forces. This information was double-edged. It meant, on the one hand, that the actress's popularity was not limited to a narrow demographics and that she had in fact support amongst various audience groups. On the other hand, it sent the studio a disturbing signal that men could view Temple as an object of sexual interest, which was not desirable considering her young age.[22]

Selznick therefore tried in various ways to prevent his under-age actress from becoming a pinup girl designated for the enjoyment of the male public. Immediately after the signing of the contract, he forbade any kind of photographs in swimsuits or negligee with the explanation that this involved cheap publicity contrary to good taste. Temple was only supposed to be photographed in clothes in which she felt comfortable, without being forced into lascivious poses with exposed body parts.[23] There was also strict supervision of her make-up and hairstyles. During the filming of *Since You Went Away*, for example, Selznick expressed dissatisfaction with her excessively pronounced lipstick, which did not correspond to the age of her character and created an unsuitable impression particularly in the prayer scene.[24] The actress was in general supposed to use "no eyeshadow, very little rouge and only a slight amount of lipstick."[25] Additionally, the studio closely cooperated with leading magazines which were interested in writing about Temple's adolescence. The emphasis was also placed on having the actress, in photographs and accompanying texts, presented tastefully, as the prototype of an elegant young woman, who her peers could safely identify with. Her photoshoot for the October issue of *Look* magazine, during which the fifteen-year-old Temple displayed her wardrobe from the renowned designer Adrian (born as Adrian Adolph Greenburg), was viewed as exemplary. True, the clothing on display included, among others, "a date dress," opening the possibility of intimate relations with men, but it was designed to cover up her entire body from the neck to her knees. The actress also assumed an upright pose with her gaze directed away from the lens of the camera in the corresponding photographs, as if she were avoiding the sight of potentially lustful readers.[26] The photoshoot aptly titled "Shirley Temple Grows Up" undoubtedly also pleased Selznick due to the fact that he was mentioned in the introductory words as the "star-saver" of the actress's career.[27]

Apart from maturation (and the emphasis on its "harmlessness"), the second pillar of the newly constructed identity of Shirley Temple was related to her patriotic zest and connection with wartime activities. *Since You Went Away* was intended as a celebration of the "unconquerable fortress" of the American home, which was assigned to the care of women after the men's departure for combat. Brig is an essential part of the family unit of the Hiltons and her temporary innocence and lack of experience in this context only serve to enhance this dimension. It is specifically Brig, as a representative of the youngest generation, who provides the reason for her father to enlist in the army and who will soon assume the burden linked with the building up of the nation. The film demonstrates that despite her young age she is aware of her individual responsibility and contribution to the shared future. She even goes as far as to express several times that what she is doing—selling war stamps, preparing bandages for the wounded, collecting scrap—is "kid's stuff" and makes a request for more serious tasks. In short, Brig was conceived in Selznick's screenplay as a young girl "in the know" who by her own choice gets involved in supporting the US military and the society impacted by the war.

The actions of the fictional character were directly mirrored in the actions of Shirley Temple as a closely observed public figure. The actress joined dozens of other Hollywood ambassadors who during the war supported the troops and spread optimism in US society.[28] The participation in pledge drives and public forums and regular contact with members of the military were not merely results of her own initiative but were amongst the activities coordinated or originated by Selznick's talent department. Temple carried out several trips around the US and Canada, during which she encouraged the sales of war bonds, met with politicians and soldiers, visited the wounded in hospitals, and christened navy ships. Her performance at the Stage Door Canteen in New York, during which she danced with a number of naval troops (until it brought about a crowd frenzy), gave out 1,400 autographs, and caused a record attendance, was met by a great response, though it once again threatened her reputation as wholly innocent and devoid of sexual overtones.[29] After the premiere of *Since You Went Away*, she participated in a prominent forum organized by the *New York Herald Tribune*, where she spoke of the importance of films for spreading democratic ideas abroad. Her speech, coauthored by Selznick himself, was subsequently published in one of the October issues.[30] These and many other activities served to construe Temple as an icon of patriotism and form a continuity with her childhood career at the time of the Depression, when a great part of US society also viewed her as a symbol of hope and optimism.

The third key ingredient in the revived career of Shirley Temple under Selznick's supervision was her link with the concepts of quality and prestige. By means of her involvement in a high-budget and star-packed film with a current, socially relevant topic, the actress was supposed to be disassociated from the cheap, schematic pictures she had made as a child. Despite the fact that she did not play the main role in *Since You Went Away* and was only billed fourth after Claudette Colbert, Jennifer Jones, and Joseph Cotten, her placement alongside established and rising stars (in addition to the already mentioned, the cast included Robert Walker, Monty Woolley, Lionel Barrymore, and Agnes Moorehead) guaranteed her respect and recognition from industry insiders as well as increased interest among the more sophisticated audiences in larger cities (while earlier her pictures were more directed at the small-town and rural public[31]).

The role in *Since You Went Away* was also designed to show off her up to now not fully utilized acting talent. It was Temple's performance skills that Selznick was thinking of when he addressed the celebrated stage actress Katharine Cornell, considered at one point for the role of Anne Hilton: "PLEASE DISMISS FROM YOUR MIND THE GENERAL SACCHARINE CONCEPTION OF SHIRLEY BASED UPON THE DREADFUL PICTURES SHE DID AS A CHILD. SHE [. . .] HAS GREAT AND UNFULFILLED PROMISE AS AN ACTRESS."[32] As I already mentioned, Brig does not undergo any complex psychological development over the course of the story but she does react to the dramatic events around her with a range of emotions from enthusiasm and joy to disappointment and sadness. The film thereby presents the actress in a much richer palette of moods than her earlier roles. Critics noticed this

Portrait of Shirley Temple from the souvenir program for *Since You Went Away*.

shift and valued her performance on par with other star actors and actresses in the film. For example, James Agee in a review for *Time* magazine stated that "Selznick placed a big bet on Shirley Temple's comeback and she pays off enchantingly as a dogged, sensitive, practical little girl with a talent for bargaining."[33] *Showmen's Trade Review* assured readers that the actress "will retain her old friendships and make new ones among the picturegoers for the manner in which she plays the Junior Miss of the Hilton household."[34] Likewise, *Variety* confirmed that "Shirley Temple, persuasively creating her first grownup role, will be one of the reasons for wide audience interest in the picture."[35]

From the very beginning of her professional alliance with Selznick, then, Temple was supposed to embody the ideal of youth and patriotism and be associated with prestige and quality. The producer cast her in a role tailor-made for her in a costly and star-studded picture and carefully controlled her activities behind the screen including photoshoots, interviews in the media, and public performances in support of the military. Follow-up films were supposed to build upon this image, but also modify it in a relevant manner and keep it always up-to-date and attractive for her fans.

TEENAGE IDOL 2: THE DEVELOPMENT AND REDEFINITION OF THE TYPE IN *I'LL BE SEEING YOU* AND *KISS AND TELL*

Shirley Temple turned sixteen in April 1944. On this occasion, Selznick used the premises of his studio to organize a birthday party for her which, however, contrasted with the large-scale events organized years prior at Twentieth Century-Fox.[36] A report about it appeared in the May issue of *Life* magazine:

> Her guests were cast and crew members who came when they quit work at 6 o'clock, and the fun ended promptly at 7 to abide by the ruling of the state school board. It was a far cry from previous Temple birthday parties, attended by hundreds of children and marked by such gifts as ponies and bicycles and miniature roller-coaster. But the simple celebration was one indication that Shirley had grown up and had to work on her birthday the same as anyone else.[37]

Selznick's company did not intend to ignore the ongoing maturing of the actress. On the contrary, the producer repeatedly declared that her next roles would "parallel her own age" in order for her to become a "representative American girl" embodying "in personality and appearance [. . .] the best ideals of young America."[38] The upcoming projects were therefore supposed to build on the prototype presented in *Since You Went Away*, while at the same time updating it, specifically in terms of appearance and sexuality. In another two pictures, both released during 1945, Temple's characters arouse the interests of men and actively pursue it by means of more daring clothes and provocative behavior.

The drama *I'll Be Seeing You* came about as a more modest follow-up to *Since You Went Away*: while Selznick's costlier production was concerned with changes linked with the departure of men to the armed forces and the situation on the home front, the loose sequel examined difficulties connected with the return of war veterans and (still during the war) boldly raised the question of post-traumatic stress syndrome. The picture was produced by Dore Schary, who as a new asset to the company was responsible for supervising A-films with medium-sized budgets, which were supposed to make the use of contract stars more effective and spread out the high operational costs.[39] The leading male role of a lonely and mentally unstable war veteran Zach went to Joseph Cotten. Ginger Rogers was hired for the role of the prisoner Mary, who receives furlough during Christmas to visit her family. Shirley Temple played the part of Mary's seventeen-year-old cousin Barbara, who feels threatened by her arrival.

Selznick did not personally produce the film, but he nevertheless maintained an essential role in terms of creative control.[40] He insisted that Barbara was conceived and publicized as Temple's "first part with make-up, high heels, et cetera."[41] While in *Since You Went Away*, the actress played a fourteen-year-old girl, in *I'll Be Seeing You* she had the role of a more or less adult young woman with an emerging sex appeal. Barbara wears more prominent lipstick (which her mother scolds her for) and, when attending a dance, chooses a dress with a pronounced neckline, which she justifies to her mother by saying it will boost the morale of the soldiers. Uniformed young men are presented as the main targets of her attempts to draw attention to herself. She first tries to attract the significantly older Zach, while later she is accompanied at the dance by a young lieutenant. Barbara's obsession with uniforms is also testified to by the list she makes in which she evaluates the attractiveness of the available men in the armed forces by phrases such as "high voltage" and "eager beaver." The film, however, carefully avoids depictions of physical contact between the girl and her suitors and her interest in the opposite sex is linked with her patriotic sensibility and consumer behavior (she enjoys picking up clothes, cosmetics, etc.). In short, Shirley Temple remains a safe model for teenage girls.

It is perhaps no coincidence that Jon Savage in his book on the topic described the emergence of teenagers as a distinct demographic group and their association with consumerism at precisely the same time the film was released: "During 1944, the words 'teenage' and 'teenager' become the accepted way to describe this new definition of youth as a discrete, mass market. Teenagers

Shirley Temple in *I'll Be Seeing You*.

were neither adolescents nor juvenile delinquents. Consumerism offered the perfect counterbalance to riot and rebellion: it was the American way of harmlessly diverting youth's disruptive energies."[42]

Barbara is not of course one-sidedly defined by merely her appearance and interest in men. In fact, she is a complex character, particularly in comparison with Brig from *Since You Went Away*. She undergoes a remarkable development during the story, primarily in relation to her cousin. She is initially cold and suspicious and views the arrival of her older relative, with whom she has to share a room, as a disruption to her privacy. She treats Mary cruelly, reminding her of her criminal past. Her less than tactful behavior begins to harm Mary's developing relationship with Zach. But Barbara sees reason in the end and, in an emotionally tense scene, asks Mary for forgiveness. The role of the erring girl, who manages to mature psychologically over a short period of time, corresponded with Selznick's plan to cast the actress in more demanding parts as well as with her own request to receive "more substantial roles" that would emphasize her acting skills. In an interview for the *Los Angeles Times*, she stated how she was "tired of 'icky' parts" and instead wanted "to be someone who isn't just obviously nice, but who is—well, interesting, too."[43] The reviews were positive once again, when for example Bosley Crowther from the *New York Times* referred to her performance in a demanding role as "splendid."[44]

The studio biography, prepared by the head of advertising Don King at the beginning of 1945, clearly depicts the tension between continuity and novelty, which characterized the treatment of Temple's star identity in her first two films for Selznick:

The little girl whose dancing feet, dimples, bobbing curls, and baby voice cheered some of the darkest hours of the century is a big girl now. The dancing, the singing, the baby personality are gone; but the same effervescent spirit which carried her through the old career has carried her into the new, and will carry her through it, too. The baby is gone, and in her place is the lovely young dramatic actress. But she is the same Shirley.[45]

Same but different: Shirley Temple was supposed to evoke nostalgic recollections amongst the public for the period of the 1930s when she spread optimism and hope as a child star among lonely people, while at the same time conveying values linked with maturation, support of the war efforts and acting skill, which were all marked as key for the revival of her career.

Both *Since You Went Away* and *I'll Be Seeing You* became big hits (grossing together almost $9 million domestically),[46] and even though Temple did not have the main role in either of them, they served to significantly improve her position in the film industry. It also appeared that they successfully reestablished her warm relationship with the public. Following a preview of *I'll Be Seeing You*, Selznick stated that "Shirley's name was received with the biggest applause [...], despite the fact that [...] Cotten is the great new romantic rage, and that Ginger [Rogers] is one of the top stars of the business."[47] The volume of fan letters also clearly testifies to her popularity: Temple received 176,388 letters in 1944, which roughly corresponded to the number of letters for Ingrid Bergman, Joan Fontaine, Jennifer Jones, and Joseph Cotten combined.[48]

While these films were being prepared for release, Selznick already started planning an "important outside picture" for Temple.[49] Soon after the opportunity fell through to lend her to Fox for an adaptation of the autobiographical bestseller by Betty Smith *A Tree Grows in Brooklyn*, her mother Gertrude came up with a proposal that she could be cast in the main role in the upcoming film version of F. Hugh Herbert's Broadway hit *Kiss and Tell*.[50] The actress was very much interested in the role of the popular teenager Corliss Archer and had already been mentioned in the press in 1943 as the preferred choice of the producer George Abbott for the Los Angeles staging.[51] The play was premiered at the Biltmore Theater in New York in March 1943, and within two years it reached almost a thousand performances.[52] The film version of the comedy was prepared under Abbott and Herbert's supervision in the

126 FROM MODEL TEENAGER TO TEENAGE MOTHER

production of independent Sol C. Siegel, with the distribution rights picked up by Columbia Pictures.

Selznick wanted to grant his actress's wish and therefore began negotiations about the loan-out with Siegel. It soon became apparent, however, that they had radically different conceptions of the part of Corliss and the entire film. Siegel wanted, for commercial purposes, to emphasize the controversial aspects of the material by presenting Temple as a sexy teenager. Selznick, in contrast, was interested in preserving the continuity of Temple's image and therefore required that the role would not differ to any great extent from the type of a decent and respectable young girl. He insisted on approval rights to the screenplay as well as the cameraman and director and also wanted to supervise the promotional materials including all the photographs with Temple.[53] Siegel understandably resisted this type of control over his film. The conflict culminated with Selznick withdrawing the actress from the production, despite the fact that her casting had already been announced in the press. *Variety* tried to shed some light on the affair:

> From the D.O.S. office comes the explanation that Miss Temple did not play because her home outfit will not allow her to appear in "sexy" roles for another year or two. Real reason, Siegel declares, was that Selznick was too insistent on supervision of scenes, rushes and stills in which his contractee took part.[54]

In a letter addressed to the columnist Louella Parsons, Selznick explained that "it is obvious that the producers [Siegel and his colleagues] are trying to exploit sex situations, however innocent they might be, and I felt that the same motives might lead them to stills that would be in bad taste, and that would be particularly offensive because of Shirley being involved."[55] *I'll Be Seeing You* had demonstrated that Selznick was willing to update Temple's star image and gradually prepare her for "adult" roles. However, *Kiss and Tell* threatened to disrupt the process by bringing about this transformation too quickly. The conflict was temporarily resolved in January 1945 when Temple returned to the cast of *Kiss and Tell*: Selznick gave up the right to more extensive interventions in the film and was assured in return that Temple's role would be conceived in line with moral standards and good taste. He continued, however, to mistrust Siegel, which led, among other things, to a refusal to cooperate on a sequel, even though this had been part of the original agreement.[56]

Caution was apparently justified as the finished film contained several suggestive and potentially controversial situations and the character of Corliss was surrounded for the entire time by a possibility of a sexual relationship. The introductory scene is already daring in the definiteness with which it completes the transformation begun in *I'll Be Seeing You*: the fifteen-year-old Corliss and her slightly older friend Mildred operate a stand with embroidered towels as part of a charity bazaar in support of the USO (United Service Organizations). But their sales are not going according to the plan and the girls decide to offer something else for a price: their kisses. The effect is immediate. Dozens of soldiers rush in to stand in line, impatiently waiting for their turn. The lucrative business is only brought to an end by the arrival of the girls' mothers, who scold them and accuse one another of being a bad influence.

Corliss, like Barbara in *I'll Be Seeing You*, is obsessed with uniformed men. This time, however, it does not remain a distant, platonic admiration: she initiates physical contact, although once again under the cloak of patriotism (the idea to give out kisses generated money for a good cause and raised the morale of an entire army unit). Her sexual aggressiveness is also manifested in her relation to her guileless neighbor Dexter, with whom she manipulates by means of blatant flirting. She is coded as a seductive flirt by her clothing, with unbuttoned blouses and sweaters and a bold top revealing a significant part of her chest.

The plot of *Kiss and Tell* focuses on the efforts by the seventeen-year-old Mildred to hide her marriage to Corliss's brother Lenny and her subsequent pregnancy. Corliss is first seen in an obstetrician's office, where she accompanied her friend, thereby creating the suspicion that it is she who is pregnant. Out of loyalty, she keeps the truth to herself, which brings about another series of misunderstandings. Everything is cleared up at the end with the wrath of the family and the disdain of the community warded off. Although it becomes apparent that Corliss behaved in an honorable manner and that all rumors surrounding her are false, the film nevertheless for the first time opens the possibility that a character played by Shirley Temple can be sexually active. The potential of an intimate relationship with a man, pregnancy, and marriage are an important line connecting the entire plot and it can be assumed that it was this aspect, based on a tension between the role and Temple's accumulated star image, still containing resonances of her childhood career, that was supposed to appeal to the public to the most extent.

The film's reception was, however, significantly influenced by an event from the actress's private life. In April 1945—while the film was still in postproduction—Temple, not yet seventeen years old, became engaged to John Agar, a soldier seven years her senior. This event was for the time being overshadowed by the news of Franklin Delano Roosevelt's death. But when the pair decided to marry five months later, on September 19, 1945, it was covered by all important media outlets. *Kiss and Tell*, ready to enter distribution after the couple's large-scale wedding, therefore gained a completely different meaning for the public: that which the story had played with merely as a fictional possibility had now become reality. Or rather, for the first time—and rather abruptly—the actress's personal life got ahead of her film roles. Commentators did not fail to notice this dimension. The influential Bosley Crowther, for example, wrote in a review of *Kiss and Tell*:

> It seems only yesterday that Shirley Temple got her first screen kiss [in *Miss Annie Rooney*]—a pious peck on her dimple, administered by a daring, beardless youth. [. . .] America's favorite moppet had reached the kissable age. No more dolls for Shirley. Little Miss Marker had grown up. Oh, boy, what a whale of a difference just a few—or, precisely, three—years make! And what a remarkable transformation the current Miss Temple represents! She is now a married woman. [. . .] And as for osculation—well, you should see her in "Kiss and Tell"![57]

The question was how Selznick's company, whose plans were disturbed by Temple's early and unexpected marriage, would react to the situation.

A TEENAGE BRIDE

Until the end of the war, harmony was maintained between Temple's roles and her public identity: the development of her film characters corresponded with the maturation of the actress so that she could become a model all-American teenager both on screen and off. Finally, paradoxically, *Kiss and Tell* quite smoothly fit into this pattern. Selznick was concerned that the characterization of Corliss had gone too far, but the engagement to and marriage with John Agar dissipated these concerns. Instead of outraged reactions to the fact that the former child star had openly flirted with several men in the film, there was more of a surprise and wonder at how quickly she had grown. Another reason for the public's conciliatory reaction was that Agar was a soldier, and thus the decision to marry him carried with it a certain patriotic subtext.

Now the studio had to decide what to do with the career of the married Shirley Temple. The young pair had initially declared that the marriage would only take place two years after the engagement,[58] and Selznick doubtless hoped that he would be able to make greater use of the actress's teenage years. In September 1945, however, he was forced to reevaluate his plans. The producer was disappointed at first that he did not have a new film ready for release which could make use of the publicity around Temple and her marriage. He did, however, encourage his colleagues to advertise *Since You Went Away* and *I'll Be Seeing You* at the places where the films were about to be released or try to return them to cinemas in a rerun.[59] Of greater importance was to plan a new project for the actress, which would reflect her marital status and reestablish a continuity between her film roles and private life. The change in strategy was declared in the revised studio biography by the new head of advertising Paul Macnamara:

> Shirley Temple has put away her dolls and is concentrating on domesticity. As Mrs. John Agar, she has embarked upon a new career, marriage. The doll house on the rear of the Temple property has been turned into a honeymoon Cottage, and Shirley is learning recipes and figuring budgets and managing her household as brides have done since the cornerstone was first laid for the institution of marriage. In an interview the first week after her marriage she said: "Marriage should come first for any girl, of course, above all else. But it is no longer necessary for the girl to sacrifice her career for the sake of the boy's career. Both can have careers in these modern times, and I think a man should be proud if his wife can have one."[60]

Temple was supposed to personify a new social order, involving, on the one hand, an increased number of new marriages with the return of men from combat and the need to care for a household and family, and, on the other hand, a higher percentage of women remaining in jobs obtained during the war. She was therefore to embody not only family values, but also hard-work, spirit of enterprise, and professionalism.

Selznick wanted to make the greatest use possible of Temple's marriage and the free publicity which immediately surrounded it. He therefore began to develop a new picture for Vanguard which would be focused on a series of mishaps in the life of a young bride and her groom. The producer had achieved the reputation of a skillful adapter of respected literary sources during his years in the film industry and the success of his films was always based on careful literary preparation of his screenplays. In this case, however, he took a completely different route: a superficially attractive title—*What Every Young Bride Should Know*—was chosen first and nothing else was known with certainty other than that the film was supposed to be a light comedy with a couple of songs.[61] Sally Benson was earmarked as a potential screenwriter, being the author of the series of short stories that led to the successful film *Junior Miss* (1945, Twentieth Century-Fox). Other candidates included F. Hugh Herbert, the creator of the original play *Kiss and Tell*, and screenwriter and novelist Marian Cockrell, the latter of whom eventually got the assignment. The picture's aim was to establish a continuity once again between Temple's roles and her personal life. This was supposed to be further enhanced by the casting. Selznick noticed as early as October 1945 that "John Agar photographs very well, judging by the wedding pictures, and it might be a terribly smart stunt to test him, and even to use him in Shirley's next picture."[62] Agar successfully underwent screen tests and signed a long-term contract with Vanguard Films in April 1946. His immediate use was complicated, however, by his insufficient experience. While undergoing extensive acting training, he was replaced in the cast by Guy Madison, a handsome actor who also belonged to Selznick's roster.[63] The realization of *What Every Young Bride Should Know* as a Selznick production was, however, prevented by the unsatisfactory screenplay, which even after numerous revisions failed to meet the producer's requirements for a film bearing his company's name.[64]

The basic concept (the troubles of a young bride and her husband-to-be) and the casting (Temple and Madison) were taken over by RKO, which developed its own screenplay, based on a story by the Austrian writer Vicki Baum, for the film *Honeymoon* (working title *Mexican Honeymoon*).[65] Soon, Selznick viewed the loan-outs of his contract stars as a mistake. He wrote his closest colleague Daniel O'Shea a telegram, stating: "I CANNOT COMMENCE TO TELL YOU HOW INCREASINGLY WORRIED I AM ABOUT WHAT 'MEXICAN HONEYMOON' WILL DO TO BOTH TEMPLE AND MADISON."[66] This revelation came too late, however, as in April 1946, when the telegram was sent, the crew had already been filming for three weeks. The project met with a range of production difficulties in the following months (a strike in the Mexican film industry as well as complicated postproduction), which resulted in postponing the premiere until May 1947, when the material had already lost its freshness as Temple and Agar's marriage took place more than a year and a half earlier. The film, directed by William Keighley, ended up being a banal and unimpressive comedy detailing the attempts of the seventeen-year-old Barbara (Temple) to find her fiancé (Madison) in Mexico City and—when she finally succeeds—to overcome the bureaucratic obstacles that emerge on their path to marriage. Shirley Temple danced and sang in the film, which recalled her childhood career with Fox, thereby contributing to the overall impression of an anachronism.[67] It didn't help that Selznick freed up from his team the producer David Hempstead to supervise the final cut at RKO. *Honeymoon* was a complete failure: the costs rose to $1.75 million, while the rentals did not even reach a million.[68] Reviews of the film were unanimously unfavorable and Selznick's fears concerning the negative impact on Temple's career seemed to have been confirmed. Bosley Crowther stated that the characterization of her character was "silly" and prophetically added that it "will not likely win her many friends."[69] The same view was shared by Otis L. Guernsey Jr. from the *New York Herald Tribune*, who wrote that "Shirley Temple is not likely to gain adult cinema stature on the basis of this effort."[70]

The negative consequences of the project were to be mitigated by the comedy *Suddenly It's Spring*, which was being readied for Vanguard by Dore Schary. Joseph Cotten was (again) supposed to appear in the main role, whereby building upon the successful link between Temple and the actor from *Since You Went Away* and *I'll Be Seeing You*. In late 1945 and early 1946, however, Selznick became involved in the complicated production of his follow-up to *Gone with the Wind*, the monumental Western *Duel in the Sun*, which used up most of his financial resources. To make things easier for the studio and obtain additional capital, he decided to sell off several upcoming projects, including *Suddenly It's Spring*, to RKO.[71] He continued to be interested in the film, however, not only because he had a contractually guaranteed percentage in its profits, but also because of the future of Shirley Temple. As he stated in July 1946, "if it is what I think it can be, it can bring Shirley up to date and increase [her] following; but on the other hand, if it isn't done with the greatest skill [. . .], then it can be extremely damaging to Shirley."[72]

The picture's quality was supposed to be guaranteed not only by the involvement of the experienced Dore Schary in the role of producer, but also by an updated casting, in which Joseph Cotten was replaced by Cary Grant and the pair was joined by Myrna Loy. Under a changed name, *The Bachelor and the Bobby-Soxer*,[73] as it was now known, the film was an entertaining light comedy with Grant as a bohemian painter who at the instigation of the prudish judge (Loy) has to feign an interest in her younger sister (Temple) to cure her of her romantic infatuation. Temple received, after *Kiss and Tell*, another opportunity to demonstrate her comedic talent and with it a gift for self-irony. In the words of Jeanine Basinger, "her playing of a typical teenager is the opposite of her roles in *Since You Went Away* and *I'll Be Seeing You*. In those two serious films, she provided a low-key honest portrait of the all-American girl. Here she is the comic counterpart of these two young women satirically mocking the self-importance and exaggerated behavior of those years."[74] In this film, awarded an Oscar for the screenplay, the actress was able to keep pace with both Cary Grant and Myrna Loy, who according to expectations finally make up the romantic couple (the disparity between the characters played by Grant and Temple, given by their age difference, is the main source of humor, and there is never a consideration of their marriage). The picture became the surprise hit of the season (earning more than $5 million and ending up in the top 5 box-office champions premiered in 1947[75]) and for her participation, Temple received positive notices in the press. This strengthening of her artistic and commercial reputation did not, however, last long. Her third and final film premiering in 1947 was the drama *That Hagen Girl*, which ended up negating the previous attempts to repeatedly link the actress with prestige and quality.

The adaptation of Edith Kneipple Roberts's novel, developed by Warner Bros., was chosen for Temple with the aim to provide her with "an acting opportunity that [. . .] she hasn't had to date."[76] The title character of Mary Hagen has grown up in a typical US small town haunted by uncertainty concerning the identity of her biological father. She has faced slander and injustice from her fellow citizens from her birth due to her uncertain origin, which even leads her to a suicide attempt. The story amounts to a condemnation of the harmful influence of gossip and prejudice and the screenplay contained sufficient dramatic situations and turns of the plot to test the expressive range of Temple. Due to other responsibilities, Selznick handed over the supervision of the film to Henry Willson, whose task was to ensure that the use of Shirley Temple would correspond to established standards. During the filming, however, news reached the company that the lighting and make-up were not always completely suitable for her type (in one scene, for example, the actress supposedly looked "too dark, like a Mexican"),[77] and the project also met with other than photographic issues. The entire story, probably written as a serious, socially relevant exposé of small-town morals, came across as unconvincing and the film ended up being a failure both commercially and artistically. Bosley Crowther, in a scornful, mocking review, stated that the screenplay created the impression that it had been written and directed by a "second-rate amateur." Shirley Temple, in his view, played the character "with the mopish dejection of a school-child who has just been robbed ob [sic] a two-scoop ice cream cone. [. . .] They shouldn't do such things to Shirley. It's downright un-American!"[78] *That Hagen Girl* failed to succeed with the public and was listed by *Variety* in January 1948 amongst several titles which not even a star cast (the male lead was played by Ronald Reagan) could help achieve satisfactory revenues.[79]

MONEY MACHINE AND THE END OF THE CONTRACT

Out of the three films with Shirley Temple released in 1947, only one, *The Bachelor and the Bobby-Soxer*, became a favorite with both the moviegoers and critics. In contrast, the remaining two—*Honeymoon* and *That Hagen Girl*—failed commercially and met with extremely negative responses in the press. It became apparent in the end that all three pillars that had been presented in *Since You Went Away* as the basis of Temple's revived career had collapsed: after the marriage with Agar and the publicity it generated, the actress could no longer easily embody the paragon of a carefree teenager (although technically she still ranked among the teenage population); she lost her link with the ideals of patriotism and serving her country after the end of the war; and finally *Honeymoon* and *That Hagen Girl* damaged her aura of a prestigious, valuable commodity, as they did not meet the commercial expectations and were viewed by respected critics as artistically inferior products.

The seven-year contract between the actress and Selznick's studio had moved at this time into the second half and the producer was forced to take a purely pragmatic approach considering the problematic financial situation of his company: the development of a specific star identity and the effort to surround Temple with an aura of prestige (and thereby contribute to the building up of his own brand) had to step aside at the expense of immediate financial returns. Until recently, the profits from loan-outs were unable to cover the expenses on the regular weekly salary for the actress. During the first option period—after the completion of *Since You Went Away* and *I'll Be Seeing You*—she was, for example, only loaned out once for *Kiss and Tell*, for which the studio received $40,000. During that same period, however, Temple earned more than twice as much in wages.[80] It was the same in the following option period when the studio received $61,666 for the loan-out for *Honeymoon*, but paid out $40,000 more to the actress.[81] Only with the assignments in *The Bachelor and the Bobby-Soxer* and *That Hagen Girl*, with the combined price of $200,000 was the studio finally guaranteed a profit on the contract.[82] A series of loan-outs in the years 1948 and 1949 was supposed to ensure the continuation of this trend.

In the late 1940s, Selznick was faced with challenges related to the growing overhead costs of his company, escalating bank debts, and the need to radically reorganize when faced with extensive changes in the postwar US film industry (especially falling attendance and growing production costs). His focus at this time was on, for example, the establishment of his own distribution company, Selznick Releasing Organization, and reorientation on the international film market.[83] He invested his remaining energy into managing the acting career of Jennifer Jones and producing a small number of his own films (*The Paradine Case* and *Portrait of Jennie*), which, in light of his legendary obsession with details and decreasing ability to delegate tasks to others, demanded more and more of his time and financial resources. These circumstances also dictated the treatment of his other contract actors and actresses, among them Shirley Temple. Archive materials indicate that the control from Selznick's side was eased up at this time and handed over to his colleagues: the head of the talent department, Henry Willson, and his assistant, Julian Blaustein. One consequence was the loss of exclusivity: if initially Temple appeared in a small number of prestigious titles, in the short period between 1947 and 1949 she was loaned out to eight films in all, out of which a number could be labeled as B-productions or programmers, routine films with medium-sized budgets. Contrary to earlier practice, interest and care was not invested into the selection of her projects, and the intention was no longer to gain symbolic capital for the actress and the studio in the form of recognition and positive responses (or at least to protect her position in the market) but to generate immediate profits to pay off Selznick's creditors. This does not mean that more significant monetization of their cooperation was not part of the plans from the very beginning. However, in all probability, it wasn't supposed to occur by means of inferior products, which could damage Selznick's company brand and his own reputation as a starmaker.

The first film in the series of loan-outs in the late 1940s still involved high production values, a star cast, and a quality screenplay. Accordingly, it was received warmly by audiences and critics alike. John Ford's Western *Fort Apache* (1948), first in his celebrated cavalry trilogy, was made for his independent company Argosy Pictures with the aim of addressing the wider viewing public.[84] The rentals of around $3 million testified to the fulfillment of these ambitions.[85] Temple played a supporting role of Philadelphia Thursday, the daughter of a strict commander of a military regiment (Henry Fonda), who argues for a different solution to the conflict with the Apaches than the lower ranked, but experienced, Captain York (John Wayne). Rather than her performance, though, the press mentioned the fact that her husband John Agar, in his film debut, appeared in the role of her love interest, a young West Point officer.[86]

The dominance of the private discourse over the professional one was enhanced even further by an event from January 30, 1948, when Temple gave birth to daughter Linda Susan. Selznick's studio received dozens of requests for interviews and photoshoots and the producer himself came up with one of the most controversial ideas in his career: during Temple's pregnancy, he discussed with Dan O'Shea the possibility of drawing up a seven-year contract with the child and paying her a regular monthly salary. He even had a legal analysis commissioned for this purpose, according to which US courts might not resist such an agreement. Temple and her daughter would then, according to these plans, appear together in a film with the working title *Then Baby Came*.[87] Selznick's questionable plan to exploit in this fashion the personal situation of his contract actress, having a parallel of sorts from two years earlier in the idea for *What Every Young Bride Should Know*, which was supposed to profit from her marriage, can serve as confirmation of the turn in his strategies. The producer, whose earlier star policy emphasized dignity and professionalism, did not hesitate to violate good taste and ethics when he found himself in financial difficulties. This time, however, he met with resistance from both parents who were not willing to subject their daughter to excessive publicity. The actress not only refused the offer, but also limited her cooperation with the media during the first few months after her daughter's birth. This did not mean, however, that interest in her person subsided. It became increasingly apparent that Temple's private existence (her life with her husband, running the household, and the raising of her daughter) generated greater interest than her films and performances.[88]

Temple and Agar were reunited in their next picture, the costume comedy *Adventure in Baltimore* (1949) from RKO. The story of a crusader for women's emancipation from the beginning of the twentieth century ended up as a definite commercial failure, and most critics condemned it for its old-fashioned nature and naiveté: instead of being a serious account of the suffragette movement, it amounted to an innocent and unsophisticated comedy made up of the romantic and family troubles of the main heroine. Apart from the screenplay, the critics also panned Temple's performance. Bosley Crowther in the *New York Times* wrote: "Whatever strides toward maturity Shirley Temple may have made in her two or three recent pictures are completely reversed by this job. As the supposedly strong, enlightened maiden, she seems a mildly precocious child whose moods are expressed either by pouting or by dimpling her chubby cheeks."[89] *Adventure in Baltimore* demonstrated that audience's increased interest in the star's private life did not necessarily convert into commercial success. In their following films, Temple and Agar went in different directions.[90]

The actress was further loaned out to the comedy *Mr. Belvedere Goes to College* (1949), produced by her former home studio Twentieth Century-Fox. The film was a sequel to the surprise hit from the previous season *Sitting Pretty* (1948), which succeeded due to the amusing character of the arrogant genius Lynn Belvedere played by Clifton Webb. The second installment, conceived from the beginning as Webb's star vehicle, also met with positive responses, but it seems that Temple's contribution was negligible: in several reviews, the romantic line surrounding her character was referred to as "incongruous," as it drew attention away from the eccentricities of the title hero, which were the actual attraction of the story.[91]

The last two films made under the contract with Selznick found their way into the cinemas shortly after one another in November 1949. As it turned out, they were also the last pictures in the entire career of Shirley Temple. *The Story of Seabiscuit* (1949) was conceived by Warner Bros. as a tribute to the racehorse champion who enthralled the nation at the turn of the 1930s and 1940s. Temple plays an Irish girl, who, because of her brother's tragic death on the horserace track, resists a romance with a young jockey. The romantic plot was again viewed as outdated and insignificant and the actress's attempt to play her character with an Irish accent was evaluated as extremely "inadequate."[92] The long-delayed sequel to the comedy *Kiss and Tell*, made by the independent company Strand Productions and released as *A Kiss for Corliss*, also met with negative comments. In the new story, the seventeen-year-old Corliss feigns an interest in an infamous and much older ladies' man (David Niven), thereby turning public opinion against her and generating the fear and anger of her parents. The prevailing position at the time was exemplified by a review in *Film Bulletin*, which stated that "far short of its forerunner, 'Kiss and

Tell' either in entertainment value or star power, the film is undistinguished in all departments. [. . .] Miss Temple's baby grimaces, [. . .] once cute but now a little palling, contribute nothing to the comedy and, under Richard Wallace's direction, the film often strains showingly to gather its laughs." The comedy was therefore viewed strictly as part of double features.[93]

As is apparent from the previous lines, the final phase of the professional association between Temple and Selznick was more than anything else characterized by stagnation, as the actress's star identity had not been systematically developed. The loan-outs were not subjected to a strict process of evaluation as had been the norm earlier, and during their filming, Selznick's company did not provide the usual service motivated by an interest in protecting its once precious commodity. Temple appeared in films of various importance and quality over the years 1947 to 1949 with the lack of consistency also evident in their genre heterogeneity (contemporary comedy, costume drama, Western, animal "biopic"). In films such as *Adventure in Baltimore* and *A Kiss for Corliss*, which were more in line with B-productions, she played the main roles, but in more significant pictures such as *Fort Apache* and *Mr. Belvedere Goes to College* she was relegated to a supporting player. This further weakened her position in the industry, which no longer approached her as a leading star capable of being the draw for more substantial productions.

Shirley Temple's confidence in Selznick's studio radically weakened as a result of this development.[94] The actress registered the low quality of the films for which she was provided and was unhappy with the fact that after *Since You Went Away* she did not star in any other title personally produced by Selznick.[95] For her employer, she became merely a reliable machine for generating money, as he banked $100,000 for each loan-out. The company was more interested in profiting from the remnants of her popularity with the public, which was still very much obsessed with her private life (engagement, marriage, motherhood), than in the ongoing quality of her films and performances.

In August 1949, Temple changed representation and moved from the talent agency MCA to Famous Artists, which began on her behalf to negotiate the conditions of her potential further cooperation with Selznick. The money was in all probability not the main criterion, as she was earning $160,000 per year and was supposed to receive $40,000 more in the final option period. She seemed to be more interested in fixing her reputation, which had suffered alarmingly. Jeanine Basinger in her book cites the actress's words clarifying her position: "Some of the critics say I've done a poor job [in the last films]. Maybe I have. But I defy anyone to have done a better job with the vapid, spineless characters I've been handed. I don't intend to play any more of them. If a good part comes along, fine. If it never comes along, that'll be fine, too."[96] Selznick was not, however, able to find a satisfactory place for the actress in his domes-

SHIRLEY TEMPLE IN THE 1940S

tic and ever-expanding overseas activities, and because, without marketable results, she represented a financial burden for the company, their cooperation came to an end on May 9, 1950. At the time, Temple was going through closely observed divorce proceedings with John Agar, which could have also played an important role in her decision to move out of the spotlight.[97]

A SUMMARY OF A REVIVED CAREER

The seven years of cooperation between Selznick's company and Shirley Temple can be divided into three distinct phases. The producer initially succeeded in transforming the former child star, who had been generally viewed as a phenomenon of the past, into the prototype of an all-American teenager of the war years. Temple thus became one of the few actresses under Selznick's tutelage with a relatively stable star identity based on her maturation and intimate relationship with the public, which had known her since her childhood. The transformation of her type went hand in hand with the renewal of confidence in her commercial potential, which seemed diminished after the failures from the turn of the 1930s and 1940s. *Since You Went Away*, *I'll Be Seeing You*, and *Kiss and Tell* became hits and brought Temple positive reviews in the press, which described her as a capable dramatic (*I'll Be Seeing You*) and comedic actress (*Kiss and Tell*). But her engagement and marriage to John Agar in 1945 ended up disturbing Selznick's plans. The studio made several attempts to reestablish the correspondence between her film roles and private life, which was always essential for her career, but all of them failed. The only success from this period was the star-packed film *The Bachelor and the Bobby-Soxer*, in which Temple returned to comedy and the type of an energetic teenager. The third and final phase came in the late 1940s and was characterized by inconsistency: Selznick, under pressure caused by the financial and organizational difficulties of his company, handed over control of Temple's career to his colleagues and was only concerned that she would generate much-needed profits through loan-outs to other producers. In addition, Temple became with increasing frequency the subject of public's attention—not for what she had accomplished professionally, but for she experienced in her private life. Motherhood, marital problems, and the divorce were sources of continuous publicity, which were not at all linked with her on-screen performances.

The lackluster conclusion to the professional alliance of Selznick and Temple might unfairly overshadow the indisputable successes which had preceded it. Under the producer's management, the actress became a sought-out adolescent star at a time when almost no one believed she could make a comeback. As the youngest member of Selznick's esteemed female star stable, her presence and highly valued performances contributed to the high returns of Selznick's war diptych *Since You Went Away* and *I'll Be Seeing You* and the outside comedy *Kiss and Tell*. This meant that the studio could demand the above-standard sum of $100,000 per film over the following years for her loan-outs. Her newly established status made it therefore possible to translate it into financial gains at a time when the studio needed it the most.

5

SELZNICK (GOES) INTERNATIONAL

Selznick's Studio and International Stars after 1945

Week by week, here in Hollywood, I go through the British and foreign film magazines because it is part of my policy to take a world-wide view of films. [. . .] During twenty-five years of production I have discovered and presented to you some of the greatest of stars. I have searched for them all over the world. I still continue to do so; and the five I have recently placed under contract can claim between them four different countries of origin. Those five, in my view, are certain stars of the future.

—DAVID O. SELZNICK IN THE ARTICLE "FIVE DARK HORSES FROM EUROPE"[1]

In November 1948, the British magazine *Picturegoer* published the article "Five Dark Horses from Europe," which was authored by David O. Selznick himself. "One of the greatest of star-makers, a man who does not back losers," as he is introduced by the magazine's editors, explains in the text his plans for international expansion, which included the use of five fresh acting faces from four European countries: Alida Valli and Rossano Brazzi from Italy, Louis Jourdan from France, Alf Kjellin from Sweden, and Hildegard Knef from Germany.[2] *Picturegoer* was not chosen randomly for the articulation of the producer's ambitious plans: the United Kingdom was historically known as the most important foreign market for Hollywood films, and the magazine, with a circulation of 325,000 copies and more than a million readers, was the most important source of information about cinema.[3]

Selznick had earlier successfully imported several stars from the other side of the Atlantic, including Freddie Bartholomew (still during his time with MGM), Ingrid Bergman, and Vivien Leigh.[4] Only after 1945, however, did stars from abroad become a priority for him. As had been the case with the development of male stars during the war, this was a reaction to the changing conditions in the US film industry and the current state of his organization. The growing importance of foreign markets, increased interest of the US public in foreign stars, and the need to update his acting stable after the departure of Joan Fontaine, Ingrid Bergman, Vivien Leigh, and Dorothy McGuire prompted Selznick to refocus on discoveries from Europe.

Selznick's archive is full of materials documenting careful research about dozens of potential stars from various parts of the continent. Their selection and evaluation were assigned to Jenia Reissar, who ran Selznick's London office for many years. As earlier with Kay Brown in New York, Reissar was on the lookout for actors and actresses from the UK, France, Italy, Germany, or Scandinavia who had a sufficiently attractive appearance, an interesting personality and talent, and who had a chance to become established in the US and—as was essential after the war—in other territories where Hollywood exported its products. It was specifically the use of these new acting acquisitions in the postwar period which differed in comparison with previous years: Valli, Jourdan, Brazzi, and others could become part of Selznick's US productions (which were increasingly focused on a global public), his forthcoming international co-productions, as well as loan-outs to both domestic and foreign producers. The name of the original company Selznick International Pictures, liquidated after 1940 for tax reasons, would have been therefore much more suitable for the postwar period which was characterized by increased international activity.

Despite all his efforts, Selznick's "five dark horses" eventually failed to meet expectations. In this chapter, I focus on three of them—Alida Valli, Louis Jourdan, and Hildegard Knef—and explore the circumstances of their engagement by Selznick and the reasons for their lack of success. I also document the more general transformation of the producer's strategies in the development of stars, considering the universal move of the film industry towards internationalization after World War II.

HOLLYWOOD'S POSTWAR INTERNATIONALIZATION AND SELZNICK'S COMPANY

In 1945 and 1946, Hollywood celebrated the victory in the war, to which it contributed significantly, as well as record revenues. The postwar optimism was, however, quickly replaced by concerns and a skeptical prognosis: the decision in the Paramount case, resulting in the divestiture of cinemas from the production and distribution companies; the anti-communist campaign and establishment of the blacklist; strike riots; ongoing conflicts with the exhibitors; struggles around censorship and the rigid Production Code; and above all the dramatically declining attendance—all of this threatened the stability of the industry and undermined the foundations of the studio system.[5]

One of the few possibilities to partially compensate for the problematic domestic situation was increased attention to foreign markets. After 1945, the ties between Hollywood and international, predominantly European markets, severely circumscribed during the war, were renewed and intensified. The revenues from the export of US films grew from 25 to 30 percent from before the war to more than 40 percent in the mid-1950s.[6] Foreign markets became essential for evaluation of the investment—they ensured profit for the companies at the time of rapidly decreasing attendance at home—and at the same time increased export activity became a means of spreading democratic ideals and a positive image of the United States, which was viewed as one of the priorities in foreign policy after the end of the global conflict.[7] Significantly, as Joseph Garncarz shows using the example of German cinema, Hollywood films had the best chance of success in Europe if they resonated with European culture by adapting a European source, being set in Europe or featuring European characters or, for that matter, stars of European origin.[8]

The strengthening of Hollywood's presence in the film markets of the up-until-recently occupied and enemy countries[9] did not take place without resistance. To make it easier for Hollywood to introduce their products and penetrate the wall of protective measures which a range of European countries introduced against American "colonizers," Hollywood established as early as 1945 the Motion Picture Export Association (MPEA), which played an important negotiating and coordinating function. Not even this, however, could accomplish much in the countries behind the Iron Curtain; attention was therefore focused on Western Europe, primarily the United Kingdom, Italy, France, West Germany, and Scandinavia.

Apart from the export of films produced domestically, Hollywood also got involved overseas at the level of production. This was partially the result of a cheaper (but still highly skilled and qualified) labor force and attractive natural and historical locations. The phenomenon of runaway productions—films completely or partially made outside the territory of the United States—involved more than 300 titles between 1949 and 1956.[10] Shooting films in Europe helped to bring them closer to the preferences of European audiences. Another important motivation for the shift was to overcome various forms of protectionist measures which were in force in the UK, France, Italy, and elsewhere. Tariffs, import and screening quotas, and so-called frozen funds (the requirement to reinvest part of the profits in the given country) resulted in the emergence of US-European co-productions and foreign subsidiary companies of large studios. By such means, Hollywood producers could finally (paradoxically) obtain various forms of government support, which was established to stimulate the local film industries damaged by the war.[11]

Cultural and business exchange between Hollywood and the rest of the world was not a one-way phenomenon though. After the war, a growing number of films from abroad found their way to US cinemas, primarily from the United Kingdom (films by David Lean, Laurence Olivier, and Michael Powell and Emeric Pressburger), as well as from France (*Children of Paradise* [*Les enfants du paradis*, 1945, Pathé Cinéma] by Marcel Carné, several exemplars of the so-called tradition of quality etc.) and Italy (primarily the neorealist works of Roberto Rossellini, Vittorio De Sica, and others). Most of them only played in art cinemas located in large cities, but some of them managed to find their way into wider distribution and met with a significant commercial success, with revenues around $2 million (this was the case of Olivier's *Hamlet* [1948, Two Cities Films], which was even awarded an Oscar for the best film of the year, David Lean's *Great Expectations* [1946, Cineguild], and *The Red Shoes* [1948, The Archers] by Powell and Pressburger).[12] While the number of films produced in the US continued to fall (by 28 percent between 1946 and 1956), the supply of foreign films increased exponentially (by 223 percent over the same period).[13] This had many causes including the fragmentation of the moviegoing public and the change in taste which came about as a result of the war, the long-term exposure to newsreels, and the foreign experience which was related to foreign deployment of the military and the accessibility of travel.[14] Also worth mentioning is the fact that a small circle of businessmen originally from Europe attempted to establish themselves in the US, with an interest in breaking up the hegemony of the traditional Hollywood studios. The most significant of these was the British film magnate J. Arthur Rank, the founder of the distribution company Eagle-Lion Films, which was active in the second half of the 1940s.[15]

The internationalization of the US film industry also impacted the star system. Dozens of actors and actresses (along with representatives of other professions) flooded into the US, both before and during the war, to escape political or ethnic persecution and bloodshed. Only a few of them, however, established themselves over the long-term: as the case of Jean Gabin demonstrates, even the biggest European stars had difficulty making a lasting impression in Hollywood if they did not have sufficient language skills and if their star identity was difficult to adapt to the specifics of the studio system powered by audience interest in a small number of dominant genres and production cycles.[16] Those who had come across the Atlantic under less dramatic circumstances during the 1920s and 1930s as discoveries of producers, directors, or talent scouts usually met with greater (and more lasting) success: for example, Ronald Colman, Greta Garbo, Charles Boyer, Marlene Dietrich, Hedy Lamarr, and Ingrid Bergman (although even in these cases there was no guarantee of a positive reception by the public).

As Thomas Schatz argued, stars were still central points in the organization of film production, marketing, and publicity after the war, but their position had changed. The smaller number of films in production also meant a smaller circle of stars, which was dominated by veterans from previous years.[17] In addition, actors and actresses, with the gradual dissolution of the studio system, began to work increasingly freelance, under more financially profitable conditions than those guaranteed to them by long-term contracts with the majors. The break-up of the studio structures, growing demands of established acting personalities, and the trend towards runaway productions and increased requirements on the part of the public for ethnically "correct" casting all led to more frequent involvement of stars from abroad.[18] This tendency was most apparent starting in the mid-1950s (see the careers of Richard Burton, Yves Montand, Sophia Loren, Gina Lollobrigida, Anna Magnani, Audrey Hepburn, and others), but actors, such as James Mason and Rossano Brazzi (as part of his cooperation with David O. Selznick), tried to break into Hollywood as early as the late 1940s. The number of Hollywood actors working in Europe (in runaway productions as well as in films made with no involvement of the major studios) also grew in parallel fashion as can be seen in the examples of Orson Welles, Ingrid Bergman (in her collaboration with Roberto Rossellini), Kirk Douglas, and Anthony Quinn. The fragmentation of the domestic audience and the increased importance of foreign markets resulted in a more intensive cultural exchange and professional mobility: actors and actresses could move much more freely after the war in a more globalized space and provide services in various national or transnational contexts.

David O. Selznick was not merely a passive recipient of these extensive changes. On the contrary, he helped initiate them himself with his postwar activities. Already in the summer of 1945, he arranged for a collaboration with the British producer J. Arthur Rank, which was to be translated into a series of films produced under the banner of the newly established company English Selznick International, based in London. Rank was to become the head of the board of directors, while Selznick intended to maintain supervision over the production side.[19] The prospect of alternating between Hollywood and England excited Selznick. In a letter to actress Vivien Leigh, in which he tried to persuade her to work with him again, he wrote: "I think it will be great fun to have operations in both places and exciting for our personalities, directors, etc."[20] When the joint production plans fell through, Selznick at least offered Rank the services of some of his contract actors and actresses, including Shirley Temple.[21] The alliance with Rank failed to produce any results, but the cooperation with another British film mogul, Alexander Korda, ended up more fruitful. Selznick knew his British counterpart very well: in 1939, he acquired Vivien Leigh from him for *Gone with the Wind*, and subsequently dealt with him repeatedly when he became a partner in United Artists.[22] In May 1948, he entered into a four-film co-production deal with Korda, which in the following years resulted in *The Third Man* and *Gone to Earth* (1950, London Film Productions/Vanguard Films, released in the US in an edited version called *The Wild Heart*). Selznick, in exchange for the rights to the Western Hemisphere, provided his contract actors (Alida Valli, Joseph Cotten, Jennifer Jones) and part of the finances, which came from the frozen revenues of his pictures in the UK. As late as mid-1950, he was looking forward to "merging the qualities and freshness of European production with American showmanship,"[23] but the fulfillment of the original agreement to the intended extent (the other contemplated projects included, for example, an adaptation of Thomas Hardy's *Tess of the d'Urbervilles* and a Technicolor version of Dickens's *A Tale of Two Cities*)[24] was prevented by numerous creative and business disagreements, which finally brought Selznick and Korda to court.[25]

The United Kingdom was the most important foreign partner for Hollywood, accounting for about half of the foreign income. The economic crisis there and the strict protection measures, however, forced US producers to seek out partners elsewhere as well.[26] For Selznick, this global perspective on the film market, transcending the Anglo-American area, was typical. In 1947 and 1948, for example, he was planning an adaptation of Henrik Ibsen's *A Doll's House*, to be made in Sweden by Alf Sjöberg from a script by the then fledgling Ingmar Bergman and starring Dorothy McGuire. However, the project ran into the producer's dissatisfaction with the screenplay.[27] In Italy, Selznick tried to set up cooperation with director Roberto Rossellini and, when this also did not work out, he approached his colleague Vittorio De Sica and in a co-production with him made *Terminal Station* (*Stazione Termini*, 1953, released in the US in another cut as *Indiscretion of an American Wife*), with Jennifer Jones and Montgomery Clift in the main roles.

At least as important a component of Selznick's foreign activities as his production plans were his attempts to discover and promote new acting stars, "[the] very best talent in Europe, [. . .] the very top cream of each [. . .] continental country," as he stated in a cable from November 1947.[28] Jenia Reissar from the London office was tasked with monitoring the film industry in the UK, Italy, France, Scandinavia, and elsewhere and compiling detailed files for the most promising actors and actresses with personal information, an overview of their activities, and a set of photographs. These were then forwarded to Selznick, who could order camera tests based on the files. The most promising personalities were either hired outright or they entered a six-month trial period during which they received training in acting and diction and underwent repeated evaluations of their progress. Europe was viewed by Selznick as a rich reservoir of relatively inexpensive talent: he was most interested in those individuals

STUDIO AND INTERNATIONAL STARS AFTER 1945 145

who were already established in their local culture industries (and thus possessed considerable film or theater experience) but not yet discovered in the rest of the world. For them, the possibility of working in Hollywood meant a dream come true and a promise of material security. Only rarely were they able to resist the offer. But only a fraction of them succeeded and lived to see a multi-year contract. In the late 1940s, these were mainly the five introduced in the *Picturegoer* article: Alida Valli, Rossano Brazzi, Louis Jourdan, Alf Kjellin, and Hildegard Knef.

Selznick planned to use his foreign acquisitions in his own, star-laden productions. However, as there were fewer and fewer of them after the war, he also employed them as business articles in loan-outs to other producers and in coproductions with foreign partners. This strategic reorientation on the foreign market was supposed to reach its peak around 1950, when Selznick planned to move his entire organization to Europe. Instead of a massive foreign expansion, however, a radical decline in the producer's film and business activities followed: his company was paralyzed by mounting debts, high operating costs, an inflexible organizational structure, and numerous lawsuits. One of the reasons for the final setback was the artistic and commercial failure of *The Paradine Case*, which was intended to introduce American and international audiences to two additions to Selznick's star stable: Alida Valli and Louis Jourdan.

THE VALLI CASE

The adaptation of the lengthy, more than five-hundred-page novel by Robert Smythe Hichens, published in 1933, was planned as the culmination of Selznick's collaboration with Alfred Hitchcock, which after seven years was coming to an end. The project had been planned by Selznick for years since his time at MGM, and his personal interest in the material eventually led him to take on the script himself (based on a treatment prepared by Hitchcock, his wife Alma Reville, and assistant Barbara Keon). It was clear from the outset that this would be an expensive and star-studded film, much like the recent *Since You Went Away* and *Duel in the Sun*. Gregory Peck won the leading male role of lawyer Anthony Keane, in love with a possible murderess, after Laurence Olivier proved unavailable. His faithful wife, Gay, was played by the British actress Ann Todd, hired from J. Arthur Rank. The experienced performers Charles Laughton, Charles Coburn, Ethel Barrymore, and Leo G. Carroll were cast in other important roles. As with *Gone with the Wind* and *Rebecca*, the greatest difficulty lay in casting the female lead, the beautiful but mysterious Maddalena Anna Paradine. Selznick tried to convince Greta Garbo, who was a perfect fit in looks and personality for the enigmatic character, to return from her retirement but to no avail. After her, two other stars of European origin, Ingrid Bergman and Hedy Lamarr, turned down the role.[29] Only then did Alida Valli, an actress discovered in Italy by Jenia Reissar and Neil Agnew, vice president of Selznick's Vanguard Films, become the main candidate.

During the war, Valli had become the leading female star of the fascist-led Italian film industry. Although born as Alida Maria von Altenberger to parents with Austrian and Slovenian roots, she used the name Alida Valli since 1936 and became an idealized version of Italian femininity. As Stephen Gundle has argued, in a series of light comedies and costume dramas she became established as a representative of the "idealized average: a typical middle-class girl distinguished only by her unusual beauty and vivacity."[30] In the roles of fiancées, schoolgirls, dancers, or secretaries, she was supposed to be viewed by audiences as one of them. Her energy and beauty made her a model young woman with whom her peers could easily identify. In contrast, "[a]t no point in her pre-1945 career was Valli ever depicted as a woman of refinement or elegance."[31] Gundle further writes that "[h]er looks seemed to conform to a conventional idea of beauty while also being modern. There could be no doubt that she was a modern urban girl of bourgeois extraction."[32]

As one of the most popular and representative personalities of Italian cinema in the first half of the 1940s,[33] she could not escape the attention of Jenia Reissar, who in the summer of 1945, just a few weeks after the end of the war and Germany's surrender, sent news of her latest discovery to Hollywood. Selznick did not want "to pass up the new Dietrich or Garbo"[34] and therefore took a bold step: influenced by the enthusiasm of his London representative and close associate Neil Agnew, he gave permission to sign a contract with her without ordering the usual series of screen tests or seeing a single foot of film with the actress. This unprecedented confidence in the judgment of others can be attributed to the fact that the contracts with Ingrid Bergman and Joan Fontaine were coming to an end, threatening Selznick's brand built on the association with female stars. Communication across the ocean was long and complicated due to the postwar turmoil, but an agreement was finally reached at the beginning of November. Just as Selznick had wished, Valli signed an exclusive contract for seven years, over the course of which her weekly salary would increase from the initial $750 to $3,000.[35] Later that month, Selznick mentioned for the first time that the actress was scheduled to appear in the upcoming film directed by Alfred Hitchcock.[36] Her casting resulted in several changes in Selznick's screenplay and the conception of the main character: the "tall, slim and beautiful [woman] with natural blonde hair and cold Nordic beauty" became a brunette from Italy. However, she was still to possess "an almost blank look which is startling—and brooding eyes," making Maddalena Anne Paradine into a bewitching woman surrounded by mystery.[37]

```
CA NL CABLE CULVER CITY CALIF JULY 13 1945 (CHG VANGUARD)

JENIA REISSAR
27 KNIGHTSBRIDGE COURT
SLOANE STREET
LONDON S W 1
(ENGLAND)


VALLI STILLS LOOK EXTREMELY INTERESTING, AND THIS, TOGETHER
WITH YOUR AND MR AGNEWS ENTHUSIASM LEADS ME TO URGE THAT YOU
SHOULD PROCEED AT ONCE TO MAKE A DEAL WITH HER INSTEAD OF
WAITING FOR ME TO SEE THE FILM LEST WE LOSE HER IN THE
INTERIM STOP IMPORTANT WE GET SEVEN YEARS AND I SUGGEST YOU
TRY TO GET IT ON BASIS OF ONE PICTURE COMMITMENT WITH OPTION
EXERCISABLE THIRTY DAYS AFTER PREVIEW OF FIRST FILM STOP
OPTIONS CAN BE EITHER ON A WEEKLY SALARY BASIS AT FORTY OUT
OF FIFTYTWO WEEKS OR ON BASIS OF NUMBER OF FILMS PER YEAR
STOP IF LATTER SHOULD BE OUR OPTION WHETHER WE MAKE TWO OR
THREE YEARLY STOP PROBABLY YOU SHOULD ALLOW ENOUGH TIME FOR
HER TO LEARN OR POLISH HER ENGLISH IN HOLLYWOOD BEFORE SHE
STARTS FOR WHICH TIME WE CAN PAY HER LIVING EXPENSES AND COST
OF LESSONS STOP WILL EAGERLY AWAIT WORD STOP ALSO PLEASE
ASSIDUOUSLY PURSUE MICHELINE PRESLE AND LOUIS JOURDAN AND
TRY TO GET NEGOTIATIONS STARTED PENDING MY SEEING FILM STOP
PLEASE TRY TO SEND STILLS STOP HOWEVER DIFFICULT PRESLE MAY
BE ABOUT TERM CONTRACT SHE COULDNT BE MORE SO THAN BERGMAN
WAS STOP BEAR IN MIND NECESSITY OF LEARNING ENGLISH ENGLISH
ON ALL OF THEM AND ALSO NECESSITY OF TIME TO MAKE TESTS ETCETERA
REGARDS
                    DAVID SELZNICK
```

Telegram from David O. Selznick to Jenia Reissar urging her to sign a contract with Alida Valli.
Courtesy of Daniel Selznick.

From the beginning, the collaboration with Valli was accompanied by a number of complications. At the time of her involvement with Selznick's studio, the actress had a valid contract with the Italian company Minerva Savoia for another eighteen months, which she had to be bought out of after complicated negotiations.[38] Much more pressing was the question of her conduct during the war, which had a direct impact on her political acceptability in the US. Although Selznick had her background checked before signing the contract and insisted that she not appear on any "fascist list," a series of accusations soon surfaced that labeled her a collaborator with the regime.[39] The US consul in Italy had repeatedly refused to grant her a visa for this reason. Only the testimony of two high-ranking Allied officers and an "invest[ment] over $30,000 in the right places" forced him to change his mind, but the waiting period at this time exceeded a year.[40] At least in the meantime, Selznick's studio was given an opportunity to prepare a statement (to be used in press releases and official biographies) that the actress had not collaborated with the fascists (participation in films produced by the fascist regime was not considered collaboration) but, rather, had been forced into hiding and even joined the resistance.[41]

While the visa issues were still being solved, Selznick had to deal with another disturbing report:

> I AM HORRIFIED BY INFORMATION CASUALLY RECEIVED THAT VALLI IS FIVE FEET SIX INCHES TALL AND WEIGHS ONE HUNDRED FIFTY POUNDS STOP SINCE WE ARE CONTEMPLATING EXTREMELY COSTLY DELAY IN START OF THE PARADINE CASE BASED ON HOPE THAT VALLI WILL BE HERE FOR IT IT WOULD BE JUST TOO AWFUL AND IMPOSSIBLY COSTLY IF ON HER ARRIVAL WE FOUND THAT SHE WAS WRONG FOR AMERICAN AUDIENCES AS A CONSEQUENCE OF THIS WEIGHT STOP CERTAINLY IN THIS COUNTRY A WOMAN OF THIS HEIGHT WHO WEIGHS THIS MUCH IS CONSIDERED ANYTHING BUT ATTRACTIVE.[42]

Although the figures proved to be inflated (the error was caused by an inaccurate conversion from the metric system), Valli was indeed overweight and it was arranged for her to immediately start a medically supervised diet.[43] Even after several months, however, her body weight was not satisfactory, as evidenced by the frequency of this topic in the studio's internal correspondence.[44] Another source of anxiety was the actress's level of English: *The Paradine Case* was supposed to be her first English language film and Selznick had doubts as to whether, with minimal preparation, "SHE WILL BE ABLE AT LEAST TO DO THE LINES OF THE SCRIPT CLEARLY ENOUGH."[45]

These concerns only grew more serious as the actress's arrival in California was repeatedly delayed. Valli finally arrived on January 5, 1947—more than a year after the signing of the contract—and immediately joined the crew, which had already been working on the film since mid-December. Selznick was impressed by his first meeting with her: "SHE IS ENCHANTING AND I AM DELIGHTED WITH HER SO ALL OF OUR WORRIES ON HER WOULD APPEAR TO BE ENDED."[46] The personal affection Selznick had for the actress

STUDIO AND INTERNATIONAL STARS AFTER 1945 149

could not, however, mask the carelessness—until recently unthinkable—with which he approached the casting of the key role in his costly film. As a result of time pressure, Selznick failed to adhere to those procedures which had earlier minimized the risk of failure of his acting discoveries. Valli did not undergo elaborate costume tests, extensive acting training, or language preparation, and the cameraman Lee Garmes did not receive the opportunity to properly experiment with various kinds of lighting and camera angles to find the most flattering presentation for her. Selznick was noticeably concerned about the situation, but at the same time did not prepare any backup plan—he staked everything on one card, reasoning that it was very "DOUBTFUL WHETHER FOR YEARS, IF EVER, WE MAY BE ABLE TO GET SUCH AN OPPORTU-NITY FOR HER IN THE WAY OF ROLE, CAST, PRODUCTION, DIREC-TOR, ETC."[47] He probably hoped that the sheer scope of the production and the strong acting ensemble would offset any shortcomings associated with his newest acquisition.

With Valli's arrival in Hollywood, a massive campaign was launched to get the actress the attention of all the important players:

> We must convince the trade and the public that she is a great star from the outset. Convince is actually the wrong word, because what I mean to say is that we must assume that she is, and get this accepted by everyone else. We must treat her exactly as Marlene Dietrich was treated when Paramount brought her over here, as Anna Sten was treated when Gold-wyn brought her over here. We must have the biggest single campaign any player has ever had in the history of the screen.[48]

As with Ingrid Bergman a couple of years ago, the producer instructed his employees to avoid comparisons with famous actresses in the publicity.[49] It was nevertheless apparent that Valli was modeled as a combination of Greta Garbo and Marlene Dietrich. As described by Stephen Gundle, the actress underwent a process of glamorization that transformed her from the type of a modern-girl-next-door for which she had become famous in Italy into the epitome of refined elegance.[50] The publicity department presented her as a European beauty, surrounded by wealth and luxury. Its head at the time, Paul Macnamara, suggested, for example, that they build a reputation for her as a renowned Hollywood hostess and a woman with refined taste in clothing. The model Anita Colby, who—in an interesting publicity stunt—had been appointed during the war the "feminine director" of Selznick's studio, was available to the actress in issues connected with her wardrobe so as to meet the demands of high society.[51] In photographs, Valli was to appear mysterious and brooding, like a carefully sculpted statue of an ancient goddess.[52] When

Studio portrait of Alida Valli.

a photograph of her striking a relaxed pose and adorning her face with a broad smile appeared in *Time* magazine after *The Paradine Case* was released, Selznick chastised his subordinates as this kind of presentation was against studio policy.[53] In contrast, in order to emphasize the aura of exoticism and uniqueness, he decided that her first name would not be used in promotion and publicity (as had often been the case with Garbo) and that her last name would be displayed in a special ribbon-like font in the film's credits, on posters, and in other promotional materials.

While all of this may have seemed consistent with her role in *The Paradine Case*, the approach also created a gap between the actress and the public. The type of the exotic and inaccessible lady seemed to be outdated after the war. Authenticity, unpretentiousness, accessibility—qualities personified by Betty Grable, Doris Day, Claudette Colbert, Esther Williams, Susan Hayward, or Selznick's Ingrid Bergman (each in her own way)—were much more success-

STUDIO AND INTERNATIONAL STARS AFTER 1945   151

ful with the public, as documented by the Quigley rankings for years 1947 to 1952.[54] It is precisely the fundamentally different manner of presentation by the studio and reception by the public of Selznick's two European-born stars that is remarkable. While Bergman underwent a process that transformed her into a model of naturalness and spontaneity admired by the audience, a few years later Valli underwent a procedure that resulted in the complete opposite: the audience could not identify with her type of a reserved and unattainable female vamp.

One of the reasons for this was also Hitchcock's direction of *The Paradine Case*. Hitchcock was a proponent of so-called negative acting, by which he meant "the ability to express words by doing nothing."[55] Valli therefore spends much of the film just posing for the camera, and only at the end does she at least partially reveal her character's emotions and motivations. But by then, it is too late for a deeper identification of the audience. Hitchcock also found himself in frequent conflicts with Selznick over the camera. While the director pushed for visual austerity and coldness, Selznick demanded that cinematographer Lee Garmes, an Oscar winner for *Shanghai Express* (1932, Paramount) with Marlene Dietrich, idealize his stars and especially Valli, who was to become the new icon of glamour:

> We can't go on photographing the walls and the windows, making pass-port photos, without any modeling to the face, any lighting designed to give the woman interest and beauty and mystery, no study of her best angles and how to light and photograph them [. . .], any composition or modern camera angles on her to excite the audiences and thereby understand Keane's fascination.[56]

As documented by Leonard Leff, the filming of *The Paradine Case* was long (ninety-two days), costly (over $4 million), and fraught with many creative disagreements,[57] which all contributed to its unsatisfactory artistic qualities and cold reception. Neither an expensive promotional campaign centered on the stellar international cast and the Hitchcock-Selznick combination, nor shortening by eighteen minutes after many viewers complained about the slow pace, could prevent this.[58] Although the film cost twice as much as *Spellbound*, it only grossed $2 million and became Selznick's first commercial flop in over a decade.

A Gallup poll conducted prior to the film's wide release suggested that Valli did not score well with audiences, which was later confirmed by press reviews.[59] Some hailed her as a new exotic star, but more often there were hesitant or downright negative reactions. For example, Leo Miller published an article "Selznick, Stars, Hitch—So What?," in which he stated that all of the actors act "as if they have no interest in each other," and Valli "has little else to do but be beautiful in the low-key close-ups."[60] Others also criticized the actress's coldness and indifference. Kaspar Monahan wrote for a Pittsburgh newspaper that Valli in *The Paradine Case* "has little opportunity to live up to her advance notices from her native Italy where she reportedly captivated audiences in some films or more. She is beautiful but her rigid Mona Lisa expression becomes monotonous."[61] Selznick's decision to present the new discovery only as Valli, without a first name, also caused embarrassment from the start. Kyle Crichton summed up the attitude of many others when he wrote for the popular magazine *Collier's*: "We suggest to Mr. David O. Selznick that he give this little girl a name; we mean a first name. That chance of confusion with Rudy [Vallee—American singer, bandleader, and actor—author's note]. Ugh!"[62]

The failures of *The Paradine Case* and Alida Valli in her first American role proved to be interconnected: the film did not appeal to audiences because of, among other things, the coldness of the title character (which was a direct result of Selznick's script and Hitchcock's direction), and the actress suffered from the fact that she entered the shoot without adequate preparation and that the entire film was plagued by disagreements between the director and the producer, whose relationship became more strained by the day.[63] Selznick later regretted the choice of Valli as it was, in his view, her who caused the commercial fiasco, stating in November 1949: "WE HAD HUGE LOSS AS RESULT OF LAUNCHING HER IN PARADINE WHICH OBVIOUSLY COULD HAVE BEEN GREATLY MINIMIZED [OR] COMPLETELY NULLIFIED BY CASTING ESTABLISHED STAR."[64] The lukewarm reception of the actress in the role also negatively influenced the further development of her career. *The Paradine Case* failed to create the expected interest in her persona, and the following three pictures which she made in the US did not reach a high level either. The financial returns on Selznick's investment were also affected: the loan-outs, which the producer negotiated for the actress, did not bring the kind of financial compensation which he had hoped for.

While still completing *The Paradine Case*, she was loaned out to independent producer Jesse L. Lasky for the spiritual drama *The Miracle of the Bells* (1948). The role of Polish-born actress Olga Treskovna, who is given the opportunity of a lifetime to act in the large-scale Hollywood production of Joan of Arc but does not live to see the result due to a terminal illness, did allow Valli to exhibit a warmer, more sentimental side of her personality,[65] but the film was a failure with moviegoers and ended up with a loss of $640,000 for Lasky and the distributor RKO.[66] Because of its subject matter (Olga's tragic death is supposed to cause a miracle in the mining community), the film was labeled blasphemous and representing "the depths of bad taste"[67] with Valli also being subjected to criticism. Bosley Crowther in the *New York Times* commented that she "is evidently burdened with the notion that she is playing Camille, plus Joan of Arc, plus Olga Treskovna, yet not quite certain which one she really is."[68]

The next two films did not manage to correct this negative impression. The drama *Walk Softly, Stranger*, in which Valli played the wealthy industrialist's daughter in a wheelchair, was completed in the spring of 1948, but the new head of RKO, Howard Hughes, decided to postpone its premiere until the fall of 1950—in all probability to take advantage of the US premiere of *The Third Man*, which also relied on the combination of Valli and Joseph Cotten.[69] Selznick received $125,000 for the actress's services which was an improvement of $50,000 in comparison with *The Miracle of the Bells*,[70] but the film did her career no favors, when it ended up with a huge loss approaching one million dollars.[71] In the following film, the mountain-climbing drama *The White Tower*, produced once again by RKO, the financial compensation for the actress was back to the original amount of $75,000 (while Glenn Ford, the main star of the film, received $125,000).[72] The film, partially filmed in the French Alps, did not have such devastating reviews, but it did not break into the Top 100 highest-grossing films of 1950,[73] nor did it succeed in updating the actress's image to resonate with contemporary American audiences. In the words of Stephen Gundle, "[i]n all her films, her face was turned into an icon in the Garbo mold, while her body was more or less ignored. Given the focus on the figures of postwar stars like [Rita] Hayworth and Jane Russell, this gave Valli a classic rather than a contemporary inflection."[74]

As with Shirley Temple, Selznick's interest in the development of the actress's career waned considerably at the end of the decade. The selection of her projects was not driven by a desire to build up an image consistent with the requirements of the postwar public or with the idea of establishing her as a commercial commodity endowed with prestige. Instead, it was propelled by the need for immediate financial gain. Preoccupied with the organizational difficulties of his company, Selznick did not conduct the previously routine quality control of scripts or camerawork on films made outside his studio, leaving supervision to his less authoritative subordinates. The resignation is evident, for example, in a memorandum concerning the terms of Valli's loan-out for the ultimately unrealized project *Lovers' Meeting*:

> I have no desire to have final word on the script. I may not even have time to give comments. I would like to be free to give comments, but under no obligation to do so, and would be perfectly willing to have it specified that the producer's word was final, once Valli and ourselves had approved the role submitted, and provided that the contract would provide the role would undergo no drastic changes or

reductions—although these considerations are not important in the case of Valli at this moment, for we must recognize too that Valli is not yet in a position where we can make such demands.[75]

Selznick was aware of his failure, being unable in the five years from the signing of the contract to turn Alida Valli into a leading star, and his current situation offered him little opportunity to turn things around.

The actress's most successful film became *The Third Man*, which was prepared as a co-production between Selznick and Alexander Korda. In it, Valli portrayed the Czechoslovak actress Anna Schmidt, who is left bitter and unprotected from the Viennese occupation authorities by the (presumed) death of her lover, the bootlegger Harry Lime (Orson Welles). Selznick commented on Graham Greene's screenplay and was instrumental in expanding Valli's part, which also ensured her more media attention when the film became an unexpected hit.[76] It was *The Third Man* that represented the direction that the collaboration with the actress could take in the following years. For this reason, Valli did not figure in the massive 1949 deal in which the producer sold the contracts with several of his performers to Warner Bros.[77] He was convinced that her acting and language skills would enable her to become a pillar of his planned production activities in Italy, France, the UK, or Scandinavia: "It is my intention and believe [*sic*] that her future base, so to speak, should be Europe because it will be the scene of most of our future operations," he declared hopefully in May 1950.[78] However, these ambitious plans quickly fell apart. Selznick's increasingly conflicted nature led to the premature termination of his dealings with Korda, and his company's existential difficulties made significant foreign expansion impossible for good. Projects with Valli that were ultimately not undertaken included, for instance, the remake of Hitchcock's *The Man Who Knew Too Much* with Joseph Cotten and the adaptation of Henry James's *The Wings of the Dove*, where she was supposed to play alongside Jennifer Jones. Eventually, the actress's growing demands, dissatisfaction with the way she was currently used, the change in her family situation (in February 1950, she and her husband Oscar De Mejo had a son, Lorenzo), and the psychological strain resulting from her unwanted stay in the US contributed to the end of her Hollywood engagement.[79] In the second half of 1950, Selznick allowed her to appear in the French-Italian film *Miracles Only Happen Once* (*Les miracles n'ont lieu qu'une fois*, 1951, Films Sacha Gordine/Excelsa Film), for which he received the equivalent of $80,000 (half in lire and half in francs),[80] and finally, after a long and tense negotiation, he agreed to a termination of the contract with her at the beginning of 1952. By then, her price had dropped below $50,000 per film, so she was more of a liability than an asset to the studio.

The reasons behind her failure must be sought out, however, much earlier: the unfortunate circumstances of her involvement, in a prominent role, in *The Paradine Case* and the inability on the producer's part to create an attractive and original identity for her led to Valli's failure with American audiences. The studio was thus unable to emulate the triumphant US debuts of Ingrid Bergman and Vivien Leigh, who immediately became public favorites. The actress's failure in her first Hollywood role determined the course of her further cooperation with Selznick. As she did not become a sought-after star as Selznick had hoped, her participation was limited to less prestigious films, where she was partnered with more well-known male performers (Fred MacMurray, Joseph Cotten, Glenn Ford). Her most successful title from this period was the Euro-American co-production *The Third Man* (which grossed over $2 million in the US alone),[81] but there she was only one of many audience attractions.

After her return to Europe, Valli's career was negatively affected by the tragic death of the model Wilma Montesi (in April 1953), with whom the actress's new partner, Piero Piccioni, was allegedly having an affair. (According to some theories, he was even involved in her murder.) The scandal filled the pages of the press, and Valli had to withdraw from the film industry for a while (Visconti's *Senso* [1954, Lux Film], completed before the scandal broke out, still managed to reach the cinemas). In the second half of the 1950s, however, she made a successful comeback when she appeared in Antonioni's *Il grido* (1957, SpA Cinematografica/Robert Alexander Productions). In the years that followed, she continued to work with famous directors, such as Pier Paolo Pasolini (*Oedipus Rex* [*Edipo re*, 1967, Arco Film/Somafis]), Bernardo Bertolucci (*The Spider's Stratagem* [*Strategia del ragno*, 1970, RAI/Red Film], *Novecento* [1976, Produzioni Europee Associate/Les Productions Artistes Associés/Artemis Film], *La luna* [1979, Fiction Cinematografica/Twentieth Century-Fox]) and Dario Argento (*Suspiria* [1977, Seda Spettacoli], *Inferno* [1980, Produzioni Intersound]). From time to time, she also starred in international co-productions, and was nominated for a Golden Globe for her role in the Mexican film *The Paper Man* (*El hombre de papel*, 1963, Ismael Rodríguez).

FROM LOVER TO ENTERTAINER: LOUIS JOURDAN

The commercial fiasco of *The Paradine Case* had a negative impact on the career of another European personality who was introduced to the US moviegoing public through the film. Louis Jourdan had already acted in a dozen French comedies and melodramas produced during the war when he came to the attention of Jenia Reissar. Selznick immediately saw in the handsome actor a candidate for a popular screen lover and instructed his employee to draw up a contract with him:

> I cannot commence to tell you the extent of my enthusiasm for Jourdan. I think he is an absolute certainty for great stardom and for <u>immediate</u> zooming to a position that has not been occupied by any Latin actor in many, many years. I think that in two pictures, or three at the most, he will be bigger than [Charles] Boyer ever was, assuming that we can get the right roles for him.[82]

In addition to his attractive looks, Jourdan also had good language skills. Thanks to his studies in the UK, he knew excellent English and the accent which he still had was not an obstacle, but was viewed, on the contrary, as "enchanting."[83]

He first had the opportunity to demonstrate it in the role of the butler André Latour in *The Paradine Case*. Although Gregory Peck was the film's main star attraction, the promotion was not to neglect Jourdan: he was supposed to be prominently included, along with Valli, in all of the advertising materials, in order for the public to register him as a rising star.[84] The first viewers reacted to him more positively than to Valli and the responses in the press were also universally favorable.[85] Typical, for example, is the review published in the *Motion Picture Herald*: "Jourdan, the other newcomer, is dark and attractive in a way which suggests he may prove to be a bobby soxer's delight when he gets sufficient screen circulation. His performance here indicates he can also act."[86]

As Hilary Radner noted, "with his darkly handsome looks, chiseled profile, long graceful hands and melodic, cultivated accent, the young actor appeared poised for success."[87] His physical attractiveness, evoking, for example, the star of silent era Rudolph Valentino, particularly impressed the female public[88] (while men, in contrast, mostly identified after the war with rougher models of masculinity—Gary Cooper, Humphrey Bogart, or John Wayne, all prominently featured in Quigley's star rankings from this period). However, although he appeared in other high-profile films after *The Paradine Case* alongside established stars (Joan Fontaine in *Letter from an Unknown Woman* [1948, Rampart Productions/Universal] and Jennifer Jones in *Madame Bovary* [1949, MGM]), he never achieved the comparable acclaim as his predecessors Maurice Chevalier and Charles Boyer. His American career was both enabled and limited by the fact that he represented the stereotypical image of the French (or more generally European) lover. Selznick took advantage of both his gender and ethnicity to establish him as a successor to this tradition, but at the same time this prevented him from playing more ambitious roles, which would transcend the type of a hypersexual Southern European.[89] This was also true of his colleagues Boyer and Chevalier, each a generation older than him, who still managed to establish themselves as top Hollywood stars. Another, and more important, reason why Jourdan did not quite fulfil his potential (Robin Wood even referred to him as "among the most wasted stars of the Hollywood cinema"),[90] was the dismal state of Selznick's company: the producer's preoccupation with the studio's existential problems simply did not allow him to pay enough attention to the development of the actor's career. A great number of ambitious plans for his next projects appeared in the press, but none of them were realized in the end. For example, Jourdan was to play the lead role in a sequel to Selznick's adventure film *The Prisoner of Zenda*;[91] together with Alida Valli and Rossano Brazzi, he was to form the cast of an adaptation of George du Maurier's (grandfather of Daphne du Maurier, author of *Rebecca*) popular novel *Trilby*;[92] with Jennifer Jones, he was to appear in the Technicolor costume film *Victoria Grandolet*, based on Henry Bellamann's novel of the same name, being prepared by Warner Bros,[93] or in Selznick's own production of *Romeo and Juliet*;[94] and among the projects under consideration was a Paris-set sequel to the successful comedy starring Shirley Temple with the working title *The Frenchman and the Bobby-Soxer*.[95] Another aspect that undermined the successful development of Jourdan's career was that the films he was loaned out to during his contract by Selznick did not meet with adequate audience response. Like *The Paradine Case*, Max Ophüls's melodrama *Letter from an Unknown Woman* ended up in the red (the losses amounted to $804,000, making the film one of the greatest commercial failures in the postwar history of Universal),[96] and a similar fate was met by the comedy *No Minor Vices* (with worldwide grosses of around $650,000)[97] and the adaptation of Gustave Flaubert's literary classic *Madame Bovary* (*Variety* estimated the receipts at a disappointing $2 million).[98] Thus, Selznick's plan to make Louis Jourdan a leading male star and a valuable commodity over "two, maximum three films" decidedly failed.

Nothing illustrates this failure and the troubles of the entire Selznick organization more eloquently than the tour organized in late 1949 under the name *Selznick Stars of 1950*. The event was intended to make use of the producer's symbolic capital, which had been accumulated over the previous decade by means of his successes with both male and female stars, and convert it into much-needed cash. The show was of such poor quality, however, that it, paradoxically, rather harmed Selznick's brand based on quality and prestige.

The tour involved selected members of Selznick's stable of actors with long-term contracts, who were paid a substantial fee each week, but at the same time were not properly used in feature films. The stars that Selznick considered his most valuable properties, notably Jennifer Jones and Alida Valli, were spared from participation; the acting ensemble consisted exclusively of those performers who were positioned lower in the studio hierarchy. After several experiments, the line-up was settled on the foursome of Louis Jourdan, John Agar, Rhonda Fleming, and Rory Calhoun who were joined by Calhoun's wife, the dancer Lita Baron, performing under the stage name Isabelita. Although the tour bore Selznick's name and was intended to capitalize on his long-standing reputation as a starmaker, his involvement was minimal. The show was produced by Paul Small with Paul Macnamara and Daniel O'Shea from the studio overseeing it.

The program, consisting of acting, dancing, and singing routines, was to rotate through a few select cities in the US Midwest and in the New York State, and if successful, move to other densely populated territories in Texas and Florida and, eventually, to New York City. The agreement with the cinemas in which the tour took place guaranteed Selznick's company 50 percent of ticket sales and a minimum weekly revenue of $10,000. If successful, Selznick promised himself a total net profit of up to a quarter of a million dollars. After the first stop, however, it was clear that such an estimate was overly optimistic.

The tour began on November 2, 1949, in Loew's State Theatre in St. Louis. Jourdan became the central point of the marketing, as his roles in *The Paradine Case* and *Madame Bovary* (the latter in theaters since August 1949) made him the biggest star. John Agar was best known as Shirley Temple's husband (although their marriage was coming to an end), and Rory Calhoun and Rhonda Fleming were still awaiting their breakthrough roles (although Fleming had drawn attention to herself earlier that year with a prominent supporting role in the musical adaptation of Mark Twain's *A Connecticut Yankee in King Arthur's Court* [1949, Paramount]). Each of the participants was introduced on stage through a film excerpt (for Jourdan, it was a scene from *The Paradine Case*). This opening segment was followed by a series of comedy sketches and dramatic performances interspersed with dancing and singing. The program culminated in a finale featuring the entire ensemble.

The hour-long show met with sharp criticism in the press as many reviewers pointed out its incoherence and a generally low level of execution. It was not helped by its awkward combination with Anthony Mann's procedural crime film *Border Incident* (1949, MGM), the screening of which was part of the admission price. Though the producer Small telegraphed Selznick that "UNIT PLAYING BEAUTIFULLY. ALL THE ACTORS SEEM VERY HAPPY. THEY ALL LOOK GOOD, HAVE EXCELLENT MATERIAL, GREAT DIGNITY, PROPER PRESENTATION,"[99] Selznick and O'Shea had received different accounts. According to Howard Burkhart, the head of Loew's Midland Theater in Kansas City, which was to be the next stop on the tour, the program was extremely disappointing:

I DEFINITELY WOULD NOT CONNECT THE NAME OF SELZ-
NICK WITH A SHOW OF THIS TYPE. A NAME RESPECTED IN

> THIS BUSINESS AND WHICH TOOK YEARS TO BUILD IS BEING
> HURT AND IT IS HURTING THE YOUNG PLAYERS WHO ARE
> IN IT. I HAVE PLAYED SELZNICK PICTURES MANY YEARS. HIS
> NAME IS TOO BIG TO BE CONNECTED WITH THIS SHOW.[100]

Selznick was concerned that his long-established brand would be harmed considerably. He therefore canceled the Kansas City stop, engaged the theater director Burt Shevelove, and entrusted him with the task of having the actors prepare new material over a two-week period. With a partially revamped production team, the show opened in Cleveland in late November. Attendance remained low, however, and reviews, although somewhat more sympathetic, still criticized the show's lack of coherence and the inadequate preparation of the performers, who clearly did not have the experience necessary for live performances. The most highly rated was Jourdan, who in one self-conscious scene fantasized about breaking out of the stereotypical role of the French lover and playing a cowboy or a gangster.[101] The tour closed in Buffalo and Rochester without any significant improvement in reviews or sales. This brought a definite end to all considerations about prolonging the tour at additional locales on the East Coast or in the South.

While Selznick's company blamed Small for the artistic and commercial fiasco, he viewed the cause of the failure elsewhere: "It was a very good show. The only trouble was that the audiences didn't know the people or weren't interested in them and did not come which is best evidenced by the fact that all the opening shows were weak even before they saw the performances."[102] Selznick had expected that his name alone in the title of the program would be sufficient to ensure a satisfactory turnout. This did not prove to be the case—the show featuring lesser-known actors from his stable and accompanied by negative feedback concerning the quality of its execution ended up threatening a laboriously won reputation built on the highest standards.

Louis Jourdan got the best reaction from the audience out of the entire cast, primarily owing to his attractive appearance, charm, and acting skills, but not even he could avert the disaster of the whole tour. Despite positive mentions in the press, Selznick failed to mold him into a desirable lead performer and instead reduced him to an entertainer in a variety program of poor quality, intended only to generate immediate profits. The actor enjoyed a personal friendship with the producer (he even served as the best man at his wedding to Jennifer Jones on July 13, 1949), but he was also aware that, under Selznick's guidance, his career had reached a dead end.[103] In January 1950, periodicals reported that "Jourdan is rapidly, through no fault of his own, becoming one of Hollywood's forgotten men."[104] After several weeks of negotiations, Selznick allowed Jourdan to buy out the rest of his contract. In May, the actor signed a new agreement with Darryl Zanuck at Twentieth Century-Fox, where he was supposed to become the successor to Tyrone Power, famous for playing heroic roles in a series of adventure films.[105]

In the following years he moved between Europe and the United States, working in both film and television. He was most successful in Vincente Minnelli's Oscar-winning musical *Gigi* (1958, MGM) and went on to play the title character in the French-Italian co-production *The Story of the Count of Monte Cristo* (*Le Comte de Monte Cristo*, 1961, J. J. Vital/Rene Modiano/Royal/SNEG) and, at a later age, the villain Kamal Khan in the Bond film *Octopussy* (1983, United Artists/MGM).

STAR MACHINE'S COLLAPSE: HILDEGARD KNEF

The crisis of Selznick's company, which led to a significant reduction in star development and trade, is aptly illustrated by my final case study in this chapter focused on the German-born actress Hildegard Knef. The producer had high hopes for her, but in the end was unable to secure a single suitable project for her and after several months released her from his services.

Knef was considered a remarkably talented actress with a dramatic life story that was of particular interest to the media. After the war, she managed to make a name for herself in the restored German film industry thanks to her roles in the so-called rubble films (*Trümmerfilme* in German), which, in a realist mode, thematized collective guilt, the trauma of a lost war, and the need for social renewal. The most significant representatives of this trend with Knef's participation were *The Murderers Are Among Us* (*Die Mörder sind unter uns*, 1946, DEFA), *Between Yesterday and Tomorrow* (*Zwischen gestern und morgen*, 1947, Bavaria Film/ NDF), and *Film Without a Title* (*Film ohne Titel*, 1948, Bavaria Film/Camera-Filmproduktion). As Ulrike Sieglohr writes, "[w]ith her tall, blonde and expressive fresh-faced features, she embodied the resilient survivor and became the most promising new German actress of the era."[106] News of her success in her homeland reached overseas, and in May 1947, the lavishly illustrated magazine *Life* devoted a full six pages to her in an article entitled "New German Star."[107] After reading it and discovering that the actress had dreams of a Hollywood career,[108] Selznick instructed his staff to investigate the situation and gather more information.[109] After receiving her photographs in October, he stated that he was not "overboard" about Knef, but continued to express moderate interest in her.[110] This was solidified after viewing several scenes from her German films. In January 1948, the actress traveled to the United States, which made further negotiations much easier. The producer first gathered his impressions from his East Coast representatives (Robert Ross, for example, appreciated her accent and wrote that she had a "LOVELY AND ORIGINAL" face)[111] and finally met with her in person in February. After her political background had been thoroughly checked and any possibility of accusations of collaboration with Hitler's regime had been safely ruled out,[112] Selznick offered her a six-month trial period with an option of a standard, seven-year contract. Knef accepted the offer, and on April 1 became an employee of the studio at a salary of $250 per week.[113] (This made her the first German actress to sign a contract with a US producer or studio after the war.)[114] During her trial, she was to improve her English, work on eliminating her foreign accent, and attend acting lessons, which were paid for by the studio. In the meantime, the publicity and advertising department worked to create an appealing public identity for her.

The basis for this was her life story with the dramatic development of wartime and postwar Germany in the background. The official studio biography, in which she appears under the Americanized name Hildegarde Neff,[115] presents her as "a victim of the march of history" and further adds that "it took the rape of Czechoslovakia, mass murders, flights to freedom, the American Army and pure chance to bring it about, but Hildegarde Neff is now a happy, almost carefree war-bride, with a Selznick contract, a handsome husband, and a future toward which she looks with confidence." The thirteen-page document prepared by Mervin Houser, Selznick's head of publicity in the late 1940s and early 1950s, took painstaking care to dispel any possible doubts about the actress's wartime activities[116] and instead drew a parallel with the films she starred in: just as their stories were set against the rubbles of bombed-out cities and chronicled the gradual rebuilding of a decimated nation, so too Hildegard Knef's (or rather Hildegarde Neff's) German career had to rise from the ashes and face various external obstacles, such as imprisonment in a Russian prison camp. Only through her moral strength and resilience was she able to succeed and become "Europe's most brilliant postwar star."[117]

The reference point for the actress's buildup was the successful career of Marlene Dietrich. This time, Selznick was not so reluctant to draw comparisons with another popular star—probably because he believed that this might alleviate the possible animosity towards a citizen of a hitherto hostile nation. Dietrich, who became a US citizen in 1939, was renowned for her patriotism and service for her new home during the war, and the publicity centered around Knef was supposed to similarly emphasize her admiration and love for the American nation and its values. The parallels did not end there, however: both actresses were reportedly happy housewives and excellent cooks[118] and even had similar looks—they prided themselves on their slender figures and their faces were dominated by prominent cheekbones.

Knef was to become another item in Selznick's rich portfolio, confirming his global expansion and growing position in the market with internationally bankable stars. The studio's policy was succinctly articulated in the previously mentioned biography of the actress written by Mervin Houser: "In motion pictures, David O. Selznick continues to prove there are no national boundaries, no language boundaries. His 'One World' concept has resulted in an impressive group of actors, all originating in other countries, becoming an integral part of the American screen." As in the case of Jourdan and Valli, Knef was to work primarily in Hollywood, at least initially, but "her work was to be for the whole world, in keeping with Selznick's concept based on the idea that films are international."[119]

To "over-night be as important as Dietrich was in her first picture," it was necessary to secure her a prominent role in an important film.[120] For this, however, Selznick's company was increasingly ill-equipped. It was only sporadically active in film production after 1948, and the lead roles in the handful of films it produced or co-produced went to Jennifer Jones and Alida Valli, leaving no room for Knef. More importantly, however, Selznick's standing in the film industry declined after the commercial failure of *The Paradine Case* and the unconvincing management of some of his contract actors and actresses of recent times. As a result, he was unable to negotiate similarly lucrative loan-outs that had been instrumental in bringing Ingrid Bergman, Dorothy McGuire, and Jennifer Jones to prominence at the beginning of the decade. Selznick planned to market Knef as an exclusive commodity, but at the same time did not want to discourage potential bidders with too high a price. He therefore decided to request between $50,000 and $75,000 for the actress's services.[121] Negotiations for the female lead in the drama *Tokyo Joe* (1949, Santana Pictures/Columbia) alongside Humphrey Bogart and in an unnamed production by MGM, however, fell apart—partly because Knef, although rated as a capable actress, was said to be insufficiently "GLAMOROUS AND BEAUTIFUL."[122] Selznick argued that poorly executed screen tests and an unflattering presentation (especially the hairstyle) were to blame, but he was unable to turn the situation around.[123]

Some industry interest was aroused by a screening of *Film Without a Title*, one of Knef's German pictures, at the Academy Theater in Inglewood on January 9, 1949. The event was attended by two thousand members of the Academy of Motion Picture Arts and Sciences and several dozen journalists. Among those invited were "top agents, actors and producers" (e.g., Fritz Lang, Otto Preminger, and Charles Feldman), who were given the opportunity to learn about the personality and acting skills of Knef, who had won an award for her performance at the Locarno Film Festival the previous year.[124] For Selznick, it was welcome free publicity as all the costs of the evening were covered by the Academy. However, although the reactions of the participants were apparently positive, they did not result in any concrete offer.

Selznick's negotiating position was increasingly weaker at the end of the 1940s in comparison with the beginning of the decade. His earlier, almost unfailing judgment had been called into doubt by a series of failures that involved both the films he produced (which, apart from *The Paradine Case*, consisted of the commercially unsuccessful *Portrait of Jennie*) and the stars he developed, as the examples discussed in this chapter have shown. In addition, the financial straits in which the studio found itself did not allow adequate investments in fresh acquisitions from abroad and thus their adaptation in a new environment. In Knef's case, for example, Selznick refused to pay for surgery on her teeth to correct what he perceived as a major flaw in her appearance.[125]

In desperation, the producer reduced the price he was asking for her loan-out to just $20,000, hoping that these terms would entice a bidder to sign a contract with his company for a larger number of films.[126] He also lowered his standards for the quality of the productions in which Knef was to appear. Whereas he had previously categorically refused her participation in B-movies, he was now willing to provide her, for example, for the British film *State Secret* (1950, London Film Productions), which he described as "THIRD-RATE OLD-FASHIONED HITCHCOCKIAN MATERIAL."[127] All of this was intended to recoup at least some of the company's costs, which had reached $15,000 in wages alone by the end of March (Knef had been receiving $500 a week since October 1948). Negotiations with Jack Warner seem to have gone the furthest, but even these produced no result.

There was a belief in the studio that Knef was a "SPLENDID ACTRESS," but "WITHOUT DEFINITIVE PART TO WHICH SHE IS IDEALLY SUITED PHYSICALLY AND BY NATIONALITY, I DON'T THINK WE OUGHT TO PROCEED WITH HER."[128] While the first option was taken up after her trial period, in April 1949 Selznick stated that "IT IS ONLY WHAT HAS HAPPENED TO HOLLYWOOD PLUS OUR OWN INACTIVITY THAT MAKES IT IMPOSSIBLE FOR US TO PICK UP OPTION ON HER AT THIS TIME."[129] Thus, Selznick and Knef's collaboration ended without any tangible result.

In the following months, the producer took an interest in the further development of the actress's career in Hollywood, although he did so to a certain extent to satisfy his own ego. This is suggested, for example, by a sentence found in a letter to Jack Warner, through which he again argued for Knef to be given an opportunity (this time without financial benefit to his studio): "I'm very proud of my record on the people that I brought over here, both those that are still with me and those that are not, and I would like the record to be completed with Miss Neff's success."[130]

The actress did make her Hollywood debut, but it was not in a Warner Bros. film. After starring in the scandalous German production of *The Sinner* (*Die Sünderin*, 1951, Deutsche Styria Film/Junge Film-Union Rolf Meyer), she was cast in the war drama *Decision Before Dawn* (1951, Twentieth Century-Fox),

164   SELZNICK (GOES) INTERNATIONAL

which was shot by a crew led by director Anatole Litvak in authentic West German locations. Shortly thereafter, she returned to the US as a "new discovery" of Twentieth Century-Fox. After completing three films in quick succession (*Diplomatic Courier, The Snows of Kilimanjaro,* and *Night Without Sleep* [all 1952, Twentieth Century-Fox]), she embarked on a successful international career as an actress and chanson singer. Thus, Selznick's assessment of her potential for the global market proved correct, even though he himself did not have the means to fully develop it.

CONCLUSION

Selznick's plans for internationalization, which included the development and use of foreign stars in an effort to build a truly cosmopolitan star roster, were ambitious, but in the end they were not implemented to the extent intended. His company was most successful in the first half of the 1940s. As late as the 1945–46 season, it was still prospering thanks to hit films and the ingenious handling of contract actors and actresses. But the situation soon changed. Ingrid Bergman, Joan Fontaine, and Dorothy McGuire, who had provided the studio with high income and prestige, left in quick succession, and new acting acquisitions from Europe failed to adequately replace them. Selznick's reputation as a starmaker was beginning to take a serious hit: on closer inspection, all the major discoveries (including Bergman, Fontaine and McGuire as well as Joseph Cotten, Gregory Peck, and Jennifer Jones) took place prior to 1945. The lower success rate in the development of stars had many interconnected causes: Selznick could no longer rely on the judgment of his almost infallible talent scout Kay Brown, who left the studio in 1942; the financial difficulties his company ran into after the war made it impossible to invest appropriately in new acquisitions; the cumbersome structure of the studio required complex reorganization that never materialized; the advertising and publicity department was subject to too many personnel changes, contributing to a lack of continuity; the producer's increasingly confrontational manner had a negative impact when dealing with important partners, such as J. Arthur Rank and Alexander Korda; *The Paradine Case* met with a negative reception and did not make leading stars of Alida Valli and Louis Jourdan; and finally, the ever-decreasing number of films Selznick personally produced almost exclusively starred Jennifer Jones. In July 1949, the producer married his longtime partner and throughout the 1950s served as her de facto agent and manager, while his other activities were severely curtailed. It was Jones who, through her work between two continents, eventually fulfilled, at least in part, the idea of transnational stardom that Selznick envisioned for his other actors and actresses.[131]

The ultimate failure of Selznick's "five dark horses from Europe" is therefore undeniable: Valli, Jourdan, and Knef—as well as Rossano Brazzi and Alf Kjellin, who during their tenure with Selznick were only cast into one supporting role each (Brazzi in *Little Women* [1949, MGM] and Kjellin, who went by the stage name Christopher Kent, in *Madame Bovary*)—were not transformed into internationally sought-after and financially lucrative Hollywood stars. The paralyzed studio had to gradually get rid of them, because they were a burden rather than a financial gain. At the same time, though, we should not miss the fact that Selznick remained a visionary, or at least a good judge, in this respect, too: indeed, the further development of the US film industry was moving in the direction of intensified internationalization, and most of the personalities singled out by Selznick, especially Valli, Jourdan, and Knef, managed to build successful and long-lasting international careers from the early 1950s onwards.

6

THE MOST FAITHFUL OF THEM ALL

Jennifer Jones after *The Song of Bernadette*

David's love for Jennifer was very real and touching but in it lay the seeds of the failures that marked the last years of his life. Everything he did was for Jennifer. His
whole life centered upon her, to the detriment of his good judgment.
—JOHN HUSTON[1]

In the chapter on Selznick's loan-outs of contract actresses during World War II,
I have described how Jennifer Jones, with a single role, became a leading Hollywood star. The title part in Twentieth Century-Fox's production of *The Song
of Bernadette* secured her the attention of the industry, the media, and the
public, transforming her almost overnight from an unknown actress with a few
B-movie credits into an admired performer and sought-after commodity. For
Selznick, however, she was not just another addition to his portfolio of attractive contract players: according to many accounts, during the filming of her
next film, *Since You Went Away*, Jones became his lover which had a significant
impact on the further development of their collaboration.[2] Just one day after
she accepted her Academy Award for her portrayal of St. Bernadette, she began
divorce proceedings with actor Robert Walker (then under contract at MGM),
with whom she was raising two sons. Their marriage was formally ended in June
1945. David O. Selznick and Irene Mayer's divorce did not become official until
January 1949, but from at least the middle of the decade the couple—like Walker
and Jones, the parents of two sons—lived apart, with Selznick's extramarital affair with Jones no secret in Hollywood.[3] The lovers were eventually married on
June 13, 1949, and their longtime union finally received a stamp of legitimacy.

To speak of Selznick and Jones's careers without mentioning the private
aspect of their relationship is impossible, for everything depended on it. As
Selznick's partner, Jones was a fixture in his star stable, while the remaining

JENNIFER JONES AFTER *THE SONG OF BERNADETTE* 167

members were coming and going: if Ingrid Bergman, Joan Fontaine, and Dorothy McGuire left Selznick when their contracts expired and went on to freelance or find other, more lucrative engagements, in Jones's case the question of ending her collaboration with Selznick's company was never on the agenda. The actress was loyal to her employer and life partner throughout the 1940s and 1950s, and he reciprocated this loyalty by gradually curtailing most of his activities and working as her personal agent and manager.

Their personal and professional relationship is often described as unequal: in many interpretations, Selznick is likened to Svengali, the (in)famous character from George du Maurier's novel *Trilby* who controls and abuses a young Irish girl and uses hypnosis to turn her into a successful singer.[4] Selznick's influence seems to have been significant, perhaps even dominant in many ways, but at the same time I do not believe there is any reason to portray him exclusively in the negative light that the analogy implies. The extent of the actress's autonomy is difficult to determine, as her voice is rarely represented in archival documents. Moreover, she was a very shy, private person who, as far as possible, avoided publicity and contact with media and did not leave behind her autobiography to correct the information disseminated through other channels. According to the accounts of her collaborators (directors and acting partners), however, she was not a passive puppet controlled by the more experienced Selznick, seventeen years her senior,[5] but an intelligent professional with good judgment regarding her choice of roles and performances.[6] Even Selznick himself repeatedly acknowledged these skills and generally held her in high regard. There is no reason to assume that he would make an important decision concerning her career without previous consultation or even against her will as some suggest.[7] On the contrary, in an interview published in February 1958, he admitted that he had disapproved of her participation in *Good Morning, Miss Dove* (1955) and *The Man in the Gray Flannel Suit* (1956, both Twentieth Century-Fox) but "she went ahead, anyway. She has a fine mind of her own, and she uses it."[8]

Because Selznick's work during the 1940s and 1950s—and especially in the postwar period—was so strongly linked to Jones's (we can even say that he in many respects adapted and submitted to her career's progress), it seems fitting to end the book with an overview of their collaboration after *The Song of Bernadette*. The actress's star identity brings together many of the ideas that Selznick had long championed, and so it is also a good opportunity to recapitulate some of his principles of star development. In the second part of the chapter, I use case studies of two projects—*Carrie* (1952), for which Jones was loaned out to Paramount, and *Terminal Station*, which Selznick developed with the Italian director Vittorio De Sica—to illustrate the way in which Selznick operated in the latter part of his career, when he largely abandoned production activities and acted mainly as adviser and manager to his wife. As we will see, despite good intentions, the outcomes of his actions were not always positive.

CULTIVATING VERSATILITY

On the occasion of the UK premiere of *Carrie*, based on Theodore Dreiser's classic novel, *Picturegoer* magazine featured a portrait of Jennifer Jones, "the star who always wants to be different." In the article, Paul Holt called the actress "the oddest and most original star of the screen since Garbo let her hair go loose. [. . .] She achieves, by some alchemy of personality, exactly the unexpected in everything she attempts."[9] Jones was an enigma to journalists. As a shy, reclusive person, she carefully guarded her privacy and kept a distance from everyone, thus resembling Garbo, who also had a reputation as an inaccessible star. The bits of information that leaked out suggested that she was a woman of contradictions: she did not seek out the company of other people but could be a charming hostess when the situation called for it; she loved fashion from leading designers, but could equally be found at home in an old skirt or apron; and, as for her character, "[. . .] she is capable [. . .] of being tough, moody, gay or simple at will." As Holt noticed, this lack of consistency "has proved puzzling to such observers of the Hollywood scene as Louella O. Parsons or Hedda Hopper, for these imperious ladies of the Press like to pin-point their victims and be sure of them."[10]

The same instability characterized the actress's choice of roles. Jones was not associated with an established type, thus breaking from standard Hollywood practice, for which typecasting was one of the key tactics in establishing and developing stars. During her fifteen-year tenure with Selznick, the actress appeared in roles and films that—beyond very general characteristics—had little in common. As columnist Jimmie Fidler noted in 1949: "No characterization seems to be beyond her reach. She's played ethereal ladies, earthy peasant gals, sexy sirens, 'typical' American roles; she's sparked in comedy and scored in tragedy. In fact, she's portrayed such an array of diversified characters that, more than any other Hollywood actress perhaps, she's obscured her off-screen personality."[11] On the producer's part, the bet on versatility and universality was a conscious choice, applied not only to Jones but also to other contract actors and actresses—namely, Bergman, McGuire, and Peck. It was Jones, however, who became the most distinct personification of these qualities, for she, more than anyone else, lacked the richly nurtured publicity that could have compensated for the diversity of characters portrayed on screen.

The systematically built profile of a versatile actress, unencumbered by a stable type or association with a single genre, had its origins in the very beginnings of the actress's collaboration with Selznick. After appearing in the hugely popular *The Song of Bernadette*, there was a threat that Jones would be identified with this fragile, spiritual character. To create "sensational contrast with Bernadette"[12] and to prove that she was "an extremely attractive young American girl not to be classified as simply a gawky, young, one-part character actress,"[13] Selznick soon cast her in his epic paean to the plight of women during World War II, *Since You Went Away*. Her character Jane—the elder daughter of Tim and Anne Hilton—is the personification of the modern, resilient American girl who, in her dedicated service to her country, is not broken even by the tragic death of her beloved. In addition, compared to the source material—a novel in letters written by a woman to her husband in the armed forces—Selznick, himself the author of the screenplay, expanded her role considerably, so that in the star-studded film, Jones was second in importance only to Claudette Colbert who played her mother. Jones was nominated for an Academy Award for Best Supporting Actress for her sensitive performance, and critics at this early stage of her career were already praising the diversity of her expression. Louella Parsons was delighted to note that the actress "belies the whisper that she is a 'one-picture' girl," and James Agee in *Time* magazine praised Selznick for being the one who "brought [her] out of cloister and made her an All-American girl."[14]

An even bigger surprise for the industry and the moviegoing public, however, was Selznick's scandalous "super-Western" *Duel in the Sun*, in which the actress played the mixed-race Pearl, torn between two opposing brothers. Many scenes of the spectacular film emphasized the instinctive, sexual attraction between Pearl and Lewt (Gregory Peck), an aspect that figured prominently in the film's extensive $2 million promotional campaign. As *Time* magazine put it, it was to be "the costliest, the most lushly Technicolored, the most lavishly cast, the loudest ballyhooed, and the sexiest horse opera ever made."[15] Jones's exaggerated performance, bordering on camp and emphasizing the sensual and impulsive side of her character, shocked many viewers, who still remembered her best as the gentle Bernadette. A reviewer for the Florida newspaper *The Independent*, for example, warned that those "who saw Jennifer Jones in *The Song of Bernadette* will never recognize her as 'Pearl.' [. . .] I liked her very much better in her first picture. [. . .] [*Duel in the Sun*] most certainly plays everything from the sex angle and at times is decidedly broad in its inferences."[16]

Although the film ended up being a hit, grossing over $10 million (against a $5 million cost),[17] and Jones was nominated for an Oscar for her performance for the fourth time in four years (she received her third nomination for her role as a traumatized girl in *Love Letters*), it also did a lot of damage. It was negatively received by much of the trade press as well as the Catholic Legion of Decency, which condemned its low tone and emphasis on sexual lust.[18] Most affected was the reputation of Selznick himself, as is evident from his letter to Paul Macnamara, then his head of publicity:

> I really think [. . .] that I have got to prepare to spend a great deal of money [. . .] on the regaining of my personal position as it was before *Duel*. Even the advertising and ballyhoo on *Duel* was damaging, and was a complete contradiction of our former "Tiffany" standards [. . .] in view of the consequent great loss of prestige with the trade and press and public, I think the campaign on me is needed very badly.[19]

Selznick planned a similar "cleansing" campaign for his leading actress. Despite her Oscar nomination, it was she who became the target of harsh criticism and the reason why many commentators accused the film of bad taste. When the impact of *Duel in the Sun* became fully apparent, Selznick began pushing for Jones to appear in an upcoming film about Joan of Arc, a star vehicle with a contemporary setting, or a quality adaptation of some literary classic. He was unable to get her into the big Walter Wanger-produced film about the Maid of Orléans (the role went to Ingrid Bergman, for whom it had been a dream project), and an adaptation of *Little Women*, equally selected as a possibility for Jones, was made by MGM with June Allyson as Jo. The much-needed corrective eventually came with *Portrait of Jennie*, Selznick's own production that finally hit the screens in 1948; an adventure film dealing with Cuba's recent political history, *We Were Strangers* (1949, Horizon Pictures/Columbia); and an adaptation of Gustave Flaubert's acclaimed novel *Madame Bovary*. All these films again demonstrated that Jones was an actress of many faces.

By the time of the release of *Carrie*, an adaptation of Dreiser's naturalistic novel that was directed and produced by William Wyler, Jones's versatility was already well established and functioned as her trademark. The pressbook for the film stressed that "she has managed to portray some of the most diverse and provocative characters in the annals of cinema amour. Her roles range in scope from the profoundly devout girl of *The Song of Bernadette* [. . .] to the recklessly romantic young woman in *Carrie*."[20] The diversity that Selznick aimed for was evident both at the level of genre classification and individual characters: Jones alternated between historical and contemporary material; she starred in a war drama (*Since You Went Away*), literary adaptations (*Madame Bovary*, *Carrie*), Westerns (*Duel in the Sun*), and comedy (Lubitsch's *Cluny Brown* [1946, Twentieth Century-Fox]); her characters were both childishly innocent (*The Song of Bernadette*, *Portrait of Jennie*) and aggressive and sexually direct (*Cluny Brown*, *Duel in the Sun*, *Ruby Gentry* [1952, Bernhard-Vidor Productions]) and represented different racial and ethnic identities (the mixed-race daughter of a white father and a Native American mother in *Duel in the*

Sun, British in *Cluny Brown*, French in *The Song of Bernadette* and *Madame Bovary*, Cuban in *We Were Strangers*, daughter of a Welsh Gypsy in *Gone to Earth* [1950], and, later, Eurasian in the romance *Love Is a Many-Splendored Thing* [1955, Twentieth Century-Fox]).

What might appear to be inconsistency in the approach to her career was, on the contrary, part of a conscious strategy to secure her a strong position in the film industry. In other words, her versatility and lack of a stable type were meant to be an advantage, not an obstacle, when negotiating for attractive roles. In this context, it is worth recalling the changes that took place in Hollywood in the latter half of the 1940s, which also affected the market for stars. After the decision in the historic Paramount case, which marked the definitive end of vertical integration and thus the separation of production and distribution centers from theater chains, the studios found themselves without a guaranteed outlet for their films. Since Hollywood companies "could no longer function as 'factories' turning out hundreds of films annually by methods that were similar to (if always different in important respects from) the industrial assembly line," they shifted to a different system organized around individual pictures (the so-called *package-unit system*).[21] As historian Janet Staiger has pointed out, the new system intensified the "need to differentiate the product on the basis of its innovations, its story, stars, and its director. [. . .] the use of a studio brand name became only another (if slightly larger) line on the poster. Instead, the names of individuals and the unique package were marketed."[22] One consequence was the gradual dissolution of carefully built acting stables: instead of actors with long-term contracts at the big studios, there was an increase in the number of those who freelanced with the help of their agents and managers.[23] This created more room for negotiating for substantial financial benefits and greater creative involvement. On the other hand, these opportunities were open only to a small circle of performers—the "veterans" whose films had been consistently profitable in the past, and a handful of newcomers who had the potential to appeal to younger audiences.

Although she was only in her late twenties, Jones clearly belonged to the former group. Along with David Selznick, she was able to use her accumulated symbolic capital (in the form of artistic renown, positive critical reception, and various awards) to gain desirable and well-paid engagements. Versatility was more of an advantage in the new system—it made Jones employable in a wide range of projects, and she did not have to wait for the "right role" or the "right film" to come along. Her skills allowed her to play almost any type of character across a variety of genres. As she stated at one point: "When I play a part, it's like an author writing a book. After I finish it, I put it out of my mind, and look for something new. I was never Bernadette, nor was I Pearl Chavez. Each was simply a role which I as an actress tried to interpret."[24] This eliminated the need to make the roles correspond to some consistent image being created on and off screen. Rather, the roles that Jones played were to be as diverse as possible, and, likewise, different from her "real" self, which remained shrouded in mystery to the public anyway. If the actress's personality was to be associated with anything, it was her professionalism and productive association with her husband and mentor Selznick.

Selznick's main concern was therefore to secure projects for his partner that would not jeopardize but rather strengthen her position in the market, in line with his belief that she was "a tremendous drawing card and an established star of the first rank."[25] The choices were therefore primarily based on an assessment of the importance of the material and the actress's collaborators. Jennifer Jones most often starred in adaptations of recent bestsellers (*The Song of Bernadette*, from the novel by Franz Werfel; *Duel in the Sun*, from the novel of the same name by Niven Busch; *Portrait of Jennie*, from the fantasy novel by Robert Nathan, etc.) or highly regarded classics (*Madame Bovary*, based on the novel by Gustave Flaubert; *Carrie*, adapted from the celebrated novel by Theodore Dreiser; *Farewell to Arms*, based on Ernest Hemingway's book of the same name)—that is, projects with literary origins whose popularity and high cultural status (their "pre-sold" qualities) reduced the risk of failure of the film versions derived from them. Jones's acting partners were exclusively leading Hollywood figures, including Joseph Cotten (on four occasions), Gregory Peck (twice), Charles Boyer, John Garfield, Van Heflin, Laurence Olivier, Charlton Heston, Montgomery Clift, Humphrey Bogart, William Holden, and Rock Hudson. Films starring her were directed by Henry King, John Cromwell, William Dieterle, King Vidor, Ernst Lubitsch, John Huston, Vincente Minnelli, and William Wyler, all considered masters of the craft, and in other key positions (camera, costumes, make-up) Selznick, too, insisted on having experienced and respected professionals.[26] At the turn of the 1940s and 1950s, he tried to further enhance her prestige through collaborations with European directors Michael Powell and Vittorio De Sica, although this association—as I will shortly demonstrate—was very uneasy and ultimately did not bring the expected benefits. The image of the esteemed star, whose fame derived not from tabloid-worthy escapades but from her acting skills, also had its origins in the coordination of the actress's off-screen existence. On her behalf, Selznick refused offers for cheesecake photos and advertising campaigns for commercial products. Her reticence in dealing with the media ultimately contributed to the impression of a consummate professional, fully focused on doing her best as an actress. Thus, like Ingrid Bergman and Dorothy McGuire, Jones also broke away from the traditional conception of a female star, albeit in a slightly different way. As Gaylyn Studlar has noted, "her star persona was unusual for the time in its almost exclusive textual focus. As an offscreen persona she barely existed other than in her association with Selznick."[27]

Name of Film	Studio	Director	Cast	Proposed Starting Date	Status
Gertrude Lawrence Story					
THE GARDENIA	Warners release	Robson ?			
GREEN LIGHT	Warners				
HILDA CRANE					
29 Wagonloads of Cotton / The Unsatisfactory Supper / HELLO FROM BERTHA / The Last of My Solid Gold Watches	Warners	Kazan		May – 6 weeks Mississippi	awaiting (Tenn. Williams)
HELEN MORGAN STORY	Warners				
LA OTRA	Warners				
LOTUS OF THE MOON		M. Powell		India	
MADAME BUTTERFLY					
MAGNOLIA	20th Century	Zanuck? Sen-lin Sou?			
MAGIC FACE LADY (Ketti Frings)	Universal prod. Albert Cohen	REFUSED			
MAURICE GUEST	Paramount	Vidor		Aug.–Sept.	Goetz are writing
MEXICAN VILLAGE	Metro		Lennox, Mardillan, Grace ann		
Marjorie Lawrence	Metro		Goldwyn August Bogart	Sept.– Oct. 1952	
THE MOON IS BLUE	Preminger				
MY COUSIN RACHEL	Fox	Cukor			
MR. AND MRS. SMITH	RKO–Hughes	Clark ?			
NELL GWYN					
PILATE'S WIFE	RKO–Hughes	Stevens?		June–July– Aug.	Feldman disc. Steven with Ideright
PRINCESS O'ROURKE	Warners – Musical				
THE PRESIDENT'S LADY	Fox			April 1–5 May 15	forgot to tell us—musical
RUBY GENTRY	Jos. Bernhard	King Vidor			Wyler not interested
THE RAIN GIRL	Paramount?	Wyler Stevens?			

A list of possible projects for Jennifer Jones. Courtesy of Daniel Selznick.

SELZNICK'S IN(TER)VENTIONS: *CARRIE*[28]

The way Selznick managed his wife's career to maintain or even improve her position in the industry is well illustrated by his involvement in the production of William Wyler's adaptation of Dreiser's *Sister Carrie* for Paramount. A great deal of attention and effort had always been invested in the selection of the actress's projects, but even so, her films of the late 1940s—*Portrait of*

Jennie, We Were Strangers, and *Madame Bovary*—did not end up the commercial and critical successes Selznick had hoped for. On the contrary, their box-office performance was disappointing (in particular, Selznick's costly *Portrait of Jennie* ended up as a worldwide flop),[29] and Jones was often blamed in reviews for their dismal results. The prospect of working with the two-time Academy Award-winning director (for *Mrs. Miniver* and *The Best Years of Our Lives* [1946, Samuel Goldwyn]) therefore promised to reverse the negative trend. Selznick, however, was not content to play the role of a distant observer and instead assertively entered all phases of *Carrie's* development—from selecting key crew and cast members and literary preparation through shooting to postproduction and theatrical release. In addition to his sincere interest in his wife's career, he may have compensated in this way for the diminished operations of his own production company, which was active only sporadically after the fiascos of *The Paradine Case* and *Portrait of Jennie.*

Since the mid-1930s, William Wyler ranked among Hollywood's most reliable and esteemed filmmakers. Despite disagreements which arose during the making of *Intermezzo: A Love Story,* which resulted in Wyler's (forced or voluntary) departure from the film,[30] Selznick held him in high professional regard, especially after the triumphs of *Mrs. Miniver* and *The Best Years of Our Lives,* which managed to combine critical acclaim with exceptionally high box-office receipts.[31] His latest film, *The Heiress* (1949, Paramount), based on Henry James's 1880 novel *Washington Square,* repeated the artistic success of its predecessors (it won four Oscars and received the same number of nominations), but with weaker earnings: it made only $2.3 million and barely covered its production costs.[32] The director's credit remained unblemished, however, and when it was announced that his next project would be the adaptation of Theodore Dreiser's famous and, at the time of its release at the turn of the century, controversial novel, Selznick immediately sensed that this would be a great opportunity for Jones.[33] In a letter to Wyler from June 1950, he summarized the concept of the central female character, an inexperienced country girl named Carrie who comes to Chicago to fulfill her American dream, and emphasized that she could not be played by any Hollywood beauty:

> Clearly the story has no point unless Carrie is a girl of obvious quality of obvious gentleness, despite her lack of outstanding talent and despite her lack of educational opportunities. The audience must understand why the man [Hurstwood], in such circumstances, falls hopelessly and irrevocably in love with <u>Carrie</u>, and goes headlong into doom and disaster.[34]

The casting of Jones was intended to give Carrie the credibility and audience sympathy that Selznick felt most Hollywood stars were unable to provide.[35]

But Jones was not the only candidate for the coveted role. After Laurence Olivier was confirmed as the male lead in the role of Hurstwood, the manager of a posh restaurant who loses his job and social status as a result of his affair with Carrie, Wyler considered younger actresses: Elizabeth Taylor and Jeanne Crain. Selznick viewed Wyler's behind-the-scenes actions as a betrayal, as he lived under the assumption that he had made a deal with the director that was supposed to guarantee him priority access to information regarding the casting of the title role.[36] Moreover, it was he who at an early stage—against Wyler's initial intuition—recommended Olivier as the only actor who possessed "every single thing the part [Hurstwood] requires."[37] Wyler's favorites eventually proved unavailable, and so the director apologetically returned to his original idea of giving the role to Jones.[38] Seeing great potential for artistic triumph and a commercial hit in the Wyler-Olivier-Jones-Dreiser combination, Selznick significantly lowered his usual demands: he was to collect $125,000 for the loan-out of the actress, plus an additional $25,000 once the film reached its negative cost in receipts; he also reluctantly waived approval rights for the cinematographer, make-up artist, and costume designer, and agreed to bill Olivier first in the credits and promotional materials.[39] All of these concessions were made in the hope that working with the best would result in a film of exceptional quality "that will be remembered for many years to come."[40]

During the making of *Carrie*, Selznick repeatedly declared that it was not his intention to interfere with Wyler and his colleagues.[41] In reality, however, he followed the film's development very closely, attempting at every opportunity to steer its course according to his own interests. Sometimes he was asked to send comments by Wyler, who was interested in the opinion of an experienced colleague and successful adaptor of literary classics (even though his credit had been damaged by recent failures). At other times, he did so unprompted. The credits of the resulting film do not reflect his input, but it is clear from the available material that it was not insignificant.[42]

As early as November 1949—at a time when Jones had not yet been confirmed in the role—Selznick read one of the early versions of the script by the married couple Ruth and August Goetz (also the writers of Wyler's previous film, *The Heiress*). Although his opinion was generally positive, he did have a range of suggestions concerning the construction of Carrie's character as well as the overall trajectory of the story. According to Selznick, the film could only achieve the desired artistic and commercial success by becoming "a love story. [. . .] The whole thing has to be re-examined from the standpoint of the girl in love."[43] In a letter addressed to Wyler, the producer repeatedly decried the inconsistency of Carrie, whose actions were not properly motivated by the script, were subject to sudden, inexplicable reversals in attitude and mood, and for that reason would not inspire sufficient audience participation. To change this, Selznick argued, it was necessary to create "a full, three-dimensional portrait: what she is, what she thinks and feels, what she wants—and all of these changing as her life changes."[44] The thirteen-page letter also contained twenty-nine specific reservations and proposed solutions. The final passage then bluntly revealed Selznick's motives for taking such an interest in the script's development:

> I hope you'll come up with a role that will be a really great challenge to Jennifer. [. . .] But there's no point in having her attempt to play a character whom even you couldn't describe to me when I challenged you; and whose story isn't worth telling because we know nothing about her, because it has no beginning, no middle, and no end. [. . .] so soon after Bovary, neither of us wants her to play another shallow character [. . .] without a thought in her head except marriage and pretty clothes, without motivations or purpose, without objectives or either progression or retrogression, without viewpoint, without understandable dramatic climaxes or conclusion, without change or variety—merely a creature of circumstance who goes all the way up the ladder from the bottom to the first rung.[45]

It seems that according to Selznick, Dreiser's version of determinism, where there is almost no room for human free will and individual life circumstances change due to invariable social mechanisms, was incompatible with the principles of good cinematic storytelling and character construction.

After reading the revised version of the script in July 1950, Selznick stated with satisfaction that the character of Carrie had undergone a major evolution and had come closer to the form he had so strenuously advocated. Nevertheless, in his opinion, she still acted like a naïve "idiot" in several places (for example, in a scene taken almost verbatim from the novel, where Hurstwood lures her out of the house under false pretenses), and in the end came across as unnecessarily cold when she did not react to Hurstwood's social downfall with feeling and understanding (here again, the screenwriters stuck closely to the literary original, which depicts the relationship of the former lovers without a hint of sentimentality).[46] Selznick, on the other hand, sought to further humanize Carrie: she was not to be so obsessed with material pleasures and the desire to live in luxury, and she was also to win the audience's sympathy by leaving Hurstwood not for selfish reasons but in the belief that it would do him good. In a lengthy letter of nearly thirty pages, Selznick presented himself as an expert on the tastes of the public, which he felt needed to be stimulated not only intellectually but also emotionally. For this reason, the ending of the script, which in its current form (in keeping with the novel) ended with Hurstwood's suicide, had to be significantly modified. Selznick did not advocate a classic happy ending—he knew that it would be inappropriate—but suggested closing the film with at least a hint of joy or optimism. Months later, when filming was nearing completion and the problem with the ending still persisted, he even devised three versions of the final scene, in which a desperate Carrie seeks out Hurstwood and, in a final monologue, declares her determination to spend the rest of her life by his side.[47] Here and in other screenplay drafts and commentaries, Selznick interpreted Dreiser's work as a tragic love story: the lovers were separated not as a result of differing natures or ideas of wellbeing, but because of a fatal misunderstanding concerning Hurstwood's theft, of which Carrie had no idea. In addition, Selznick knew that while the first half of the film focused on Carrie and her arrival from the country to the big city, the second half prioritized Hurstwood and the dramatic line of his social downfall. To present the ending from Carrie's perspective would mean to highlight Jones's performance at a key moment in the film that audiences would undoubtedly remember. While Wyler and the Goetzes did rewrite the final dialogue to make Carrie emerge as generous (rather than indifferent) and removed the suicide scene (leaving only a hint of it, with Hurstwood fiddling with the gas valve),[48] they did not act on Selznick's other suggestions: the film ends with Hurstwood leaving Carrie without saying goodbye to meet an uncertain fate. Still, Selznick provided strong feedback to the filmmakers, and many of his comments eventually found their way to the screen.

With the start of filming in mid-August, Selznick's involvement did not lessen. He was very uncomfortable with the cinematographer George Barnes, an experienced professional who had shot *Rebecca* (for which he was awarded an Oscar) and *Spellbound* for Selznick, but who had also been fired by him while working on *Since You Went Away* because he had failed to get satisfactory footage with Jennifer Jones. The producer feared that the same might happen this time. Because he had given up the approval right for the cinematographer and other crew members, he had to put pressure on Wyler informally. During the screen tests, he informed the director that Barnes, although one of the top cameramen in the industry, was "the only cameraman who has not been able to 'get' Jennifer."[49] At the same time, he criticized Paramount's antiquated make-up practices: the department, headed by Wally Westmore, reportedly indulged in heavy make-up (Selznick spoke of "war paint")[50] that was long outdated and not flattering to his wife. Selznick insisted that Barnes and Westmore conform to his actress, not the other way around, and sent detailed instructions through Wyler on how they should ideally proceed: Jones was to be photographed with only a minimum of make-up around her eyes; she was to use a darker shade of lipstick in moderate amounts; Barnes was to adjust the lighting and filters to her complexion; and there were also to be minor changes in the laboratory processing of the material in order to achieve a more satisfactory result.[51] Selznick's pressure eventually led to Barnes being removed from the film and replaced by Victor Milner, formerly a longtime Paramount contract cameraman and frequent collaborator with Cecil B. DeMille (he won his only Oscar for DeMille's *Cleopatra* [1934, Paramount]). Selznick was apparently pleased with this choice, as no significant criticism of the camera was made in further correspondence with Wyler.

In early December, Selznick viewed a rough cut of *Carrie* and compiled another list of objections and recommendations. In addition to the obligatory criticism of the ending, he commented on numerous other scenes, paying particular attention to the clarity of the story: he objected to the continuity of individual shots and the quality of the sound recording. He also commented on Jones's appearance; in one scene he did not like her eyebrows, in another the position of her hat and the camera angle.[52] These minor shortcomings were simply to be resolved by reshoots, but an unfortunate event occurred during their realization: on December 16, 1950, Jones suffered a miscarriage. She started filming the movie while already pregnant but kept it a secret from Wyler so as not to lose the part. When the director found out, there was no turning back. An unusually large number of scenes were therefore shot in close-ups and medium close-ups. In the full shots, the actress insisted on wearing tight corsets to disguise her condition. However, according to some accounts, they also contributed to her losing her child shortly after the filming was completed.[53] In January, she was still recovering, but gradually became involved in the reshoots and dubbing sessions, which were scheduled partly in response to Selznick's barrage of comments.

Two months later, a shorter cut was prepared, which solved most of the technical problems (awkward transitions between shots, poor sound quality), but at the same time, according to Selznick, damaged the emotional impact of the story and the performances of Jones and Olivier. In his thorough, fifteen-page analysis, the producer tried to convince Wyler to push for longer screen time with Paramount executives to allow for deeper characterizations of Carrie and Hurstwood and stronger emotional intensity of certain moments; in all, he cited fifteen scenes that suffered unnecessarily from the ill-advised shortening: "I don't say, mind you, that what is left isn't magnificent; but I do say, and most emphatically, that you have thrown away moments that would belong in any anthology of the great scenes of motion picture history. And for what? WHY?"[54]

Selznick was convinced that the film could succeed commercially only if it first attracted a selective art-house audience willing to pay higher admission prices—the same audience that made hits out of foreign imports like *The Red Shoes* and *Hamlet*: "Its great chance [. . .] was that it would build such tremendous prestige out of this additional and highly lucrative audience

Jennifer Jones and Laurence Olivier in a publicity still for *Carrie*.

as to make it a 'must' with the more conventionally minded, average movie-goer."[55] *Carrie*, therefore, should have been treated, according to Selznick, as a prestige title that would first build a reputation in smaller theaters in large cities, and only positive word-of-mouth would help it into wider distribution, where it would not be missed even by audiences who do not normally seek out art films.[56]

Paramount executives, however, saw the situation differently. Not only did they reject a running time that would have exceeded two hours (the distribution version ran 118 minutes), but they finally decided to postpone the premiere until July 1952—almost a year and a half after the film's completion. Selznick pressured company president Barney Balaban and vice president Y. Frank Freeman to consider at least a limited release in the fall of 1951 for a chance to contend for the Oscars. However, his pleading letters (in one of which, for example, he urged Freeman with the words, "Please, Frank, give 'Carrie' its chance")[57] were ignored. Paramount seemed to lack the willingness to give the film the extra care it required on the level of postproduction and promotion. While Selznick or Samuel Goldwyn in their days of glory would have made sure it got the necessary media and public attention, Paramount's strategy favored the more traditional spectacle *The Greatest Show on Earth*, which was scheduled to open in January 1952.[58] At the Academy Awards the following year, somewhat ironically, it was DeMille's big-budget blockbuster that won the award for Best Picture, whereas *Carrie* had to settle for only two nominations for sets and costumes in black-and-white. The box-office results were similar: *The Greatest Show on Earth* was the highest-grossing film of the year with $12 million, while *Carrie* was among the losers with less than $2 million.[59]

Trade journals had already predicted that the film would not have an easy time attracting moviegoers. *Variety* reported that the target audience for this old-fashioned and gloomy story was mainly mature adults, but this would not be enough to ensure a profit.[60] The *Hollywood Reporter* similarly hinted that this serious material would not correspond with the preferences of the majority of moviegoers, who tended to seek out light entertainment and spectacular scenes filmed in Technicolor.[61] Wyler's *Carrie* may not have been equipped to compete in the market with films like *David and Bathsheba* (1951, Twentieth Century-Fox), *Quo Vadis* (1951), and *Ivanhoe* (1952, both MGM), which were among the biggest commercial hits of the early 1950s, but it did not even come close to the success of the adaptation of another Dreiser novel, *An American Tragedy*, also produced by Paramount and directed by George Stevens under the title *A Place in the Sun* (1951). Starring young stars Elizabeth Taylor, Montgomery Clift, and Shelley Winters, the film won six Academy Awards and grossed $3.5 million.[62] While Stevens was successful in adapting and updating the sprawling subject matter to find resonance with intellectuals and younger audiences, Wyler in his attempt to do the same utterly failed. As we have seen, however, Selznick's interference may have played a significant role. The producer warned Wyler that the film must not "sit on two chairs," that it must become an artistic triumph to succeed commercially.[63] However, his interference related to the characterization of Carrie and the overall construction of the story prevented exactly that. Too often, critics of the time lamented the film's softening or dumbing down of the subject matter and unwarranted departures from Dreiser's well-established literary original, which were exactly those elements which Selznick had so vehemently promoted.[64]

Lowell E. Redelings complained in the *Hollywood Citizen-News* that the heroine, as played by Jones, was "whitewashed until she's as pure as the driven snow. [. . .] In Dreiser's novel, the heroine had some gray and black shadings to go with her all-white traits; she was thus a more convincing character."[65] Bosley Crowther in the *New York Times* called Carrie "a weak and distorted shadow of the young woman whom Theodore Dreiser drew in his classic novel. [. . .] This arrant distortion of Carrie—and the coy performance Miss Jones gives—reduces the theme of the drama to that of hopeless, death-less love, with most of the human implications and social ironies of the novel removed."[66] Crowther was so distressed by the result that he addressed the film in a separate article published a few days after the original review. There he re-iterated that the heroine was very far from Dreiser's fallen woman and went on to ponder the reasons for such a drastic distortion: it could have been the Production Code Administration with its regulations, Wyler and the Para-mount studio seeking commercial success, or Jones herself, who "didn't wish (or wasn't able) to portray a woman for whom the feminine audience might not have overflowing sympathy."[67]

As the surviving correspondence shows, however, Crowther was wrong: it was chiefly Selznick who pushed for changes in the conception of the title character and transformation of the whole film into a romantic melodrama concerning tragic love. Although he held no official position on the film, he claimed considerable influence; the loan-out of his contract star gave him an excuse to be involved in its making on many levels. Through constant pressure, he forced even an experienced filmmaker like Wyler into a series of concessions that, in sum, contributed to the film's near elimination of the social criticism present in the novel and brought the main character closer to the virtuous heroines of women's films. Selznick appealed to his experience and expertise, arguing that he wanted to benefit the entire film, but his main concern was his wife's reputation and the potential financial gain that might result. Wyler tolerated his meddling—and probably shared some of his reservations—but when the opportunity arose, he refused further collaboration with Jones (and thus the prospect of a re-encounter with Selznick).[68] Ultimately, *Carrie* failed to live up to the potential arising from the celebrated book, generous budget, and combination of established personalities in key positions, and ended in a clear disappointment for all involved.

INDISCRETION OF AN AMERICAN PRODUCER:
TERMINAL STATION

In the late 1940s and early 1950s, while *Carrie* was under development, David O. Selznick was planning a major expansion of his company's operations in Europe.[69] This project included co-productions with foreign partners, in which Jennifer Jones was to play a prominent role. However, the attempt to raise his and his wife's prestige through collaboration with renowned European film-makers did not quite work out: Selznick's obsessive nature, his increasingly pressing urge to control every stage of the films' production, and differing ideas about the shape of the final products led to disagreements, lawsuits, and ultimately to the creation of different screen versions for the European and American markets, which revealed the incompatibility of Selznick's approach not only with European tastes but also with the demands of a transformed American audience. The use of Jones in the two films that emerged under these complicated circumstances was also an important point of contention.

The adaptation of Mary Webb's novel *Gone to Earth* was, like *The Third Man*, co-produced by David O. Selznick and Alexander Korda. Under the direction of the established duo of Michael Powell and Emeric Pressburger (*A Matter of Life and Death* [1946], *Black Narcissus* [1947, both The Archers], *The Red Shoes*) Jones portrayed the superstitious half-Gypsy girl Hazel, torn between two men: the country squire Reddin (David Farrar), to whom she is attracted by an animalistic passion, and the vicar Marston (Cyril Cusack), who in turn awakens in her restraint and refinement. The story, reminiscent of *Duel in the Sun*, is set against the rural backdrop of Shropshire in the West Midlands region of England (on the border with Wales) in the late nineteenth century.

Selznick monitored the making of the film from afar and began to exercise his authority only after the rough cut was completed: the picture, in his opinion, deviated too much from the book and the approved script. His objections concerned in particular "an excessively English resistance to portrayal of emotions [. . . and] a fantastic obsession against making things clear."[70] However, both the directors and Korda as co-producer refused to make the required adjustments and the whole case went to court. The ruling stated that the film adhered sufficiently to the novel, but that if Selznick had reservations, he could prepare his own version for distribution in the Western Hemisphere at his own expense (while Korda controlled the rights for the Eastern Hemisphere).[71] With the help of director Rouben Mamoulian and the original cast, he therefore filmed several new scenes in California, while a range of others were eliminated. On this basis, Selznick assembled his own eighty-minute cut under the title *The Wild Heart*, which differed in many ways from the British, 110-minute version. Joseph Cotten narrated the prologue, which introduced the setting and the main players and gave the whole film an ominous atmosphere by framing it as "a tale of pagan cruelty." Other elements were added to clarify certain motives or plot points; these included inscriptions and the protagonist's voice-over in a scene in which she performs a pagan ritual. Further, the fairy-tale-like dimension of the story was emphasized, with the sexually predatory Reddin repeatedly likened to the mythical Black Rider.[72] The most important changes, however, concerned the presentation of Jennifer Jones. Clearly dissatisfied with the quality and quantity of his wife's shots, Selznick had cinematographer Christopher Challis shoot additional close-ups of her face as well as new scenes in which she was presented in different and more daring costumes. This, along with the elimination of episodic scenes in which Hazel's character did not figure, resulted in *The Wild Heart* feeling more like a Hollywood product centered around the psychologically motivated protagonist as a key driver of the plot and thus privileging the performance of a star actress.

The cost of the altered version was a not inconsiderable $165,000, but Selznick was able to sell the distribution rights to RKO for half a million. However, the film was not a commercial or critical success in either version,[73] and it did not make any significant contribution to Jones's reputation as a renowned dramatic actress. Moreover, the conflict between Selznick and Korda thwarted the prospects for further collaborations, such as an adaptation of Hardy's *Tess of the d'Urbervilles*, which could have provided Jones with one of the biggest opportunities of her career to date.

The one-time professional alliance with the Italian director Vittorio De Sica also had an unfortunate outcome, one that is worth looking at in more detail, as it promised an even more unlikely combination of Hollywood elegance, refinement, and grandeur, all qualities personified by Selznick, with the poetics of Italian neorealism, which usually used location shooting and non-professional actors to focus on working-class characters in everyday situations, often struggling against the hardships in the aftermath of the war.[74] The initiative came from Selznick, who approached De Sica as a more reliable replacement for his original choice, the award-winning but also erratic and unpredictable director Roberto Rossellini. The joint project between the megalomaniacal Hollywood producer and one of the founders of the neorealist movement in Italy (*Children Are Watching Us* [*I bambini ci guardano*, 1944, Invicta Film/Scalera Film], *Shoeshine* [*Sciuscià*, 1946, CG Entertainment/Societa Cooperativa Alfa Cinematografica], *The Bicycle Thief* [*Ladri di biciclette*, 1948, Produzioni De Sica]) was riddled with confusion and disagreements from the start. As David Thomson remarked, "co-production requires self-deception on all sides. David wanted art, prestige, Continental sophistication; the Italians wanted American money, big stars, and a chance of getting to Hollywood."[75]

Selznick had already been interested in co-producing *The Bicycle Thief*, in part "to profitably use millions of lire that belonged to [him] as his share of receipts from films previously shown in Italy,"[76] but he and De Sica could not agree on the casting of the leading man in the English-language version, which was to be made after or alongside the Italian version. For commercial reasons, Selznick advocated big Hollywood names such as Cary Grant, Bing Crosby, and Danny Kaye, which was out of the question for De Sica.[77] Later, De Sica was considered for an engagement in Hollywood, but as Henry Hart, editor of *Films in Review*, noted, instead of making a film about Italian Americans overseas, as he had originally planned, De Sica ended up making a film about an

American in Rome.[78] Selznick agreed to pursue the idea of screenwriter Cesare Zavattini (a key collaborator of De Sica's), dealing with the final moments of a love affair between a well-to-do American housewife and a young Italian American college professor. While the character of Mary was intended from the outset for Jones, various actors were considered for the male lead, including Marlon Brando, Richard Burton, Farley Granger, and Louis Jourdan, before the choice fell on Montgomery Clift, who by then had already enjoyed success in *Red River* (1948, Monterey Productions/United Artists), *The Heiress*, and *A Place in the Sun.*

The production was beset by troubles of various kinds.[79] The screenplay for *Stazione Termini*, or *Terminal Station*, as the project was called from the beginning, was very difficult to complete, and half a dozen writers worked on it, including Zavattini, Paul Gallico, Alberto Moravia, Carson McCullers, and Truman Capote, who was eventually credited in both versions as the author of the English dialogue.[80] Work on the set (from October to December 1952) was hampered by the language barrier between the Italian and American-British sections of the crew, as well as filming in the newly opened terminal of the Rome train station, which had to take place exclusively at night due to the busy traffic. At the time, Jennifer Jones was still recovering from the tragic death of her first husband, Robert Walker (who died suddenly on August 28, 1951, at the age of thirty-two), and, according to witnesses, was often nervous and irritable.[81] Last but not least, De Sica had to endure the scrutiny of his American business partner. According to his own account, he received daily multi-page memoranda with detailed instructions, but soon stopped reading them and instead did things his own way.[82] The facts, however, show that he made some significant concessions during the filming. He admitted that the whole film "was made for Jones,"[83] which was reflected, among other things, in Selznick's extreme concern for the quality of her photography. It soon became apparent that the work of De Sica's preferred man, Aldo Graziati (known as G. R. Aldo; he had shot *Miracle in Milan* [*Miracolo a Milano*, 1951, Produzioni De Sica] and *Umberto D.* [1952, Rizzoli Film/Amato Film]), did not meet the producer's high standards, as the DOP preferred the natural setting and lighting at the expense of the attractive presentation of the two Hollywood stars. For this reason, a young British cinematographer, Oswald "Ossie" Morris, was hired. In an interview with David Thomson, he recalled his assignment as follows: "It was made absolutely clear to me by D.O.S. that he held me responsible for Jennifer's appearance in the movie, that I was to tell him exactly where Aldo was going wrong and all her scenes were to be retaken!"[84] While Graziati and De Sica were determined to capture in authentic fashion the bustle of the train station, Morris worked to capture the physical beauty and elegance of Jones and Clift as flatteringly as possible using glamorizing close-ups (by means of carefully selected lenses, soft lighting, and diffusers). The resulting film (in both versions) shows the incompatibility of these two approaches: one seeks an almost documentary-like depiction of a specific time and place, while the other, through the idealization of the star actors, leads to a sentimentalization of their amorous outburst typical for Hollywood melodrama.[85]

Despite his close supervision of the filming process, Selznick was dissatisfied with De Sica's cut: the narrative contained too many digressions that were distracting from the romance of Mary and Giovanni. In the words of David Thomson: "The realist [De Sica] saw a panorama that had to be filmed in a real station (in Rome), with many stories, or incidents, spilling over so that the viewer could see how insignificant each story was in the sea of affairs." By contrast, Selznick wanted to see only one dominant storyline, with his Hollywood stars as the main players.[86] The response to the screening of De Sica's version at the Cannes Film Festival confirmed Selznick's conviction: too often, moviegoers were bored and did not understand the connection between the central story and the other episodes.[87] Selznick therefore decided to shorten the film considerably (from the original 88 to 63 minutes)[88] and, as with *Gone to Earth*, prepared his own cut for use in the Western Hemisphere, confident that "the public generally will like the re-edited version much better, distributors and exhibitors will prefer it, and [. . .] it will have greater success than the longer, original, slower version."[89] Again, then, the two distribution versions—American and European—were not planned but instead resulted from the different ideas of the producer and director and their estimation of their respective markets.

Unlike the British co-production discussed above, however, this time Selznick did not order any new footage to be shot: his editor, Jean Barker, worked solely with the material shot by De Sica in Rome. Some of the changes were purely technical (for example, the re-recording of a number of lines for better clarity). Other alterations, however, led to significant differences between the two versions, with the use of stars playing an important role throughout the process.[90] The opening titles (De Sica's version is introduced by the image of a train, Selznick's by the silhouette of the embracing lovers) and the conception of the first scene differ considerably: the Italian version unfolds in a slower tempo, detailing Mary's hesitation whether to visit Giovanni's apartment or to leave without saying goodbye, as well as her journey from Piazza Navona to the central station, where the rest of the action is set; the American version, on the other hand, opens with a title (by screenwriter Ben Hecht) that introduces Rome as "eternal city of culture, of legend . . . and of love," and Mary's insecurity is dealt with via flashback. It takes De Sica sixteen minutes to introduce the character played by Montgomery Clift; the American version manages it in half that time. All this signals from the outset the different intentions of the two cuts: the Italian version shows more interest in atmosphere and setting, while the American is more clearly defined as a romance with two principal protagonists.[91]

The biggest difference concerns the emphasis placed on the central story line. De Sica populated the station with episodic characters who always claim the viewer's attention for a time: the camera waits for them after Mary or Giovanni leave the frame, giving them space to utter one or two lines or perform a simple action. These moments usually do not last more than a few seconds, but they nevertheless contribute to the decentralization of the narrative, as they show that there are other dramas going on at the station than the parting of the central couple. In the spirit of neorealism, completely in line with Zavattini's philosophy that "cinema should take as its subject the daily existence and condition of the Italian people,"[92] the director documents the everyday while simultaneously providing a cross-section of Italian society as we encounter individuals of different social status. The viewer's attention is thus distracted, and although we always return to the central plot line, we are thereby shown that Mary and Giovanni are as much (or as little) a part of the social fabric as anyone else.

In Selznick's version, these atmospheric vignettes are not eliminated entirely (two scenes with a group of priests, for example, remain), but their number was noticeably reduced: the narrative, in keeping with the conventions of classical Hollywood cinema, focuses on clearly profiled individuals and thus privileges star discourse. In such instances, Selznick's cut interrupts De Sica's longer running scenes immediately after Mary or Giovanni leave the scene (or even before this can happen), thus eliminating episodic characters. As the video essayist kogonada notes, all this material was viewed by Selznick as excessive, distracting the viewer's attention as it did not contribute in any fashion to the main plot line. For De Sica, by contrast, it represented the essence of his neorealist approach, helping to present the train station as a vibrant place brimming with social activity.[93]

However, the scenes between Mary and Giovanni were shortened as well because, according to Selznick, some of their dialogue was repetitive (especially in the restaurant scene). While the US cut seemed to accommodate the American audience, which was not accustomed to a slower paced narrative, it also disrupted De Sica's concept, where the 90-minute running length corresponded to the time of the plot, which covers the period from 7 to 8:30 p.m., when the lovers finally part. Even the choice of titles for the two distribution versions ultimately suggested an overall re-polarization: the title *Terminal Station* emphasizes the setting and prepares the audience for a certain degree of descriptiveness, while the title *Indiscretion of an American Wife* frames the

Jennifer Jones wearing a costume from Dior in a publicity still for *Indiscretion of an American Wife*.

central motive of the film in sensationalist terms and foregrounds the title character and, by extension, the star actress playing her.

Amy Lawrence, the author of a monograph on Montgomery Clift, further noted that "Selznick removed any sign of adult sexuality in favor of sentimentality and romance." In her view, the producer was too anxious about his wife's reputation and chose to portray her more positively than De Sica—as a reserved and chaste wife and mother[94] (much as he had tried in *Carrie*). While there is something to it, this interpretation is not entirely valid: his cut, for example, uses a longer version of the scene in which an old snooper announces to another onlooker at the station that Mary and Giovanni have been caught "making love" in the compartment of an abandoned train carriage. Later, during the interrogation in the office of the commissioner investigating the circumstances of this incident, part of a dialogue, according to which the pair indulged only in conversation, is in contrast omitted. The addition in the first case and omission in the second case cause a shift in meaning, more explicitly pointing to the fact that the pair were caught *in flagrante*.

The American version thus contributes even more to the characterization of Mary as a woman of contradictions: she is a seemingly ordinary Philadelphia housewife, but she walks around the railway station in an elegant Dior costume (as the opening credits unambiguously announce); in close-ups, she is filmed as a saint, but at the same time she succumbs to sudden bursts of passion with a man she had met only a few days before. The role thereby combined two contrasting types of a devoted wife and mother and a reprehensible sinner, as the US trailer also pointed out. Jones, it said, mixed "the tenderness of her award-winning Bernadette with the fire of *Duel in the Sun*" in this new character. Thus, as in *Gone to Earth*, the various shades were here squeezed into a single characterization, once again highlighting the actress's versatility but also rendering the character's motivations and actions contradictory and hard to decipher.

Selznick's cut was acquired for distribution by Columbia Pictures, which paid $500,000 for it. To compensate for its modest hour-long running time, which was more often associated with B-movie productions, the studio commissioned a musical prologue from Selznick to give the audience the feeling that they were getting something extra for their money.[95] William Cameron Menzies (a production designer who played a key role in the making of *Gone with the Wind*) was directing, with the equally famous James Wong Howe behind the camera. In an eight-minute pre-film shot in a chic New York apartment, complete with decorations in the style of ancient Rome, singer Patti Page sings two songs ("Autumn in Rome" and "Indiscretion") that evoke in mood and lyrics the situation of a lonely woman who has gone through a love affair with an unfortunate outcome. With the involvement of a popular performer (her 1950 hit "Tennessee Waltz" lasted thirty weeks on the *Billboard* magazine music chart)[96] and a slick visual style that relies on lingering close-ups, soft lighting, and sumptuous surroundings, the prologue establishes the star discourse characteristic of the American distribution version, even though here it is directed at Page, who becomes Jones's substitute for a few minutes.[97]

The advertising campaign further exploited the tabloid-style element inherent in the American title. The use of a newspaper headline on some posters and the slogan "Suddenly the whole world knew her secret!" promised to cross socially acceptable boundaries and evoked the recent scandal caused by the much-publicized affair between Ingrid Bergman and Roberto Rossellini. But audiences remained immune to this aggressive mode of address: unlike other "Roman" films of the time—such as *Roman Holiday* (1953, Paramount) or *Three Coins in the Fountain* (1954, Twentieth Century-Fox)—the film was a commercial flop, and even the critics were not particularly kind to it. Many reviewers blamed it for its awkward fusion of Italian neorealism with Hollywood sentiment and compared it unflatteringly to similar European productions: Henry Hart described it as an unsatisfactory copy of David Lean's *Brief Encounter* (1945, Cineguild), writing that "it wholly lacks the integrity, emotional and artistic, of that excellent British picture,"[98] while Bosley Crowther stated that the story was devoid of the social resonance of *The Bicycle Thief*, as it revolved around the protagonist's transgression and the petty question of whether to stay with her Italian lover or return to her family.[99] But the negative reaction in the press could not have come as a complete surprise to Selznick. Prior to the film's release, he had tested both versions in front of American audiences and, as it turned out, the shortening did not help: "both versions received recurring complaints of an inadequate story, overlong duration, slow pace, and stilted dialogue."[100] Not even another series of alterations and reductions in Selznick's cut changed the audience's general stance. As concluded by Dylan Levy, "it appears that both Italian and American viewers could not get past the film's central plot, which, in hindsight for Selznick, was fundamentally flawed to the point that it could not be fixed through cutting and re-editing."[101]

CONCLUSION

Selznick's versions of his two European co-productions starring Jennifer Jones showed that the formerly almost infallible producer was not particularly sensitive to the tastes and demands of the American public in the 1950s, even though it was specifically the American public that he wanted to accommodate with his alterations. One of the main problems was the often-excessive emphasis on stars. As Thomas Schatz observed, Selznick "became increasingly obsessed with the power and commercial value of stars, to a point where he seemed to evaluate any project only on its merits as a star vehicle."[102] Schatz made this remark in the context of the producer's activities in the mid-1940s, but I believe it even better describes his operations in the following decade, when he tied his activities so closely to his wife's career. While he had previously declared repeatedly that he preferred a weaker role in a first-rate film for his contract actors and actresses over a strong role in a lower-quality film (the part of Detective Brian Cameron for Joseph Cotten in *Gaslight* is a good example),[103] he increasingly broke this principle as time went on. Both in his own productions and in loan-outs to other studios, he vehemently advocated changes that resulted in all components of the film's production and promotion being subordinated to the star, regardless of other qualities.

Selznick's last film as a producer, an adaptation of Ernest Hemingway's war novel *A Farewell to Arms*, made under a deal with Twentieth Century-Fox, can

Jennifer Jones in a publicity still for *A Farewell to Arms*.

serve as the final case in point. Selznick was oblivious to the fact that the thirty-eight-year-old Jones was not a good fit for Hemingway's fifteen-years-younger heroine, and instead pushed for her to have more space in the film than in the original book. Accordingly, he chose to emphasize the romance at the expense of the wartime storyline, which led to the replacement of the original director, John Huston, with the more malleable Charles Vidor.[104] Selznick also pushed cinematographer Ossie Morris to subordinate the spectacle to intimacy and to ensure that Catherine Barkley (Jones) and Frederick Henry (played by Rock Hudson) would be "romantic and beautiful people. The audience must be in love with them visually from the beginning."[105] The reworking of a famous literary subject into a long, miscast sentimental romance led to its commercial and critical failure. As Bosley Crowther noted in the *New York Times*, "Selznick's picture [. . .] lacks that all-important awareness of the inescapable presence and pressure of war. [. . .] [Except for two reminders], you scarcely know a war is going on." And further: "As a pure romance, too, it has shortcomings. The essential excitement of a violent love is strangely missing. [. . .] The show of devotion between two people is intensely acted, but not realized. It is questionable, indeed, whether Mr. Hudson and Miss Jones have the right personalities for these roles."[106] Selznick clearly failed to learn from his earlier mistakes and refused to admit until the very end that he had erred in his management of his wife's career or in his approach to the stories he handled.

The inglorious end of Selznick's collaboration with Jones can easily obscure its successful beginnings. As David Thomson noted, "[s]o many people believed she did her best work when David was too far away to advise her."[107] But I think such an assessment is too harsh. Selznick was instrumental in turning an unknown actress of dubious professional background into a leading Hollywood star. Jones regularly garnered Oscar nominations in the mid-1940s, and although she never appeared in the list of top box-office draws according to exhibitors, her films *The Song of Bernadette*, *Since You Went Away*, and *Duel in the Sun* were among the biggest hits of the decade (all three were in the top 5 for the respective years). After 1947, her position faded: she received only one Academy Award nomination in the following ten years (for *Love Is a Many-Splendored Thing*), and even the proportion of hits in her filmography declined precipitously. Elizabeth Forrest introduced her December 1953 profile article about Jones with the following words:

> Poor Jenny! She's beautiful. She's talented. And she's been a film star for ten of her thirty-two years. Yet something is always going wrong for Jennifer Jones. That's the way it's been these last five years. Where the parts were right, the films were wrong. Where the films were right, Jennifer wasn't on form. And where both were right, the films were box office disappointments.[108]

In the 1950s, her career stagnated rather than progressed, but she was not alone among female stars: Greer Garson, Gene Tierney, Joan Fontaine, and Teresa Wright had similar career trajectories. For one, the factor of age and changing appearance is more significant for women than for men. As Leo C. Rosten (writing in 1941) showed, four-fifths of Hollywood actresses had had careers of less than a decade, while more than 40 percent of men had enjoyed careers longer than that.[109] This trend was only reinforced after the war, as the development of the American film industry tended to favor men.[110] Jones's career of more than fifteen years at the top is therefore clearly above average.

For these reasons, it is not easy to judge whether Selznick was a salvation or a curse for his wife, an engine or an obstacle to her success. He undoubtedly made her a star in the first phase of her career, but later his notoriously conflicted nature and tendency to interfere in the creation of the projects for which he lent her may have been more of a hindrance, as the examples given in this chapter show.[111] Nevertheless, Jones remained loyal to him and continued to personify his vision of fame and stardom, even though it no longer resonated with audiences as strongly as it had in the mid-1940s.

Conclusion

THE SELZNICK BRAND

In the Tradition of Quality and Prestige

I have never gone after "honors instead of dollars" but I have understood the relationship between the two.
—DAVID O. SELZNICK[1]

In the last few chapters, I have been documenting Selznick's activities after World War II, at a time when his studio was no longer as successful: his independent production company was unable to adjust to the new industry realities and although Selznick himself remained a visionary (he foresaw the growth of foreign markets and the onset of television, for example), a number of his ideas concerning production of films and stars ended up being ill-suited for the postwar period. The book's second half therefore ends up emphasizing the trajectory of the producer's professional decline, which is inevitable with almost every successful filmmaker whose work is dependent on the interest of the public and the fluctuating market, both of which are difficult to predict. I would like, however, to return in the conclusion to the first half of the 1940s, when Selznick prospered as a producer of star identities and was able to implement his own version of stardom, which met with great success and allowed him to compete with the Hollywood majors. It was only when he began to violate some of his own principles after 1945 that the gradual collapse of his brand and position in the market resulted.

A 1941 poll among 550 Hollywood professionals revealed that Selznick's name, more than that of any other personality in the film industry, was associated with prestige and the highest artistic standards.[2] This was no accident. The producer understood that only through building up a powerful, easily recognizable brand would he be able to compete with traditional studios which could rely upon a stable foundation and rich financial and personal resources.[3] Selznick achieved this by pushing for, apart from financial rewards, accumulation of symbolic capital in the form of awards, recognition, and prestige. By these means, he systematically built up a unique identity, which, in the words of Kyle Dawson Edwards, helped "cultivate relationships and maintain good will with prospective and current employees, industrial counterparts, and cinema audiences."[4] The investment in his own brand also led, in the long run, to financial success. Along with Samuel Goldwyn, Selznick was in all probability the most renowned film producer (better known than most of the moguls at large studios), which allowed him to differentiate products more effectively in the market and address all important players including exhibitors and moviegoers. It was specifically this close link between business and art, financial profits and personal reputation, economic and symbolic capital that formed the cornerstone of Selznick's business strategies. In 1961, when his career was effectively over, he summed up his activities in the following, characteristically immodest manner:

> No pictures in the history of the industry ever received, picture for picture, as many honors as my own; no pictures in the history of the industry, picture for picture, have ever achieved comparable grosses or comparable profits. [. . .] I have seen studio administration after administration go under, because of the failure to realize that honors in the picture business are not only a satisfaction to the recipients, and proper rewards for work well done, but (a) worth millions in gross; (b) an incentive to better work; (c) invaluable to a studio's morale, and to its *commercial* [. . .] results on an over-all basis.[5]

The films made by Selznick were usually based on culturally highly regarded literary sources (*Little Lord Fauntleroy, The Prisoner of Zenda, The Adventures of Tom Sawyer*, and, in particular, *David Copperfield, Anna Karenina*, and *A Tale of Two Cities*, the last three made while he was still at MGM) or current bestsellers (*Gone with the Wind, Rebecca*). They were distinguished by high budgets and production values (lavish sets and costumes, Technicolor, elaborate special effects) as well as an above-standard level of craftsmanship. Leading representatives of the respective professions worked on them (directors, screenwriters, cameramen, designers, etc.) and established stars or carefully chosen personalities earmarked for stardom played in the leading and supporting roles. The literary aspect of the pictures and their serious character were emphasized at the level of advertising, not only in the sense that the stories were derived from respected literary sources, but also as a contrast to comedy or action, which were mostly domains of titles with a lower cultural status. In this way they appealed to sophisticated and middlebrow audiences in larger cities (in the US as well as abroad), whose support helped to legitimize this kind of film production as an alternative to reading or going to the theater. Selznick consistently made use of his reputation secured by his previous successes, which had been confirmed by a range of awards: the first page of the pressbook for *Since You Went Away* contained, for example, a list of more than twenty awards received by his films thus far.[6] The carefully mounted advertising campaigns were tailored to fit his films' release patterns. The roadshow format was preferred, in which the films played in selected upscale movie palaces with expensive admission and only then, after this lucrative market was exhausted, did they find their ways into lower-ranking cinemas frequented by less-well-to-do patrons. Finally, the pompous colonial facade of Selznick's office building in Culver City, which formed the company's logo introducing every picture, also helped support the desired image.[7] Kyle Dawson Edwards summarized this succinctly when he wrote that

> [Selznick International Pictures] depended heavily on the quality of its films and the intensity of its marketing campaigns: a Selznick picture had to be more than a night at the movies, it had to be an event that could invoke both "good feelings" from an audience and the desire to see current and future SIP releases again and again; in turn, promoting and presenting pictures in this manner could allow the company to leverage favorable terms from distributors and exhibitors.[8]

My research has demonstrated that identical principles were used in Selznick's treatment of contract actors and actresses. The goal of this last section is to summarize the ways in which the producer maintained and developed his associations with concepts of quality and prestige in the first half of the 1940s, that is at a time when his business activities related to developing and selling stars took precedence over production of films.[9]

To begin with, it is important to note that Selznick's stars were in no way the same or interchangeable. Their gender, age, name, appearance, origin, voice and accent, performance style, and interaction with the public—all of that distinguished them and made them unique. Vivien Leigh was a strong-minded Brit of dark features and refined demeanor, which is why she, more than anyone else, was suitable for playing Scarlett O'Hara in *Gone with the Wind*. On the other hand, Joan Fontaine had subtler and lighter features and as an actress was more adept at evoking insecurity and awkwardness, which helped her to get the part of the unnamed heroine in *Rebecca*. Even though both Ingrid Bergman and Jennifer Jones had reputations as versatile professionals, Bergman was further characterized by her Swedish origin and open and relaxed relationship with the public, while Jones—born and raised in

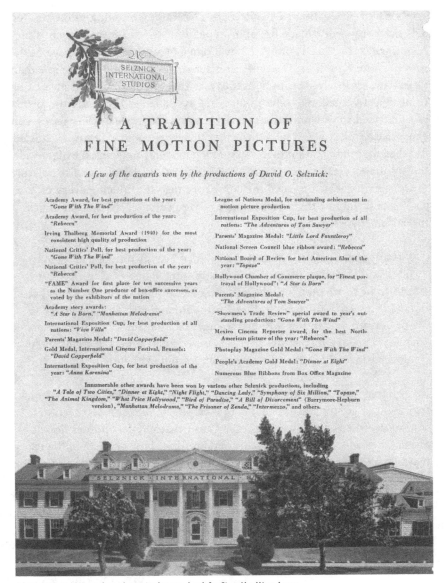

A list of Selznick's awards as shown in the pressbook for *Since You Went Away*.

Oklahoma—preferred to avoid interactions with the press and her fans as much as possible. Similarly, audiences had no trouble in distinguishing between the towering Gregory Peck, who projected strong authority, Joseph Cotten, ten years older and a model of old-school charm, and the elegant and refined Alan Marshal. Nevertheless, all these actors and actresses were associated with several general attributes that in the wartime Hollywood dominated by large studios were not the default norm.

To illustrate this more clearly, I decided to add a comparison with Twentieth Century-Fox's contract star Betty Grable. I am not arguing that Grable represents a typical or average Hollywood star as there was no such thing. But she did personify one possible star modus (extremely popular and frequently imitated) that stood in sharp contrast to the policy of Selznick's studio. Among other things, the comparison will thus allow me to discuss side by side certain practices of Selznick as an independent producer and Twentieth Century-Fox as a representative of Hollywood majors.

Betty Grable ranked among the biggest female stars during the war and postwar period. Between 1942 and 1951, she consistently placed in the top ten of the most lucrative actors and actresses according to exhibitors, and in the year 1943 she became the only woman in this time frame to end up in the first position.[10] Selznick was well aware of her market value, but, in a memo from June 1946, nevertheless stated that he was not interested in her services, not even if this opportunity was given to him.[11] How can one explain the lack of interest of this successful film producer and businessman, who should be primarily interested in profit, in one of the most popular (and thus most easily marketable) Hollywood stars? The answer lies in the attributes which surrounded Grable. The actress was not associated with prestige and did not possess great potential to make a neat fit with Selznick's established brand, which, apart from accumulation of economic capital, was aimed at symbolic evaluation in the form of recognition from colleagues in the trade, members of the press, and the moviegoing public.

Selznick built up an aura of quality and exclusivity amongst the members of his star stable by casting them in or loaning them out to only a small number of carefully chosen high-profile pictures. Inactivity was preferred over involvement in less important films that might have been financially advantageous but could also harm the reputation of the individual and establish a dangerous precedence negatively influencing negotiations concerning future contracts. For this reason, B-productions were out of the question for Selznick's most important actors and actresses. High-budget adaptations of literary works, Hollywood versions of successful Broadway productions, or historical films were preferred—in other words, priority was given to projects that were associated with seriousness and dignity and that announced themselves as works with artistic ambitions. Equally important was the connection with middle-class or higher-class values which these films and their stories' settings provided. In contrast, Westerns, gangster films, light-hearted musicals, detective stories, or pictures with working-class milieu, which did not have such lofty and distinguished aspirations, were usually dismissed by Selznick. For example, Joan

Fontaine played in seven films over the years 1940 to 1945, most of which were adaptations: *Rebecca* and *The Frenchman's Creek* were based on novels by Daphne du Maurier, *This Above All* (1942, Twentieth Century-Fox) was derived from the contemporary novel by Eric Knight, *The Constant Nymph* was based on a novel and popular play by Margaret Kennedy, and *Jane Eyre* was a screen version of Charlotte Brontë's literary classic.

Over the same time, Betty Grable at Twentieth Century-Fox played in fifteen pictures, mostly Technicolor musicals with romantic-comic plots. The regular supply of films, made possible by the studio's effective organization and strict division of labor, ensured that the actress was constantly in the public eye, appearing in a new film as the main character every five months on average. Her pictures, "with threadbare plots and promising titles that were quite literally constructed around her performances and her figure,"[12] represented typical Hollywood studio products in the sense that they depended on standardization and predictability: the differences between them (especially after 1941) were minimal.[13] The characters which the actress played over and over were similarly constant. Usually, she portrayed an attractive girl next door: energetic, strong-willed, friendly, and easily accessible. Grable was attractive and sexy, but not in a threatening way; she was equally liked by men of all age categories and professions (including soldiers) and women who did not view her as an unwelcome competitor. According to Jeanine Basinger, she became a perfect emblem of the time; along with Greer Garson she was an important icon of the war years, because she symbolized perseverance and determination.[14] However, while one could easily imagine the elegant Englishwoman Garson as part of Selznick's stable, the much more folksy, all-American Grable would be completely out of place.

Grable, like most stars employed by large Hollywood studios, was subject to typecasting. There existed a distinct continuity among the characterizations of her roles which served to form the assumptions of the audience: even before seeing the film, the public had clear expectations of what they were going to see. Selznick, in contrast, did not want his stars to be linked with one kind of production or character type.[15] His goal was instability or unpredictability: whenever there was a threat that one of his contract actors or actresses would become identified with one distinct character (Jennifer Jones with Bernadette, Gregory Peck with Father Chisholm in *The Keys of the Kingdom*, Joseph Cotten with Uncle Charlie in *Shadow of a Doubt*), he or she was cast in a different or even contradictory role. As the previous chapters demonstrated, this was to some extent a necessity: as an independent producer making relatively few films, he could not provide his actors and actresses with a regular supply of standardized roles as was the case at large studios producing up to fifty titles per year. At the same time, however, Selznick could build up a discourse around his stars based on versatility and superb mastery of the acting craft. Jennifer Jones, Ingrid Bergman, Gregory Peck, Dorothy McGuire, and Joseph Cotten were presented as remarkably competent performers, capable of portraying a wide range of characters—from virtuous heroes and saints to villains and scoundrels. If in the case of Betty Grable (as with John Wayne, Mickey Rooney, Rita Hayworth, and many others) the fictional characters could have been viewed as extensions of her public persona (perceived by most of the viewers as her true self), with Selznick's actors and actresses, they remained exclusively effects of their performances. With the use of Barry King's useful distinction, one could argue that for Selznick's stars the practice of impersonation, when the identity of the actor or actress dissolves into the fictional character, was the standard. In contrast, and in accordance with widespread Hollywood norms of the time, Betty Grable represented the mode of personification, as her physiognomy, previous roles, and public appearances infiltrated her characters and vice versa. This "personal monopoly" was supposed to lead toward improved success in the market as it emphasized the individual's distinct qualities, which were not shared with anyone else.[16] In order for Selznick to compensate for this seeming deficit, he emphasized the remarkable talent and acting skills of his stars, enabling them to achieve impressive results when embodying a variety of characters: Ingrid Bergman was accepted—and widely celebrated— both as a loose woman in *Dr. Jekyll and Mr. Hyde* and as a Mother Superior in *The Bells of St. Mary's*; Gregory Peck was equally convincing as a traumatized man suffering from memory loss in *Spellbound* and as the sexually predatory Lewt in *Duel in the Sun*.[17]

This casting strategy depending on versatility and professionalism finally also led to numerous awards: all the important members of Selznick's star stable, except for Shirley Temple and Joseph Cotten, received at least one Oscar nomination between 1940 and 1948, and Vivien Leigh, Joan Fontaine, Jennifer Jones, and Ingrid Bergman all became Academy Award winners. The press praised them and celebrated their abilities, which distinguished them from other (or most) Hollywood stars. Bergman, after her performance in Paramount's *For Whom the Bell Tolls*, was referred to as "the first lady of Hollywood,"[18] as she "has greater versatility than any actress on the American screen. [. . .] Her roles have demanded an adaptability and a sensitiveness of characterization to which few actresses could rise."[19] Betty Grable, in contrast, did not receive any similar honors and in lieu of warm reception from the critics or the recognition from her peers she could "only" rely on the support of the crowds.[20] Adrienne L. McLean stated aptly that "she was a musical star who could not sing or dance well and whose acting was average,"[21] and even Grable herself had a quite sober view of her skills, as is testified to by the following statement for *Screen Guide* magazine: "I don't sing too well. I don't

Gregory Peck and Jennifer Jones in a publicity still for *Duel in the Sun*.

dance too well. I don't act too well. It's on the combination of doing all three just passably that I get by."[22]

When recruiting new actors and actresses, Selznick was interested in exceptionally talented and experienced professionals. He mostly discovered them in theater after they had had some success on Broadway (Joseph Cotten, Gregory Peck, Dorothy McGuire), or abroad, where the tried and tested talent scouts Kay Brown and Jenia Reissar would recommend actors and actresses from various local film industries (Ingrid Bergman, Vivien Leigh, or, in the later period, Alida Valli and Louis Jourdan). Only rarely did he consider complete newcomers without basic acting training. A connection with theater was of particular importance as this respected form of cultural production (at least in comparison with popular cinema) once again enhanced the prestige which Selznick's actors and actresses were supposed to be surrounded by. The producer therefore supported the theater activities of his stars even after the signing of a contract and their arrival in Hollywood (for example, he encouraged the activities of the La Jolla Playhouse established by Gregory Peck, Dorothy McGuire, and Mel Ferrer) and he himself (with the assistance of John Houseman) developed in the early 1940s cooperation with the Lobero Theatre in Santa Barbara, which functioned as a training ground or acting laboratory where Alan Marshal, Ingrid Bergman, and Jennifer Jones could refine their skills with immediate feedback from the audience.[23] In short, theatrical activities were encouraged as long as they did not interfere with film assignments and other duties.

Selznick's actors and actresses derived most of their performance techniques from legitimate theater though some measure of adaptation to the requirements of the film medium was of course necessary. The same style, standardized with the coming of sound in the late 1920s and early 1930s, was preferred by the producer when it came to other professionals hired for leading and supporting roles in his films such as *Rebecca* (Laurence Olivier, Judith Anderson) and *Since You Went Away* (Monty Woolley, Lionel Barrymore, Agnes Moorehead). According to David Sterritt, an actor working in this mode "was expected to put on a fetching show—to look appealing, speak fluently, and move stylishly— even when playing a reprehensible villain or a family drunk."[24] Selznick viewed acting as a skill based on flawless mastering of facial expressions, gestures, movements, and voice—that is, those tools that, along with the techniques of the film medium, contributed to the construction of the character. Members of his acting stable had at their disposal experienced coaches and advisors who were available to help them overcome all challenges and obstacles related to specific roles. The result still involved a certain level of ostentatiousness as the star performance tended to usurp the viewers' attention; it wasn't meant to obscure the fact that the film is indeed a spectacle mounted for the pleasure of the audience.[25] In this way, the style differed from the Method (or method acting), Lee Strasberg's interpretation (or, according to some, distortion)[26] of Stanislavski's teachings, which spread to Hollywood in the late 1940s and early 1950s and whose goal and effect was very often an illusion of spontaneity and a tight emotional and psychological fit or merger between the performer and the fictional character.[27]

As trained professionals, chosen for their roles not only on the basis of their appearance and personality but also specifically due to their acting talent and ability, they did not require the gradual buildup—from minor walk-on parts to supporting roles to leading roles—that usually took place at large studios, which would test, one step at a time, the reaction of the public so as not to risk the fate of a costly film.[28] Selznick paid increased attention to acting and personality tests and internal evaluations, which preceded each signing of a contract. Once an individual was hired, however, he treated him or her as a major star who could not play anything but a leading role. This was the case with the film debut of Dorothy McGuire in the title role in *Claudia*; with Joan Fontaine, who, despite her reputation as a not particularly talented actress (as a result of several lackluster years at RKO), was cast in the demanding lead role in *Rebecca*; Ingrid Bergman, who was presented to the US public in the main female role in *Intermezzo: A Love Story*; Jennifer Jones, who was loaned out for the title role in Fox's *The Song of Bernadette*; and Vivien Leigh who won over hundreds of competitors and obtained the much sought-out role of Scarlett O'Hara in *Gone with the Wind*. These bets on actors and actresses mostly unknown to the US public—who, however, had already amassed precious experiences in theater or in foreign productions—allowed Selznick to build up an aura of an unerring filmmaker with a unique, almost magical sense for discovering talent.

A comparison with Betty Grable is once again illustrative. The actress had been working in Hollywood since the beginning of the 1930s. She had started as a chorus girl for Fox Film Corporation and Samuel Goldwyn during the boom of sound film. After the audience interest in musical revues declined, she signed a contract with RKO, which cast her in episode and supporting roles in films of various genres. Only with her employment with Twentieth Century-Fox (after a short tenure with Paramount) was she promoted to leading roles. Fox's executives experimented with various genres (the film noir [in contemporary jargon, murder melodrama] *I Wake Up Screaming*, the romantic war drama *A Yank in the R.A.F.* [both 1941]), until they realized that Betty Grable was most suitable for backstage musicals with a romantic plot. As soon as they found a successful formula, they stuck to it, introducing only a minimum of variation. Grable finally achieved stardom after ten years in the film industry and more than fifty roles (including short films). It would be difficult to identify one specific title which definitively made her into a star: it was instead a cumulative result of a long process, in which luck also played a role (one of her early successes with Fox—and a stimulus for the development of Grable's career—was the musical *Down Argentine Way* [1940], in which she replaced Alice Faye, who became ill).[29] She achieved her height of popularity during the war, when she became a favorite with soldiers and those who supported the struggle against the enemy in factories and on the home front. Fox did not feel it necessary to combine her with other top stars from their stable—her partners were, for example, John Payne or Victor Mature, competent actors to be sure who nonetheless never achieved the level of popularity of, say, Tyrone Power, who only appeared alongside Grable a single time, in 1941. As Thomas Schatz recorded, it was only and exclusively Grable who was expected to be the draw for films like *Song of the Islands, Springtime in the Rockies* (both 1942), *Coney Island, Sweet Rosie O'Grady* (both 1943), *Pin Up Girl* (1944), and *Diamond Horseshoe* (1945).[30] Fox also did not feel the need to link her with the leading directors at their disposal,[31] instead entrusting these straightforward genre films to reliable craftsmen such as Walter Lang (six films), Irving Cummings (four films), and H. Bruce Humberstone (two films).

IN THE TRADITION OF QUALITY AND PRESTIGE 203

David O. Selznick, in contrast, was a firm believer in what we can call star accumulation or—using an anachronistic term—star synergy. He was extremely attentive to ensuring that his actors and actresses were surrounded by additional popular and respected figures, even though it often involved complicated negotiations and significant financial costs. A remarkable accumulation of star personalities can be seen, for example, in *Gone with the Wind* (Clark Gable, Vivien Leigh, Olivia de Havilland, Leslie Howard, Thomas Mitchell, Hattie McDaniel, and many others), *Rebecca* (Laurence Olivier, Joan Fontaine, George Sanders, Judith Anderson, C. Aubrey Smith, Leo G. Carroll), *Since You Went Away* (Claudette Colbert, Jennifer Jones, Shirley Temple, Joseph Cotten, Robert Walker, Monty Woolley, Lionel Barrymore, Hattie McDaniel, Agnes Moorehead, Alla Nazimova), *Duel in the Sun* (Jennifer Jones, Joseph Cotten, Gregory Peck, Lionel Barrymore, Herbert Marshall, Lillian Gish, Walter Huston, Charles Bickford, Harry Carey) and *The Paradine Case* (Gregory Peck, Ann Todd, Charles Laughton, Charles Coburn, Ethel Barrymore, Louis Jourdan, Alida Valli, Leo G. Carroll). He also paid great care to the selection of key members of the crew: directors, cameramen, costume designers, make-up artists, etc. The same criteria of excellence were required for his stars' loan-outs: the contract often guaranteed approval rights for the male or female costars as well as directors, scriptwriters, cameramen, etc. The members of Selznick's star stable were, in other words, supposed to be associated only with leading professionals and masters of their crafts; cooperation with Ingrid Bergman, Jennifer Jones, or Joseph Cotten was a privilege, available only to the best.

Selznick ranked among those producers who were greatly involved in the creative process. He closely supervised the writing of the screenplays[32] as well as the actual filming and was not hesitant to replace a director or cameraman if he was not fully satisfied with their work. He also supervised the editing process and ordered retakes if necessary. All of this allowed him to effectively shape the images of his contract actors and actresses on the screen. Additionally, he extended his influence on films which came about outside his own production company. In a series of loan-outs, he persistently pushed for influence over the script, costume design, and the visual presentation at the level of camera and lighting, often disregarding that this could result in making enemies and damaging friendly working relations. What many perceived as undesirable meddling was viewed by Selznick as essential protection of his stars. When he, for example, provided Ingrid Bergman to Paramount for *For Whom the Bell Tolls*, he commented on the choice of her costumes, her make-up (eyebrows, eyelashes, lipstick), her hairstyle, and the work of the director Sam Wood and the director of photography Ray Rennahan.[33] With the same intensity, he monitored Bergman's screen tests and the final cut of the film.

No detail was too small for his interest, everything required the same level of attention. This possessive, often confrontational approach was for Selznick the only possible way of ensuring the highest standard for outside productions and thereby protecting his own brand and the reputation of his stars.

Stars are not, however, only formed by fictional characters on the screen. Equally important is the supervision of their presentation in advertising and publicity. Amongst other things, Selznick made sure that his actors and actresses had a suitable billing on posters or in advertisements in the press, which would correspond to their importance. Further, he categorically rejected cheesecake photographs of the pinup type (widespread during the war), which would present his female stars as sexual objects. It was inconceivable that Vivien Leigh, Joan Fontaine, Ingrid Bergman, Shirley Temple, or Dorothy McGuire would appear in revealing dresses or in swimsuits in positions showing off their legs, chest, or other body parts.[34] Instead, portrait pictures were preferred which would accent their natural beauty, casualness, immediacy, as opposed to exaggerated luxury, exoticism, or seductiveness—in other words those attributes associated with traditional conceptions of Hollywood glamour.

This was also why Selznick had such a critical attitude to their being linked with commercial goods. Participation in tie-ins for cosmetic products, fashion brands, or cigarettes, quite common in Hollywood as it generated additional income, was out of the question for his stars, as this would once again undermine their image as respected performers. His stars were, in other words, not supposed to become icons of consumption. Paul Macnamara, one-time head of Selznick's PR department, recalled in his memoirs that Jennifer Jones was only supposed to wear clothes and accessories from her own wardrobe during photography shoots for magazines, as opposed to items provided by fashion houses (even leading ones) as they would have made her into a mere model or figurine.[35]

Finally, Selznick also sought to minimize the gossip discourse, which could be harmful considering his plans for his stars. He thereby often ignored the industry maxim according to which even negative publicity is better than no publicity. It was quite impossible to get by in Hollywood of the 1940s without the cooperation of influential columnists such as Hedda Hopper, writing for the *Los Angeles Times*, and Louella Parsons, whose articles for the *San Francisco Chronicle* were syndicated by dozens of papers throughout the country and abroad. Selznick's PR department, however, carefully controlled what kind of information was released, coordinated interviews with the press and the radio, and generally took great care that the presentation of all actors and actresses under contract would be tasteful and emphasize their professional achievements as opposed to their private lives: Jennifer Jones was supposed to be known to the public as a remarkably talented actress, not as a cook

IN THE TRADITION OF QUALITY AND PRESTIGE 205

or housewife; Joseph Cotten was supposed to have the reputation of being a talented actor, not a sought-out lover, etc. For these reasons, Selznick's studio preferred communicating with the public by means of magazines such as *Life* and *Look*, which had high standards for its texts and photographs, as opposed to tabloids or fan magazines such as *Photoplay, Screenland,* and *Modern Screen.* That doesn't mean that cooperation with these magazines was impossible, but if there was a choice, more highbrow periodicals were preferred. This once again indicates that his stars were supposed to be constructed as admired artists, not celebrities defined by love affairs, scandals, and various excesses which took place off-screen. The only exception was Shirley Temple, who as a former child star met with enormous public attention and whose engagement, marriage, and divorce as well as the birth of her daughter were covered thoroughly by all kinds of media outlets. Temple's popularity was based upon her intimate relationship with her fans, and Selznick's studio thereby worked as effectively as possible to coordinate her contact with the public instead of interrupting it.

If we take a final look at the comparison with Grable, essential differences will once again be apparent. Although the actress was not associated with any serious scandals, the press closely covered her personal life including her divorce from the former child star Jackie Coogan (in 1939) and her marriage (four years later) with Harry James, the frontman of a popular big band. The public manifested enormous interest in her privacy and this unmitigated demand was met with numerous articles in fan magazines and other periodicals dealing with Hollywood stars. The photographs which made Grable during the war into "The Queen of the Pinup Girls" were also widely circulated.[36] The pictures emphasized (and thereby fragmented and commodified) her body: her attractive face, platinum-blond hair, and in particular her "million-dollar legs,"[37] which were exhibited for (men's) admiration thanks to carefully selected clothes (short skirts, swimsuits, etc.). One photograph of the actress—the famous picture where she poses in a one-piece swimsuit and looks seductively over her shoulder—became so popular that it even led to a film entitled *Pin Up Girl.* These static photographs,[38] which were owned in large numbers by US soldiers to remind them about "what they were fighting for," most likely contributed to Grable's iconic status more than her numerous film roles. The actress became the (male) ideal of US femininity in the 1940s, as she combined beauty and eroticism with values of patriotism and homeland, thereby providing an image which was, in the words of Adrienne L. McLean, "at once easily obtainable and impossibly perfect."[39]

Just as Grable, with her appearance, personality type, and acting, dancing, and singing skills (although sometimes called into doubt), perfectly fitted in with the optimistic, patriotic musicals of Twentieth Century-Fox, Gregory Peck, Joseph Cotten, Ingrid Bergman, Joan Fontaine, Vivien Leigh, Dorothy

Betty Grable in a series of pin-up photographs.

McGuire, and Jennifer Jones became ideal members of Selznick's acting stable, which was based on the concepts of prestige, dignity and professionalism. Grable would have undoubtedly been unable to succeed as a serious, respected actress in films like *Rebecca* and *The Song of Bernadette*, but equally absurd and improbable is the notion of Ingrid Bergman playing leading parts in films such as *Springtime in the Rockies* and *Pin Up Girl*. Selznick's actors and actresses became bearers of those values which the producer perceived as desirable: they were selected in a sophisticated process and their careers were managed, after signing their contracts, with this single goal in mind.

Bergman, Jones, Fontaine, Leigh, Peck, and Cotten rank among the legends of the Hollywood studio era. Thanks to their competent and often masterful performances and charisma they come across as autonomous individuals who act out on the screen that which they have a natural talent for: embodying fictional characters and thereby providing us with entertainment, emotional experience, or space for identification. However, as I've tried to demonstrate in this book, someone else was responsible for their success: David O. Selznick devised such mechanisms which transformed unknown or little-known individuals into popular and admired personalities. Therefore, we should not forget that he was not only a producer of legendary films, but also of permanently popular star identities. As his former colleague and successful talent agent Henry Willson stated: "Selznick was a starmaker, perhaps the last of that breed."[40]

APPENDIX:
SELZNICK'S STAR STABLE IN NUMBERS

The following tables provide an overview of the roles of Selznick's most prominent stars during the period they were under long-term contract with his studio. Included are both Selznick's own productions and loan-outs to other companies. Films made outside of the collaboration with Selznick are generally not listed. Among the awards tracked are the Academy Awards (AA), Golden Globes (GG), National Board of Review Awards (NBR), and the New York Film Critics Circle Awards (NYFCC). Box-office figures are taken from accounting reports available in archives or reproduced in trade publications, or from annual rankings published in *Variety*. Unless stated otherwise, they are worldwide theatrical rentals. For some titles, a reliable figure could not be ascertained.

INGRID BERGMAN (ACTIVE UNDER SELZNICK 1939–46)

Title	Year of Release	Production Studio	Director	Costar(s)	Awards	Box-office in million $
Intermezzo: A Love Story	1939	Selznick International	Gregory Ratoff	Leslie Howard	-	1.0
Adam Had Four Sons	1941	Columbia	Gregory Ratoff	Warner Baxter	-	-
Rage in Heaven	1941	MGM	W. S. Van Dyke	Robert Montgomery	NBR	-
Dr. Jekyll and Mr. Hyde	1941	MGM	Victor Fleming	Spencer Tracy	-	2.35
Casablanca	1943	Warner Bros.	Michael Curtiz	Humphrey Bogart, Paul Henreid	-	6.9
For Whom the Bell Tolls	1943	Paramount	Sam Wood	Gary Cooper	AA nomination	7.1 (only US)
Gaslight	1944	MGM	George Cukor	Charles Boyer, Joseph Cotten	AA, GG, NBR, NYFCC nomination	4.6
The Bells of St. Mary's	1945	Rainbow Productions	Leo McCarey	Bing Crosby	GG, NYFCC, AA nomination	11.15
Spellbound	1945	David O. Selznick Productions	Alfred Hitchcock	Gregory Peck	NYFCC	5.0 (only US)
Saratoga Trunk	1945	Warner Bros.	Sam Wood	Gary Cooper	-	7.8
Notorious	1946	RKO	Alfred Hitchcock	Cary Grant	-	7.1

JOSEPH COTTEN (1943–50)

Title	Year of Release	Studio	Director	Costar(s)	Awards	Box-office in million $
Shadow of a Doubt	1943	Universal	Alfred Hitchcock	Teresa Wright	-	1.2 (only US)
Hers to Hold	1943	Universal	Frank Ryan	Deanna Durbin	-	1.7 (only US)
Gaslight	1944	MGM	George Cukor	Ingrid Bergman	-	4.6
Since You Went Away	1944	David O. Selznick Productions	John Cromwell	Claudette Colbert, Jennifer Jones	-	over 7.0
I'll Be Seeing You	1944	Vanguard Films	William Dieterle	Ginger Rogers, Shirley Temple	-	over 6.0
Love Letters	1945	Paramount	William Dieterle	Jennifer Jones	-	3.2 (only US)
Duel in the Sun	1946	David O. Selznick Productions	King Vidor	Jennifer Jones, Gregory Peck	-	11.3 (only US)
The Farmer's Daughter	1947	RKO	H. C. Potter	Loretta Young	-	4.3
Portrait of Jennie	1948	David O. Selznick Productions	William Dieterle	Jennifer Jones	-	1.5 (only US)
Under Capricorn	1949	Transatlantic Pictures	Alfred Hitchcock	Ingrid Bergman	-	2.7
Beyond the Forest	1949	Warner Bros.	King Vidor	Bette Davis	-	1.7
The Third Man	1949	London Film Productions	Carol Reed	Alida Valli	-	2.0 (only US)
Walk Softly, Stranger	1950	RKO	Robert Stevenson	Alida Valli	-	1.4
September Affair	1950	Paramount	William Dieterle	Joan Fontaine	-	1.4 (only US)

JOAN FONTAINE (1940–46)

Title	Year of Release	Studio	Director	Costar(s)	Awards	Box-office in million $
Rebecca	1940	Selznick International	Alfred Hitchcock	Laurence Olivier	NBR, AA nomination, NYFCC nomination	6.0
Suspicion	1941	RKO	Alfred Hitchcock	Cary Grant	AA, NBR, NYFCC	1.8 (only US)
This Above All	1942	Twentieth Century-Fox	Anatole Litvak	Tyrone Power	-	2.4 (only US)
The Constant Nymph	1943	Warner Bros.	Edmund Goulding	Charles Boyer	AA nomination	3.5
Jane Eyre	1943	Twentieth Century-Fox	Robert Stevenson	Orson Welles	-	1.75
Frenchman's Creek	1944	Paramount	Mitchell Leisen	Arturo de Córdova	-	3.5
The Affairs of Susan	1945	Hal Wallis Productions	William A. Seiter	George Brent	-	-
From This Day Forward	1946	RKO	John Berry	Mark Stevens	-	-

JENNIFER JONES (1943–62)

Title	Year of Release	Studio	Director	Costar(s)	Awards	Box-office in million $
The Song of Bernadette	1943	Twentieth Century-Fox	Henry King	William Eythe, Charles Bickford	AA, GG	4.7 (only US)
Since You Went Away	1944	David O. Selznick Productions	John Cromwell	Joseph Cotten, Robert Walker	AA nomination	over 7.0
Love Letters	1945	Paramount	William Dieterle	Joseph Cotten	AA nomination	3.2 (only US)
Cluny Brown	1946	Twentieth Century-Fox	Ernst Lubitsch	Charles Boyer	-	1.0 (only US)
Duel in the Sun	1946	David O. Selznick Productions	King Vidor	Joseph Cotten, Gregory Peck	AA nomination	11.3 (only US)
Portrait of Jennie	1948	David O. Selznick Productions	William Dieterle	Joseph Cotten	-	1.5 (only US)
We Were Strangers	1949	Horizon Pictures	John Huston	John Garfield	-	-
Madame Bovary	1949	MGM	Vincente Minnelli	Van Heflin, James Mason, Louis Jourdan	-	2.0 (only US)
Gone to Earth (released in the US as *The Wild Heart*)	1950/1952	London Film Productions, Vanguard Films	Michael Powell and Emeric Pressburger	Cyril Cusack, David Farrar	-	-
Carrie	1951	Paramount	William Wyler	Laurence Olivier	-	1.8 (only US)

(*continued*)

JENNIFER JONES (1943–62) (*continues*)

Title	Year of Release	Studio	Director	Costar(s)	Awards	Box-office in million $
Ruby Gentry	1952	Bernhard-Vidor Productions	King Vidor	Charlton Heston	-	1.75
Terminal Station (released in the US as *Indiscretion of an American Wife*)	1953/1954	Produzioni De Sica, Selznick Releasing Organization	Vittorio De Sica	Montgomery Clift	-	-
Beat the Devil	1953	Romulus Films, Santana Pictures	John Huston	Humphrey Bogart	-	-
Love Is a Many-Splendored Thing	1955	Twentieth Century-Fox	Henry King	William Holden	AA nomination, NYFCC nomination	4.0 (only US)
Good Morning, Miss Dove	1955	Twentieth Century-Fox	Henry Koster	Robert Stack	-	-
The Man in the Gray Flannel Suit	1956	Twentieth Century-Fox	Nunnally Johnson	Gregory Peck	-	4.35 (only US)
The Barretts of Wimpole Street	1957	MGM	Sidney Franklin	John Gielgud, Bill Travers	-	1.1
A Farewell to Arms	1957	Twentieth Century-Fox, Selznick Co.	Charles Vidor	Rock Hudson	-	6.9
Tender Is the Night	1962	Twentieth Century-Fox	Henry King	Jason Robards	-	1.25 (only US)

SELZNICK'S STAR STABLE IN NUMBERS

LOUIS JOURDAN (1947–49)

Title	Year of Release	Studio	Director	Costar(s)	Awards	Box-office in million $
The Paradine Case	1947	David O. Selznick Productions	Alfred Hitchcock	Alida Valli	-	2.1
Letter from an Unknown Woman	1948	Rampart Productions	Max Ophüls	Joan Fontaine	-	loss of 0.8
No Minor Vices	1948	Enterprise Productions	Lewis Milestone	Lilli Palmer, Dana Andrews	-	0.64
Madame Bovary	1949	MGM	Vincente Minnelli	Jennifer Jones	-	2.0 (only US)

VIVIEN LEIGH (1939–45)

Title	Year of Release	Studio	Director	Costar(s)	Awards	Box-office in million $
Gone with the Wind	1939	Selznick International	Victor Fleming	Clark Gable, Leslie Howard	AA, NBR, NYFCC	20.0 (as of May 1940), 49.0 (as of 1956)
Waterloo Bridge	1940	MGM	Mervyn LeRoy	Robert Taylor	NBR	2.5

ALAN MARSHAL (1936–44, ONLY FILMS SINCE 1941 ARE LISTED)

Title	Year of Release	Studio	Director	Costar(s)	Awards	Box-office in million $
Tom, Dick and Harry	1941	RKO	Garson Kanin	Ginger Rogers	-	1.6
Lydia	1941	London Film Productions	Julien Duvivier	Merle Oberon	-	-
The White Cliffs of Dover	1944	MGM	Clarence Brown	Irene Dunne	-	6.3
Bride by Mistake	1944	RKO	Richard Wallace	Laraine Day	-	1.8 (only US)

DOROTHY MCGUIRE (1943–47)

Title	Year of Release	Studio	Director	Costar(s)	Awards	Box-office in million $
Claudia	1943	Twentieth Century-Fox	Edmund Goulding	Robert Young	-	2.5 (only US)
A Tree Grows in Brooklyn	1945	Twentieth Century-Fox	Elia Kazan	James Dunn	-	3.0 (only US)
The Enchanted Cottage	1945	RKO	John Cromwell	Robert Young	-	2.8
The Spiral Staircase	1945	RKO	Robert Siodmak	George Brent	-	4.0
Claudia and David	1946	Twentieth Century Fox	Walter Lang	Robert Young	-	1.65 (only US)
Till the End of Time	1946	RKO	Edward Dmytryk	Guy Madison, Robert Mitchum	-	3.2
Gentleman's Agreement	1947	Twentieth Century-Fox	Elia Kazan	Gregory Peck, John Garfield	AA nomination, NYFCC nomination	3.9

Title	Year of Release	Studio	Director	Costar(s)	Awards	Box-office in million $
Days of Glory	1944	RKO, Casey Robinson	Jacques Tourneur	Tamara Toumanova	-	0.8
The Keys of the Kingdom	1944	Twentieth Century-Fox	John M. Stahl	Thomas Mitchell, Vincent Price	AA nomination	2.4 (only US)
The Valley of Decision	1945	MGM	Tay Garnett	Greer Garson	-	8.1
Spellbound	1945	David O. Selznick Productions	Alfred Hitchcock	Ingrid Bergman	-	5.0 (only US)
The Yearling	1946	MGM	Clarence Brown	Jane Wyman	GG, AA nomination	7.6
Duel in the Sun	1946	David O. Selznick Productions	King Vidor	Jennifer Jones, Joseph Cotten	-	11.3 (only US)
The Macomber Affair	1947	Benedict Bogeaus Productions	Zoltan Korda	Joan Bennett	-	1.6 (only US)
Gentleman's Agreement	1947	Twentieth Century-Fox	Elia Kazan	Dorothy McGuire, John Garfield	AA nomination	3.9
The Paradine Case	1947	David O. Selznick Productions	Alfred Hitchcock	Alida Valli, Ann Todd	-	2.1
Yellow Sky	1948	Twentieth Century-Fox	William Wellman	Anne Baxter	-	2.8 (only US)
Twelve O'Clock High	1949	Twentieth Century-Fox	Henry King	Hugh Marlowe	NYFCC, AA nomination	4.3
The Gunfighter	1950	Twentieth Century-Fox	Henry King	Helen Westcott	-	2.8
Only the Valiant	1951	William Cagney Productions	Gordon Douglas	Barbara Payton	-	3.1

SHIRLEY TEMPLE (1944–50)

Title	Year of Release	Studio	Director	Costar(s)	Awards	Box-office in million $
Since You Went Away	1944	David O. Selznick Productions	John Cromwell	Claudette Colbert, Jennifer Jones, Monty Woolley	-	over 7.0
I'll Be Seeing You	1944	Vanguard Films	William Dieterle	Ginger Rogers, Joseph Cotten	-	over 6.0
Kiss and Tell	1945	Columbia	Richard Wallace	Jerome Courtland	-	-
Honeymoon	1947	William Keighley Productions	William Keighley	Guy Madison, Franchot Tone	-	1.8
The Bachelor and the Bobby-Soxer	1947	RKO	Irving Reis	Cary Grant, Myrna Loy	-	5.6
That Hagen Girl	1947	Warner Bros.	Peter Godfrey	Ronald Reagan	-	2.1
Fort Apache	1948	Argosy Pictures	John Ford	John Agar, Henry Fonda, John Wayne	-	4.4
Mr. Belvedere Goes to College	1949	Twentieth Century-Fox	Elliott Nugent	Clifton Webb	-	3.7
Adventure in Baltimore	1949	RKO	Richard Wallace	John Agar, Robert Young	-	loss of 0.8
The Story of Seabiscuit	1949	Warner Bros.	David Butler	Lon McCallister, Barry Fitzgerald	-	-
A Kiss for Corliss	1949	Strand Productions	Richard Wallace	David Niven	-	-

ALIDA VALLI (1947–52)

Title	Year of Release	Studio	Director	Costar(s)	Awards	Box-office in million $
The Paradine Case	1947	David O. Selznick Productions	Alfred Hitchcock	Gregory Peck, Louis Jourdan	-	2.1
The Miracle of the Bells	1948	Jesse L. Lasky Productions	Irving Pichel	Fred MacMurray, Frank Sinatra	-	2.6
The Third Man	1949	London Film Productions	Carol Reed	Joseph Cotten, Orson Welles	-	2.0 (only US)
The White Tower	1950	RKO	Ted Tetzlaff	Glenn Ford	-	2.1
Walk Softly, Stranger	1950	RKO	Robert Stevenson	Joseph Cotten	-	1.4

ARCHIVE COLLECTIONS USED

Bill Douglas Cinema Museum, Exeter (UK)
 Oswald Morris Papers
British Film Institute, London (UK)
 Special Collections
Cinema Archives, Wesleyan University, Middletown (US)
 Ingrid Bergman Collection
Harry Ransom Center, University of Texas at Austin (US)
 The David O. Selznick Collection
Margaret Herrick Library, Academy of Motion Picture Arts and Sciences,
 Los Angeles (US)
  The Core Collection
  Motion Picture Association of America, Production Code
   Administration Records
  Special Collections, Gregory Peck Papers
  Special Collections, Henry King Papers
  Special Collections, Paramount Pictures contract summaries
  Special Collections, William Wyler Papers
Victoria & Albert Museum, London (UK)
 Theatre and Performance Collections, Vivien Leigh Archive
Wisconsin Center for Film and Theater Research, Madison (US)
 United Artists Records

To access articles from the daily press, I have generally used free online platforms such as the Media History Digital Library (http://mediahistoryproject.org/) and the Internet Archive (https://archive.org/), or subscription-based services such as the *New York Times*' TimesMachine (https://timesmachine.nytimes.com/).

NOTES

PROLOGUE: *A STAR IS BORN*
AS THE QUINTESSENTIAL HOLLYWOOD MYTH

1. M. W., "Star-maker Becomes a Star Himself," *Picturegoer*, November 11, 1944, 6.

2. Jib Fowles, *Starstruck: Celebrity Performers and the American Public* (Washington and London: Smithsonian Institution Press, 1992), 257.

3. I adopt the term from Steven Cohan, *Hollywood by Hollywood* (Oxford: Oxford University Press, 2019).

4. The star narrative was also part of the backstage musical *Dancing Lady* (1933, produced by Selznick for MGM), which was set in Broadway theaters.

5. Cited in Rudy Behlmer and Tony Thomas, *Hollywood's Hollywood: The Movies About the Movies* (Secaucus, NJ: Citadel Press, 1975), 81.

6. Memo from David O. Selznick, January 7, 1937, cited in Rudy Behlmer, *Memo from David O. Selznick* (New York: Viking Press, 1972), 109.

7. The letter "O" in the middle of the producer's name stood for Oliver. The nineteen-year-old Selznick, a great admirer of Charles Dickens, chose it in 1921 to give oneself a certain respectability and dignity. For more on this, see Bob Thomas, *Selznick: The Man Who Produced* Gone with the Wind (Beverly Hills: New Millennium Press, 2001), 4–5; and David Thomson, *Showman: The Life of David O. Selznick* (New York: Alfred A. Knopf, 1992), 39.

8. "The Making of *A Star Is Born*, undated," *A Star Is Born*, The Core Collection, Margaret Herrick Library, Academy of Motion Picture Arts and Sciences, Los Angeles (hereinafter MHL).

9. See Cohan, *Hollywood by Hollywood*, 107.

10. Cited in Behlmer, *Memo from David O. Selznick*, 98.

11. In this regard, the creators were inspired by the fates of several Hollywood actors including John Barrymore, John Gilbert, and John Bowers who died during the filming of *A Star Is Born*. See Behlmer and Thomas, *Hollywood's Hollywood*, 81. In *What Price Hollywood?*, it is the formerly successful director Max Carey (Lowell Sherman) whose career is irrevocably destroyed due to excessive consumption of alcohol and who ends up killing himself.

12. For more on this, see Christopher Ames, *Movies About the Movies: Hollywood Reflected* (Lexington: University Press of Kentucky, 1997), 21–51.

224   NOTES

13. Cohan writes about back-studio pictures in general that they "go behind the scenes to demystify production as a condition for remystifying it" (Steven Cohan, "Another Hollywood Picture? *A Star Is Born* (1937) and the Self-Reflexivity of the Backstudio Picture," in *Resetting the Scene: Classical Hollywood Revisited*, eds. Philippa Gates and Katherine Spring [Detroit: Wayne State University Press, 2021], 85).

14. Richard Maltby, *Hollywood Cinema* (Malden, MA: Blackwell Publishing, 2003), 151.

15. The acceptance of the story by the audiences was simplified by the fact that the role of the newly born star Esther was played by Janet Gaynor, a very capable actress (Oscar recipient from 1929) for whom the film represented a return to form (and fame) after several lean years.

INTRODUCTION

1. Marcella Rabwin, *Yes, Mr. Selznick: Recollections of Hollywood's Golden Era* (Pittsburgh: Dorrance Publishing, 1999), 157.

2. Cited in Behlmer, *Memo from David O. Selznick*, xiii.

3. A list drawn up by David O. Selznick from August 25, 1962, Tests 1948–1953, b. 2298, f. 1, The David O. Selznick Collection, Harry Ransom Center, University of Texas at Austin, Texas (hereinafter HRC).

4. Thomson, *Showman*.

5. Ronald Haver, *David O. Selznick's Hollywood* (New York: Random House, 1980).

6. Thomas Schatz, *The Genius of the System: Hollywood Filmmaking in the Studio Era* (New York: Pantheon Books, 1988).

7. Leonard J. Leff, *Hitchcock & Selznick: The Rich and Strange Collaboration of Alfred Hitchcock and David O. Selznick in Hollywood* (New York: Weidenfeld & Nicolson, 1987).

8. Behlmer, *Memo from David O. Selznick*.

9. Nathan Platte, *Making Music in Selznick's Hollywood* (Oxford: Oxford University Press, 2018).

10. Ronald Bowers, *The Selznick Players* (South Brunswick and New York: A. S. Barnes and Company, 1976).

11. Leonard J. Leff, "Star Struck: Guy Madison and David Selznick in Postwar Hollywood," *Film History* 23, no. 4 (2011): 376–85.

12. Stephen Gundle, "Alida Valli in Hollywood: From Star of Fascist Cinema to 'Selznick Siren,'" *Historical Journal of Film, Radio and Television* 32, no. 4 (2012): 559–87.

13. David Smit, "Marketing Ingrid Bergman," *Quarterly Review of Film and Video* 22, no. 3 (2005): 237–50; David Smit, *Ingrid Bergman: The Life, Career and Public Image* (Jefferson, NC, and London: McFarland & Company, 2012).

14. Gaylyn Studlar, *Precocious Charms: Stars Performing Girlhood in Classical Hollywood Cinema* (Berkeley, Los Angeles, and London: University of California Press, 2013), 51–89, 159–201.

15. Letter from Ernest L. Scanlon, October 18, 1941, b. 20, f. 4, United Artists Records 5A, Wisconsin Center for Film and Theater Research, Madison.

16. The contracts with Martha MacVicar and Gene Kelly were sold soon after to Universal and MGM. These transactions represented another form of revenue.

NOTES

17. In this section I make considerable use of Haver, *David O. Selznick's Hollywood*; and Behlmer, *Memo from David O. Selznick*.

18. The oldest brother, Howard, suffered from mental illness and was not involved in the film industry.

19. See Haver, *David O. Selznick's Hollywood*, 60–62.

20. Beginning in the early 1930s, Whitney was involved in the company Pioneer Pictures, which was established with the aim of introducing the new Technicolor process on the market. This role was in the mid-1930s taken over by Selznick's firm, whose films were usually made in color.

21. Cited in Alan Vertrees, *Selznick's Vision: Gone with the Wind and Hollywood Filmmaking* (Austin: University of Texas Press, 1997), 9.

22. Cited in Haver, *David O. Selznick's Hollywood*, 171.

23. Behlmer, *Memo from David O. Selznick*, xv.

24. Emily Carman, "Going Independent in 1930s Hollywood: Freelance Star and Independent Producer Collaborations at United Artists," in *United Artists*, eds. Peter Krämer, Gary Needham, Yannis Tzioumakis, and Tino Balio (London and New York: Routledge, 2020), 60.

25. On Selznick's intentions to develop his own stars, see, for example, the article by Susan Myrick, "David O. Selznick Eager to Discover Talent," *Atlanta Journal*, December 15, 1939, 56–57.

26. Between December 1939 and May 1940, *Gone with the Wind* grossed $20 million and became, by far, the highest-grossing film of all time. Most of the profits, however, went to MGM, which received the distribution rights in exchange for the services of Clark Gable and part of the $4 million budget.

27. Selznick still profited a great deal from these deals: for a package containing the rights to the literary original, the screenplay, part of the cast, and in certain cases the director, he received a share of the profits, which usually amounted to hundreds of thousands of dollars. On Schary's involvement with Vanguard and his departure for RKO, see Thomas Schatz, *Boom and Bust: The American Cinema in the 1940s* (New York: Charles Scribner's Sons, 1997), 189–91.

28. Schatz, *The Genius of the System*, 405.

29. Thomas F. Brady, "Selznick Closing Selling Outlets; Releasing Organization Shutting 'Most Branch Offices in U.S.'—New Policy to Be Set," *New York Times*, January 27, 1949, 19.

30. See Lloyd Shearer, "The Man Who Makes Hollywood Tremble," *Ottawa Citizen: Weekend Magazine*, February 1, 1958, 51–54. The two-hour program *Light's Diamond Jubilee*, prepared on the seventy-fifth anniversary of the invention of the light bulb, ranked among the producer's isolated postwar triumphs and was run on all four television channels of the day in October 1954. On this, see Christopher Anderson, "David O. Selznick and the Making of *Light's Diamond Jubilee*," in *Hollywood TV: The Studio System in the Fifties* (Austin: University of Texas Press, 1994), 101–32.

31. On this see, for example, Haver, *David O. Selznick's Hollywood*, 353.

32. On this see Labor, "Star Costs Bar Cheaper Pix," *The Film Daily*, March 8, 1948, 1.

33. The overblown, kitschy *Duel in the Sun* met with extremely negative responses and Selznick had to face for the first time in his career accusations of lack of taste, cheapness and amorality.

34. After *A Farewell to Arms*, Selznick worked on an adaptation of F. Scott Fitzgerald's novel *Tender Is the Night*, but the project was completed by Twentieth Century-Fox under the supervision of Henry T. Weinstein.

35. Preface by Thomas Schatz in a book by Alan Vertrees *Selznick's Vision*, xiii.

36. Paul McDonald, *Hollywood Stardom* (Malden, MA: Wiley-Blackwell, 2013), 2. See also his other books on the topic: *The Star System: Hollywood's Production of Popular Identities* (London: Wallflower, 2000) and *George Clooney* (London: Bloomsbury, British Film Institute, 2019).

37. For more on my position on this, see Milan Hain, "From Stars to Starmakers: Spotlighting the Producers of Popular Screen Identities," *Slovenské divadlo* 69, no. 3 (2021): 307–21.

38. Emily Carman, *Independent Stardom: Freelance Women in the Hollywood Studio System* (Austin: University of Texas Press, 2016), 4–5. This may no longer be true. According to the USC's website, the Warner Bros. archive is "closed until further notice." See Warner Bros. Archive Collection Overview, *University of Southern California*, https://cinema.usc.edu /about/warnerbrosarchives.cfm.

39. See Jeanine Basinger, *The Star Machine* (New York: Alfred A. Knopf, 2007), 126.

40. For an overview of the discipline, see Martin Shingler, *Star Studies: A Critical Guide* (London: Palgrave Macmillan, 2012), 14–23. For different takes on the same, see Paul McDonald, "Star Studies," in Joanne Hollows and Mark Jancovich, eds., *Approaches to Popular Film* (Manchester and New York: Manchester University Press, 1995), 79–97; and Paul McDonald, "Reconceptualising Stardom" (supplementary chapter), in Richard Dyer, *Stars* (London: British Film Institute, 1998), 175–200.

41. James Chapman, Mark Glancy and Sue Harper refer to *agency* and *process* as "buzzwords" of the so-called new film history, which in their view is marked by a higher level of methodological sophistication (in comparison with earlier approaches to film history), significant use of primary sources and an understanding of films as specific cultural artefacts. All these tenets inform my present research. See James Chapman, Mark Glancy, and Sue Harper, "Introduction," in James Chapman, Mark Glancy and Sue Harper, eds., *The New Film History: Sources, Methods, Approaches* (Basingstoke and New York: Palgrave Macmillan, 2009), 6–8. The concept of agency is the main element in the theory of structuration by the British sociologist Anthony Giddens, see Anthony Giddens, *The Constitution of Society: Outline of the Theory of Structuration* (Cambridge: Polity Press, 1984). An empirical, historically grounded model of research has been frequently employed in recent years in relation to film authorship, see, for example, Sarah Kozloff, *The Life of the Author* (Montreal: caboose, 2014); C. P. Sellors, *Film Authorship: Auteurs and Other Myths* (New York: Wallflower Press, 2010).

42. I have taken the concepts of economic and symbolic capital from Pierre Bourdieu. Economic capital consists of financial resources and material property while symbolic capital exists in the form of recognition or acknowledgement and is therefore dependent on social valorization. See, for example, the collection of Bourdieu's essays on arts gathered by Randal Johnson and available as Pierre Bourdieu, *The Field of Cultural Production: Essays on Art and Literature* (New York: Columbia University Press, 1993). Bourdieu's concepts are also used by Paul McDonald, see his *Hollywood Stardom*, 215–24.

43. Leo C. Rosten wrote as early as the beginning of the 1940s, that there is "little distinction between Hollywood's social and professional life." Leo C. Rosten, *Hollywood: The Movie Colony, the Movie Makers* (New York: Harcourt, Brace and Company, 1941), 181. The idea

NOTES

of Hollywood as a "business world embedded within a social network (and vice versa)" is developed by Tom Kemper in his excellent study of Hollywood talent agents active from the 1920s to the 1940s (this also included Selznick's brother Myron): Tom Kemper, *Hidden Talent: The Emergence of Hollywood Agents* (Berkeley, Los Angeles, and London: University of California Press, 2010), ix.

44. A number of cases exist when the public failed to accept a star identity developed and widely advertised with major financial expenses. For example, Samuel Goldwyn was unable, despite great effort, to make a star of the Ukrainian native Anna Sten in the mid-1930s.

45. See McDonald, *Hollywood Stardom*, 16.

46. Ingrid Bergman and Alan Burgess, *Ingrid Bergman, My Story* (New York: Delacorte Press, 1980); Joan Fontaine, *No Bed of Roses* (New York: Berkley Books, 1979).

47. For this, see, for example, Thomas Schatz, "'A Triumph of Bitchery': Warner Bros., Bette Davis, and *Jezebel*," in Janet Staiger, ed., *The Studio System* (New Brunswick, NJ: Rutgers University Press, 1995), 74–92; and Ronny Regev, *Working in Hollywood: How the Studio System Turned Creativity into Labor* (Chapel Hill: University of North Carolina Press, 2018).

48. See the report by E. L. Scanlon from November 3, 1947, Ingrid Bergman—Correspondence 1947–1948, b. 536, f. 11, HRC. According to the 1940 census, the average income in the US was $1,368. See Diane Petro, "Brother, Can You Spare a Dime? The 1940 Census: Employment and Income," *Prologue* 44, no. 1 (Spring 2012), https://www.archives.gov/publications/prologue/2012/spring/1940.html.

49. I do not want to trivialize the ethical question of the division of the profits from loan-outs and the revenues from Selznick's films. It is surely an interesting topic for further consideration.

50. Shearer, "Man Who Makes Hollywood Tremble," 52. Several hundred memoranda and telegrams, covering a period of thirty-six years, were published as Behlmer, *Memo from David O. Selznick*.

51. The memo does not, of course, provide a complete picture—not all of the issues had to be necessarily recorded in writing (this concerns, for example, conferences, personal meetings, etc.) and the reactions of the addressee or the other side are often missing. It is therefore necessary to assess them on the basis of additional available materials (other written documents, data from the press, finished films etc.).

52. See Susan Ohmer, *George Gallup in Hollywood* (New York: Columbia University Press, 2006).

53. On certain failures in the Hollywood star factory, see Basinger, *The Star Machine*, 101–26.

54. On this, see Carman, *Independent Stardom*, 34–35.

1. THE CONSTRUCTION OF NATURALNESS:
INGRID BERGMAN AND *INTERMEZZO: A LOVE STORY*

1. Robin Wood, "Star and Auteur: Hitchcock's Films with Bergman," *Hitchcock's Films Revisited* (New York: Columbia University Press, 2002), 312.

2. Ora Gelley, *Stardom and the Aesthetics of Neorealism: Ingrid Bergman in Rossellini's Italy* (New York: Routledge, 2016), 51.

3. For example, Robin Wood, "Star and Auteur," 303–35; Donald Spoto, *Spellbound by Beauty: Alfred Hitchcock and His Leading Ladies* (New York: Harmony Books, 2008); Lesley L.

Coffin, *Hitchcock's Stars: Alfred Hitchcock and the Hollywood Star System* (Lanham, MD: Rowman & Littlefield, 2014).

4. Gelley, *Stardom and the Aesthetics of Neorealism*; Adrienne L. McLean, "The Cinderella Princess and the Instrument of Evil: Revisiting Two Postwar Hollywood Star Scandals," Adrienne L. McLean and David A. Cook, eds., *Headline Hollywood: A Century of Film Scandal* (New Brunswick, NJ: Rutgers University Press, 2001), 163–89; Erik Hedling, "European Echoes of Hollywood Scandal: The Reception of Ingrid Bergman in 1950s Sweden," in McLean and Cook, eds., *Headline Hollywood*, 190–205; Lisabeth During, "Saints, Scandals, and the Politics of Love: Simone Weil, Ingrid Bergman, Roberto Rossellini," *SubStance* 45, no. 3 (2016): 16–32.

5. See, for instance, Charles Affron, *Star Acting: Gish, Garbo, Davis* (New York: E. P. Dutton, 1977); Michaela Krützen, *The Most Beautiful Woman on the Screen: The Fabrication of the Star Greta Garbo* (Frankfurt am Main: Peter Lang GmbH, 1992); Gerd Gemünden and Mary R. Desjardins, eds., *Dietrich Icon* (Durham and London: Duke University Press, 2007); Erica Carter, *Dietrich's Ghosts: The Sublime and the Beautiful in Third Reich Film* (London: British Film Institute, 2007); Gaylyn Studlar, *In the Realm of Pleasure: Von Sternberg, Dietrich, and the Masochistic Aesthetic* (New York: Columbia University Press, 1993); Adrienne L. McLean, *Being Rita Hayworth: Labor, Identity, and Hollywood Stardom* (New Brunswick, NJ, and London: Rutgers University Press, 2004).

6. Kirtley Baskette, "Nordic Natural," *Photoplay* 19, no. 5 (October 1941): 86.

7. Bergman and Burgess, *Ingrid Bergman, My Story*, 66, 68–69.

8. Ethan Mordden, *Movie Star: A Look at the Women Who Made Hollywood* (New York: St. Martin's Press, 1983), 260.

9. Robin Blaetz, "Ingrid Bergman: The Face of Authenticity in the Land of Illusion," in Sean Griffin, ed., *What Dreams Were Made Of: Movie Stars of the 1940s* (New Brunswick, NJ, and London: Rutgers University Press, 2011), 51–52 (emphasis in the original). Blaetz's article attempts, somewhat unconvincingly, to present a parallel between Bergman as an authentic star and her female fans, who by means of their identification with her strengthened their own identity and independence during World War II and beyond.

10. Joseph Garncarz, "Die Schauspielerin wird Star. Ingrid Bergman—eine öffentliche Kunstfigur," in Renate Möhrmann, ed., *Die Schauspielerin—Eine Kulturgeschichte* (Frankfurt am Main: Insel Verlag, 2000), 368–93; Smit, "Marketing Ingrid Bergman"; Smit, *Ingrid Bergman: The Life, Career and Public Image*; James Damico, "Ingrid from Lorraine to Stromboli: Analyzing the Public's Perception of a Film Star," in Jeremy Butler, ed., *Star Texts: Image and Performance in Film and Television* (Detroit: Wayne State University Press, 1991), 240–53.

11. That this type was often associated with stars imported from abroad is corroborated by Richard Dyer who, in *Heavenly Bodies*, states: "the earlier sex goddesses are either foreign (actually or supposedly) and therefore of a sexuality beyond all scrutiny (Theda Bara, Dietrich, Garbo, Anna May Wong), or else they are predatory, like a man (Bow, West, Jean Harlow)." Richard Dyer, *Heavenly Bodies: Film Stars and Society*, 2nd edition (Oxon and New York: Routledge, 2004), 53.

12. Basinger also claims that "they are the women stars that appeal mostly to men. [. . .] These are the women one puts on a pedestal, the unreal astonishing beauties of the silver screen. Men may lust after them, or dream of them in a noble way, and women can wish they had their beauty, and thus their power. They reduce women to objects of desire" (Jeanine

Basinger, *A Woman's View: How Hollywood Spoke to Women, 1930–1960* [Hanover and London: Wesleyan University Press, 1993], 166).

13. Catherine Jurca, *Hollywood 1938: Motion Pictures' Greatest Year* (Berkeley, Los Angeles, and London: University of California Press, 2012), 21.

14. Jurca, *Hollywood 1938*, 109.

15. Jurca, *Hollywood 1938*, 110.

16. I discuss the casting process of *Rebecca* (and the emergence of Joan Fontaine as a star on the strength of this film) in Milan Hain, "Looking for 'I': Casting the Unnamed Heroine in Alfred Hitchcock and David O. Selznick's Adaptation of Rebecca," *Revue LISA/LISA e-journal* 19, no. 52 (2021), https://journals.openedition.org/lisa/13470.

17. Steve Wilson, *The Making of Gone with the Wind* (Austin: University of Texas Press, 2014), 65.

18. Wilson, *The Making of Gone with the Wind*, 65.

19. Behlmer, *Memo from David O. Selznick*, 98.

20. Memo from David O. Selznick, October 23, 1938, Intermezzo Casting, b. 174, f. 11, HRC.

21. Bengt Forslund, "The Melodramas of Gustaf Molander," in Mariah Larsson and Anders Marklund, eds., *Swedish Film: An Introduction and Reader* (Lund: Nordic Academic Press, 2010), 111.

22. The exact sequence of events is unclear. According to Selznick, the film was first seen at Cinèma de Paris by Elsa Neuberger, although David Thomson popularized the version in which the picture was first mentioned to Kay Brown by a Swedish lift boy in the New York seat of the company on Park Avenue. Cf. Behlmer, *Memo from David O. Selznick*, 98; Haver, *David O. Selznick's Hollywood*, 226; Donald Spoto, *Notorious: The Life of Ingrid Bergman* (Cambridge, MA: Da Capo Press, 2001), 55; David Thomson, *Ingrid Bergman* (New York: Faber and Faber, 2009), 2–3.

23. *Variety* wrote that "Miss Bergman's star is destined for Hollywood!" Cited in Daniel Herbert, "The Transnational Film Remake in the American Press," in Iain Robert Smith and Constantine Verevis, eds., *Transnational Film Remakes* (Edinburgh: Edinburgh University Press, 2017), 214. Additional US reviews of the Swedish version of *Intermezzo* are available, for example, in "At the Cinema de Paris," *New York Times*, December 25, 1937, 10; and "Intermezzo," *Film Daily*, December 30, 1937, 8.

24. See memo from David O. Selznick, October 23, 1938, Intermezzo Casting, b. 174, f. 11, HRC.

25. See memo from David O. Selznick, January 9, 1939, and the document "Suggestions for cast—INTERMEZZO," February 4, 1939, Intermezzo Casting, b. 174, f. 11, HRC.

26. Letter from David O. Selznick, July 10, 1943, For Whom the Bell Tolls—Campaign, b. 3336, f. 1, HRC.

27. Spoto, *Notorious*, 54.

28. After her arrival in Hollywood, steps were taken to conceal her involvement with the German film industry to avoid even a hint of suspicion of collaboration with the dubious (and soon openly hostile) regime. I return to the topic when addressing the actress's publicity.

29. Memo from David O. Selznick, January 10, 1939, Intermezzo Casting, b. 174, f. 11, HRC.

30. Contract between Selznick International and Ingrid Bergman from February 14, 1939, Ingrid Bergman Contracts, b. 3337, f. 2, HRC.

230   NOTES

31. The making of the entire film depended to a certain extent on this. Joseph Breen from the Production Code Administration, when evaluating the screenplay, pointed out the issue of the motive of adultery and declared that the acceptability of the material, apart from the indispensable voice of morality, "will depend upon the casting of the three leads." Giving Ingrid Bergman the role of the young adulteress Anita, who threatens the happy marriage of Holger and Margit, and emphasizing her purity, innocence, and spiritual quality, could therefore help overcome the risks in treating such a topic and contribute to the fact that the film was, despite the potentially offensive elements, approved without major difficulties. Letter from Joseph Breen, October 14, 1938, "Intermezzo," Motion Picture Association of America, Production Code Administration Records, MHL. The film's release does not seem to have caused any controversy.

32. Memo from Leslie Howard, May 18, 1939, Intermezzo Casting, b. 174, f. 11, HRC.

33. A handwritten note stating "they are using makeup" was added to the memorandum of Leslie Howard. Undated memo from David O. Selznick, Intermezzo Casting, b. 174, f. 11, HRC (underlined in the original). See also Arne Lunde, *Nordic Exposures: Scandinavian Identities in Classical Hollywood Cinema* (Seattle: University of Washington Press, 2010), 162.

34. As the biographer Donald Spoto writes, Bergman "was very fair-skinned and the bright lights evoked a ruddy gleam that had to be expertly matted with the proper powders" (Spoto, *Notorious*, 74–75).

35. Memo from Gregory Ratoff, June 24, 1939, Intermezzo Wardrobe, b. 177, f. 3, HRC.

36. See, for example, memo from David O. Selznick, October 17, 1939, Intermezzo Production, b. 176, f. 1, HRC.

37. Smit, "Marketing Ingrid Bergman," 240.

38. The candidates included, for example, Rouben Mamoulian, William Dieterle, and Michael Curtiz. The director of the Swedish version Gustaf Molander supposedly also received an official offer but turned it down for personal reasons. See Forslund, *The Melodramas of Gustaf Molander*, 112.

39. When Wyler was asked about the reasons for ending his involvement in *Intermezzo*, he only answered vaguely that he did not recall the exact circumstances. After the completion of the film, he did write (but did not send) a letter addressed to Selznick, in which he referred to the result as "butchery." The sharp tone seems to indicate that he had been extremely upset by the entire situation around his resignation/sacking and that it had hurt his artistic ego. Cf. Jan Herman, *A Talent for Trouble: The Life of Hollywood's Most Acclaimed Director, William Wyler* (New York: Da Capo Press, 1997), 203; unsent letter from William Wyler, November 10, 1939, Intermezzo—general 1939, 17.f-232, William Wyler Papers, Special Collections, MHL.

40. Harry Stradling worked in Hollywood during the 1920s but spent most of the following decade in France where he cooperated, for example, with one of the leading figures of poetic realism, Jacques Feyder. After a short stop in the UK (filming, for example, *Pygmalion* [1938], with Leslie Howard, and Hitchcock's *Jamaica Inn* [1939]) he returned to the US at the beginning of 1939, where *Intermezzo* became his first assignment.

41. Memo from David O. Selznick, June 9, 1939, Intermezzo Casting, b. 174, f. 11, HRC.

42. Toland's innovations concerned in particular depth-of-field and expressive lighting. More on this in Barry Salt, *Film Style & Technology: History & Analysis* (London: Starword, 1992), 232–34; and David Bordwell, "Deep-focus Cinematography," in David Bordwell, Janet

NOTES 231

Staiger, and Kristin Thompson, *The Classical Hollywood Cinema: Film Style & Mode of Production to 1960* (New York: Columbia University Press, 1985), 345–49.

43. Memo from David O. Selznick, June 22, 1939, Intermezzo Cameraman, b. 174, f. 10, HRC.

44. Chris Cagle, "Classical Hollywood, 1928–1946," in Patrick Keating, ed., *Cinematography* (New Brunswick, NJ: Rutgers University Press, 2014), 40. See also Patrick Keating, *Hollywood Lighting from the Silent Era to Film Noir* (New York: Columbia University Press, 2010), 3.

45. Memo from David O. Selznick, June 22, 1939, Intermezzo Cameraman, b. 174, f. 10, HRC.

46. Patrick Keating, "Shooting for Selznick: Craft and Collaboration in Hollywood Cinematography," in Steve Neale, ed., *The Classical Hollywood Reader* (London and New York: Routledge, 2012), 289. See the memo from David O. Selznick, July 28, 1939, Intermezzo Cameraman, b. 174, f. 10, HRC.

47. See memo from David O. Selznick, July 28, 1939, Intermezzo Cameraman, b. 174, f. 10, HRC.

48. Memo from David O. Selznick, July 11, 1939, Intermezzo Cameraman, b. 174, f. 10, HRC.

49. See the budget for *Intermezzo*, December 22, 1939, Intermezzo Daily Budget Reconciliation, b. 175, f. 2, HRC.

50. See memo from David O. Selznick, September 29, 1939, Intermezzo Cameraman, b. 174, f. 10, HRC. Toland did receive the Academy Award for Best Cinematography, Black-and-White, in 1939, but it was for *Wuthering Heights*.

51. Smit, "Marketing Ingrid Bergman," 243.

52. The most marked exception is *En kvinnas ansikte* (*A Woman's Face*, 1938), arguably the finest Swedish film starring Ingrid Bergman, which provided her with the most interesting opportunity in the role of the disfigured leader of a blackmail gang. It was remade in Hollywood by MGM in 1941 as *A Woman's Face*, directed by George Cukor, with Joan Crawford in the main role.

53. See, for example, Ronald L. Davis, *The Glamour Factory: Inside Hollywood's Big Studio System* (Dallas: Southern Methodist University Press, 1993).

54. Joel W. Finler gives the average cost of producing a Hollywood film in 1940 as $400,000. See Joel W. Finler, *The Hollywood Story* (London and New York: Wallflower Press, 2003), 42.

55. Budget for *Intermezzo* from December 22, 1939, Intermezzo Daily Budget Reconciliation, b. 175, f. 2, HRC.

56. See Smit, "Marketing Ingrid Bergman," 242, 245.

57. Memo from David O. Selznick, February 27, 1939, Intermezzo Publicity Cont., b. 176, f. 4, HRC.

58. Memo from David O. Selznick, July 28, 1939, Intermezzo Publicity Cont., b. 176, f. 4, HRC.

59. See the memo from David O. Selznick, February 27, 1939, Intermezzo Publicity Cont., b. 176, f. 4, HRC.

60. The romantic drama *Algiers* (1938) produced by Walter Wanger served as a model for Selznick, as it was by means of this film that Hedy Lamarr (maiden name Hedwig Eva Maria Kiesler), a native of Vienna and the star of Gustav Machatý's *Ecstasy* (1933, Elektafilm), was presented to the US public. See memo from David O. Selznick, February 27, 1939, Intermezzo Publicity Cont., b. 176, f. 4, HRC. *Algiers* also shared other details with *Intermezzo*: it was a remake of a foreign film *Pépé le Moko* (1937) and its effectiveness depended to a great extent

232 NOTES

on the powerful cinematography by James Wong Howe, who received an Oscar nomination for it.

61. Harry Friedman, "Meet New Star from Sweden," *Los Angeles Examiner*, ca. June 1939; the article is part of a collection of excerpts in the Series X Scrapbooks, 1938–1939, 1939–1940, b. 50, Ingrid Bergman Collection, Cinema Archives, Wesleyan University. Selznick's reaction is available in a memorandum from June 12, 1939, Intermezzo Publicity Cont., b. 176, f. 4, HRC.

62. Selznick was convinced that Bergman was too trusting and could be easily manipulated to make an unfortunate comment which would harm her or the film. See memo from David O. Selznick, July 28, 1939, Intermezzo Publicity Cont., b. 176, f. 4, HRC.

63. See the memo from David O. Selznick, July 28, 1939, Intermezzo Publicity Cont., b. 176, f. 5, HRC.

64. *Los Angeles Examiner*, September 21, 1939, the excerpt is part of Intermezzo Publicity Cont., b. 176, f. 4, HRC.

65. See the telegram from David O. Selznick, September 25, 1939, and telegram from Ingrid Bergman, September 29, 1939, Intermezzo Publicity Cont., b. 176, f. 4, HRC.

66. The cooperation between Ingrid Bergman and the Nazi-controlled film industry still evokes questions and speculations. In her memoirs, the actress claims that, immediately after starting her work in Berlin in April 1938 on the picture *The Four Companions*, she noticed "what was happening there." Her political naiveté and lack of interest in anything not directly linked with her profession meant that she persisted in working on the picture directed by Carl Froehlich. She also continued to count on participating in another two projects which she had committed to (one of them was supposed to be a biography of Charlotte Corday, the murderess of the leading figure of the French Revolution Jean-Paul Marat). Only the escalation of events in the summer of 1939 meant that the romantic comedy *The Four Companions* remained the only German language title in the actress's filmography. Cf. Bergman and Burgess, *Ingrid Bergman, My Story*, 51; Smit, *Ingrid Bergman*, 34–35.

67. Pressbook for *Intermezzo: A Love Story*, The Core Collection, MHL.

68. Pressbook for *Intermezzo: A Love Story*.

69. Selznick at one point considered a change in her name due to possible difficulties with its pronunciation and German appearance (the most frequently suggested alternative was "Ingrid Berriman"), only to abandon the plan soon after the actress's arrival in Hollywood. Cf. Memo from David O. Selznick, February 27, 1939, Intermezzo Publicity Cont., b. 176, f. 4, HRC; memo from David O. Selznick, May 26, 1939, Intermezzo Publicity Cont., b. 176, f. 4, HRC.

70. On this, see Spoto, *Notorious*, 66; and Basinger, *The Star Machine*, 50.

71. Cf. Spoto, *Notorious*, 16, 68; and "Natural Beauty of Ingrid Bergman Made Her Way in Hollywood," *Stars Changes*, https://starschanges.com/ingrid-bergman-height-weight-age/.

72. Selznick wanted Bergman to be "glamourous, [but] not in the usual Hollywood way." Memo from David O. Selznick, January 2, 1940, Intermezzo Publicity, b. 176, f. 3, HRC.

73. Margaret Farrand Thorp, *America at the Movies* (New Haven: Yale University Press, 1939), 65.

74. Another consideration could have been that in the previous year Garbo (along with Marlene Dietrich) was referred to as "box-office poison" by the Independent Theatre Owners Association. See Adrienne L. McLean, "Introduction: Stardom in the 1930s," in Adrienne L. McLean, ed., *Glamour in a Golden Age: Movie Stars of the 1930s* (New Brunswick, NJ: Rutgers University Press, 2011), 6.

NOTES

75. See, for example, Alexander Doty, "Marlene Dietrich, and Greta Garbo: The Sexy Hausfrau versus the Swedish Sphinx," in McLean, ed., *Glamour in a Golden Age*, 118. The construction of Garbo's star image is the subject of Michaela Krützen's *The Most Beautiful Woman on the Screen*. Her star identity is also aptly described in Louise Wallenberg, "Greta Garbo," in Alastair Phillips and Ginette Vincendeau, eds., *Journeys of Desire: European Actors in Hollywood* (London: British Film Institute, 2006), 259–61.

76. Memo from David O. Selznick, June 22, 1939, Intermezzo Cameraman, b. 174, f. 10, HRC.

77. Memo from David O. Selznick, June 22, 1939, Intermezzo Publicity Cont., b. 176, f. 4, HRC.

78. See memo from David O. Selznick, June 22, 1939, Intermezzo Publicity Cont., b. 176, f. 4, HRC and other documents in the same file.

79. See memo from David O. Selznick, July 27, 1939, Intermezzo Wardrobe, b. 177, f. 3, HRC.

80. Memo from David O. Selznick, June 22, 1939, Intermezzo Publicity Cont., b. 176, f. 4, HRC.

81. See, for example, memo from David O. Selznick, October 10, 1939, Intermezzo Credit, b. 174, f. 17, HRC. The difference in the status of both performers was indicated by the fact that Howard's name was placed in a privileged position above the film's title.

82. The term "lexicon," referring to the summary of attributes specific for a given star, is used by James Damico in the article "Ingrid from Lorraine to Stromboli," in Butler, ed., *Star Texts*, 247.

83. The child actress Ann Todd, who played the daughter of the Holgers in the film, ended up in third place with eighty-two photographs. The photographs of Edna Best, who played Margit, were requested by only fourteen people. All the data and citations come from an undated report titled "Intermezzo Previews at Pomona and Santa Barbara, California," Intermezzo Preview, b. 175, f. 15, HRC; and from a memo from David O. Selznick, August 23, 1939, Intermezzo Preview, b. 175, f. 15, HRC.

84. Memo from David O. Selznick, August 22, 1939, Intermezzo Preview, b. 175, f. 15, HRC.

85. Telegram from David O. Selznick, October 6, 1939, Intermezzo Preview, b. 175, f. 15, HRC.

86. Telegram from David O. Selznick, October 2, 1939, Intermezzo Publicity Cont., b. 176, f. 5, HRC.

87. See memos from Lowell V. Calvert (head of Selznick's sales and distribution department), October 2 and 5, 1939, Intermezzo Publicity Cont., b. 176, f. 5, HRC.

88. Memo from David O. Selznick, October 2, 1939, Intermezzo Broadcast, b. 174, f. 9, HRC.

89. Frank S. Nugent, "The Screen: Four Films in Review," *New York Times*, October 6, 1939, 31 (emphasis by MH).

90. "Intermezzo—A Love Story," *Variety*, October 4, 1939, 12.

91. See, for example, "Intermezzo—A Love Story," *Variety*.

92. See, for example, Thomas S. Hischak, *1939: Hollywood's Greatest Year* (Lanham, MD: Rowman & Littlefield, 2017). *Intermezzo* competed directly in the cinemas with, among others, the star-studded comedy *The Women* (MGM), the adventure *Beau Geste* (Paramount), the melodrama *The Old Maid* (Warner Bros.), and the musical comedy *Babes in Arms* (MGM). Other popular films premiering in 1939 included the musical fantasy *The Wizard of Oz* (MGM), the Western by John Ford *Stagecoach* (Walter Wanger/United Artists), the populist political drama by Frank Capra *Mr. Smith Goes to Washington* (Columbia), the romantic drama *Goodbye, Mr. Chips* (MGM), the comedy with Greta Garbo *Ninotchka* (MGM), and Selznick's own opus *Gone with the Wind*, which premiered in December.

234 NOTES

93. See, for example, memo from David O. Selznick, October 7, 1939, Intermezzo Publicity Cont., b. 175, b. 5, HRC.

94. In a letter to Ingrid Bergman from October 16, the producer wrote that "the principal purpose of the picture was to introduce you to American and English audiences." See letter from David O. Selznick, October 16, 1939, Intermezzo Comment, b. 174, f. 13, HRC.

95. Unnamed extract from the magazine *Picturegoer*, December 8, 1939, Series X Scrapbooks, 1938–1939, 1939–1940, b. 50, Ingrid Bergman Collection. See also *Picture Reports*, October 4, 1939, 10.

96. Dora Albert, "Bergman Is Back," *Screenland* 40, no. 6 (April 1940), 62.

97. Albert, "Bergman Is Back," 92.

98. Jack Stinnett, "One-Word Sketch of Ingrid Bergman: Different," *New York World Telegram*, January 24, 1940, Series X Scrapbooks, 1938–1939, 1939–1940, b. 50, Ingrid Bergman Collection.

99. Arne Lunde, in his book about the Hollywood conception of Scandinavian identity, writes that "Hollywood markets Bergman's Swedish milkmaid image as a virtual extension of an imagined fresh and unspoiled Nordic homeland, idyllically beautiful in its own 'undecorated state.'" Lunde, *Nordic Exposures*, 162.

100. Stinnett, "One-Word Sketch of Ingrid Bergman."

101. Wood, "Star and Auteur," 312.

102. Harry Evans, "Hollywood Diary," *Family Circle*, November 3, 1939, 10.

103. Evans, "Hollywood Diary," 22.

104. More on this in the following chapter.

105. Smit, "Marketing Ingrid Bergman," 240.

106. *Dr. Jekyll and Mr. Hyde* works in an interesting way with contrasting casting of the female roles. The part of the protagonist's girlfriend Beatrix was played by Lana Turner, promoted by MGM as the "Sweater Girl," whose star image was based on her association with glamour and whose acting was perceived as not very accomplished, both attributes in stark contrast to the qualities surrounding Bergman. I am indebted to the anonymous reviewer for this observation.

107. More on this in Garncarz, "Die Schauspielerin wird Star," 385; Smit, "Marketing Ingrid Bergman," 237–38, 250; Damico, "Ingrid from Lorraine to Stromboli," 248–52.

108. Cited in Damico, "Ingrid from Lorraine to Stromboli," 249.

2. PRODUCING PRESTIGE: LOAN-OUTS OF SELZNICK'S FEMALE STARS IN THE FIRST HALF OF THE 1940S

1. Thomas Wood, "Selznick and His Girls," *Look*, January 25, 1944, 36.

2. Robert Osborne, *85 Years of the Oscar: The Official History of the Academy Awards* (New York and London: Abbeville Press Publishers, 2013), 78.

3. Tom O'Neil, *Movie Awards: The Ultimate, Unofficial Guide to the Oscars, Golden Globes, Critics, Guild, & Indie Honors*, revised and updated edition (New York: Berkley Publishing Group, 2003), 89.

4. That same year, Ingrid Bergman also played the main female role in *Casablanca*, which received eight Oscar nominations and eventually brought Warner Bros. the award for the Best Picture.

NOTES   235

5. Two of them are reproduced in Edward Z. Epstein, *Portrait of Jennifer: A Biography of Jennifer Jones* (New York: Simon & Schuster, 1995).

6. See, for example, Thomson, *Showman*, 410.

7. See O'Neil, *Movie Awards*, 89. The story of the Oscar evening from the perspective of Jennifer Jones is described in Epstein, *Portrait of Jennifer*, 9–15.

8. Somewhere in between can be situated film packages, consisting most often of rights to literary or theatrical material, screenplay in a certain state of development and the services of Selznick's contract actors, actresses and/or directors. Selznick would usually begin to develop the material inside his company, only to decide to sell it to another studio due to time, finances, or other reasons. An example would be *Claudia*, discussed below.

9. More on the development of male stars in the following chapter.

10. Wood, "Selznick and His Girls," 36.

11. On Ingrid Bergman in *Intermezzo*, see the previous chapter.

12. The only exception was Vivien Leigh, who after being loaned out for *Waterloo Bridge* (1940, MGM) and starring in the historical romance *That Hamilton Woman* (1941) produced by Alexander Korda, preferred work in theater and service in the war efforts in her native Britain.

13. "Femme Star Costs Up 100%," *Variety*, March 8, 1944, 55 (entire article, 1, 55).

14. See Schatz, *Boom and Bust*, 102, 208; and Carman, *Independent Stardom*, 129–30.

15. "Femme Star Costs Up 100%," 55.

16. For more on this, see Schatz, *The Genius of the System*, 338.

17. Ed Raiden, "Wandering Around Hollywood," *Showmen's Trade Review*, January 15, 1944, 69.

18. I do not want to demean the contribution of the actresses themselves, as their talent, skills, and part in the decision-making process (when choosing roles, etc.) were essential for the success. My aim is, in accordance with the subject and aim of this book, to describe the role of David O. Selznick in the entire process.

19. See, for example, a memo from September 1941, where he referred to both as "atrocities." Memo from David O. Selznick, September 13, 1941, Ingrid Bergman Publicity, b. 3337, f. 3, HRC.

20. See the memo from David O. Selznick, December 10, 1940, For Whom the Bell Tolls—Campaign, b. 3336, f. 1, HRC.

21. Selznick was also interested in purchasing the rights to the novel, but did not make an offer, as, in his own words, he was exhausted after working on *Gone with the Wind* and *Rebecca*. See the memo from David O. Selznick, July 10, 1943, For Whom the Bell Tolls—Campaign, b. 3336, f. 1, HRC. He worked on an adaptation of another Hemingway's work in the mid-1950s when he produced his version of *A Farewell to Arms*.

22. It sold more than 750,000 copies over three years after its publication. See "Movie of the Week: For Whom the Bell Tolls," *Life*, July 26, 1943, 97.

23. See the memo from Kay Brown, November 29, 1940, For Whom the Bell Tolls—Campaign, b. 3336, f. 1, HRC.

24. See the memo from David O. Selznick, December 10, 1940, For Whom the Bell Tolls—Campaign, b. 3336, f. 1, HRC.

25. Cooper played another Hemingway hero ten years earlier in Paramount's adaptation of *A Farewell to Arms* (1932).

26. "The Hemingways in Sun Valley. The Novelist Takes a Wife," *Life*, January 6, 1941, 53 (entire article, 49–57). Hemingway first learned about Bergman from Martha Gellhorn, his

partner (and as of December 1940 his wife), who met the actress in January 1940 aboard the ocean liner *SS Rex* on a cruise from Genoa to New York. See Isabella Rossellini and Lothar Schirmer, eds., *Ingrid Bergman: A Life in Pictures* (San Francisco: Chronicle Books, 2015), 156.

27. Memo from David O. Selznick, January 13, 1941, For Whom the Bell Tolls—Campaign, b. 3336, f. 1, HRC.

28. Memo from David O. Selznick, January 31, 1941, For Whom the Bell Tolls—Campaign, b. 3336, f. 1, HRC. Also cited in Behlmer, *Memo from David O. Selznick*, 307.

29. The meeting was arranged at the last minute as Hemingway was preparing to leave for China. Bergman cut short her skiing holiday at June Lake to see him and flew in from Reno.

30. "Ingrid Bergman Takes a Short Holiday from Hollywood," *Life*, February 24, 1941, 46–51. Bergman elsewhere stated that Hemingway sent her the book with the dedication earlier, although the more likely version is that he handed it over to her during their meeting in San Francisco. Cf. interview with Ingrid Bergman for the station CBC, 1971, https://www .youtube.com/watch?v=kqoncx4y3ls.

31. See, for example, the later description of the occasion in Thomas Carlile and Jean Speiser, "Ingrid Bergman: Young Swedish Star Brings a New Brand of Charm to American Screen," *Life*, July 26, 1943, 106.

32. "It's Bergman or Else . . .," *Los Angeles Examiner*, undated clipping, For Whom the Bell Tolls—Campaign, b. 3336, f. 1, HRC. Hemingway's threat was clearly only a rhetorical gesture as the screenplay had already been assigned to the experienced Dudley Nichols and the studio was not planning on any significant participation on the part of the writer. His statement therefore had primarily a symbolic value.

33. See, for example, the memo from David O. Selznick, August 21, 1941, For Whom the Bell Tolls—Campaign, b. 3336, f. 1, HRC. Selznick initially did not insist on financial compensation and instead called for trading Bergman for the services of a male star from Paramount's roster—Bob Hope, Sterling Hayden, or Fred MacMurray. This offer should be seen within the context of the lack of male actors which Hollywood experienced in the early 1940s. See the memo from David O. Selznick, October 2, 1941, For Whom the Bell Tolls—Campaign, b. 3336, f. 1, HRC.

34. Memo from Frances Inglis, October 7, 1941, For Whom the Bell Tolls—Campaign, b. 3336, f. 1, HRC.

35. Ralph Vile, "Hollywood Speaking," *Film Daily*, June 25, 1941, 8.

36. "Who Will Play Maria? Four Movie Stars Are Top Candidates to Play Heroine in Hemingway Tale," *Detroit Free Press*, February 1, 1942, 13. See also the scrapbooks that are part of the Ingrid Bergman Collection, Cinema Archives, Wesleyan University.

37. Apart from the already mentioned names, the following actresses were also referred to in connection with the film: Susan Hayward, Annabella, Margo, Fay McKenzie, Madeleine Lebeau, Barbara Britton, and Esther Fernández. Most of them were either new faces developed by Paramount or actresses from abroad who had the physical and linguistic prerequisites for the role.

38. The price for Cooper's services at that time was around $125,000 per film. See "Decree Crimps Prod. Coin," *Variety*, November 27, 1940, 25.

39. For example, Dugal O'Liam, "Why Bergman Replaced Zorina," *Hollywood* 31, no. 11 (November 1942): 66–67.

NOTES

40. A letter from Ernest Hemingway addressed to Maxwell Perkins, July 27, 1942, available in Carlos Baker, ed., *Ernest Hemingway: Selected Letters, 1917–1961* (New York: Scribner, 2003), 540.

41. "Ingrid Bergman Gets Prize Maria Role in 'For Whom the Bell Tolls,'" *Showmen's Trade Review*, August 8, 1942, 43. Zorina was also supposed to undergo a new series of tests—with a new haircut and make-up—but this was only an attempt to boost her self-confidence after the fiasco. See "Ingrid Bergman Gets Prize Maria Role," 43. As consolation for the lost role, Paramount cast her in the adaptation of W. Somerset Maugham's *The Hour Before Dawn*, but in the end, she did not appear in it either (Veronica Lake took over the role after her). After starring in the musical *Follow the Boys* (1944) and the comedy *Lover Come Back* (1946, both Universal), her Hollywood career was at an end, and she continued to work only in ballet. The experience with *For Whom the Bell Tolls* basically destroyed her film career, as it undermined the industry's (and her own) confidence in her acting skills and professionalism.

42. See the memo from David O. Selznick, July 10, 1943, For Whom the Bell Tolls—Campaign, b. 3336, f. 1, HRC.

43. See the memo from David O. Selznick, July 27, 1942, For Whom the Bell Tolls—Campaign, b. 3336, f. 1, HRC.

44. The second transaction also involved obtaining the services of Olivia de Havilland for one film under the condition that Selznick pay her salary for a period of eight weeks. See the contract for the loan-out of Ingrid Bergman for *Casablanca*, April 24, 1942, Ingrid Bergman Contracts, b. 3337, f. 2, HRC.

45. See the contract for the loan-out of Ingrid Bergman for *For Whom the Bell Tolls*, August 4, 1942, For Whom the Bell Tolls—Campaign, b. 3336, f. 1, HRC.

46. This is confirmed, for example, in Thomson, *Showman*, 408.

47. Wood, "Selznick and His Girls," 36.

48. Carlile and Speiser, "Ingrid Bergman," 106.

49. Advertisement from the *Los Angeles Examiner*, August 11, 1943, part I, 15.

50. Ernest Hemingway, *For Whom the Bell Tolls* (New York: Simon & Schuster, 1995), 22.

51. Helen Weller, "Swedish Dynamo," *Hollywood* 30, no. 8 (August 1941): 46; Kirtley Baskette, "Nordic Natural," *Photoplay* 19, no. 5 (October 1941): 52; Peter Kalischer, "North Star," *Glamour of Hollywood*, April 1941, 43. See also Lunde, *Nordic Exposures*, 156–67. Hemingway's alleged statement concerning Bergman "I've seen Spaniards just like you. They're tall and blond, many of them" cannot be taken as completely convincing in this context. See Bergman and Burgess, *Ingrid Bergman: My Story*, 100.

52. It would be much more difficult to harmonize the ballerina and musical actress Zorina, whose image was based on goddess-like beauty and flashy nobility, with the character of Maria. A more detailed description of Bergman's star image and an analysis of her character in *For Whom the Bell Tolls* is beyond the framework of this study. For more on the basic components of her star persona, see, in particular, Wood, "Star and Auteur," 303–35; and Smit, *Ingrid Bergman*. On the establishment of the basic attributes of her Hollywood stardom, see the chapter on *Intermezzo*.

53. Schatz, *Boom and Bust*, 466.

54. Lee Mortimer cited in "What New York Critics Say about 'Bell Tolls,'" *Motion Picture Daily*, July 16, 1943, 3.

238   NOTES

55. According to *Film Daily*, the ratio of submitted votes was approximately 3:1 in favor of Maria in *For Whom the Bell Tolls*. "'Famous Fives' Awards to Lukas and Garson," *Film Daily*, December 22, 1943, 7.

56. Schatz, *Boom and Bust*, 466.

57. "Par's Slant on Selznick's Holdings," *Variety*, September 30, 1942, 18. The article informed about the planned, but unrealized, trade between Selznick's studio and Paramount.

58. "The Money Making Stars of 1944," *Motion Picture Herald*, December 10, 1944, 14; Schatz, *Boom and Bust*, 470. She rose to number 13 in 1945 and reached her career high of number 2 in 1946.

59. See the February 1944 report, Spellbound Audience Research, b. 228, f. 14, HRC.

60. Bergman was loaned out to Warner Bros. in February 1943 (after the premiere of *Casablanca*, but prior to the release of *For Whom the Bell Tolls*) for $125,000 to star in an adaptation of Edna Ferber's novel *Saratoga Trunk*, which was supposed to reunite her with her acting partner Gary Cooper and the director Sam Wood. In November, MGM paid twice that amount to cast her in *Gaslight* (1944). See the contract for the loan-out of Ingrid Bergman for *Saratoga Trunk*, February 22, 1943, Ingrid Bergman Contracts, b. 3337, f. 2, HRC; contract for the loan-out of Ingrid Bergman for *Gaslight*, November 9, 1943, Ingrid Bergman Contracts, b. 3337, f. 2, HRC. David Thomson and David Shipman both mentioned that Selznick in fact received $250,000 for the loan-out of Bergman for *Saratoga Trunk*, but the contract I found in Selznick's archive is for half that amount. Cf. Thomson, *Showman*, 362; David Shipman, *The Great Movie Stars 1: The Golden Years* (London: Macdonald, 1989), 58.

61. More than 300,000 copies of the Claudia novels were sold by the end of 1943, while stories in the magazine *Redbook* had more than 7,000,000 potential readers. The Broadway production of the play exceeded 700 performances and the radio plays were broadcast over 110 various stations. See the advertisement in *Film Daily*, November 10, 1943, 8.

62. "'Claudia' Becomes an Industry," *Variety*, March 19, 1941, 27.

63. Telegram from Kay Brown, February 13, 1941, Claudia—Correspondence 1 of 3, b. 855, f. 12, HRC.

64. Telegram from Robert Stevenson, March 13, 1941, Claudia—Casting, b. 855, f. 5, HRC.

65. See the documents in Keys of the Kingdom—Casting "Nora," b. 305, f. 17, HRC.

66. See the telegram from Kay Brown, May 23, 1941, Claudia 1 of 2, b. 292, f. 2, HRC.

67. Memo from Elsa Neuberger, June 9, 1941, Dorothy McGuire 2 of 2, b. 3343, f. 2, HRC.

68. Memo from David O. Selznick, June 4, 1941, Claudia 1 of 2, b. 292, f. 2, HRC.

69. Memo from David O. Selznick, June 4, 1941, Claudia 1 of 2, b. 292, f. 2, HRC.

70. On "the courtship" between Walker and Selznick's company, see Paul Green, *Jennifer Jones: The Life and Films* (Jefferson, NC, and London: McFarland, 2011), 23–25; Epstein, *Portrait of Jennifer*, 50–54; and Thomson, *Showman*, 366–68.

71. See the memo from David O. Selznick, August 11, 1941, Jennifer Jones—Correspondence, b. 554, f. 3, HRC.

72. Memo from Kay Brown, July 25, 1941, Claudia—Miscellaneous, f. 3504, f. 6, HRC.

73. Memo from David O. Selznick, November 14, 1941, Claudia—Miscellaneous, f. 3504, f. 6, HRC.

74. See the undated biography of Dorothy McGuire written by Paul Macnamara, Dorothy McGuire—Biography, b. 1592, f. 7, HRC.

NOTES 239

75. The production was on the repertoire of Booth Theatre from February 12, 1941, to March 7, 1942. It moved to St. James Theatre in May and was finally staged in Forrest Theatre from November 8, 1942, to January 9, 1943. See Claudia, *Internet Broadway Database*, https://www.ibdb.com/broadway-production/claudia-1080.

76. Memo from David O. Selznick, November 11, 1942, McGuire—20th Century-Fox Deal, 1942–1947, b. 562, f. 9, HRC. The attempt to secure the main role for Joseph Cotten also failed.

77. Letter from David O. Selznick, December 11, 1942, Dorothy McGuire—Correspondence 1943, b. 562, f. 2, HRC.

78. For the reaction to the tests, see the letter from David O. Selznick, April 21, 1943, Dorothy McGuire—Correspondence 1943, b. 562, f. 2, HRC.

79. See "Top Grossers of the Season," *Variety*, January 5, 1944, 54.

80. "Claudia," *Film Daily*, August 19, 1943, 6.

81. "Claudia," *Showmen's Trade Review*, August 21, 1943, 27.

82. For example, in a poll conducted by *Film Daily* she came in second place after Sonny Tufts. "'Famous Fives' Awards to Lukas and Garson," *Film Daily*, December 22, 1943, 7.

83. The only exception was the ten-minute recruitment short *Reward Unlimited* (1944), which was made during World War II for the United States Public Health Service. In it, McGuire portrayed a young woman volunteering to join the US Cadet Nurse Corps.

84. James R. Parish and Gene Ringgold, "Dorothy McGuire," *Films in Review* 15, no. 8 (1964): 474.

85. As of February 5, 1947, the period for which her contract was suspended amounted to seventy-four weeks. Report from Billie Edwards, February 5, 1947, Dorothy McGuire—Correspondence 1947, b. 562, f. 6, HRC.

86. See Bowers, *The Selznick Players*, 166–67.

87. *The Song of Bernadette* was another bestselling book from the early 1940s: over the course of several months from the publication of the English translation, 400,000 copies were sold in the US alone. See Green, *Jennifer Jones*, 27.

88. See Peter Lev, *Twentieth Century-Fox: The Zanuck-Skouras Years, 1935–1965* (Austin: University of Texas Press, 2013), 79–80.

89. The actress hid her previous engagements out of fear that this might harm the interest of Selznick's studio. See the memo from Kay Brown, October 23, 1941, Jennifer Jones—Correspondence, b. 554, f. 3, HRC. She also confessed to appearing in an uncredited role of a Native American girl in a Roy Rogers Western. The title, however, has not been identified. See Studlar, *Precocious Charms*, 273.

90. Memo from Whitney Bolton, February 9, 1942, Jennifer Jones—Correspondence, b. 3823, f. 13, HRC. Even the names of her parents were changed in the official materials to Jones and this form was subsequently taken over by many periodicals.

91. Memo from David O. Selznick, March 2, 1942, Jennifer Jones—Correspondence, b. 3823, f. 13, HRC.

92. Franz Werfel states in the foreword to the book: "*The Song of Bernadette* is a novel but not a fictive work. In face of the events here delineated, the skeptical reader will ask with better right than in the case of most historical epic narratives: 'What is true? What is invented?' My answer is: 'All the memorable happenings which constitute the substance of this book

took place in the world of reality. Since their beginning dates back no longer than eighty years, there beats upon them the bright light of modern history and their truth has been confirmed by friend and foe and by cool observers through faithful testimonies. My story makes no changes in this body of truth. I exercised my right of creative freedom only where the work, as a work of art, demanded certain chronological condensations or where there was need of striking the spark of life from the hardened substance'" (Franz Werfel, *The Song of Bernadette* [New York: Viking Press, 1942], 6–7).

93. *Hollywood Reporter*, October 27, 1942, 7, cited according to "The Song of Bernadette," *AFI Catalog of Feature Films*, https://catalog.afi.com/Catalog/moviedetails/676.

94. Telegram from David O. Selznick, August 25, 1942, Jennifer Jones—Correspondence, b. 554, f. 3, HRC.

95. This view is also expressed by Edward Z. Epstein in *Portrait of Jennifer*, 67.

96. Telegram from David O. Selznick, October 11, 1942, Jennifer Jones—20th Century-Fox Deal, b. 555, f. 10, HRC.

97. Telegram from David O. Selznick, October 11, 1942.

98. In the meantime, Jones took intensive acting classes with the respected acting coach Sanford Meisner, who was associated with the New York Group Theatre. Her preparations for her return to the screen also included lessons in diction and body posture. Green, *Jennifer Jones*, 207.

99. See the telegram from William Goetz, October 12, 1942, Jennifer Jones—20th Century-Fox Deal, b. 555, f. 10, HRC.

100. Telegram from David O. Selznick, October 11, 1942, Jennifer Jones—20th Century-Fox Deal, b. 555, f. 10, HRC.

101. Telegram from David O. Selznick, October 14, 1942, and telegram from William Goetz, October 15, 1942, Jennifer Jones—20th Century-Fox Deal, b. 555, f. 10, HRC.

102. See, for example, the telegram from David O. Selznick, October 16, 1942, Jennifer Jones—20th Century-Fox Deal, b. 555, f. 10, HRC.

103. The interest of the studio in Gish was reported by *Hollywood Reporter*, July 24, 1942, 2, cited in "The Song of Bernadette," *AFI Catalog of Feature Films*, https://catalog.afi.com/Catalog/moviedetails/676.

104. Dorothy O'Leary, "Practical Dreamer: Jennifer Jones," *Screenland* 50, no. 7 (May 1946): 72. Jennifer Jones later said: "Bernadette was just a normal peasant girl who happened to see a miracle. I'm playing her that way." Quoted in Green, *Jennifer Jones*, 30.

105. Official program for *The Song of Bernadette*, Henry King Papers, 3.f-43, MHL.

106. Linda Darnell was cast into the uncredited role of the Lady—the vision which Bernadette sees repeatedly.

107. "Award Jennifer Jones 'Bernadette' Title Role," *Showmen's Trade Review*, December 12, 1942, 20.

108. Cal York, "Cal York's Inside Stuff," *Photoplay* 22, no. 4 (March 1943): 13.

109. See the contract from June 14, 1943, Jennifer Jones—20th Century-Fox Agreement and Correspondence, b. 909, f. 5, HRC.

110. Memo from David O. Selznick, December 17, 1942, Jennifer Jones—20th Century-Fox Deal, b. 555, f. 10, HRC.

111. Memo from David O. Selznick, January 4, 1943, Jennifer Jones—Correspondence, b. 3823, f. 13, HRC.

NOTES 241

112. The full title card in the film reads "And Introducing Jennifer Jones (By Arrangement with David O. Selznick) As Bernadette."

113. Like *For Whom the Bell Tolls*, *The Song of Bernadette* was first shown in selected luxury first-run theaters and only in 1945 went into general release.

114. See, for example, Fredda Dudley, "Good News," *Modern Screen* 28, no. 4 (March 1944): 111.

115. *Time*, February 7, 1944, cited in Green, *Jennifer Jones*, 38.

116. Delight Evans, "Your Guide to Current Films," *Screenland* 48, no. 7 (May 1944): 8.

117. A day after the Oscar ceremony the actress started divorce proceedings with her husband Robert Walker. Green, *Jennifer Jones*, 39.

118. Schatz, *Boom and Bust*, 466; Aubrey Solomon, *Twentieth Century-Fox: A Corporate and Financial History* (Lanham, MD: Scarecrow Press, 2002), 63.

119. The official program for *The Song of Bernadette* falsely states, for example, that the actress received the Oscar for her film debut, thereby "establishing a shining precedent." Official program for *The Song of Bernadette*, Henry King Papers, 3.f-43, MHL.

120. Memo from David O. Selznick, December 22, 1943, Jennifer Jones—Correspondence 1943, b. 554, f. 1, HRC.

121. The same conditions were negotiated for the loan-outs of both performers: $100,000 up front and 5 percent from the gross receipts above $2 million. The film made approximately $3.2 million, therefore the sum of $120,000, corresponding to 10 percent of $1.2 million, was added to the amount of $200,000. See the loan-out contract from December 7, 1944, Paramount Pictures Contract Summaries, 13.f-1267, MHL.

122. More about this in the conclusion.

123. Brian Hannan, *Coming Back to a Theater Near You: A History of Hollywood Reissues, 1914–2014* (Jefferson, NC: McFarland, 2016), 353.

124. Here is the list of all Oscar nominations of Selznick's contract actresses in the period from 1940 to 1948: Vivien Leigh 1x Best Actress in a Leading Role (*Gone with the Wind*, 1940); Joan Fontaine 1x Best Actress in a Leading Role (*Suspicion* [RKO], 1942) and 2x nomination in the same category (*Rebecca*, 1941; *The Constant Nymph*, 1944); Ingrid Bergman 1x Best Actress in a Leading Role (*Gaslight*, 1945) and 2x nomination in the same category (*For Whom the Bell Tolls*, 1944; *The Bells of St. Mary's* [Rainbow Productions/RKO], 1946); Jennifer Jones 1x Best Actress in a Leading Role (*The Song of Bernadette*, 1944), 2x nomination in the same category (*Love Letters*, 1946; *Duel in the Sun*, 1947), and 1x nomination for Best Actress in a Supporting Role (*Since You Went Away*, 1945); Dorothy McGuire 1x nomination for Best Actress in a Leading Role (*Gentleman's Agreement*, 1948). Only Shirley Temple did not receive any nominations during her tenure with Selznick.

3. WHILE THEY WERE FIGHTING:
THE DEVELOPMENT OF MALE STARS DURING WORLD WAR II

1. Craig White, "Man Shortage Forces Stars to Hire Escorts!," *Hollywood* 31, no. 8 (August 1942): 28.

2. More on the development of female stars and their loan-outs to other studios in the previous chapter.

3. Schatz, *Boom and Bust*, 142.

4. Schatz, *Boom and Bust*, 206.

5. Randy Roberts, "John Wayne Goes to War," in Steven Mintz, Randy Roberts and David Weekly, eds., *Hollywood's America. Understanding History Through Film* (Malden: Wiley-Blackwell, 2016), 171.

6. For more on the employment of Van Johnson during the war, see Basinger, *The Star Machine*, 469–77.

7. For various versions as to why Rogers did not join the armed forces, see Edward Buscombe, "Gene Autry, and Roy Rogers, The Light of Western Stars," in Griffin, ed., *What Dreams Were Made Of*, 36.

8. Memo from David O. Selznick, June 28, 1940, Alan Marshal—Correspondence, b. 930, f. 15, HRC.

9. Memo from David O. Selznick July 26, 1940, Alan Marshal—Correspondence, b. 930, f. 15, HRC. Like Ginger Rogers, Anna Neagle was a contract actress at RKO. She appeared, however, in less prestigious films. In 1940, she was cast alongside Alan Marshal in the musical comedy *Irene*.

10. Memo from Daniel O'Shea, August 16, 1940, Alan Marshal—Correspondence, b. 930, f. 15, HRC.

11. The successes with Jennifer Jones and Dorothy McGuire, which were achieved through loan-outs, were still to come. See the previous chapter for more details.

12. Telegram from David O. Selznick, August 24, 1940, Alan Marshal—Correspondence, b. 931, f. 2, HRC.

13. Memo from David O. Selznick, August 18, 1941, Alan Marshal—Correspondence, b. 931, f. 2, HRC.

14. Report from E. L. Scanlon, December 31, 1941, Alan Marshal—Correspondence, b. 931, f. 2, HRC.

15. Hedda Hopper, "Hedda Hopper's Hollywood," *Los Angeles Times*, September 6, 1941, part II, 9.

16. The agents selected for the job included Frank Vincent (Columbia), Frank Orsatti (MGM), David's brother Myron Selznick (Paramount and Universal), John McCormick (Warner Bros.), and Ned Marin (Twentieth Century-Fox). See the memo from Ray Klune, November 17, 1941, Alan Marshal—Correspondence, b. 931, f. 2, HRC.

17. Memo from David O. Selznick, October 31, 1941, Alan Marshal—Correspondence, b. 931, f. 2, HRC.

18. Marshal did take part in the screen tests in April 1942, but the possibility of getting the role of Rochester was extremely remote. The main reason was to test his acting abilities and boost his self-confidence, which had suffered due to his long absence from the screen. Soon after, Selznick sold the property to Twentieth Century-Fox and Orson Welles was cast as Rochester.

19. Hedda Hopper, "My Own Super-Superlative Awards for 1941," *Photoplay* 20, no. 4 (March 1942): 43.

20. Memo from David O. Selznick, January 28, 1942, Alan Marshal—Correspondence, b. 931, f. 2, HRC.

21. Memo from David O. Selznick, September 3, 1942, Alan Marshal—Correspondence, b. 931, f. 2, HRC.

NOTES

22. Memo from David O. Selznick, February 15, 1943, Alan Marshal—Correspondence, b. 931, f. 2, HRC.

23. See memo from David O. Selznick, February 15, 1943, Alan Marshal—Correspondence, b. 931, f. 2, HRC.

24. Memo from David O. Selznick, February 11, 1943, Alan Marshal—Correspondence, b. 931, f. 1, HRC.

25. Memo from David O. Selznick, June 21, 1943, Alan Marshal—Correspondence, b. 931, f. 1, HRC. He stated in a similar spirit only two weeks later that "our publicity failure on Marshal is baffling, and is something that I can simply no longer tolerate" (Memo from David O. Selznick, July 5, 1943, Alan Marshal—Correspondence, b. 931, f. 1, HRC).

26. Memo from Henry Willson, July 30, 1943, Alan Marshal—Correspondence, b. 931, f. 1, HRC.

27. See, for example, Leon Surmelian, "He Calls Her 'Binks,'" *Photoplay* 24, no. 1 (December 1943): 50, 83; Constance Palmer, "Alan Marshal's 7 Steps to Stardom," *Screenland* 48, no. 6 (April 1944): 28–29, 65; Constance Palmer, "At Home with the Alan Marshals," www.alan marshal.com.

28. The career of Helen Ferguson and her successes with female clients are described in Mary Desjardins, "'As Told by Helen Ferguson': Hollywood Publicity, Gender, and the Public Sphere," in Kathleen A. Feeley and Jennifer Frost, eds., *When Private Talk Goes Public: Gossip in American History* (New York: Palgrave Macmillan, 2014), 161–82.

29. Memo from David O. Selznick, October 19, 1943, Alan Marshal—Correspondence, b. 931, f. 1, HRC.

30. Memo from David O. Selznick, March 16, 1944, Alan Marshal—Correspondence, b. 931, f. 5, HRC.

31. The profits amounted to $1.8 million. See Tino Balio, *MGM* (London and New York: Routledge, 2018), 149.

32. "'White Cliffs' in 7th Week at Radio City Music Hall," *Motion Picture Herald*, June 24, 1944, 88.

33. Bosley Crowther, "The Screen: The White Cliffs of Dover, Based on Poem of Alice Duer Miller, With Irene Dunne and Alan Marshal, at Music Hall," *New York Times*, May 12, 1944, https://www.nytimes.com/1944/05/12/archives/the-screen-the-white-cliffs-of-dover -based-on-poem-of-alice-duer.html.

34. Thalia Bell, "Review: Bride By Mistake," *Motion Picture Daily*, July 28, 1944, 7.

35. "Bride By Mistake," *Showmen's Trade Review*, July 29, 1944, 8.

36. Memo from David O. Selznick, October 29, 1947, Alan Marshal—Correspondence, b. 931, f. 3, HRC.

37. Although he wasn't endowed with an athletic figure, he did have an attractive smile and seductive look.

38. Marshal was unable to work due to mental and family issues until 1950 when he appeared in several television series. He worked in later years in television, theater, and occasionally in films. He died on July 9, 1961, at the age of fifty-two. (Information concerning the date of his premature death differs. I am basing this on information from Marshal's son Kit who until recently administered the website http://alanmarshal.com/.)

39. According to Cynthia Baron, "by the mid to late 1930s Hollywood professionals seem to have developed a definite consensus that training in dramatic schools and on the stage

244 NOTES

was not only valuable, but essential training for film actors." Baron states that film acting differed from stage acting not so much qualitatively but rather quantitatively: it didn't require adopting or developing new techniques as much as adjusting (usually subduing) those used in theater (due to the proximity of the camera, dimensions of the screen, sensitivity of the sound recording equipment etc.). Cynthia Baron, "Crafting Film Performances: Acting in the Hollywood Studio Era," in Pamela Robertson Wojcik, ed., *Movie Acting. The Film Reader* (Routledge: New York and London, 2004), 86–90 (quotation on page 87).

40. Memo from Kay Brown, January 28, 1941, Gene Kelly—Correspondence, b. 911, f. 4, HRC.

41. Kelly, along with his brother Fred, was supposed to first work on a staging of the fantasy play by William Saroyan *Sweeney in the Trees*, but this never materialized. Several periodicals mentioned this plan; see, for example, "Selznick Signs Kelly; 'Pal Joey' Will Close," *The Film Daily*, July 23, 1941, 9. Kelly had been cast in and developed the choreography for the Broadway version of another play by Saroyan, *The Time of Your Life*, in the years 1939 and 1940.

42. Selznick later championed an identical approach with Dorothy McGuire, who had her film debut in the title role in *Claudia*, which she had already played with success on Broadway. See the previous chapter.

43. Columbia released the film version of *Pal Joey* in 1957, with Frank Sinatra in the title role.

44. Coincidentally, after the deal was finalized, one of the directors under consideration for *The Keys of the Kingdom* was Alfred Hitchcock. He preferred, however, to make *Lifeboat* (1944), and Fox complied with his wishes. See Patrick McGilligan, *Alfred Hitchcock: A Life in Darkness and Light* (New York: HarperCollins, 2010), ePub edition, chapter 9.

45. *Anchors Aweigh* secured Kelly his only Oscar nomination of his career.

46. The final papers were signed on February 13, 1943. See the documents in Gene Kelly—Correspondence, b. 911, f. 4, HRC.

47. Memo from Kay Brown, February 3, 1941, Gregory Peck—Correspondence, b. 568, f. 5, HRC.

48. Memo from Kay Brown, February 3, 1941, Gregory Peck—Correspondence, b. 568, f. 5, HRC.

49. Telegram from David O. Selznick, March 7, 1941, Gregory Peck—Correspondence, b. 568, f. 5, HRC.

50. Memo from David O. Selznick, March 11, 1941, Gregory Peck 1941–47, b. 3344, f. 3, HRC. Also cited in Behlmer, *Memo from David O. Selznick*, 309. Douglas Fairbanks Jr. played the role of Richard Carleton in Selznick's film version.

51. In the following years, possibly because of the experience with Gregory Peck, Selznick paid increased attention to appropriate technical conditions and professional supervision for the screen tests.

52. Memo from Frances Inglis, October 29, 1942, Gregory Peck—Correspondence, b. 568, f. 5, HRC.

53. See Gerard Molyneaux, *Gregory Peck: A Bio-Bibliography* (Westport, CT, and London: Greenwood Press, 1995), 6.

54. *New York World Telegram*, September 15, 1942, cited in Molyneaux, *Gregory Peck*, 58.

55. "Gregory Peck, The Average Man on the Flying Trapeze," *Time*, January 12, 1948, 53.

NOTES

56. See, for example, Molyneaux, *Gregory Peck*, 10. RKO was originally involved in the negotiations as well, but their share was taken over by Selznick. Publicly, this less-than-transparent arrangement was presented not as a result of a fierce competitive struggle, but as an expression of solidarity during difficult times: struck by the acute lack of young actors, the studios supposedly reached a gentleman's agreement on dividing Peck's services so as to allow all of them to get their fair share. See "Selznick, RKO In Talent Pool," *Motion Picture Herald*, May 1, 1943, 45.

57. See, for example, the review from Bosley Crowther, "'Days of Glory,' starring Tamara Toumanova and Gregory Peck, at Palace," *New York Times*, June 17, 1944, https://www.nytimes.com/1944/06/17/archives/days-of-glory-starring-tamara-toumanova-and-gregory-peck-at-palace.html.

58. Mary Morris, "Leading Man," *PM*, January 31, 1944, cited in Molyneaux, *Gregory Peck*, 72.

59. See Solomon, *Twentieth Century-Fox*, 64.

60. The undated excerpt is part of the collection The Keys of the Kingdom—clippings, b. 344, f. 3509, Gregory Peck Papers, Core Collection, MHL.

61. *New York World Telegram*, December 29, 1944, cited in Molyneaux, *Gregory Peck*, 72.

62. As stated in a profile article in the *New York Times*, "this time Hollywood rather than the paying customers can take credit for recognizing a gold mine." Thomas M. Pryor, "Taking a Peek at Peck," *New York Times*, January 7, 1945, 3.

63. Pryor, "Taking a Peek at Peck," 3.

64. Amy Porter, "Growth of the Yearling," *Collier's*, September 29, 1945, 77, cited in Molyneaux, *Gregory Peck*, 79.

65. Schatz, *Boom and Bust*, 467.

66. See, for example, Peter Martin, "Phantom Star," *Saturday Evening Post*, September 22, 1945, 14–15.

67. See the December 1946 report in Spellbound Publicity Advertising, August 1945–December 1945, b. 229, f. 13, HRC.

68. Gregory Peck, "The Average Man on the Flying Trapeze," 54.

69. Information concerning the rejection of Peck back in March 1941 was of course kept a secret from the public as this would have put Selznick's reputation as an unerring judge in discovering stars in jeopardy.

70. Memo from David O. Selznick, February 14, 1945, Gregory Peck—Correspondence, b. 568, f. 5, HRC.

71. Gregory Peck, "The Average Man on the Flying Trapeze," 54.

72. See the memo from Ray Klune, January 21, 1942, Joseph Cotten—Correspondence 1940–1942, b. 541, f. 4, HRC.

73. Telegram from David O. Selznick, April 20, 1942, Joseph Cotten—Correspondence 1940–1942, b. 541, f. 4, HRC.

74. Telegram from David O. Selznick, April 20, 1942, Joseph Cotten—Correspondence 1940–1942, b. 541, f. 4, HRC.

75. Joseph Cotten played the main role and contributed to the screenplay (co-written by Welles).

76. See Joseph Cotten, *Vanity Will Get You Somewhere: An Autobiography* (Lincoln, NE: toExcel Press, 2000), 54–55.

77. See "Top Grossers of the Season," *Variety*, January 5, 1944, 54.

246 NOTES

78. E. A. Cunningham, "Shadow of a Doubt," *Motion Picture Herald*, January 9, 1943, 34.

79. Bosley Crowther, "Shadow of a Doubt a Thriller, with Teresa Wright, Joseph Cotten, at Rivoli," *New York Times*, January 13, 1943, https://www.nytimes.com/1943/01/13/archives /shadow-of-a-doubt-a-thriller-with-teresa-wright-joseph-cotten-at.html.

80. I use the correct Czech version of the name, although the character is listed as "Franticek Svoboda" in most of the materials.

81. Memo from David O. Selznick, August 22, 1942, Joseph Cotten—Correspondence 1940–1942, b. 541, f. 4, HRC.

82. See, for example, memo from David O. Selznick, August 21, 1942, Joseph Cotten— Correspondence 1940–1942, b. 541, f. 4, HRC. The film was released in 1943 as *Lady of Burlesque*. For the same reason, Selznick rejected an offer for a loan-out of Cotten for the role of the murderer in the thriller *The Lodger* (1944, Twentieth Century-Fox). See the telegram from Harriett Flagg, January 26, 1943, Joseph Cotten—Correspondence 1943, b. 861, f. 13, HRC.

83. Letter from David O. Selznick, December 17, 1942, Joseph Cotten—Correspondence 1940–1942, b. 541, f. 4, HRC.

84. Telegram from David O. Selznick, December 18, 1942, Joseph Cotten—Correspondence 1940–1942, b. 541, f. 4, HRC.

85. The film's working title was *Three Smart Girls Join Up*. When it became apparent that the characters of the two sisters from the previous installments will not feature in the story, the title was changed to *Hers to Hold*.

86. "Hers to Hold," *The Film Daily*, July 16, 1943, 6.

87. See "Top Grossers of the Season," *Variety*, January 5, 1944, 54.

88. The article was published in *Hollywood Citizen News*, March 15, 1943, and is part of the file Joseph Cotten—Correspondence 1943, b. 541, f. 6, HRC.

89. Memo from David O. Selznick, March 19, 1943, Joseph Cotten—Correspondence 1943, b. 541, f. 6, HRC.

90. See the memo from David O. Selznick, March 5, 1943, Joseph Cotten—talent files 1943, b. 3338, f. 4, HRC.

91. Memo from Daniel O'Shea, August 28, 1942, Joseph Cotten—talent files 1943, b. 3338, f. 4, HRC.

92. In selecting his examples, the producer seems to have overlooked the fact that Cagney was over forty years of age (he was born in 1899) and Errol Flynn was Australian and did not become a naturalized American citizen until August 15, 1942. See Basinger, *The Star Machine*, 247.

93. Memo from David O. Selznick, August 29, 1942, Joseph Cotten—Correspondence 1940–1942, b. 541, f. 4, HRC.

94. The screenplay was authored by Selznick himself who adapted it from the book by Margaret Buell Wilder *Since You Went Away: Letters to a Soldier from His Wife* (originally serialized in a magazine and published as a book in 1943).

95. See, for example, *Since You Went Away*, a commemorative program, author's collection, unpaginated.

96. May Mann, "Joseph Cotten Turns to Romance," *Screenland* 48, no. 4 (February 1944): 38.

97. In the commemorative program for *Since You Went Away*, the following lines appear: "Recognizing the personality that was later developed to such surprising advantage, Mr. Selznick put Mr. Cotten under exclusive contract and declined role after role, no matter how important, that might further identify him as a character actor. [Instead,] precisely

NOTES 247

the correct roles were sought, and eventually secured and created" (*Since You Went Away*, commemorative program, author's collection, unpaginated).

98. Memo from David O. Selznick, June 7, 1943, Joseph Cotten—Correspondence 1943, b. 541, f. 6, HRC.

99. Memo from David O. Selznick, January 24, 1944, cited in Behlmer, *Memo from David O. Selznick*, 352.

100. Memo from David O. Selznick, January 24, 1944, cited in Behlmer, *Memo from David O. Selznick*, 352.

101. The filmmakers did accept, however, many other recommendations. See Behlmer, *Memo from David O. Selznick*, 349–53.

102. "'Going,' 'Since' 1–2," *Variety*, January 3, 1945, 134. See also Schatz, *Boom and Bust*, 467.

103. "Production Notes from the Studios: Cotten Set for Four Films This Year," *Showmen's Trade Review*, January 22, 1944, 54.

104. Leff, *Hitchcock & Selznick*, 134.

105. Cf. Cotten's loan-out contract with Universal Pictures for *Shadow of a Doubt* from July 24, 1942, Joseph Cotten—Vanguard contracts 1945—1951, b. 861, f. 13, HRC; and a contract summary concerning the loan-out of Joseph Cotten by Paramount Pictures for *Love Letters* from December 7, 1944, Paramount Pictures contract summaries, 6.f-514, Joseph Cotten, Special Collections, MHL.

106. Memo from David O. Selznick, September 10, 1945, Joseph Cotten—Correspondence 1945, b. 541, f. 8, HRC. See also memo from David O. Selznick, June 4, 1945, Joseph Cotten—Correspondence 1945, b. 541, f. 8, HRC.

107. See the report from December 1944, Fan Mail Reports 1944, b. 10, f. 2, HRC; and a report from January 1946, Fan Mail Reports 1946, b. 3939, f. 21, HRC. In contrast, Alan Marshal only received 3,374 letters in his most successful year 1944, which further indicates that he had a reserved relationship with the public.

108. His profile in *Liberty* magazine stated that he counts among "Hollywood's top quickeners of the feminine pulse" (Alyce Canfield, "King Cotten," *Liberty*, October 26, 1946, 24).

109. See "The Money Making Stars of 1945," *Motion Picture Herald*, December 29, 1945, 14. Cotten's debut in the top 25 was the only appearance on the list in his career, while Peck in contrast appeared on the list non-stop until 1954; he was highest when eighth in 1947 and 1951.

110. See "The Money Making Stars of 1945," *Motion Picture Herald* and the report from December 1946, Fan Mail Reports 1946, b. 3939, f. 21, HRC.

111. Leff, "Star Struck," 376.

112. Madison achieved the status of a star (although a minor one) in the 1950s thanks in particular to the title role in the television series *Adventures of Wild Bill Hickok* (1951–58).

113. Lee Server, *Robert Mitchum: "Baby I Don't Care"* (New York: St. Martin's Press, 2001), 153–54.

4. FROM MODEL TEENAGER TO TEENAGE MOTHER:
SHIRLEY TEMPLE AS SELZNICK'S CONTRACT STAR IN THE 1940S

1. Helen Markel, "Goldilocks Grows Up, But Definitely," *New York Times Magazine*, February 11, 1945, 18, 35.

248 NOTES

2. Irene Mayer Selznick, *A Private View* (New York: Alfred A. Knopf, 1983), 258.

3. Telegram from David O. Selznick, October 3, 1939, Shirley Temple 1943, b. 3345, f. 11, HRC. A successful adaptation of *Pollyanna* (Mary Pickford Company/United Artists), with Mary Pickford in the main role, was made in 1920. Over the course of the 1930s, Shirley Temple was often compared to Pickford, and as the successor to title of "America's sweetheart," she even appeared in four remakes of her silent pictures (*Curly Top* [1935], *Poor Little Rich Girl* [1936], *Rebecca of Sunnybrook Farm* [1938] and *The Little Princess* [1939, all Twentieth Century-Fox]). The idea to cast her in *Pollyanna* was therefore based on an already established model.

4. Memo from John Hay Whitney, October 4, 1939, Shirley Temple 1943, b. 3345, f. 11, HRC.

5. Memo from David O. Selznick, September 16, 1940, Shirley Temple—correspondence 1943, b. 584, f. 4, HRC.

6. See Studlar, *Precocious Charms*, 56–57.

7. The contradictions embodied in the star image of Shirley Temple and the characters she played are the subject of a frequently anthologized article by Charles Eckert: "Shirley Temple and the House of Rockefeller," *Jump Cut*, no. 2 (July–August 1974): 1, 17–20, reprinted, for example, in Butler, ed., *Star-Texts*, 184–202. More as well in Studlar, *Precocious Charms*, 51–90; and George F. Custen, *Twentieth Century's Fox: Darryl F. Zanuck and the Culture of Hollywood* (New York: Basic Books, 1997), 201–3. The importance of the actress for the US society afflicted by the consequences of the Depression has been dealt with by the cultural historian John F. Kasson in *The Little Girl Who Fought the Great Depression: Shirley Temple and 1930s America* (New York and London: W. W. Norton & Company, 2014).

8. Lev, *Twentieth Century-Fox*, 35.

9. Kathryn Fuller-Seeley, "Shirley Temple: Making Dreams Come True," in McLean, ed., *Glamour in a Golden Age*, 49.

10. Fuller-Seeley, "Shirley Temple: Making Dreams Come True," 62.

11. Custen, *Twentieth Century's Fox*, 222.

12. The letters were initially published as a regular column in *Dayton Journal Herald*. Only after serialization by the popular women's magazine *Ladies' Home Journal* and the purchase of the filming rights by Selznick (for $30,000) were they also published as a book: Margaret Buell Wilder, *Since You Went Away . . . Letters to a Soldier from His Wife* (New York and London: Whittlesey House, 1943).

13. See Schatz, *Boom and Bust*, 256–61.

14. The quotation comes from a Theodor Strauss's review of *Miss Annie Rooney* published in the *New York Times*; the author also rhetorically asked: "Couldn't Miss Temple be kept in school for just a little while?" (Theodor Strauss, "Miss Annie Rooney, Starring Shirley Temple, Opens at the Rivoli," *New York Times*, June 8, 1942, 11).

15. Memo from Frances Inglis, March 6, 1943, Shirley Temple 1943, b. 3345, f. 11, HRC. According to some accounts, Temple was paid up to $300,000 per film at the height of her popularity. See Shipman, *The Great Movie Stars 1*, 565; Robert Windeler, *The Films of Shirley Temple* (Secaucus, NJ: Citadel Press, 1979), 43.

16. Memo from Frances Inglis, March 4, 1943, Shirley Temple 1943, b. 3345, f. 11, HRC.

17. Contract between Vanguard Films and Shirley Temple from August 3, 1943, Shirley Temple 1943, b. 3345, f. 11, HRC.

18. Cited in the program for *Since You Went Away*, author's collection.

NOTES 249

19. "I have decided not to lend SHIRLEY TEMPLE until I have introduced her in my own next picture, so she is [. . .] out of the question for the part." Letter from David O. Selznick, June 7, 1943, Shirley Temple—correspondence 1943, b. 584, f. 4, HRC.

20. See, for example, a telegram from David O. Selznick, September 22, 1943, Shirley Temple 1943, b. 3345, f. 11, HRC.

21. See the materials in the file Since You Went Away—Advertising August 1944–1945, b. 195. f. 5, HRC.

22. On this, Selznick said: "I hope this [. . .] isn't anything for the Psychiatric Division of the Army!" Memo from David O. Selznick, December 17, 1943, Shirley Temple—correspondence 1943, b. 584, f. 4, HRC. It is worth mentioning, that there had already been questions, in connection with Temple's childhood career, as to the character of her attraction for the male part of the audience. Concerns connected with taboos involving child sexuality and possible pedophilia had their roots in a series of parodic one-reelers Baby Burlesks from 1932 and 1933, in which Temple and other child performers played adult roles. According to Lori Merish, her later pictures with Fox "flirt with illicit sexuality, especially pedophilia and (father-daughter) incest. [. . .] That the overtly sexual scenarios and references [. . .] did not scandalize 1930s audiences suggests less the fabled 'innocence' of those times than the structure of sexual disavowal in which the cute Shirley was embedded" (Lori Merish, "Cuteness and Commodity Aesthetics: Tom Thumb and Shirley Temple," in Rosemarie Garland Thomson, ed., *Freakery: Cultural Spectacles of the Extraordinary Body* [New York and London: New York University Press, 1996], 195). See also Fuller-Seeley, "Shirley Temple," 45, 55–59.

23. See memo from David O. Selznick, August 27, 1943, Shirley Temple 1943, b. 3345, f. 11, HRC.

24. Memo from David O. Selznick, November 22, 1943, Since You Went Away Casting—Brig, b. 196, f. 11, HRC.

25. Windeler, *The Films of Shirley Temple*, 67.

26. In contrast, pinup photographs tended to aim at the most direct communication between the photographed object and the recipients. In the most celebrated pinup photograph of the war, Betty Grable posed in a one-piece swimsuit with her back to the camera, gazing over her shoulder and with her agreeable smile directed at the addressees "on the other side."

27. "Shirley Temple Grows Up," *Look*, October 19, 1943, 64–70. Selznick praised his head of advertising Joseph Steele for the successful cooperation with *Look* magazine. See a memo from David O. Selznick, October 14, 1943, Shirley Temple 1943, b. 3345, f. 11, HRC.

28. See, for example, Schatz, *Boom and Bust*, 208.

29. Telegram addressed to Don King, July 2, 1944, Shirley Temple 1944, b. 3345, f. 12, HRC.

30. In one of the telegrams Selznick stated that he wrote most of the text himself. See telegram from David O. Selznick, October 19, 1944, Shirley Temple 1944, b. 3345, f. 12, HRC. The text was published under the title "Shirley Temple Declares Films Should Teach U.S. Ideal Abroad," in the *New York Herald Tribune*, October 22, 1944, section VII, 8.

31. See Fuller-Seeley, "Shirley Temple," 48–49.

32. Telegram from David O. Selznick, May 6, 1943, Since You Went Away Casting—Anne, b. 196, f. 8, HRC.

33. James Agee, "Cinema: New Picture, Jul. 17, 1944," *Time*, July 17, 1944, http://content.time .com/time/subscriber/article/0,33009,885558-2,00.html.

34. "Since You Went Away," *Showmen's Trade Review*, July 22, 1944, 10.

35. Quoted in "'Variety' Praises Jennifer In Terms of Academy Awards," *Hollywood Reporter*, August 4, 1944, 43.

36. Compare with Patsy Guy Hammontree, *Shirley Temple Black: A Bio-Bibliography* (Westport, CT, and London: Greenwood Press, 1998), 99–100.

37. "Life Goes to Shirley Temple's Birthday Party," *Life*, May 15, 1944, 117.

38. Memo from David O. Selznick, October 19, 1944, Shirley Temple 1944, b. 3345, f. 12, HRC; memo from David O. Selznick, April 16, 1945, Shirley Temple—1945–1946, b. 3345, f. 13, HRC.

39. See Schatz, *Boom and Bust*, 189.

40. See, for example, Dore Schary, *Heyday: An Autobiography* (Boston: Little, Brown and Company, 1979), 137.

41. Memo from David O. Selznick, April 8, 1944, Shirley Temple 1944, b. 3345, f. 12, HRC.

42. Jon Savage, *Teenage: The Creation of Youth Culture* (New York: Viking Press, 2007), 453.

43. Edwin Schallert, "Sweet Role Now Bores La Temple," *Los Angeles Times*, June 25, 1944, 23.

44. Bosley Crowther, "THE SCREEN; I'll Be Seeing You, Drama of a Shell-Shocked Soldier, With Joseph Cotten, Ginger Rogers, Opens at Capitol," *New York Times*, April 6, 1945, https://www.nytimes.com/1945/04/06/archives/the-screen-ill-be-seeing-you-drama-of-a-shell shocked-soldier-with.html.

45. Shirley Temple's undated studio biography written by Don King, Shirley Temple—1945–1946, b. 3345, f. 13, HRC.

46. Schatz, *Boom and Bust*, 190, 467.

47. Memo from David O. Selznick, November 3, 1944, cited in Behlmer, *Memo from David O. Selznick*, 356.

48. See report from December 1944, Fan Mail Reports 1944, b. 10, f. 2, HRC.

49. Memo from David O. Selznick, January 27, 1944, Shirley Temple 1944, b. 3345, f. 12, HRC.

50. See letter from Gertrude Temple, August 10, 1944, Shirley Temple—correspondence 1944, b. 584, f. 5, HRC.

51. "George Abbott Seeks Shirley Temple for 'Kiss,'" *Variety*, May 5, 1943, 3.

52. "Kiss and Tell," *Internet Broadway Database*, https://www.ibdb.com/broadway -production/kiss-and-tell-1278.

53. See the draft of the loan-out contract for Shirley Temple, September 13, 1944, Shirley Temple—correspondence 1944, b. 584, f. 5, HRC.

54. "Inside Stuff—Pictures," *Variety*, December 20, 1944, 15.

55. Letter from David O. Selznick addressed to Louella Parsons, November 30, 1944, Shirley Temple 1944, b. 3345, f. 12, HRC.

56. See, for example, telegram from David O. Selznick, January 6, 1945, Shirley Temple—correspondence 1945, b. 584, f. 6, HRC.

57. Bosley Crowther, "THE SCREEN; 'Kiss and Tell,' With Shirley Temple in Leading Role of Delightful Contrasts, Has Its Premiere at the Capitol," *New York Times*, October 26, 1945, https://www.nytimes.com/1945/10/26/archives/the-screen-kiss-and-tell-with-shirley-temple -in-leading-role-of.html.

58. Anne Edwards, *Shirley Temple: American Princess* (Guilford, CT: Lyons Press, 2017), Kindle edition, loc 2355.

NOTES 251

59. Telegram from David O. Selznick, September 22, 1945, Shirley Temple—1945–1946, b. 3345, f. 13, HRC.

60. Shirley Temple's studio biography written by Paul Macnamara, March 1946, Shirley Temple, Core Collection, MHL.

61. Memo from David O. Selznick, November 19, 1945, Shirley Temple—1945–1946, b. 3345, f. 13, HRC.

62. Memo from David O. Selznick, October 11, 1945, Shirley Temple—1945–1946, b. 3345, f. 13, HRC.

63. See, for example, the press release from Mervin Houser, April 12, 1946, Shirley Temple—1945–1946, b. 3345, f. 13, HRC.

64. Selznick declared two years later that "NOTHING BUT DOOM WOULD AWAIT US IF WE PROCEEDED WITH FILMS OF THIS QUALITY" (telegram from David O. Selznick, April 26, 1948, Shirley Temple—1947–1948, b. 3346, f. 1, HRC). In the same document, he stated that the production or distribution of "JUNK FILMS" was not the solution even at times of the greatest crisis.

65. A third Selznick actor, Joseph Cotten, was to be loaned out for the film as well. He refused to participate, however, not wanting to play the potential suitor of a character played by a generation younger actress. He was punished for this by a temporary suspension of the contract. See letter from Joseph Cotten, February 25, 1946, Joseph Cotten—Correspondence 1946, b. 541, f. 9, HRC.

66. Telegram from David O. Selznick, April 18, 1946, Shirley Temple—1945–1946, b. 3345, f. 13, HRC.

67. Jeanine Basinger wrote that "during the thirties, it might have been done with style, wit, and cast of funny supporting characters, and a maximum of laughter. As a 1947 release, it suffered from tired blood" (Basinger, *Shirley Temple* [New York: Pyramid Publications, 1975], 117–19).

68. See "Stars Alone Not Enough," *Variety*, January 7, 1948, 62.

69. Bosley Crowther, "'Honeymoon,' Starring Shirley Temple, Franchot Tone and Guy Madison, Opens at Palace," *New York Times*, May 19, 1947, 27.

70. Cited in Edwards, *Shirley Temple*, loc 2543.

71. More in Schatz, *Boom and Bust*, 190.

72. Memo from David O. Selznick, July 11, 1946, Shirley Temple—1945–1946, b. 3345, f. 13, HRC.

73. Paramount had the rights to the original title and used it for their romantic comedy starring Paulette Goddard and Fred MacMurray which was in production at the same time. The popular term bobby-soxer referred to "middle-class white teenagers thought to be obsessed with swing music, 'jive talk,' and exploring their budding sexuality by stealthily circumventing parental authority" (Studlar, *Precocious Charms*, 175).

74. Jeanine Basinger, *Shirley Temple*, 119.

75. See Schatz, *Boom and Bust*, 467. According to *Variety*, the gross receipts were around $4.5 million, see "Top Grossers of 1947," *Variety*, January 7, 1947, 63.

76. Memo from Henry Willson, May 14, 1947, Shirley Temple—Correspondence 1946, b. 584, f. 7, HRC.

77. Memo from Henry Willson, June 24, 1947, Shirley Temple—Correspondence 1946, b. 584, f. 7, HRC.

78. Bosley Crowther, "The SCREEN; 'That Hagen Girl,' With Shirley Temple, at Strand," *New York Times*, October 25, 1947, 13. Additional responses are cited in Edwards, *Shirley Temple*, loc 2664.

79. "Stars Alone Not Enough," 62.

80. Specifically, she pocketed $90,000 (40 weeks times $2,250). See report from Billie Edwards, March 27, 1945, Shirley Temple—Correspondence 1945, b. 584, f. 6, HRC.

81. Undated report from Billie Edwards, Shirley Temple—Correspondence 1946, b. 584, f. 7, HRC.

82. See, for example, the report from Billie Edwards, June 12, 1947, Shirley Temple—Correspondence 1947, b. 584, f. 8, HRC.

83. See Schatz, *The Genius of the System*, 404–407. More about this in the following chapter.

84. See, for example, Brog., "Fort Apache," *Variety*, March 10, 1948, 10.

85. See "Top Grossers of 1948," *Variety*, January 5, 1949, 46.

86. Their different positions in the industry were expressed in monetary terms: while Temple's loan-out brought the studio $100,000, Selznick received only $5,000 for Agar. See the report from Daniel O'Shea, May 21, 1947, Shirley Temple—Correspondence 1947, b. 584, f. 8, HRC.

87. See the memoranda from Daniel O'Shea, August 1, and David O. Selznick, October 5, and the legal analysis from John J. Hayes, July 30, 1947, Shirley Temple—Correspondence 1947, b. 584, f. 8, HRC. The fact that this was a controversial topic is indicated by the heading "extremely confidential" in the report by Daniel O'Shea.

88. For example, *Modern Screen* magazine published on her twenty-first birthday a special edition (the first in its history) with seventeen pages of articles and photographs. See *Modern Screen* 38, no. 5 (April 1949): 37–53.

89. Bosley Crowther, "THE SCREEN IN REVIEW; Shirley Temple, Robert Young, John Agar Share 'Adventure in Baltimore,' at Capitol," *New York Times*, April 29, 1949, 27.

90. Rumors began to circulate at the same time concerning their marital problems, which could have also contributed to their division on screen.

91. For example, Gene Arneel, "Mr. Belvedere Goes to College," *Motion Picture Daily*, April 1, 1949, 3. The series was wrapped up two years later with the third part entitled *Mr. Belvedere Rings the Bell* (Twentieth Century-Fox).

92. See "The Story of Seabiscuit with Shirley Temple, Lon McCallister and Barry Fitzgerald," *Harrison's Reports*, October 29, 1949, 175; A. W., "Seabiscuit Center of Strand Movie," *New York Times*, November 12, 1949, 8.

93. See "A Kiss for Corliss Fair Program Comedy," *Film Bulletin* 18, no. 14 (July 3, 1950): 9.

94. In this part I use information derived from various documents in Shirley Temple, b. 617, f. 2, and Shirley Temple—1949–1958, b. 2305, f. 1, HRC.

95. Around 1946, she was supposed to be a part of the attractive cast in Selznick's adaptation of *Little Women* along with Jennifer Jones, Dorothy McGuire, and Diana Lynn, but the project was abandoned and completed at MGM without Selznick's contract actresses. She was also considered for the title role in *Portrait of Jennie*, but Jennifer Jones was chosen over her.

96. Cited in Basinger, *Shirley Temple*, 129.

97. Temple's divorce was finalized on December 5, 1950. She married for the second time eleven days later the businessman Charles Alden Black. Temple never returned to film, but in the late 1950s and early 1960s she hosted her television program *Shirley Temple's Storybook*.

NOTES   253

She was primarily involved in diplomatic activities in later years, serving as US Ambassador to Czechoslovakia between 1989 and 1992.

5. SELZNICK (GOES) INTERNATIONAL:
SELZNICK'S STUDIO AND INTERNATIONAL STARS AFTER 1945

1. David O. Selznick, "Five Dark Horses from Europe," *Picturegoer*, November 20, 1948, 16.

2. Selznick, "Five Dark Horses from Europe," 16.

3. The numbers are taken from Mark Glancy, "*Picturegoer*: The Fan Magazine and Popular Film Culture in Britain During the Second World War," *Historical Journal of Film, Radio and Television* 31, no. 4 (December 2011): 474.

4. Additionally, he also had in his employ during the 1940s British directors Alfred Hitchcock and Robert Stevenson.

5. For more on this, see Schatz, *Boom and Bust*, 285 and further.

6. Michael Conant, "The Impact of the Paramount Decrees," in Balio, ed., *The American Film Industry*, 361–62.

7. Thomas H. Guback, "Hollywood's International Market," in Balio, ed., *The American Film Industry*, 396.

8. Joseph Garncarz, "Hollywood in Germany: The Role of American Films in Germany, 1925–1990," in David W. Ellwood and Rob Kroes, eds., *Hollywood in Europe: Experiences of Cultural Hegemony* (Amsterdam: VU University Press, 1996), 94–135.

9. For example, in Italy, US films dominated the screens after the war and had a share of around 75 percent in total rentals (data for 1949). Anna Maria Torriglia, *Broken Time, Fragmented Space. A Cultural Map for Postwar Italy* (Toronto and Buffalo: University of Toronto Press, 2002), 101.

10. See Peter Lev, *The Fifties: Transforming the Screen, 1950–1959* (Berkeley and Los Angeles: University of California Press, 2003), 150.

11. For more on this, see Guback, "Hollywood's International Market," 387–409; Schatz, *Boom and Bust*, 297–303; and Daniel Steinhart, *Runaway Hollywood: Internationalizing Postwar Production and Location Shooting* (Berkeley and Los Angeles: University of California Press, 2019), 1–55.

12. Schatz, *Boom and Bust*, 295.

13. Steve Neale, "Arties and Imports, Exports and Runaways, Adult Films and Exploitation," in Neale, ed., *The Classical Hollywood Reader*, 403.

14. The topic of foreign films on US screens after World War II has been examined in detail by Tino Balio in *The Foreign Film Renaissance on American Screens, 1946–1973* (Madison: University of Wisconsin Press, 2010).

15. See Balio in *The Foreign Film Renaissance on American Screens, 1946–1973*, 64. I examined one of these cases, situated at the very edge of the US film industry, in the book *Hugo Haas a jeho (americké) filmy* (Praha: Casablanca, 2015).

16. On the challenges which actors and actresses from abroad faced in Hollywood, see Alastair Phillips and Ginette Vincendeau, "Film Trade, Global Culture and Transnational Cinema: An Introduction," in Phillips and Vincendeau, eds., *Journeys of Desire*, 3–18.

17. Schatz, *Boom and Bust*, 354.

18. For more on this, see Drew Casper, *Postwar Hollywood, 1946–1962* (Malden, MA: Blackwell Publishing, 2007), 44.

19. See Selznick, "Rank Join in English Production," *Showmen's Trade Review*, August 4, 1945, 8.

20. See the letter from David O. Selznick, November 9, 1945, GB 71 THM/433/2/19, Vivien Leigh Archive, Theater and Performance Collections, Victoria & Albert Museum. The collaboration is mentioned in Geoffrey Macnab, *J. Arthur Rank and the British Film Industry* (London and New York: Routledge, 1993), 72.

21. See the telegram from David O. Selznick, July 2, 1946, Shirley Temple—correspondence 1946, b. 584, f. 7, HRC.

22. On this, see Tino Balio, *United Artists: The Company Built by the Stars, Volume 1, 1919–1950* (Madison: University of Wisconsin Press, 2009), 181–85; Charles Drazin, *Korda: Britain's Only Movie Mogul* (London: Sidgwick & Jackson, 2002), 245–51.

23. Stephen Watts, "The Fabulous Mr. Selznick," *Picturegoer*, July 15, 1950, 13.

24. "What Will Selznick Pull Out of Hat Next?," *Film Bulletin*, June 7, 1948, 24.

25. On this see Charles Drazin, *In Search of The Third Man* (London: Methuen, 2000), 110–22. On the cooperation between Selznick and Korda, see also Charles Drazin, "Anglo-American Collaboration: Korda, Selznick and Goldwyn," in Paul Cooke, ed., *World Cinema's 'Dialogues' with Hollywood* (Basingstoke: Palgrave Macmillan, 2007), 63–66.

26. See Schatz, *Boom and Bust*, 297.

27. See various materials in the file Dorothy McGuire—correspondence 1948–1949, b. 562, f. 7, HRC.

28. Cited in Steve Eaton, "To Catch a *Bicycle Thief*: David O. Selznick's Failed Attempt to Co-Opt the Neorealist Classic," *The Italianist* 39, no. 2 (2019): 222.

29. I have based my account of the casting of *The Paradine Case* as well as the production history of the picture on materials in Selznick's archive as well as on a detailed description by Leonard J. Leff in *Hitchcock & Selznick*, 224–64.

30. Stephen Gundle, *Mussolini's Dream Factory: Film Stardom in Fascist Italy* (Oxford: Berghahn Books, 2013), Kindle edition, loc 152.

31. Gundle, *Mussolini's Dream Factory: Film Stardom in Fascist Italy*, loc 5495.

32. Gundle, *Mussolini's Dream Factory: Film Stardom in Fascist Italy*, loc 5381.

33. See Antonella Palmieri, "'America is Home . . . America is her Oyster!' The Dynamics of Ethnic Assimilation in Alida Valli's American Star Persona," in Andrea Bandhauer and Michelle Royer, eds., *Stars in World Cinema: Screen Icons and Star Systems Across Cultures* (London and New York: I. B. Tauris, 2015), 82.

34. Telegram from David O. Selznick, July 6, 1945, Alida Valli 1945, b. 3346, f. 4, HRC.

35. See the report from Robert H. Dann, November 3, 1945, and the contract with Alida Valli from the same day, Alida Valli 1945, b. 3346, f. 4, HRC.

36. See the memo from David O. Selznick, November 28, 1945, Alida Valli 1945, b. 3346, f. 4, HRC.

37. Unnamed and undated document, The Paradine Case—Casting Suggestions, b. 2409, f. 8, HRC.

38. See memo from David O. Selznick, November 28, 1945, Alida Valli 1945, b. 3346, f. 4, HRC.

39. Memo from David O. Selznick, August 18, 1945, Alida Valli 1945, b. 3346, f. 4, HRC.

NOTES

40. Thomson, *Showman*, 484. See also the telegram from Daniel O'Shea, May 1, 1946, and the telegram from Neil Agnew, December 4, 1946, Alida Valli 1946, b. 3346, f. 5, HRC.

41. Alida Valli's studio biography written by Whitney Bolton, Alida Valli Biography, b. 1635, f. 13, HRC.

42. Telegram from David O. Selznick, August 9, 1946, Alida Valli 1946, b. 3346, f. 5, HRC.

43. See, for example, the telegram from Jenia Reissar, August 11, 1946, Alida Valli 1946, b. 3346, f. 5, HRC.

44. On this see, for example, Selznick's memo from January 17, 1947, in which he suggested reducing the actress's weight by a combination of a diet, sports, special massages, and hormonal treatment; Alida Valli 1946, b. 3346, f. 5, HRC. All the filming and photoshoots for the magazines were arranged so as "to conceal her figure deficiencies." See the memo from Paul Macnamara, January 30, 1947, Alida Valli 1946, b. 3346, f. 5, HRC. Her official studio biography contained intentionally faulty information, according to which the actress only weighed 114 pounds; see Alida Valli's studio biography written by Whitney Bolton, Alida Valli Biography, b. 1635, f. 13, HRC.

45. Telegram from David O. Selznick, December 5, 1946, Alida Valli 1946, b. 3346, f. 5, HRC.

46. Telegram from David O. Selznick, January 8, 1947, Alida Valli 1947, b. 3346, f. 6, HRC.

47. Telegram from David O. Selznick, September 12, 1946, Alida Valli 1946, b. 3346, f. 5, HRC.

48. Memo from David O. Selznick, December 21, 1946, Alida Valli 1946, b. 3346, f. 5, HRC.

49. See the memo from David O. Selznick, November 27, 1946, Alida Valli 1946, b. 3346, f. 5, HRC.

50. See Stephen Gundle, "Alida Valli in Hollywood: From Star of Fascist Cinema to 'Selznick Siren,'" *Historical Journal of Film, Radio and Television* 32, no. 4 (2012): 569.

51. Memo from Anita Colby, February 13, 1947, Alida Valli 1947, b. 3346, f. 6.

52. She appeared in a photograph in *Life* magazine wearing an antique-style white gown with a caption that made the allusion explicit: "In her white gown with its flowing draperies, Alida Valli resembles a Greek goddess caught pausing for a pensive moment in the evening mist." "Valli," *Life* 21, no. 12 (September 22, 1947): 75.

53. "Cast of Characters," *Time*, March 1, 1948, 84.

54. Grable, Williams, Colbert, Day, Hayward, and Bergman are the only female stars who made it to Top 10 in this time frame.

55. Cited in Leff, *Hitchcock & Selznick*, 245.

56. Leff, *Hitchcock & Selznick*, 250.

57. See Leff, *Hitchcock & Selznick*, 224–64.

58. *Film Daily*, March 8, 1948, 6.

59. See Leff, *Hitchcock & Selznick*, 263.

60. Leo Miller, "Selznick, Stars, Hitch—So What?," *Bridgeport Herald*, August 29, 1948, The Paradine Case—clippings, 53.f-531, Gregory Peck Papers, Special Collections, MHL.

61. Kaspar Monahan, "Hitchcock 'Touch' Aids 'Paradine Case,'" *Pittsburgh, PA. Press*, August 20, 1948, The Paradine Case—clippings, 53.f-531, Gregory Peck Papers, Special Collections, MHL.

62. Kyle Crichton, "Veni, Vidi, Valli," *Collier's*, January 3, 1948, Alida Valli, The Core Collection, MHL.

63. More on this in Leff, *Hitchcock & Selznick*, 251; and Schatz, *The Genius of the System*, 404.

256 NOTES

64. Telegram from David O. Selznick, November 20, 1949, Alida Valli 1949/1950 1 of 2, b. 3347, f. 1, HRC.

65. According to Antonella Palmieri, the film served to tame and downplay the actress's otherness related to her foreign origin and make it easier for her to assimilate to the image of a "good immigrant" and the values which were viewed as beneficial and desirable in the postwar US (see Palmieri, "America is Home . . . America is her Oyster!," 89–91).

66. Richard B. Jewell, *Slow Fade to Black: The Decline of RKO Radio Pictures* (Oakland: University of California Press, 2016), 79. According to *Variety*, the film made less than *The Paradine Case* and only found itself in the latter half of the Top 100 highest-grossing films of the year ("Top Grossers of 1948," *Variety*, January 5, 1949, 46).

67. Harold Conway, "The Miracle of the Bells," *Evening Standard*, September 10, 1948, Clippings, b. 3814, f. 13, HRC. Additional excerpts of the film's reviews can be found in the same file.

68. Bosley Crowther, "Miracle of the Bells, RKO Film, Starring MacMurray, Valli and Sinatra, Opens on Rivoli," *New York Times*, March 17, 1948, 30. By coincidence, a costly biopic of Joan of Arc was being readied at the same time starring Ingrid Bergman in the title role. Hedda Hopper referred to the scenes from *The Miracle of the Bells*, in which Valli appeared in the costume of the French martyr, as "a dirty trick" on the actress, as the inevitable comparison with the more famous Swedish colleague could not turn out in her favor (Hedda Hopper, *Los Angeles Times*, March 23, 1948, Clippings, b. 3814, f. 12, HRC).

69. See Bosley Crowther, "Walk Softly, Stranger, With Alida Valli, Joseph Cotten, Starts Run at Globe," *New York Times*, October 16, 1950, 30.

70. See telegram from David O. Selznick, April 26, 1948, Alida Valli 1948, b. 3346, f. 7, HRC. Selznick also provided Joseph Cotten and the director Robert Stevenson for the production.

71. Richard B. Jewell and Vernon Harbin, *The RKO Story* (New Rochelle, NY: Arlington House, 1982), 253.

72. "The White Tower," *AFI Catalog of Feature Films*, https://catalog.afi.com/Film/26568 -THE-WHITE-TOWER.

73. See "Top Grossers of 1950," *Variety*, January 3, 1951, 58.

74. Gundle, "Alida Valli in Hollywood," 576.

75. Memo from David O. Selznick, December 21, 1950, Alida Valli 1949/1950 1 of 2, b. 3347, f. 1, HRC.

76. See Drazin, *In Search of The Third Man*, 26. On Selznick's role in the creation of *The Third Man*, see Charles Ramírez Berg, "'The Third Man's Third Man: David O. Selznick's Contribution to 'The Third Man,'" *Library Chronicle*, no. 36 (1986): 92–113.

77. See "Selznick Takes Time Out," *Life* 26, no. 12 (March 21, 1949): 69.

78. Memo from David O. Selznick, May 5, 1950, Alida Valli 1949/1950 1 of 2, b. 3347, f. 1, HRC.

79. More on this in Gundle, "Alida Valli in Hollywood," 578–80.

80. See memo from Jenia Reissar, August 1, 1950, Alida Valli 1949/1950 1 of 2, b. 3347, f. 1, HRC.

81. See "Top Grossers of 1950," *Variety*, January 3, 1951, 58.

82. Memo from David O. Selznick, April 11, 1946, Louis Jourdan—correspondence 1945, 46, 47, b. 556, f. 2, HRC.

83. Memo from David O. Selznick, April 11, 1946, Louis Jourdan—correspondence 1945, 46, 47, b. 556, f. 2, HRC.

NOTES

84. See the telegram from David O. Selznick, December 15, 1947, The Paradine Case Advertising, b. 1498, f. 13, HRC.

85. See Leff, *Hitchcock & Selznick*, 263.

86. William R. Weaver, "The Paradine Case," *Motion Picture Herald*, January 2, 1948, 4001 (section Product Digest).

87. Hilary Radner, "Louis Jourdan—The 'Hyper-sexual' Frenchman," in Phillips and Vincendeau, eds., *Journeys of Desire*, 125.

88. Radner, "Louis Jourdan—The 'Hyper-sexual' Frenchman," 126.

89. On this, see also Phillips and Vincendeau, "Film Trade, Global Culture and Transnational Cinema," in Phillips and Vincendeau, eds., *Journeys of Desire*, 13.

90. Robin Wood, "Louis Jourdan," in Tom Pendergast and Sara Pendergast, eds., *International Dictionary of Films and Filmmakers, Volume 3, Actors and Actresses* (Farmington Hills, MI: St. James Press, 2000), 629.

91. *Box Office Barometer*, November 15, 1947, 126.

92. "SRO to Handle 'Trilby,'" *Box Office*, April 10, 1948, 55.

93. See the advertisement in *Motion Picture Daily*, April 21, 1949, 13.

94. "Jennifer to Play Juliet," *New York World-Telegram*, November 15, 1947, Jennifer Jones, The Core Collection, MHL.

95. See telegram from David O. Selznick, June 19, 1949, Shirley Temple, b. 617, f. 4, HRC.

96. See Gaylyn Studlar, "Masochistic Performance and Female Subjectivity in *Letter from an Unknown Woman*," *Cinema Journal* 33, no. 3 (Spring 1994): 51. Only later did the film achieve "canonical status within cinema studies," especially amongst feminist critics. See Studlar, "Masochistic Performance and Female Subjectivity," 35.

97. Data taken from the financial records of MGM and cited in "No Minor Vices," *Wikipedia*, https://en.wikipedia.org/wiki/No_Minor_Vices#cite_note-Mannix-1.

98. "Top-Grossers of 1949," *Variety*, January 4, 1950, 59.

99. Telegram from Paul Small, November 4, 1949, Personal Appearances—Paul Small Co.—Selznick Stars 1950, b. 568, f. 8, HRC.

100. Quoted in the telegram from David O. Selznick, November 5, 1949, Personal Appearances—Paul Small Co.—Selznick Stars 1950, b. 568, f. 8, HRC.

101. Omar Rammey, "Stage & Screen: Movie Stars at State Try Hard but Lack Stage Savvy," *Cleveland Press*, November 26, 1949, Hollywood Stars, b. 1398, f. 3, HRC.

102. Letter from Paul Small, January 20, 1950, Files 113 Vanguard Films Inc. Selznick Stars of 1950 Tour, b. 101, f. 13, HRC.

103. For more, see the letter from Louis Jourdan (written prior to the tour), May 12, 1949, Louis Jourdan—correspondence 1945, 46, 47, b. 556, f. 4, HRC.

104. "Fidler in Hollywood," *Nevada State Journal*, January 11, 1950, 4.

105. Cal York, "Inside Stuff: Cal York's Gossip of Hollywood," *Photoplay* 38, no. 2 (August 1950): 10.

106. Ulrike Sieglohr, "Hildegard Knef," in Phillips and Vincendeau, eds., *Journeys of Desire*, 323.

107. "New German Star," *Life* 22, no. 20 (May 1947): 129–35.

108. Her partner at the time, and husband as of December 1947, was Kurt Hirsch, an American Jew of Czech origin who worked as a lower official in the occupied German film industry. See Ulrike Sieglohr, "Hildegard Knef: From Rubble Woman to Fallen Woman," in

Ulrike Sieglohr, ed., *Heroines without Heroes: Reconstructing Female and National Identities in European Cinema, 1945–51* (London and New York: Cassell, 2000), 115.

109. Telegram from David O. Selznick, May 17, 1947, Hildegard Knef, b. 3340, f. 5, HRC.

110. Memo from David O. Selznick, October 25, 1947, Hildegard Knef correspondence, b. 565, f. 1, HRC.

111. Telegram from Robert Ross, January 29, 1948, Hildegard Knef, b. 3340, f. 5, HRC.

112. See, for instance, telegram from David O. Selznick, February 2, 1948, Hildegard Knef correspondence, b. 565, f. 1, HRC.

113. Contract with Hildegard Knef from March 1, 1948, Hildegard Knef contracts and correspondence, b. 913, f. 4, HRC.

114. See Hildegard Knef's studio biography written by Mervin Houser, undated (ca. 1948), Hildegard Knef, The Core Collection, MHL.

115. Despite the efforts of Selznick's studio to "normalize" her name, newspaper and magazine articles, as well as promotional materials occasionally give her name as Hildegard. A certain inconsistency accompanied the actress throughout the rest of her career.

116. This aspect was also emphasized in articles in the press. In March 1948, for example, Louella Parsons wrote that "[t]he German actress, Hilde Knef, signed by David Selznick, is described as blonde, beautiful and, of course, anti-Nazi." See her article from March 4, 1948, which is part of Clippings 1946–1948, b. 3814, f. 1, HRC.

117. Hildegard Knef's studio biography written by Mervin Houser, undated (ca. 1948), Hildegard Knef, The Core Collection, MHL.

118. More on this in Alexander Doty, "Marlene Dietrich and Greta Garbo," 108–28.

119. Hildegard Knef's studio biography written by Mervin Houser, undated (ca. 1948), Hildegard Knef, The Core Collection, MHL.

120. Memo from David O. Selznick, August 13, 1948, Hildegard Knef correspondence, b. 565, f. 1, HRC.

121. Memo from David O. Selznick, September 16, 1948, Hildegard Knef correspondence, b. 565, f. 1, HRC.

122. Telegram from David O. Selznick, October 5, 1948, Hildegard Knef, b. 3340, f. 5, HRC.

123. See the telegrams from David O. Selznick from October 8 to 21, 1948, Hildegard Knef correspondence, b. 565, f. 1, HRC. Florence Marly, a French actress of Czech origin, eventually got the role in *Tokyo Joe*.

124. See the report from Mervin Houser, January 10, 1949, Hildegard Knef correspondence, b. 565, f. 1, HRC.

125. See the report from Mervin Houser, January 10, 1949, Hildegard Knef correspondence, b. 565, f. 1, HRC and the memo from David O. Selznick, September 30, 1948, Hildegard Knef, b. 3340, f. 5, HRC.

126. Memo from David O. Selznick, March 16, 1949, Hildegard Knef, b. 3340, f. 5, HRC.

127. Telegram from David O. Selznick, February 26, 1949, Hildegard Knef, b. 3340, f. 5, HRC.

128. Telegram from Daniel O'Shea, April 23, 1949, Hildegard Knef, b. 3340, f. 5, HRC.

129. Telegram from David O. Selznick, April 25, 1949, Hildegard Knef correspondence, b. 565, f. 1, HRC.

130. Letter from David O. Selznick, November 9, 1949, Hildegard Knef, b. 3340, f. 5, HRC.

131. More on this in the final chapter.

NOTES 259

6. THE MOST FAITHFUL OF THEM ALL:
JENNIFER JONES AFTER *THE SONG OF BERNADETTE*

1. John Huston, *Open Book* (Cambridge, MA: Da Capo Press, 1994), 268–69.

2. On this, see Jeffrey L. Carrier, *Jennifer Jones: A Bio-Bibliography* (New York: Greenwood Press, 1990), 11.

3. See Thomson, *Showman*, 440–46. The marriage of Jennifer Jones and Robert Walker and her affair with David O. Selznick are the subject of a book by Beverly Linet, *Star-Crossed: The Story of Robert Walker and Jennifer Jones* (New York: Berkley Books, 1988).

4. See Thomson, *Showman*, 448; Studlar, *Precocious Charms*, 166.

5. For example, Paul Green referred to Selznick as a "puppet master" (Green, *Jennifer Jones*, 9).

6. See Carrier, *Jennifer Jones*, xiv.

7. On the complicated psychosexual dynamics of their relationship, see Studlar, *Precocious Charms*, 159–201.

8. Shearer, "Man Who Makes Hollywood Tremble," 15. See also Aline Mosby, "Jennifer Jones Says Selznick Leaves Her Career Alone," *Stars and Stripes*, May 4, 1955, 15.

9. Paul Holt, "Gone to Earth? No, Back to Work," *Picturegoer*, July 26, 1952, 14.

10. Holt, "Gone to Earth?," 15.

11. Jimmie Fidler, "Jennifer Jones: Lady of Many Characters," *Indianapolis News*, February 7, 1949, 12.

12. Memo from David O. Selznick addressed to the head of production Ray Klune, cited in Green, *Jennifer Jones*, 46.

13. Memo from David O. Selznick from January 26, 1944, addressed to Darryl F. Zanuck, cited in Studlar, *Precocious Charms*, 179.

14. Both citations are taken from Green, *Jennifer Jones*, 51–52. On the casting of Jones in *Since You Went Away* and the intention to vary her roles from the very beginning, see the article "Selznick, It Seems, Knew His Jennifer Jones," *New York Herald Tribune*, April 23, 1944, Jennifer Jones, The Core Collection, MHL.

15. "The New Pictures," *Time*, March 17, 1947, 99.

16. Cited in Green, *Jennifer Jones*, 77.

17. *Variety* subsequently named Jones the highest-grossing star of the year, see "Top-Grossing Stars of 1947," *Variety*, January 7, 1948, 63.

18. For an example of a sharply negative review, see Bosley Crowther, "'Duel in the Sun,' Selznick's Lavish Western That Stars Jennifer Jones, Gregory Peck, Opens at Loew's Theatres," *New York Times*, May 8, 1947, 30. As *Life* magazine cynically noted, criticism from conservative circles could have only benefited the film commercially: "Condemned last week by California branches of Catholic, Protestant, and Jewish organizations, by the D.A.R., the American Legion Auxiliary, the Girl Scouts and other groups, and threatened with a possible ban by the Legion of Decency, *Duel* reaped the usual reward: a 30% rise at the box office" ("Duel in the Sun," *Life*, February 10, 1947, 68).

19. Memo from David O. Selznick, August 13, 1947, cited in Behlmer, *Memo from David O. Selznick*, 373.

20. Pressbook for *Carrie*, PBM-25705, Special Collections, British Film Institute.

21. R. Barton Palmer, "Introduction: Stardom in the 1950s," in R. Barton Palmer, ed., *Larger Than Life: Movie Stars of the 1950s* (New Brunswick, NJ, and London: Rutgers University Press, 2010), 11.

22. Janet Staiger, "The Package-Unit System: Unit Management after 1955," in David Bordwell, Janet Staiger, and Kristin Thompson, *The Classical Hollywood Cinema: Film Style & Mode of Production to 1960* (New York: Columbia University Press, 1985), 332.

23. The number of actors and actresses employed at the Hollywood studios fell between 1946 and 1956 from 804 to 229. See Regev, *Working in Hollywood*, 197.

24. Hedda Hopper, "Meet Miss Jones," *Chicago Sunday Tribune*, March 2, 1947, 16.

25. Memo from David O. Selznick from January 4, 1952, cited in Studlar, *Precocious Charms*, 275.

26. For example, he provided Jones for *Love Letters* under the provision that the Oscar-winning cinematographer Lee Garmes would be hired by the film's producer Hal Wallis. See Green, *Jennifer Jones*, 55.

27. Studlar, *Precocious Charms*, 201.

28. I deal with the collaboration between Selznick and Wyler in more detail in Milan Hain, "Clash of the Titans: The Hidden Collaboration of William Wyler and David O. Selznick on *Carrie* (1952)," in John Price, ed., *ReFocus: The Films of William Wyler* (Edinburgh: Edinburgh University Press, forthcoming in 2023).

29. The cost, mainly due to the spectacular finale, reached $4 million, while worldwide gross receipts amounted only to $1.5 million. See Green, *Jennifer Jones*, 88.

30. For more on this, see the chapter "The Construction of Naturalness: Ingrid Bergman and *Intermezzo: A Love Story*."

31. Winner of seven Academy Awards, *The Best Years of Our Lives* became the highest-grossing film of the decade. See Schatz, *Boom and Bust*, 466–68.

32. See "Top-Grossers of 1950," *Variety*, January 3, 1951, 58. Wyler blamed Paramount, which he said had focused on promoting the biblical epic *Samson and Delilah* (1949), directed by Cecil B. DeMille, instead of *The Heiress*. See Jan Herman, *A Talent for Trouble: The Life of Hollywood's Most Acclaimed Director, William Wyler* (New York: Da Capo Press, 1997), 314.

33. The novel, considered a key work of American naturalism, concerns themes such as bigamy and social inequality. Since I discuss some of the shifts in the story and the conception of the main characters in the film adaptation, I find it useful to briefly summarize the plot of the novel. *Sister Carrie* tells the story of a simple Wisconsin girl who decides to try her luck in the big city. On the train to Chicago, she meets a businessman, Drouet, who helps her financially to get started in her new home. The pair begin living together in a pretend marriage, but their relationship falls apart when Carrie meets the dashing manager of an upscale restaurant, Hurstwood. Hurstwood falls in love with the girl but is married and to escape scandal and to remain financially secure, he commits theft. Although he recovers most of the stolen money, the stigma of the crime haunts him even after he moves to New York and prevents him from finding a steady, well-paying position. His inevitable social downfall negatively affects his relationship with Carrie, who one day leaves him. As she gradually becomes a respected stage actress, Hurstwood loses everything and scrapes along as a homeless beggar. Eventually, he cannot bear the situation and commits suicide. Carrie,

NOTES

261

meanwhile, has achieved professional success and material security, but nevertheless remains lonely and unhappy.

34. Letter from David O. Selznick, June 22, 1950, Carrie—correspondence, 1.f-19, William Wyler Papers, MHL.

35. As an example of failed casting, Selznick cited Lana Turner in the adaptation of Sinclair Lewis's novel *Cass Timberlane* (1947, MGM). While commercially successful, the film did not represent the first-rate qualities Wyler should have aspired to, according to Selznick. See letter from David O. Selznick, June 22, 1950, Carrie—correspondence, 1.f-19, William Wyler Papers, MHL.

36. On this see the telegram from David O. Selznick, 14 June 1950, Carrie—correspondence, 1.f-19, William Wyler Papers, MHL.

37. Letter from David O. Selznick, November 11, 1949, Carrie—correspondence, 1.f-19, William Wyler Papers, MHL. Selznick suggested Ronald Colman, Charles Boyer, Humphrey Bogart, Vittorio De Sica, William Powell, John Wayne, and Fredric March as other candidates for Hurstwood but he had strong reservations about each of them, such as their being too old (Colman) or their type being too "exotic" (Boyer).

38. See letter from William Wyler, June 19, 1950, Carrie—correspondence, 1.f-19, William Wyler Papers, MHL.

39. Loan-out agreement for Jennifer Jones from July 10, 1950, Jennifer Jones—Loanouts, b. 908, f. 24, HRC. The same file contains an addendum to the contract from August 14, 1950. Previously, Selznick had received $200,000 or more for loaning out Jones, see the report from Robert Dann, June 30, 1950, Jennifer Jones—Paramount Deal, b. 555, f. 5, HRC.

40. Letter from David O. Selznick, July 29, 1950, Carrie—correspondence, 1.f-19, William Wyler Papers, MHL.

41. This is explicitly mentioned, for example, in a letter from November 15, 1950, Carrie—correspondence, 1.f-19, William Wyler Papers, MHL.

42. This statement is not undermined by the fact that while some of his suggestions were accepted, many others were ignored. See below.

43. Letter from David O. Selznick, November 11, 1949, Carrie—correspondence, 1.f-19, William Wyler Papers, MHL. Correspondence between Selznick and Wyler is also part of the Selznick archive at the Harry Ransom Center. However, the Margaret Herrick Library materials also contain, in many cases, Wyler's handwritten notes, which indicate the director's attitude towards his colleague's reservations and recommendations.

44. Letter from David O. Selznick, November 11, 1949, Carrie—correspondence, 1.f-19, William Wyler Papers, MHL.

45. Letter from David O. Selznick, November 11, 1949, Carrie—correspondence, 1.f-19, William Wyler Papers, MHL.

46. Letter from David O. Selznick, July 29, 1950, Carrie—correspondence, 1.f-19, William Wyler Papers, MHL.

47. See letter from David O. Selznick, October 18, 1950, Carrie—correspondence, 1.f-19, William Wyler Papers, MHL.

48. Moreover, the change was mainly due to the pressure from the Production Code Administration (Joseph Breen had warned of the unacceptability of the suicide as early as May 1950) and Paramount executives who did not want to release such a depressing and

262 NOTES

pessimistic film in a time of Cold War and pervasive skepticism. On this see Herman, *A Talent for Trouble*, 330–31.

49. Letter from David O. Selznick, August 11, 1950, Carrie—correspondence, 1.f-19, William Wyler Papers, MHL.

50. Letter from David O. Selznick, August 24, 1950, Carrie—correspondence, 1.f-19, William Wyler Papers, MHL.

51. Letter from David O. Selznick, August 26, 1950, Carrie—correspondence, 1.f-19, William Wyler Papers, MHL.

52. See letter from David O. Selznick, December 4, 1950, Carrie—correspondence, 1.f-19, William Wyler Papers, MHL.

53. See Epstein, *Portrait of Jennifer*, 261; Herman, *A Talent for Trouble*, 328. Ironically, the main character in the film version of *Carrie* also suffers a miscarriage, while this motive does not appear in the original book.

54. Letter from David O. Selznick, March 10, 1951, Carrie—correspondence, 1.f-19, William Wyler Papers, MHL.

55. Letter from David O. Selznick, March 10, 1951, Carrie—correspondence, 1.f-19, William Wyler Papers, MHL.

56. On this see the letter from David O. Selznick, December 4, 1950, Carrie—correspondence, 1.f-19, William Wyler Papers, MHL.

57. Letter from David O. Selznick, November 20, 1951, Carrie—correspondence, 1.f-19, William Wyler Papers, MHL.

58. According to Wyler, Paramount was not equipped in those days to handle two major films simultaneously. See the letter from William Wyler, November 29, 1951, Carrie—correspondence, 1.f-19, William Wyler Papers, MHL. The postponement of the film's release may also have been caused by renewed investigations of film industry personnel for suspected Communist sympathies: Theodore Dreiser was a leftist, and a film based on his novel might have been considered un-American in the turbulent Cold War atmosphere. On this, see Carolyn Geduld, "Wyler's Suburban Sister: *Carrie* 1952," in Gerald Peary and Roger Shatzkin, eds., *The Classic American Novel and the Movies* (New York: Frederick Ungar Publishing, 1977), 152–64; and Herman, *A Talent for Trouble*, 330. *Carrie* thus eventually entered theaters after Wyler's subsequent film, *Detective Story* (1951, Paramount), which was filmed in February and March 1951.

59. According to *Variety* it reached the fifty-fourth position. See "Top Grossers of 1952," *Variety*, January 7, 1953, 61.

60. "Carrie," *Variety*, June 11, 1952, 6.

61. "Carrie," *Hollywood Reporter*, June 9, 1952, the excerpt is part of the file Carrie, The Core Collection, MHL.

62. "Top Grossers of 1951," *Variety*, January 2, 1952, 70.

63. See letter from David O. Selznick, March 10, 1951, Carrie—correspondence, 1.f-19, William Wyler Papers, MHL.

64. The uneasy combination of Dreiser and romance aimed at a female audience was reflected in the promotional campaign. Posters, print ads, and other materials often referenced the original novel, but also promised a "love story that you will love with all your heart! [...] The whispers were everywhere . . . but their love stopped at nothing!" Pressbook for *Carrie*, PBM-25705, Special Collections, British Film Institute. Selznick was involved in the advertising

NOTES   263

campaign (as evidenced by a letter from Barney Balaban), but I have been unable to ascertain the exact extent of his contributions. See the letter from Barney Balaban, February 20, 1952, Carrie—correspondence, 1.f-19, William Wyler Papers, MHL.

65. Lowell E. Redelings, "Carrie," *Hollywood Citizen-News*, August 20, 1952, the excerpt is part of the file Carrie, The Core Collection, MHL.

66. Bosley Crowther, "The Screen in Review; Carrie, With Laurence Olivier and Jennifer Jones, Is New Feature at the Capitol," *New York Times*, July 17, 1952, 20:2.

67. Bosley Crowther, "Halleluiah, Sister! Carrie Becomes a Good Girl on the Screen," *New York Times*, July 20, 1952, 2:1. Later commentators gave a similar assessment of the film and its heroine. Lawrence E. Hussman stated that the film's Carrie was "the most unrecognizable character. [. . .] Dreiser's self-absorbed, dreaming drifter [. . .] becomes a model of virtue and 'wifely' devotion" (Lawrence E. Hussman, "Adaptations, Film," in Keith Newlin, ed., *A Theodore Dreiser Encyclopedia* [Westport, CT, and London: Greenwood Press, 2003], 2). See also the commentary by the same author in "Squandered Possibilities: The Film Versions of Dreiser's Novels," where he mentions, among other things, that the film eliminated Carrie's materialism and fascination with the products of consumer society (Lawrence E. Hussman, "Squandered Possibilities: The Film Versions of Dreiser's Novels," in Miriam Gogol, ed., *Theodore Dreiser: Beyond Naturalism* [New York and London: New York University Press, 1995], 195). In a thorough comparison of the film version and the literary original, Robert E. Morsberger concluded that the film "turned a grimly naturalistic novel into a romantic soap opera" (Robert E. Morsberger, "'In Elf Land Disporting': Sister Carrie in Hollywood," *Bulletin of the Rocky Mountain Modern Language Association* 27, no. 4 [December 1973]: 219). The comparison between the film and the novel is also the subject of Geduld, "Wyler's Suburban Sister," 152–53.

68. Selznick repeatedly asked Wyler about the possibility of further cooperation. In April 1951, Wyler evasively replied that none of his projects were suitable for Jennifer Jones. In January 1952 he turned down a remake of the wartime romance *The Shopworn Angel* (1928, Paramount, and 1938, MGM), and in March he responded in the same way to the possibility of adapting *The Rain-Girl. A Romance of Today* by Herbert Jenkins. See the telegrams from William Wyler from April 23, 1951, January 2, 1952, and March 3, 1952, Carrie—correspondence, 1.f-19, William Wyler Papers, MHL.

69. More on this in the previous chapter, where I discuss the postwar context and the main motivations that led American producers to intensify international trade connections.

70. Cited in Green, *Jennifer Jones*, 112.

71. On this see the contract from August 1, 1950, A-203(i), London Film Productions, Special Collections, British Film Institute. See also Drazin, *Korda*, 322 and further. Although Drazin's interpretation is based on the study of archive materials, it is quite one-sided in favor of Korda.

72. Additional changes were carried out at the instigation of the Production Code Administration.

73. For an extremely negative contemporary review of Korda and Powell's version, see Stephen Watts, "Gone to Earth and All That!," *Picturegoer*, November 4, 1950, 10–11. Selznick's cut was intended, among other things, to clarify the motivations of the characters, to tone down the symbolic and allegorical tone of some scenes, and thus to make the story more comprehensible to the mainstream (North American) moviegoers; the result, however, was

rather the opposite. According to one Canadian exhibitor, the film was "jumpy" and "business was terrible." See "What the Picture Did for Me," *Motion Picture Herald*, December 20, 1952, 48. *Gone to Earth* grossed only £110,000 in the UK, and *The Wild Heart* did not rank in the list of the Top 100 highest-grossing Hollywood titles for 1952 and 1953. See Vincent Porter, "The Robert Clark Account: Films Released in Britain by Associated British Pictures, British Lion, MGM, and Warner Bros., 1946–1957," *Historical Journal of Film, Radio and Television* 20, no. 4 (2000): 492; "Top Grossers of 1952," *Variety*, January 7, 1953, 61; "Top Grossers of 1953," *Variety*, January 13, 1954, 10–11. At the time, the failure of *Gone to Earth* was seen as a signal of Powell and Pressburger's artistic decline (contributed to by the similar failure of *The Elusive Pimpernel* [1950], a co-production with another Hollywood producer, Samuel Goldwyn), but in retrospect the film has been hailed as a mature and visually refined masterpiece. *The Wild Heart*, on the other hand, has been mostly condemned by commentators as a butchered version of a compelling, lyrical film. On this see, for example, the commentary by Pam Cook, "Retrospective: Gone to Earth," *Monthly Film Bulletin* 53, no. 643 (November 1986): 353–54.

74. A definition of neorealism along these lines can be found in Annette Kuhn and Guy Westwell, *Oxford Dictionary of Film Studies* (Oxford: Oxford University Press, 2020), 329–30.

75. Thomson, *Showman*, 582.

76. Eaton, "To Catch a *Bicycle Thief*," 223.

77. For more details on the case, see Eaton, "To Catch a *Bicycle Thief*," 223. See also "An Interview with Charles Thomas Samuels," in Howard Curle and Stephen Snyder, eds., *Vittorio De Sica: Contemporary Perspectives* (Toronto: University of Toronto Press, 2000), 34.

78. Henry Hart, "Indiscretion of an American Wife," *Films in Review* 8, no. 5 (May 1954): 191.

79. Some aspects of the film's troubled production history are discussed by Paola Bonifazio in her article "Unlikely Partners: Salvo d'Angelo, David O. Selznick, and Zavattini's 'Stazione Termini,'" *The Italianist* 39, no. 2 (2019): 231–41.

80. Capote's involvement in the film is described in Tison Pugh, *Truman Capote: A Literary Life at the Movies* (Athens and London: University of Georgia Press, 2014), 43–86.

81. See e.g., Patricia Bosworth, *Montgomery Clift: A Biography* (New York: Limelight Editions, 2007), 245.

82. "An Interview with Charles Thomas Samuels," 42. Jenia Reissar had earlier warned Selznick that Italian directors were not "used to working under supervision—they invariably act as producers, and they are scared stiff of having to bow to somebody else's wishes" (Memo from Jenia Reissar, May 4, 1947, cited in Bonifazio, "Unlikely Partners," 234–35).

83. "An Interview with Charles Thomas Samuels," 42.

84. Thomson, *Showman*, 584.

85. See also Dylan Levy, "Atoning for an Indiscretion: The Impact of Reception, Publicity, and Censorship on the Re-editing of *Stazione Termini*," *The Italianist* 39, no. 2 (2019): 253. Recently, the film's troubled production history has been recounted in detail in Catherine O'Rawe, "Italian Neorealism and the 'Woman's Film': Selznick, De Sica and *Stazione Termini*," *Screen* 61, no. 4 (Winter 2020): 505–24.

86. Thomson, *Showman*, 582.

87. On this see Leonard J. Leff's audio commentary, *Indiscretion of an American Wife*, DVD (Criterion Collection, 2003). As documented by Dylan Levy, the audience in Italy was split "in a manner that paralleled the film's own conflict between De Sica's neorealist approach and the conventions of Hollywood melodrama at work. Some critics who praised the film's

NOTES 265

treatment of the real Stazione Termini and focus on peripheral characters did so on the basis of neorealism's prestige. [. . .] Other Italian critics, however, allegedly praised and criticized the film for the exact opposite reasons; that is, they felt the film was better as an exercise in melodrama than in neorealism" (Levy, "Atoning for an Indiscretion," 254).

88. Selznick was convinced that each story dictates its own ideal length and there is no universal rule for how long a film should be. In 1939, for example, he completed both the nearly four-hour epic *Gone with the Wind* and the seventy-minute *Intermezzo*. See the telegram from David O. Selznick, October 4, 1944, cited in Behlmer, *Memo from David O. Selznick*, 345.

89. Cited in Levy, "Atoning for an Indiscretion," 256.

90. A comparison of the two versions of the film is also the subject of the video essay "What Is Neorealism?" created by kogonada for *Sight & Sound*, http://www.bfi.org.uk/news -opinion/sight-sound-magazine/comment/video-essay-what-neorealism. An analysis of the film focusing on, among other things, gender relations is included in Torriglia, *Broken Time, Fragmented Space*, 101–9.

91. Clift's rather late arrival on the scene (in both versions) suggests that the film privileged Jones. Sam Gaglio argues that Clift's role in the film was to "reinforce Jones' character and star-power by imitating an Italian lover, which fits seamlessly with Selznick's agenda to keep her at the forefront of the film." Gaglio also claims that Clift's inept, emasculated character undermines traditional concepts of masculinity (Sam Gaglio, "Indiscretions of an Italian Lover: Montgomery Clift, Masculinity, and Melodrama," *The Italianist* 39, no. 2 [2019]: 242–50).

92. Cited in Levy, "Atoning for an Indiscretion," 253.

93. See kogonada, "What Is Neorealism?"

94. Amy Lawrence, *The Passion of Montgomery Clift* (Berkeley and Los Angeles: University of California Press, 2010), 278. A similar view is expressed by Dylan Levy who mentions "Selznick's acquiescence to censorship" as the most probable cause (see Levy, "Atoning for an Indiscretion," 262–64).

95. On this see "Indiscretion of an American Wife," *Variety*, December 31, 1953, https://variety.com/1953/film/reviews/indiscretion-of-an-american-wife-1200417676/.

96. See Green, *Jennifer Jones*, 133.

97. Selznick considered having Jones herself perform in the prologue, merely imitating the vocals of a professional singer. In the end, however, he decided to go ahead with Patti Page instead. See Green, *Jennifer Jones*, 133.

98. Hart, "Indiscretion of an American Wife," 191.

99. Crowther also blamed the filmmakers for the inclusion of an eight-minute "juke-box short" that adds nothing to the film; however, he rated Jones's performance positively (Bosley Crowther, "The Screen in Review: Jennifer Jones Stars in Drama at Astor," *New York Times*, June 26, 1954, 7).

100. Levy, "Atoning for an Indiscretion," 256–57.

101. Levy, "Atoning for an Indiscretion," 264.

102. Schatz, *The Genius of the System*, 336.

103. See the memo from David O. Selznick, January 24, 1944, cited in Behlmer, *Memo from David O. Selznick*, 352. More on this in the chapter on male stars.

104. John Huston later recalled: "From the moment I saw the script, David and I were in conflict. Through David's influence on Hecht, the Hemingway story had simply become a vehicle for the female lead—Jennifer Jones" (Huston, *Open Book*, 302).

266 NOTES

105. See the eleven-page memo from David O. Selznick, March 6, A Farewell to Arms, EXEBD 37538, Oswald Morris Papers, Bill Douglas Cinema Museum.

106. Bosley Crowther, "The Screen: David Selznick's 'A Farewell to Arms,'" *New York Times*, January 25, 1958, 14. The film, which cost over $4 million to make, grossed $6.9 million worldwide, falling short of other 1950s blockbusters. See Thomson, *Showman*, 633.

107. Thomson, *Showman*, 546.

108. Elizabeth Forrest, "Still No Joy for Jennifer," *Picturegoer*, December 19, 1953, 7.

109. Rosten, *Hollywood: The Movie Colony, the Movie Makers*, 338.

110. See J. E. Smyth, *Nobody's Girl Friday: The Women Who Ran Hollywood* (Oxford: Oxford University Press, 2018), 239–44.

111. In addition to the films discussed here, Selznick interfered in various ways in the actress's remaining projects—most noticeably in *We Were Strangers*, *Ruby Gentry*, and *Beat the Devil* (1953, Romulus Films/Santana Pictures).

CONCLUSION. THE SELZNICK BRAND:
IN THE TRADITION OF QUALITY AND PRESTIGE

1. Cited in Vertrees, *Selznick's Vision*, 8.

2. Another independent producer Samuel Goldwyn ended up in the second position. Out of the large studios, MGM dominated over Warner Bros. with the rest lagging more significantly. Rosten, *Hollywood: The Movie Colony, the Movie Makers*, 175.

3. The brand is represented by a set of values and characteristics which help increase awareness of the product and distinguish it from the competition. This differentiation is based primarily on the name/title, the appearance (including the logo), and promotion. The goal is to create a positive relationship between the product and the consumer. See McDonald, *Hollywood Stardom*, 41–43.

4. Kyle Dawson Edwards, "Brand-Name Literature: Film Adaptation and Selznick International Pictures' *Rebecca* (1940)," *Cinema Journal* 45, no. 3 (spring 2006): 33.

5. Memo from David O. Selznick, December 8, 1961, cited in Vertrees, *Selznick's Vision*, 8–9.

6. Pressbook for *Since You Went Away*, author's collection.

7. On the signs of quality and prestige in film, see Geoff King, *Quality Hollywood: Markers of Distinction in Contemporary Studio Film* (London and New York: I. B. Tauris, 2016), 45–80; Tino Balio defines the prestige film as one of the main production trends in the 1930s Hollywood and lists Selznick as its main representative (Tino Balio, *Grand Design: Hollywood as a Modern Business Enterprise, 1930–1939* [Berkeley, Los Angeles, and London: University of California Press, 1995], 179–80, 207–11).

8. Edwards, "Brand-Name Literature," 36.

9. While Selznick completed eleven pictures in his own production in the years 1936 to 1940, over the following five-year period there were only two titles.

10. A complete overview is available as "Top Ten Money Making Stars Poll," *Wikipedia*, https://en.wikipedia.org/wiki/Top_Ten_Money_Making_Stars_Poll. It wasn't until 1960 that another woman (Doris Day) ranked in the first spot. Grable's ten consecutive Top 10 finishes is an extraordinary feat, surpassed among women only by Mary Pickford in the 1910s and 1920s.

NOTES

11. See the memo from David O. Selznick, June 26, 1946, Talent, b. 985, f. 9, HRC.

12. Schatz, *Boom and Bust*, 211.

13. On the star image of Betty Grable during the war and her association with the musicals of Twentieth Century-Fox, see Lev, *Twentieth Century-Fox*, 87–95.

14. Basinger, *The Star Machine*, 514–19.

15. Only Shirley Temple, who was supposed to embody the type of an energetic teenager, and, partially, Joseph Cotten, who was transformed into a romantic hero during the war, can be regarded as exceptions.

16. Barry King, "Articulating Stardom," in Butler, ed., *Star Texts*, 125–54. King also notes that stardom based on a stable type usually lasts shorter as it quickly leads to saturation of audience demand. This was not, however, the case for Betty Grable—she was a prominent star for approximately fifteen years.

17. Paul McDonald makes a distinction between genre stars (usually associated with big-budget blockbusters) and actorly and prestige stars: while the first group primarily focuses on economic valorization in the form of high revenues, the latter is aimed at ensuring artistic valorization in the form of recognition and honors. Even here, however, the final goal is to transform symbolic capital into economic capital as "they achieve commerce through art" (McDonald, *Hollywood Stardom*, 33).

18. Cited in Smit, "Marketing Ingrid Bergman," 249.

19. Carlile and Speiser, "Ingrid Bergman," 108.

20. During her long career she was never nominated for an Oscar or a Golden Globe. The Internet Movie Database lists the star on the Hollywood Walk of Fame as the only award bestowed upon her. See "Betty Grable Awards," *Internet Movie Database*, https://www.imdb .com/name/nm0002107/awards.

21. Adrienne L. McLean, "Betty Grable and Rita Hayworth: Pinned Up," in Griffin, ed., *What Dreams Were Made Of*, 170.

22. Cited in McLean, "Betty Grable and Rita Hayworth," 170.

23. On this, see Mary Mallory, "Hollywood Heights: Santa Barbara's Lobero Theatre: David O. Selznick's Summer Playhouse," *Daily Mirror*, June 8, 2015, https://ladailymirror .com/2015/06/08/mary-mallory-hollywood-heights-santa-barbaras-lobero-theatre-david-o -selznicks-summer-playhouse/; and "Strawhatting At Santa Barbara To Season Players, Ferret Pic Yarns," *Variety*, June 18, 1941, 2.

24. David Sterritt, "Postwar Hollywood, 1947–1967," in Claudia Springer and Julie Levinson, eds., *Acting* (New Brunswick, NJ: Rutgers University Press, 2015), 77.

25. The term ostentation or ostentatiousness is used by James Naremore to describe the extent to which the performance announces itself to the audience as a construct (see James Naremore, *Acting in the Cinema* [Berkeley, Los Angeles, and London: University of California Press, 1988], 34–45).

26. Cynthia Baron, *Modern Acting: The Lost Chapter of American Film and Theatre* (London: Palgrave Macmillan, 2016).

27. Lee Strasberg proclaimed that his actors often didn't distinguish between themselves and their characters. See Sterritt, "Postwar Hollywood, 1947–1967," 77.

28. On this practice, see Basinger, *The Star Machine*, 45.

29. See Basinger, *The Star Machine*, 515.

30. Schatz, *Boom and Bust*, 211.

31. As was the case with her acting partners, Fox made use of its own resources; it did not invest further financial expenses to ensure that Grable had more suitable and more competent collaborators with contracts at other studios.

32. Selznick himself authored screenplays for *Since You Went Away*, *Duel in the Sun*, and *The Paradine Case*.

33. See the memo from David O. Selznick, July 28, 1942, For Whom the Bell Tolls—Campaign, b. 3336, f. 1, HRC.

34. Focus on the female body, mediated by more distant framings of the camera, was more frequent for starlets, industry newcomers, or aspiring actresses who were often shot outdoors wearing swimsuits or dresses with low necklines. As remarked by Šárka Gmiterková, the "emphasis on close-ups imbued the star with a degree of polish and sophistication, which contrasted with the more 'natural' feeling of the young, active female body captured in medium shots." The close-ups were also viewed as signs of the stars' more prominent professional status. Šárka Gmiterková, "Importing Modern Venus: Hollywood, Starlets, and the Czech Star System of the Early-to-Mid 1930s," *Iluminace* 27, no. 1 (2015): 30.

35. Paul Macnamara, *Those Were the Days, My Friend: My Life in Hollywood with David O. Selznick and Others* (Metuchen, NJ, and London: Scarecrow Press, 1993), 58–61.

36. Basinger, *The Star Machine*, 515. Betty Grable posed for more pinup photographs than any other Hollywood star. See Basinger, *The Star Machine*, 516.

37. Twentieth Century-Fox reportedly valued her legs to such an extent that they had them insured for a quarter of a million dollars. See Shipman, *The Great Movie Stars 1*, 272.

38. The phenomenon of the pinup girls viewed through the feminist lens is the focus of Maria Elena Buszek. Her book, covering the 150-year-long history of the pinup, challenges the traditional perspective and shows that these pictures could have served as instruments of female (sexual) empowerment (see Maria Elena Buszek, *Pin-Up Grrrls. Feminism, Sexuality, Popular Culture* [Durham and London: Duke University Press, 2006]).

39. McLean, "Betty Grable and Rita Hayworth," 167.

40. Cited in Whitney Stine, *Stars and Star Handlers: The Business of Show* (Santa Monica, CA: Roundtable Publishing, 1985), 205.

BIBLIOGRAPHY

Only monographs, book chapters, and scholarly journal articles are listed. Articles in the daily press and contemporary magazines are cited in the notes.

Affron, Charles. *Star Acting: Gish, Garbo, Davis.* New York: E. P. Dutton, 1977.

Ames, Christopher. *Movies About the Movies: Hollywood Reflected.* Lexington: University Press of Kentucky, 1997.

Anderson, Christopher. *Hollywood TV: The Studio System in the Fifties.* Austin: University of Texas Press, 1994.

Baker, Carlos, ed. *Ernest Hemingway: Selected Letters, 1917–1961.* New York: Scribner, 2003.

Balio, Tino. *The Foreign Film Renaissance on American Screens, 1946–1973.* Madison: University of Wisconsin Press, 2010.

Balio, Tino. *Grand Design: Hollywood as a Modern Business Enterprise, 1930–1939.* Berkeley, Los Angeles, and London: University of California Press, 1995.

Balio, Tino. *MGM.* London and New York: Routledge, 2018.

Balio, Tino. *United Artists: The Company Built by the Stars, Volume 1, 1919–1950.* Madison: University of Wisconsin Press, 2009.

Baron, Cynthia. "Crafting Film Performances: Acting in the Hollywood Studio Era." In *Movie Acting. The Film Reader,* 83–94. Edited by Pamela Robertson Wojcik. New York and London: Routledge, 2004.

Baron, Cynthia. *Modern Acting: The Lost Chapter of American Film and Theatre.* London: Palgrave Macmillan, 2016.

Basinger, Jeanine. *Shirley Temple.* New York: Pyramid Publications, 1975.

Basinger, Jeanine. *A Woman's View: How Hollywood Spoke to Women, 1930–1960.* Hanover and London: Wesleyan University Press, 1993.

Basinger, Jeanine. *The Star Machine.* New York: Alfred A. Knopf, 2007.

Behlmer, Rudy. *Memo from David O. Selznick.* New York: Viking Press, 1972.

Behlmer, Rudy, and Tony Thomas. *Hollywood's Hollywood: The Movies About the Movies.* Secaucus, NJ: Citadel Press, 1975.

Berg, Charles Ramírez. "'The Third Man's Third Man: David O. Selznick's Contribution to 'The Third Man.'" *Library Chronicle,* no. 36 (1986): 92–113.

Bergman, Ingrid, and Alan Burgess. *Ingrid Bergman, My Story.* New York: Delacorte Press, 1980.

BIBLIOGRAPHY

Blaetz, Robin. "Ingrid Bergman: The Face of Authenticity in the Land of Illusion." In *What Dreams Were Made Of: Movie Stars of the 1940s*, 50–69. Edited by Sean Griffin. New Brunswick, NJ, and London: Rutgers University Press, 2011.

Bonifazio, Paola. "Unlikely Partners: Salvo d'Angelo, David O. Selznick, and Zavattini's 'Stazione Termini.'" *The Italianist* 39, no. 2 (2019): 231–41.

Bordwell, David, Janet Staiger, and Kristin Thompson. *The Classical Hollywood Cinema: Film Style & Mode of Production to 1960*. New York: Columbia University Press, 1985.

Bosworth, Patricia. *Montgomery Clift: A Biography*. New York: Limelight Editions, 2007.

Bourdieu, Pierre. *The Field of Cultural Production: Essays on Art and Literature*. New York: Columbia University Press, 1993.

Bowers, Ronald. *The Selznick Players*. South Brunswick and New York: A. S. Barnes and Company, 1976.

Buell Wilder, Margaret. *Since You Went Away . . . Letters to a Soldier from His Wife*. New York and London: Whittlesey House, 1943.

Buscombe, Edward. "Gene Autry and Roy Rogers: The Light of Western Stars." In *What Dreams Were Made Of: Movie Stars of the 1940s*, 33–49. Edited by Sean Griffin. Brunswick, NJ, and London: Rutgers University Press, 2011.

Buszek, Maria Elena. *Pin-Up Grrrls: Feminism, Sexuality, Popular Culture*. Durham and London: Duke University Press, 2006.

Cagle, Chris. "Classical Hollywood, 1928–1946." In *Cinematography*, 34–59. Edited by Patrick Keating. New Brunswick, NJ: Rutgers University Press, 2014.

Carman, Emily. "Going Independent in 1930s Hollywood: Freelance Star and Independent Producer Collaborations at United Artists." In *United Artists*, 57–74. Edited by Peter Krämer, Gary Needham, Yannis Tzioumakis, and Tino Balio. London and New York: Routledge, 2020.

Carman, Emily. *Independent Stardom: Freelance Women in the Hollywood Studio System*. Austin: University of Texas Press, 2016.

Carrier, Jeffrey L. *Jennifer Jones: A Bio-Bibliography*. New York: Greenwood Press, 1990.

Carter, Erica. *Dietrich's Ghosts: The Sublime and the Beautiful in Third Reich Film*. London: British Film Institute, 2007.

Casper, Drew. *Postwar Hollywood, 1946–1962*. Malden, MA: Blackwell Publishing, 2007.

Chapman, James, Mark Glancy, and Sue Harper, eds. *The New Film History: Sources, Methods, Approaches*. Basingstoke and New York: Palgrave Macmillan, 2009.

Coffin, Lesley L. *Hitchcock's Stars: Alfred Hitchcock and the Hollywood Star System*. Lanham, MD: Rowman & Littlefield, 2014.

Cohan, Steven. "Another Hollywood Picture? *A Star Is Born* (1937) and the Self-Reflexivity of the Backstudio Picture." In *Resetting the Scene: Classical Hollywood Revisited*, 84–96. Edited by Philippa Gates and Katherine Spring. Detroit: Wayne State University Press, 2021.

Cohan, Steven. *Hollywood by Hollywood*. Oxford: Oxford University Press, 2019.

Conant, Michael. "The Impact of the *Paramount* Decrees." In *The American Film Industry*, 346–70. Edited by Tino Balio. Madison: University of Wisconsin Press, 1976.

Cotten, Joseph. *Vanity Will Get You Somewhere: An Autobiography*. Lincoln, NE: toExcel Press, 2000.

Curle, Howard, and Stephen Snyder, eds. *Vittorio De Sica: Contemporary Perspectives*. Toronto: University of Toronto Press, 2000.

BIBLIOGRAPHY

Custen, George F. *Twentieth Century's Fox: Darryl F. Zanuck and the Culture of Hollywood.* New York: Basic Books, 1997.

Damico, James. "Ingrid from Lorraine to Stromboli: Analyzing the Public's Perception of a Film Star." In *Star Texts: Image and Performance in Film and Television*, 240–53. Edited by Jeremy Butler. Detroit: Wayne State University Press, 1991.

Davis, Ronald L. *The Glamour Factory: Inside Hollywood's Big Studio System.* Dallas: Southern Methodist University Press, 1993.

Desjardins, Mary. "'As Told by Helen Ferguson': Hollywood Publicity, Gender, and the Public Sphere." In *When Private Talk Goes Public: Gossip in American History*, 161–82. Edited by Kathleen A. Feeley and Jennifer Frost. New York: Palgrave Macmillan, 2014.

Doty, Alexander. "Marlene Dietrich and Greta Garbo: The Sexy Hausfrau versus the Swedish Sphinx." In *Glamour in a Golden Age: Movie Stars of the 1930s*, 108–28. Edited by Adrienne L. McLean. New Brunswick, NJ: Rutgers University Press, 2011.

Drazin, Charles. "Anglo-American Collaboration: Korda, Selznick and Goldwyn." In *World Cinema's 'Dialogues' with Hollywood*, 52–68. Edited by Paul Cooke. Basingstoke: Palgrave Macmillan, 2007.

Drazin, Charles. *In Search of The Third Man.* London: Methuen, 2000.

Drazin, Charles. *Korda: Britain's Only Movie Mogul.* London: Sidgwick & Jackson, 2002.

During, Lisabeth. "Saints, Scandals, and the Politics of Love: Simone Weil, Ingrid Bergman, Roberto Rossellini." *SubStance* 45, no. 3 (2016): 16–32.

Dyer, Richard. *Heavenly Bodies: Film Stars and Society*, second edition. Oxon and New York: Routledge, 2004.

Dyer, Richard. *Stars*, revised and updated edition. London: British Film Institute, 1998.

Eaton, Steve. "To Catch a *Bicycle Thief*: David O. Selznick's Failed Attempt to Co-Opt the Neorealist Classic." *The Italianist* 39, no. 2 (2019): 222–30.

Eckert, Charles. "Shirley Temple and the House of Rockefeller." *Jump Cut*, no. 2 (1974): 1, 17–20.

Edwards, Anne. *Shirley Temple: American Princess.* Guilford, CT: Lyons Press, 2017.

Edwards, Kyle Dawson. "Brand-Name Literature: Film Adaptation and Selznick International Pictures' *Rebecca* (1940)." *Cinema Journal* 45, no. 3 (2006), 32–58.

Epstein, Edward Z. *Portrait of Jennifer: A Biography of Jennifer Jones.* New York: Simon & Schuster, 1995.

Finler, Joel W. *The Hollywood Story.* London and New York: Wallflower Press, 2003.

Fontaine, Joan. *No Bed of Roses.* New York: Berkley Books, 1979.

Forslund, Bengt. "The Melodramas of Gustaf Molander." In *Swedish Film: An Introduction and Reader*, 109–18. Edited by Mariah Larsson and Anders Marklund. Lund: Nordic Academic Press, 2010.

Fowles, Jib. *Starstruck: Celebrity Performers and the American Public.* Washington and London: Smithsonian Institution Press, 1992.

Fuller-Seeley, Kathryn. "Shirley Temple: Making Dreams Come True." In *Glamour in a Golden Age: Movie Stars of the 1930s*, 44–65. Edited by Adrienne L. McLean. New Brunswick, NJ: Rutgers University Press, 2011.

Gaglio, Sam. "Indiscretions of an Italian Lover: Montgomery Clift, Masculinity, and Melodrama." *The Italianist* 39, no. 2 (2019): 242–50.

Garncarz, Joseph. "Die Schauspielerin wird Star. Ingrid Bergman—eine öffentliche Kunstfigur." In *Die Schauspielerin. Zur Kulturgeschichte der weiblichen Bühnenkunst*, 368–93. Edited by Renate Möhrmann. Frankfurt am Main: Insel Verlag, 2000.

Garncarz, Joseph. "Hollywood in Germany: The Role of American Films in Germany, 1925–1990." In *Hollywood in Europe: Experiences of Cultural Hegemony*, 94–135. Edited by David W. Ellwood and Rob Kroes. Amsterdam: VU University Press, 1996.

Geduld, Carolyn. "Wyler's Suburban Sister: *Carrie* 1952." In *The Classic American Novel and the Movies*, 152–64. Edited by Gerald Peary and Roger Shatzkin. New York: Frederick Ungar Publishing, 1977.

Gelley, Ora. *Stardom and the Aesthetics of Neorealism: Ingrid Bergman in Rossellini's Italy*. New York: Routledge, 2016.

Gemünden, Gerd, and Mary R. Desjardins, eds. *Dietrich Icon*. Durham and London: Duke University Press, 2007.

Giddens, Anthony. *The Constitution of Society: Outline of the Theory of Structuration*. Cambridge: Polity Press, 1984.

Glancy, Mark. "*Picturegoer*: The Fan Magazine and Popular Film Culture in Britain During the Second World War." *Historical Journal of Film, Radio and Television* 31, no. 4 (2011): 453–78.

Gmiterková, Šárka. "Importing Modern Venus: Hollywood, Starlets, and the Czech Star System of the Early-to-Mid 1930s." *Iluminace* 27, no. 1 (2015): 29–42.

Green, Paul. *Jennifer Jones: The Life and Films*. Jefferson, NC, and London: McFarland, 2011.

Guback, Thomas H. "Hollywood's International Market." In *The American Film Industry*, 387–409. Edited by Tino Balio. Madison: University of Wisconsin Press, 1976.

Gundle, Stephen. "Alida Valli in Hollywood: From Star of Fascist Cinema to 'Selznick Siren.'" *Historical Journal of Film, Radio and Television* 32, no. 4 (2012): 559–87.

Gundle, Stephen. *Mussolini's Dream Factory: Film Stardom in Fascist Italy*. Oxford: Berghahn Books, 2013.

Hain, Milan. "Clash of the Titans: The Hidden Collaboration of William Wyler and David O. Selznick on *Carrie* (1952)." In *ReFocus: The Films of William Wyler*. Edited by John Price. Edinburgh: Edinburgh University Press, forthcoming in 2023.

Hain, Milan. "From Stars to Starmakers: Spotlighting the Producers of Popular Screen Identities." *Slovenské divadlo* 69, no. 3 (2021): 307–21.

Hain, Milan. *Hugo Haas a jeho (americké) filmy*. Praha: Casablanca, 2015.

Hain, Milan. "Looking for 'I': Casting the Unnamed Heroine in Alfred Hitchcock and David O. Selznick's Adaptation of Rebecca." *Revue LISA/LISA e-journal* 19, no. 52 (2021). https://journals.openedition.org/lisa/13470.

Hannan, Brian. *Coming Back to a Theater Near You: A History of Hollywood Reissues, 1914–2014*. Jefferson, NC: McFarland, 2016.

Haver, Ronald. *David O. Selznick's Hollywood*. New York: Random House, 1980.

Hedling, Erik. "European Echoes of Hollywood Scandal: The Reception of Ingrid Bergman in 1950s Sweden." In *Headline Hollywood: A Century of Film Scandal*, 190–205. Edited by Adrienne L. McLean and David A. Cook. New Brunswick, NJ: Rutgers University Press, 2001.

Hemingway, Ernest. *For Whom the Bell Tolls*. New York: Simon & Schuster, 1995.

Herbert, Daniel. "The Transnational Film Remake in the American Press." In *Transnational Film Remakes*, 210–23. Edited by Iain Robert Smith and Constantine Verevis. Edinburgh: Edinburgh University Press, 2017.

BIBLIOGRAPHY

Herman, Jan. *A Talent for Trouble: The Life of Hollywood's Most Acclaimed Director, William Wyler*. New York: Da Capo Press, 1997.

Hischak, Thomas S. *1939: Hollywood's Greatest Year*. Lanham, MD: Rowman & Littlefield, 2017.

Hussman, Lawrence E. "Squandered Possibilities: The Film Versions of Dreiser's Novels." In *Theodore Dreiser: Beyond Naturalism*, 176–200. Edited by Miriam Gogol. New York and London: New York University Press, 1995.

Huston, John. *Open Book*. Cambridge, MA: Da Capo Press, 1994.

Jewell, Richard B. *Slow Fade to Black: The Decline of RKO Radio Pictures*. Oakland: University of California Press, 2016.

Jewell, Richard B., and Vernon Harbin. *The RKO Story*. New Rochelle, NY: Arlington House, 1982.

Jurca, Catherine. *Hollywood 1938: Motion Pictures' Greatest Year*. Berkeley, Los Angeles, and London: University of California Press, 2012.

Kasson, John F. *The Little Girl Who Fought the Great Depression: Shirley Temple and 1930s America*. New York and London: W. W. Norton & Company, 2014.

Keating, Patrick. *Hollywood Lighting from the Silent Era to Film Noir*. New York: Columbia University Press, 2010.

Keating, Patrick. "Shooting for Selznick: Craft and Collaboration in Hollywood Cinematography." In *The Classical Hollywood Reader*, 280–95. Edited by Steve Neale. London and New York: Routledge, 2012.

Kemper, Tom. *Hidden Talent: The Emergence of Hollywood Agents*. Berkeley, Los Angeles, and London: University of California Press, 2010.

King, Barry. "Articulating Stardom." In *Star Texts: Image and Performance in Film and Television*, 125–54. Edited by Jeremy Butler. Detroit: Wayne State University Press, 1991.

King, Geoff. *Quality Hollywood: Markers of Distinction in Contemporary Studio Film*. London and New York: I. B. Tauris, 2016.

Kozloff, Sarah. *The Life of the Author*. Montreal: caboose, 2014.

Krützen, Michaela. *The Most Beautiful Woman on the Screen: The Fabrication of the Star Greta Garbo*. Frankfurt am Main: Peter Lang GmbH, 1992.

Kuhn, Annette, and Guy Westwell. *Oxford Dictionary of Film Studies*. Oxford: Oxford University Press, 2020.

Laurence, Frank M. *Hemingway and the Movies*. Cambridge, MA: Da Capo Press, 1981.

Lawrence, Amy. *The Passion of Montgomery Clift*. Berkeley and Los Angeles: University of California Press, 2010.

Leff, Leonard J. *Hitchcock & Selznick: The Rich and Strange Collaboration of Alfred Hitchcock and David O. Selznick in Hollywood*. New York: Weidenfeld & Nicolson, 1987.

Leff, Leonard J. "Star Struck: Guy Madison and David Selznick in Postwar Hollywood." *Film History* 23, no. 4 (2011): 376–85.

Lev, Peter. *The Fifties: Transforming the Screen, 1950–1959*. Berkeley and Los Angeles: University of California Press, 2003.

Lev, Peter. *Twentieth Century-Fox: The Zanuck-Skouras Years, 1935–1965*. Austin: University of Texas Press, 2013.

Levy, Dylan. "Atoning for an Indiscretion: The Impact of Reception, Publicity, and Censorship on the Re-editing of *Stazione Termini*." *The Italianist* 39, no. 2 (2019): 251–66.

BIBLIOGRAPHY

Linet, Beverly. *Star-Crossed: The Story of Robert Walker and Jennifer Jones*. New York: Berkley Books, 1988.

Lunde, Arne. *Nordic Exposures: Scandinavian Identities in Classical Hollywood Cinema*. Seattle: University of Washington Press, 2010.

Macnab, Geoffrey. *J. Arthur Rank and the British Film Industry*. London and New York: Routledge, 1993.

Macnamara, Paul. *Those Were the Days, My Friend: My Life in Hollywood with David O. Selznick and Others*. Metuchen, NJ, and London: Scarecrow Press, 1993.

Maltby, Richard. *Hollywood Cinema*. Malden, MA: Blackwell Publishing, 2003.

Mayer Selznick, Irene. *A Private View*. New York: Alfred A. Knopf, 1983.

McDonald, Paul. *George Clooney*. London: British Film Institute, 2019.

McDonald, Paul. *Hollywood Stardom*. Malden, MA: Wiley-Blackwell, 2013.

McDonald, Paul. "Star Studies." In *Approaches to Popular Film*, 79–97. Edited by Joanne Hollows and Mark Jancovich. Manchester and New York: Manchester University Press, 1995.

McDonald, Paul. *The Star System: Hollywood's Production of Popular Identities*. London: Wallflower, 2000.

McGilligan, Patrick. *Alfred Hitchcock: A Life in Darkness and Light*. New York: HarperCollins, 2010.

McLean, Adrienne L. *Being Rita Hayworth: Labor, Identity, and Hollywood Stardom*. New Brunswick, NJ, and London: Rutgers University Press, 2004.

McLean, Adrienne L. "Betty Grable and Rita Hayworth: Pinned Up." In *What Dreams Were Made Of: Movie Stars of the 1940s*, 166–91. Edited by Sean Griffin. New Brunswick, NJ, and London: Rutgers University Press, 2011.

McLean, Adrienne L. "The Cinderella Princess and the Instrument of Evil: Revisiting Two Postwar Hollywood Star Scandals." In *Headline Hollywood: A Century of Film Scandal*, 163–89. Edited by Adrienne L. McLean and David A. Cook. New Brunswick, NJ: Rutgers University Press, 2001.

McLean, Adrienne L., ed. *Glamour in a Golden Age: Movie Stars of the 1930s*. New Brunswick, NJ: Rutgers University Press, 2011.

Merish, Lori. "Cuteness and Commodity Aesthetics: Tom Thumb and Shirley Temple." In *Freakery: Cultural Spectacles of the Extraordinary Body*, 185–206. Edited by Rosemarie Garland Thomson. New York and London: New York University Press, 1996.

Molyneaux, Gerard. *Gregory Peck: A Bio-Bibliography*. Westport, CT, and London: Greenwood Press, 1995.

Mordden, Ethan. *Movie Star: A Look at the Women Who Made Hollywood*. New York: St. Martin's Press, 1983.

Morsberger, Robert E. "'In Elf Land Disporting': *Sister Carrie* in Hollywood." *Bulletin of the Rocky Mountain Modern Language Association* 27, no. 4 (1973): 219–30.

Naremore, James. *Acting in the Cinema*. Berkeley, Los Angeles, and London: University of California Press, 1988.

Neale, Steve. "Arties and Imports, Exports and Runaways, Adult Films and Exploitation." In *The Classical Hollywood Reader*, 399–411. Edited by Steve Neale. London and New York: Routledge, 2012.

Newlin, Keith, ed. *A Theodore Dreiser Encyclopedia*. Westport, CT, and London: Greenwood Press, 2003.

BIBLIOGRAPHY

Ohmer, Susan. *George Gallup in Hollywood.* New York: Columbia University Press, 2006.

O'Neil, Tom. *Movie Awards: The Ultimate, Unofficial Guide to the Oscars, Golden Globes, Critics, Guild, & Indie Honors,* revised and updated edition. New York: Berkley Publishing Group, 2003.

O'Rawe, Catherine. "Italian Neorealism and the 'Woman's Film': Selznick, De Sica and *Stazione Termini.*" *Screen* 61, no. 4 (winter 2020): 505–24.

Osborne, Robert. *85 Years of the Oscar: The Official History of the Academy Awards.* New York and London: Abbeville Press Publishers, 2013.

Palmer, R. Barton, ed. *Larger Than Life: Movie Stars of the 1950s.* New Brunswick, NJ, and London: Rutgers University Press, 2010.

Palmieri, Antonella. "'America is Home . . . America is her Oyster!' The Dynamics of Ethnic Assimilation in Alida Valli's American Star Persona." In *Stars in World Cinema: Screen Icons and Star Systems Across Cultures,* 81–91. Edited by Andrea Bandhauer and Michelle Royer. London and New York: I. B. Tauris, 2015.

Pendergast, Tom, and Sara Pendergast, eds. *International Dictionary of Films and Filmmakers, Volume 3 Actors and Actresses.* Farmington Hills, MI: St. James Press, 2000.

Phillips, Alastair, and Ginette Vincendeau. "Film Trade, Global Culture and Transnational Cinema: An Introduction." In *Journeys of Desire: European Actors in Hollywood,* 3–18. Edited by Phillips and Vincendeau. London: British Film Institute, 2006.

Phillips, Alastair, and Ginette Vincendeau, eds. *Journeys of Desire: European Actors in Hollywood.* London: British Film Institute, 2006.

Platte, Nathan. *Making Music in Selznick's Hollywood.* Oxford: Oxford University Press, 2018.

Porter, Vincent. "The Robert Clark Account: Films Released in Britain by Associated British Pictures, British Lion, MGM, and Warner Bros., 1946–1957." *Historical Journal of Film, Radio and Television* 20, no. 4 (2000): 469–511.

Pugh, Tison. *Truman Capote: A Literary Life at the Movies.* Athens and London: University of Georgia Press, 2014.

Rabwin, Marcella. *Yes, Mr. Selznick: Recollections of Hollywood's Golden Era.* Pittsburgh: Dorrance Publishing, 1999.

Radner, Hilary. "Louis Jourdan—The 'Hyper-sexual' Frenchman." In *Journeys of Desire: European Actors in Hollywood,* 125–32. Edited by Alastair Phillips and Ginette Vincendeau. London: British Film Institute, 2006.

Regev, Ronny. *Working in Hollywood: How the Studio System Turned Creativity into Labor.* Chapel Hill: University of North Carolina Press, 2018.

Roberts, Randy. "John Wayne Goes to War." In *Hollywood's America: Understanding History Through Film,* 166–83. Edited by Steven Mintz, Randy Roberts, and David Weekly. Malden, MA: Wiley-Blackwell, 2016.

Rossellini, Isabella, and Lothar Schirmer. *Ingrid Bergman: A Life in Pictures.* San Francisco: Chronicle Books, 2015.

Rosten, Leo C. *Hollywood: The Movie Colony, the Movie Makers.* New York: Harcourt, Brace and Company, 1941.

Salt, Barry. *Film Style & Technology: History & Analysis.* London: Starword, 1992.

Savage, Jon. *Teenage: The Creation of Youth Culture.* New York, Viking Press, 2007.

Schary, Dore. *Heyday: An Autobiography.* Boston: Little, Brown and Company, 1979.

Schatz, Thomas. *Boom and Bust: The American Cinema in the 1940s*. New York: Charles Scribner's Sons, 1997.

Schatz, Thomas. *The Genius of the System: Hollywood Filmmaking in the Studio Era*. New York: Pantheon Books, 1988.

Schatz, Thomas. "'A Triumph of Bitchery': Warner Bros., Bette Davis, and *Jezebel*." In *The Studio System*, 74–92. Edited by Janet Staiger. New Brunswick, NJ: Rutgers University Press, 1995.

Sellors, C. P. *Film Authorship: Auteurs and Other Myths*. London: Wallflower Press, 2010.

Server, Lee. *Robert Mitchum: "Baby I Don't Care."* New York: St. Martin's Press, 2001.

Shingler, Martin. *Star Studies: A Critical Guide*. London: Palgrave Macmillan, 2012.

Shipman, David. *The Great Movie Stars 1: The Golden Years*. London: Macdonald, 1989.

Sieglohr, Ulrike. "Hildegard Knef: From Rubble Woman to Fallen Woman." In *Heroines without Heroes: Reconstructing Female and National Identities in European Cinema, 1945–51*, 113–27. Edited by Ulrike Siehlohr. London and New York: Cassell, 2000.

Smit, David. *Ingrid Bergman: The Life, Career and Public Image*. Jefferson, NC, and London: McFarland & Company, 2012.

Smit, David. "Marketing Ingrid Bergman." *Quarterly Review of Film and Video* 22, no. 3 (2005): 237–50.

Smyth, J. E. *Nobody's Girl Friday: The Women Who Ran Hollywood*. Oxford: Oxford University Press, 2018.

Solomon, Aubrey. *Twentieth Century-Fox: A Corporate and Financial History*. Lanham, MD: Scarecrow Press, 2002.

Spoto, Donald. *Notorious: The Life of Ingrid Bergman*. Cambridge, MA: Da Capo Press, 2001.

Spoto, Donald. *Spellbound by Beauty: Alfred Hitchcock and His Leading Ladies*. New York: Harmony Books, 2008.

Steinhart, Daniel. *Runaway Hollywood: Internationalizing Postwar Production and Location Shooting*. Berkeley and Los Angeles: University of California Press, 2019.

Sterritt, David. "Postwar Hollywood, 1947–1967." In *Acting*, 74–94. Edited by Claudia Springer and Julie Levinson. New Brunswick, NJ: Rutgers University Press, 2015.

Stine, Whitney. *Stars and Star Handlers: The Business of Show*. Santa Monica, CA: Roundtable Publishing, 1985.

Studlar, Gaylyn. *In the Realm of Pleasure: Von Sternberg, Dietrich, and the Masochistic Aesthetic*. New York: Columbia University Press, 1993.

Studlar, Gaylyn. "Masochistic Performance and Female Subjectivity in *Letter from an Unknown Woman*." *Cinema Journal* 33, no. 3 (1994): 35–57.

Studlar, Gaylyn. *Precocious Charms: Stars Performing Girlhood in Classical Hollywood Cinema*. Berkeley, Los Angeles, and London: University of California Press, 2013.

Thomas, Bob. *Selznick: The Man Who Produced* Gone with the Wind. Beverly Hills: New Millennium Press, 2001.

Thomson, David. *Ingrid Bergman*. New York: Faber and Faber, 2009.

Thomson, David. *Showman: The Life of David O. Selznick*. New York: Alfred A. Knopf, 1992.

Thorp, Margaret Farrand. *America at the Movies*. New Haven: Yale University Press, 1939.

Torriglia, Anna Maria. *Broken Time, Fragmented Space: A Cultural Map for Postwar Italy*. Toronto: University of Toronto Press, 2002.

Vertrees, Alan. *Selznick's Vision:* Gone with the Wind *and Hollywood Filmmaking*. Austin: University of Texas Press, 1997.

Werfel, Franz. *The Song of Bernadette*. New York: Viking Press, 1942.

Wilson, Steve. *The Making of Gone with the Wind*. Austin: University of Texas Press, 2014.

Windeler, Robert. *The Films of Shirley Temple*. Secaucus, NJ: Citadel Press, 1979.

Wood, Robin. *Hitchcock's Films Revisited*. New York: Columbia University Press, 2002.

INDEX

Page numbers in **bold** indicate illustrations.

Abbott, George, 125
Adam Had Four Sons (1941), 55
Adams, Christopher, 110
Adrian (Adrian Adolph Greenberg), 119
Adventure in Baltimore (1949), 135–36
Adventures of Tom Sawyer, The (1938), 9, 194
After the Thin Man (1936), 84
Agar, John, 127–30, 132, 134–35, 137, 158, 252n86
Agee, James, 122, 169
Agnew, Neil, 146
Albert, Dora, 46
Algiers (1938), 231n60
Allyson, June, 170
Ameche, Don, 104
Anchors Aweigh (1945), 94, 244n45
Anderson, Judith, 201, 203
Anderson, Mary, 76
Andrews, Dana, 83
Anna Karenina (1935), 7, 42, 194
Antonioni, Michelangelo, 155
Argento, Dario, 155
Arthur, Jean, 3, 6, 27, 52
Astaire, Fred, 3, 7

Bachelor and the Bobby-Soxer, The (1947), 11, 131–33, 137
Balaban, Barney, 179, 263n64
Barker, Jean, 185
Barnes, George, 66, 177–78
Baron, Lita (Isabelita), 158

Barrymore, Ethel, 145, 203
Barrymore, John, 223n11
Barrymore, Lionel, 120, 201, 203
Bartholomew, Freddie, 3, 9, 139
Basinger, Jeanine, 13, 22, 131, 136, 198
Bathing Beauty (1944), 108
Baum, Vicki, 130
Baxter, Anne, 73, 76
Beat the Devil (1953), 266n111
Beery, Wallace, 7
Behlmer, Rudy, 4, 9, 15
Bellamann, Henry, 157
Bells of St. Mary's, The (1945), 100, 199
Bennett, Constance, 27
Benny, Jack, 51
Benson, Sally, 129
Bergman, Ingmar, 144
Bergman, Ingrid, 3–5, 9–10, 12, 14–17, 19–50, **32**, **33**, **36**, **37**, **41**, 51–63, **62**, 65, 72, 75, 79–81, 82, 84, 96, 99, 107–9, 111–12, 116, 125, 139–40, 142–43, 146, 149–50, 155, 162, 164, 167, 170, 172, 188, 195, 199–201, 203–6, 230n31, 232n66, 238n60
Berkeley, Busby, 93
Bertolucci, Bernardo, 155
Best, Edna, 28–29, 45, 233n83
Best Years of Our Lives, The (1946), 174, 260n31
Between Yesterday and Tomorrow (1947), 160
Bickford, Charles, 203
Bicycle Thief, The (1948), 183

279

280 INDEX

Bill of Divorcement, A (1932), 6
Bird of Paradise (1932), 6
Birdwell, Russell, 7
Black Narcissus (1947), 182
Blaetz, Robin, 21
Blaustein, Julian, 133
Blue Bird, The (1940), 115
Bogart, Humphrey, 62, 156, 162, 172, 261n37
Bolton, Whitney, 72, 86
Border Incident (1949), 158
Born to Be Bad (1950), 90
Bowers, John, 223n11
Bowers, Ronald, 4
Boyer, Charles, 9, 25, 82, 107, 142, 156–57, 172, 261n37
Brando, Marlon, 184
Brazzi, Rossano, 3, 139–40, 143, 145, 157, 165
Breen, Joseph, 230n31, 261n48
Bride by Mistake (1944), 88–90
Brief Encounter (1945), 189
Brontë, Charlotte, 198
Brontë, Emily, 28
Brown, Katharine (Kay), 7, 12, 20, 25–27, 56–57, 64, 66, 91, 95–97, 140, 164, 200, 229n22
Buell Wilder, Margaret, 115, 117
Burke, Billie, 24
Burkhart, Howard, 158
Burnett, Frances Hodgson, 9
Burton, Richard, 143, 184
Busch, Niven, 172

Cagle, Chris, 30
Cagney, James, 105, 246n92
Calhoun, Rory, 12, 158
Camille (1936), 42
Capote, Truman, 184
Carey, Harry, 203
Carman, Emily, 9, 13
Carné, Marcel, 142
Carrie (1952), 167–68, 170, 172–81, 187
Carroll, Leo G., 145, 203
Carson, Robert, x–xi
Casablanca (1943), 49, 54–55, 59–60, 62–63, 234n4, 238n60
Cass Timberlane (1947), 90, 261n35
Challis, Christopher, 182

Children Are Watching Us (1944), 183
Children of Paradise (1945), 142
Chopin, Fryderyk, 88
Citizen Kane (1941), 101–2, 106
Claudia (1943), 10, 54–55, 63–71, **68**, 74–75, 88, 93, 103–4, 201, 238n61, 244n42
Claudia and David (1946), 70
Cleopatra (1934), 178
Clift, Montgomery, 144, 172, 180, 184–87, 265n91
Cluny Brown (1946), 170–71
Coburn, Charles, 83, 145, 203
Cockrell, Marian, 129
Colbert, Claudette, 10, 63, 105, 108, 120, 150, 169, 203
Colby, Anita, 149
Colman, Ronald, 9, 25, 82, 86, 90, 105, 142, 261n37
Come to the Stable (1949), 72
Coney Island (1943), 202
Connecticut Yankee in King Arthur's Court, A (1949), 158
Conquest (1937), 42, 84
Constant Nymph, The (1943), 52, 54, 74, 112, 198
Coogan, Jackie, 205
Cooper, Gary, 56, 58–60, **62**, 95, 99, 156, 235n25, 238n60
Cooper, Merian C., 3, 6
Cornell, Katharine, 97, 121
Cotten, Joseph, 3, 5, 10–11, 18, 79, 84, 93, 101–11, **106**, **110**, 117, 120, 123, 125, 131, 144, 153–55, 164, 172, 182, 189, 196, 198–200, 203, 205, 207, 239n76, 245n75, 245n82, 246n97, 247n109, 251n65, 256n70, 267n15
Cover Girl (1944), 94
Crain, Jeanne, 175
Crawford, Joan, 22, 231n52
Crichton, Kyle, 152
Cromwell, John, 6, 172
Cronin, A. J., 65, 93
Crowther, Bosley, 89, 102, 124, 128, 130, 132, 135, 153, 180–81, 189–90, 265n99
Cukor, George, 6–7, 66, 107, 231n52
Cummings, Irving, 202
Cunningham, E. A., 102

INDEX

Curly Top (1935), 248n3
Curtiz, Michael, 230n38
Cusack, Cyril, 182

Damico, James, 21
Dancing Lady (1933), 7, 223n4
Dane, Clemence, 6
Darnell, Linda, 73, 76, 240n106
Davenport, Marcia, 99
David and Bathsheba (1951), 180
David Copperfield (1935), 7, 9, 194
Davis, Bette, 63
Day, Doris, 150
Day, Laraine, 89
Days of Glory (1944), 90, 100, 109
Dead End (1937), 29
Decision Before Dawn (1951), 163
de Havilland, Olivia, 63, 203, 237n44
De Mejo, Oscar, 154
DeMille, Cecil B., 58, 178, 180, 260n32
De Sica, Vittorio, 12, 142, 144, 167, 172, 183–87, 261n37, 264–65n87
DeSylva, Buddy, 59
Diamond Horseshoe (1945), 202
Dickens, Charles, 144, 223n7
Dick Tracy's G-Men (1939), 72
Dieterle, William, 72, 172, 230n38
Dietrich, Marlene, 9, 19, 22, 24, 142, 146, 149, 151, 161–62
Dinner at Eight (1933), 7, **8**, 105, 115
Dior, Christian, 188
Diplomatic Courier (1952), 164
Dollar (1938), 35
Donlevy, Brian, 103
Double Indemnity (1944), 108
Douglas, Kirk, 143
Down Argentine Way (1940), 202
Dreiser, Theodore, 168, 170, 172–77, 180–81, 262n58, 262n64, 263n67
Dr. Jekyll and Mr. Hyde (1941), 49, 55, 57, 59–60, 79, 112, 199, 234n106
DuBarry Was a Lady (1943), 94
Duel in the Sun (1946), 10–11, 79, 100, 109, 131, 145, 169–70, 172, 182, 188, 191, 199, **200**, 203, 225n33, 259n18
du Maurier, Daphne, 24, 157, 198

du Maurier, George, 157, 167
Dunne, Irene, 86, **87**, 89
Durbin, Deanna, 88, 104, 108

Ecstasy (1933), 231n60
Edwards, Kyle Dawson, 194–95
El Greco, 34
Elusive Pimpernel, The (1950), 264n73
Enchanted Cottage, The (1945), 70, 89–90
Evans, Delight, 77
Evans, Harry, 47

Fairbanks, Douglas, Jr., 9, 24, 244n50
Farewell to Arms, A (1932), 235n25
Farewell to Arms, A (1957), 13, 172, 189–91, **190**, 235n21
Farmer's Daughter, The (1947), 11
Farrar, David, 182
Faye, Alice, 202
Feldman, Charles, 162
Ferber, Edna, 49, 238n60
Fidler, Jimmie, 168
Field, Betty, 58
Film Without a Title (1948), 160
Fitzgerald, Barry, 83
Flaubert, Gustave, 157, 170, 172
Fleming, Rhonda, 158
Flynn, Errol, 105, 246n92
Follow the Boys (1944), 237n41
Fonda, Henry, 83, 93, 99, 101, 134
Fontaine, Joan, 3, 5, 10, 12, 15, 24, 52–54, 67, 69, 71, 74–75, 79, 81–82, 84, 111–12, 116, 125, 140, 146, 156, 164, 167, 191, 195, 198–99, 201, 203–5, 207
Ford, Glenn, 153, 155
Ford, John, 134
For Me and My Gal (1942), 93–94
Forrest, Elizabeth, 191
Fort Apache (1948), 134
For Whom the Bell Tolls (1943), 52, 54–64, 72–73, 79, 112, 199, 203, 235n21, 236n32, 237n41, 238n55
Four Companions, The (1938), 26, 232n66
Francis, Kay, 3, 6
Franken, Rose, 63–64, 66
Freed, Arthur, 92–93

282 INDEX

Freeman, Frank Y., 56, 179
Frenchman's Creek (1944), 86, 198
Friedman, Harry, 39
Fuller-Seeley, Kathryn, 114–15

Gabin, Jean, 142
Gable, Clark, 7, 58, 82–85, 90, 100, 105, 225n26
Gallico, Paul, 184
Gallup, George, 17, 100, 151
Garbo, Greta, 19, 22, 41–42, 84, 100, 142, 145–46, 149–50, 153, 168, 232n74
Garden of Allah, The (1936), 9, 65, 82, 84
Garfield, John, 172
Garland, Judy, 94
Garmes, Lee, 149, 151, 260n26
Garncarz, Joseph, 21, 141
Garson, Greer, 52, 99, 191, 199
Gaslight (1944), 99, 107–8, 189, 238n60
Gaynor, Janet, ix–x, **x**, 3, 9, 24, 224n15
Gelley, Ora, 19
Gentleman Jim (1942), 86
Gentleman's Agreement (1947), 70
Gigi (1958), 160
Gilbert, John, 223n11
Ginsberg, Henry, 56
Gish, Lillian, 76, 203
Goddard, Paulette, 9, 24–25, 58, 251n73
Goebbels, Joseph, 39
Goetz, August, 175, 177
Goetz, Ruth, 175, 177
Goetz, William, 67, 73–75, 103
Going My Way (1944), 99, 108
Goldwyn, Samuel, 14, 29, 39, 46, 58–59, 147, 149, 180, 194, 202, 227n44, 264n73, 266n2
Gone to Earth (1950), 144, 171, 182–83, 185, 188, 263–64n73
Gone with the Wind (1939), 4–5, 10, 24, 35, 38, 42, 51–52, 55–56, 58–59, 62, 79, 82, 107, 131, 143, 145, 188, 194–95, 202–3, 225n26, 235n21, 265n88
Good Morning, Miss Dove (1955), 167
Goulding, Edmund, 67–69
Grable, Betty, 150, 197–200, 202, 205–7, **206**, 249n26, 266n10, 268n31, 268n36
Grand Hotel (1932), 42
Granger, Farley, 184

Grant, Cary, 101, 131, 183
Grayson, Kathryn, **94**
Graziati, Aldo (G. R. Aldo), 184
Greatest Show on Earth, The (1952), 180
Great Expectations (1946), 142
Green, Richard, 99
Greene, Graham, 154
grido, Il (1957), 155
Guernsey, Otis L., 130
Gundle, Stephen, 4, 146, 149, 153
Gurie, Sigrid, 39, 46
Guy Named Joe, A (1943), 83, 99

Hamilton, Neil, 110
Hamilton, Patrick, 107
Hamlet (1948), 142, 178
Hangmen Also Die! (1943), 103, 105
Hardy, Thomas, 144, 183
Hart, Henry, 183, 189
Haver, Ronald, 4, 15
Hayden, Sterling, 236n33
Hayward, Leland, 64, 66, 92–93. 97, 102
Hayward, Susan, 3, 150, 236n37
Hayworth, Rita, 19, 153, 199
Heaven Can Wait (1943), 103–4
Hebert, William, 39
Hecht, Ben, 92, 185, 265n104
Heflin, Van, 83, 101, 172
Heiress, The (1949), 174–75, 184, 260n32
Hellinger, Mark, 11
Hemingway, Ernest, 13, 52, 56–61, 172, 189, 235n21, 235n25, 235–36n26, 236n29, 236n30, 236n32, 237n51, 265n104
Hempstead, David, 130
Henie, Sonia, 22
Hepburn, Audrey, 143
Hepburn, Katharine, 3, 7, 65, 69
Herbert, Hugh F., 125, 129
Hers to Hold (1943), 104–5, 108, 246n85
Heston, Charlton, 172
Heydrich, Reinhard, 103
Hichens, Robert Smythe, 145
Hitchcock, Alfred, 4–5, 10, 12, 19, 49, 52, 92–93, 99, 102–3, 108, 145–46, 151–52, 154, 244n44
Hobson, Valerie, 103
Holden, William, 172

Holt, Paul, 168
Honeymoon (1947), 130, 132–33
Hope, Bob, 236n33
Hopper, Hedda, 86, 168, 204, 256n68
Hornblow, Arthur, 107
Houseman, John, 101, 200
Houser, Mervin, 161–62
Howard, Leslie, 27, 29, 34, 39–41, **41**, 43–45, 83, 203, 230n40, 233n81
Howe, James Wong, 188, 232n60
Hudson, Rock, 13, 172, 190–91
Hughes, Howard, 153
Hugo, Victor, 84
Humberstone, H. Bruce, 202
Hunchback of Notre Dame, The (1939), 84
Hunt, Marsha, 89
Huston, John, 13, 172, 190, 265n104
Huston, Walter, 203

Ibsen, Henrik, 144
I'll Be Seeing You (1944), 11, 108, 122–28, **124**, 131, 133, 137–38
Indiscretion of an American Wife. See *Terminal Station*
Inferno (1980), 155
Inglis, Frances, 97
Intermezzo (1936), 17, 20, 23, 25, 29, 35, **37**
Intermezzo: A Love Story (1939), 9, 17, 19–50, **32**, **33**, 52, 55, 65, 80, 82, 85, 174, 202, 230n31, 265n88
Irene (1940), 242n9
Irene (Irene Maud Lentz), 27
Isley, Phylis. *See* Jones, Jennifer
Ivanhoe (1952), 180
Ivy (1947), 90
I Wake Up Screaming (1941), 202

Jamaica Inn (1939), 230n40
James, Harry, 205
James, Henry, 154, 174
Jane Eyre (1943), 10, 67, 69, 86, 93, 198
Johnny Eager (1941), 101
Johnson, Van, 83
Jones, Jennifer, 3–5, 10, 13–14, 17–18, 52–55, 63, 67, 71–81, **78**, 82, 96, 103, 105, 108–9, **110**, 111–12, 117–18, **118**, 120, 125, 133, 144, 154,
156–57, 159, 162, 164, 166–92, **173**, **179**, **187**, **190**, 195, 198–99, **200**, 201–4, 206–7, 239n90, 240n98, 240n104, 241n117, 252n95, 263n68, 265n91, 265n97, 265n104
Jourdan, Louis, 3, 12, 18, 139–40, 145, 155–60, 162, 164–65, 184, 200, 203
Journey Into Fear (1943), 102, 105
Junior Miss (1945), 129
Jurca, Catherine, 22–23

Kathleen (1941), 115
Kazan, Elia, 70
Keating, Patrick, 31
Keighley, William, 130
Kelly, Gene, 5, 84, 91–95, **94**, 101–2, 109, 224n16, 244n41, 244n45
Kelly, Tommy, 3, 9
Kendrick, Richard, 110
Kennedy, Margaret, 198
Kent, Christopher. *See* Kjellin, Alf
Keon, Barbara, 145
Keys of the Kingdom, The (1944), 10, 65, 67, 69, 72, 93, 98–102, 109, 198, 244n44
King, Barry, 199
King, Don, 125
King, Henry, 73, 75–76, 172
King Kong (1933), 3, 6
Kiss and Tell (1945), 125–29, 131, 133, 135, 137–38
Kiss for Corliss, A (1949), 135–36
Kitty Foyle: The Natural History of a Woman (1940), 84
Kjellin, Alf, 139, 145, 165
Klune, Ray, 9
Knef, Hildegard, 139–40, 145, 160–65, 258nn115–16
Kneipple Roberts, Edith, 132
Knight, Eric, 95, 198
Koerner, Charles, 11, 102
kogonada, 186
Korda, Alexander, 12, 85, 101–2, 109, 143–44, 154, 164, 182–83, 235n12, 263n71

Ladd, Alan, 83
Lady in the Dark (1944), 86
Lady of Burlesque (1943), 246n82
Lamarr, Hedy, 22, 25, 142, 146, 231n60

Lang, Fritz, 103, 105, 162
Lang, Walter, 202
Lasky, Jesse L., 152
Laughton, Charles, 145, 203
Lawrence, Amy, 187
Lean, David, 142, 189
Leave Her to Heaven (1945), 100
Lee, Gypsy Rose, 103
Leff, Leonard J., 4, 108, 110, 151
Leigh, Vivien, 3–5, 9–10, 24, 38, 44, 52–53, 58, 75, 79, 81–82, 84, 112, 139–40, 143, 155, 195, 199–200, 202–5, 207, 235n12
LeRoy, Mervyn, 86
Letter from an Unknown Woman (1948), 156–57, 257n96
Lev, Peter, 114
Lewin, Albert, 86
Lewis, Sinclair, 261n35
Lewton, Val, 9
Lifeboat (1944), 244n44
Lindström, Petter, 26, 38
Little Lord Fauntleroy (1936), 9, 194
Little Princess, The (1939), 248n3
Little Women (1949), 165, 170, 252n95
Litvak, Anatole, 164
Lodger, The (1944), 246n82
Loew, David, 86
Lollobrigida, Gina, 143
Lombard, Carole, 9, 17, 24
Loren, Sophia, 143
Love Is a Many-Splendored Thing (1955), 171, 191
Love Letters (1945), 79, 108–9, 169, 260n26
Lover Come Back (1946), 237n41
Loy, Myrna, 22, 131
Lubitsch, Ernst, 103–4, 170, 172
Luna, La (1979), 155
Lydia (1941), 85, 101
Lynn, Diana, 252n95

Machatý, Gustav, 231n60
MacMurray, Fred, 155, 236n33, 251n73
Macnamara, Paul, 129, 149, 158, 170, 204
MacVicar, Martha. *See* Vickers, Martha
Madame Bovary (1943), 52, 156–58, 165, 170–72, 174

Madame Curie (1943), 52
Made for Each Other (1939), 9, 24–25, 82
Madison, Guy, 3–4, 12, 109–10, 130
Magnani, Anna, 143
Magnificent Ambersons, The (1942), 101–2
Maltby, Richard, xii
Mamoulian, Rouben, 182, 230n38
Manhattan Melodrama (1934), 7
Man in the Gray Flannel Suit, The (1956), 167
Mann, Anthony, 158
Man Who Knew Too Much, The (1934), 154
March, Fredric, ix, **x**, 9, 82, 261n37
Marin, Ned, 242n16
Marly, Florence, 258n123
Married and in Love (1940), 84
Marshal, Alan, 5, 82, 84–93, **87**, 101–2, 104, 109, 196, 201, 203, 242n18, 243n25, 243n38, 247n107
Marshall, Herbert, 203
Mason, Jason, 143
Matter of Life and Death, A (1946), 182
Mature, Victor, 99, 202
Mayer, Edith, 74
Mayer, Irene (Selznick), 74, 166
Mayer, Louis B., 7, 86, 92, 107
McClintic, Guthrie, 97
McCormick, John, 242n16
McCullers, Carson, 184
McDaniel, Hattie, 203
McDonald, Paul, 13, 267n17
McGuire, Dorothy, 3, 5, 10, 12, 17, 52–55, 63–71, 70, 75, 79, 81–82, 88, 96, 103–4, 112, 140, 144, 162, 164, 167–68, 172, 199–201, 204, 206, 239n83, 244n42, 252n95
McLean, Adrienne L., 199, 205
Menjou, Adolphe, ix, **x**
Menzies, William Cameron, 188
Meredith, Burgess, 85, 93
Milestone, Lewis, 6
Milland, Ray, 83
Miller, Leo, 151
Milner, Victor, 178
Minnelli, Vincente, 94, 160, 172
Miracle in Milan (1951), 184
Miracle of the Bells, The (1948), 152–53, 256n68

INDEX

Miracles Only Happen Once (1951), 154
Misérables, Les (1935), 29
Miss Annie Rooney (1942), 115
Mitchell, Margaret, 10, 24
Mitchell, Thomas, 203
Mitchum, Robert, 110
Molander, Gustaf, 25, 230n38
Monahan, Kaspar, 152
Montand, Yves, 143
Montesi, Wilma, 155
Montgomery, Robert, 83
Moon and Sixpence, The (1942), 86
Moorehead, Agnes, 120, 201, 203
Moravia, Alberto, 184
Mordden, Ethan, 21
More the Merrier, The (1943), 52
Morris, Maynard, 97
Morris, Oswald, 184, 190
Mortimer, Lee, 62
Mr. Belvedere Goes to College (1949), 135
Mr. Belvedere Rings the Bell (1951), 252n91
Mrs. Miniver (1942), 89, 99, 174
Murderers Are Among Us, The (1946), 160
Murphy, George, 85

Nathan, Robert, 172
Nazimova, Alla, 203
Neagle, Anna, 84, 242n9
Neff, Hildegarde. *See* Knef, Hildegard
Neuberger, Elsa, 25, 65, 229n22
New Frontier (1939), 72
Nichols, Dudley, 236n32
Night Without Sleep (1952), 164
Niven, David, 83, 90, 135
No Minor Vices (1948), 157
Nothing Sacred (1937), 9, 82
Notorious (1946), 10, 49
Novecento (1976), 155
Nugent, Frank S., 44–45

Oberon, Merle, 25, 85
O'Brien, Margaret, 83
O'Brien, Willis, 3
Octopussy (1983), 160
Oedipus Rex (1967), 155
Olds, Virginia, 86

Oliver, Gordon, 110
Olivier, Laurence, 82–83, 85, 90, 142, 145, 172, 175, 178, **179**, 201, 203
Only One Night (1939), 35, **37**
On the Sunny Side (1936), 35
Ophüls, Max, 157
Orsatti, Frank, 242n16
O'Shea, Daniel, xi, 7, 84–86, 105, 130, 134, 158

Page, Patti, 188, 265n97
Pal Joey (1957), 244n43
Paper Man, The (1963), 155
Paradine Case, The (1947), 12, 133, 145–52, 155–58, 162–64, 174, 203
Parnell (1937), 84
Parsons, Louella, 126, 168–69, 204
Pasolini, Pier Paolo, 155
Payne, John, 99, 202
Pearson, Beatrice, 76
Peck, Gregory, 3–5, 10, 12, 14, 18, 69, 84, 88, 91, 95–102, **96, 98**, 108–9, 111, 145, 156, 164, 168–69, 172, 196, 198–200, **200**, 203, 205, 207, 244n51, 245n56, 245n69, 247n109
Pépé le Moko (1937), 231n60
Perlberg, William, 67, 73–75
Piccioni, Pier, 155
Pickford, Mary, 248n3, 266n10
Pilot #5 (1943), 93
Pin Up Girl (1944), 202, 205, 207
Place in the Sun, A (1951), 180, 184
Platte, Nathan, 4
Pollyanna (1920), 248n3
Poor Little Rich Girl (1936), 248n3
Portrait of Jennie (1948), 12, 133, 163, 168, 170, 172, 174, 252n95
Powell, Michael, 142, 172, 182, 263–64n73
Powell, William, 3, 6–7, 25, 261n37
Power, Tyrone, 83, 99, 101, 160, 202
Preminger, Otto, 162
Pressburger, Emeric, 142, 182, 263–64n73
Prisoner of Zenda, The (1937), 9, 82, 157, 194
Pryor, Thomas M., 99
Pygmalion (1938), 43, 230n40

Queen Christina (1933), 42
Quinn, Anthony, 143

Quo Vadis (1951), 180

Radner, Hilary, 156
Rage in Heaven (1941), 55
Raiden, Ed, 54
Random Harvest (1942), 82, 86
Rank, Arthur J., 142–43, 145, 164
Rapf, Harry, 6
Ratoff, Gregory, 28–29
Reagan, Ronald, 132
Rebecca (1940), 5, 10, 24, 35, 51–52, 55–56, 75, 82, 107, 145, 157, 177, 194–95, 198, 201, 203, 206
Rebecca of Sunnybrook Farm (1938), 248n3
Redelings, Lowell E., 180
Red River (1948), 184
Red Shoes, The (1948), 142, 178, 182
Reed, Carol, 12
Reissar, Jenia, 25, 140, 144, 146, 155, 200, 264n82
Rennahan, Ray, 203
Reville, Alma, 145
Reward Unlimited (1944), 239n83
Roberts, Randy, 83
Roberts, Ruth, 28
Robinson, Casey, 97–99
Rockwell, Norman, 77
Rogers, Ginger, 11, 27, 84–85, 108, 123, 125
Rogers, Roy, 83, 239n89
Roman Holiday (1953), 188
Romeo and Juliet (1936), 43
Rooney, Mickey, 199
Roosevelt, Franklin Delano, 127
Ross, Robert, 95, 160
Rossellini, Roberto, 19, 21, 49, 142–44, 183, 188
Rosson, Harold, 65
Rosten, Leo C., 191
Ruby Gentry (1952), 170, 266n111
Rudolph Valentino and His 88 American Beauties (1923), 6
Russell, Jane, 153

Samson and Delilah (1949), 260n32
Saratoga Trunk (1945), 49, 86, 238n60
Saroyan, William, 74, 244n41
Schary, Dore, 11, 108, 123, 131

Schatz, Thomas, 4, 11, 13, 15, 83, 143, 189
Schulberg, B. P., 6
Selznick, David O.: adaptations, 7, 9, 13, 145, 172, 197–98; awards, x–xi, 10–11, 51–52, 54, 80–81, 171, 193–95, 199; career overview, 5–13; company brand, 11, 193–207; company problems, 113, 133–34, 145, 157, 160–65, 189–91; coproductions, 12, 140–41, 144, 154–55, 181–89; David O. Selznick Productions, 4, 10; internationalization, 18, 139–65; literature on, 4–5; male stars, 82–111; screen tests, ix, 7, 16, 25–28, 35, 59, 65–68, 75–76, 92, 95–97, 99, 102, 130, 146, 162, 177, 203, 242n18, 244n51; as screenwriter, xi, 6, 115, 117, 120, 146, 169, 177, 203; Selznick International Pictures, 3, 7, 25–26, 84, 140, 143, 195; Selznick Releasing Corporation, 11, 133; star discoveries, 3–4, 200–201; star loanouts, 52–81, 173–81; star makeup, xi, 20, 23, 27, 34–35, 67, 123, 132, 175, 177; Vanguard Films, 4, 11, 108, 116, 129–31, 144, 146
Selznick, Howard, 225n18
Selznick, Lewis J., 6–7, 17, 53, 57
Selznick, Myron, 7, 242n16
Senso (1954), 155
Server, Lee, 110
Shadow of a Doubt (1943), 102–5, 108, 198
Shanghai Express (1932), 151
Shaw, George Bernard, 85, 97
Shearer, Norma, 7
Shevelove, Burt, 159
She Went to the Races (1945), 90
Shoeshine (1946), 183
Sidney, George, 93
Siegel, M. J., 11
Siegel, Sol C., 126
Sieglohr, Ulrike, 160
Sinatra, Frank, 244n43
Since You Went Away (1944), 10, 77, 79–80, 105–10, 115–25, **118**, **121**, 128, 131–33, 136–38, 145, 166, 169–70, 177, 191, 195, 201, 203, 246n94, 248n12
Sinner, The (1951), 163
Sitting Pretty (1948), 135
Sjöberg, Alf, 144
Skouras, Spyros, 72

INDEX 287

Small, Paul, 158–59
Smit, David, 4, 21, 28, 34
Smith, Betty, 125
Smith, C. Aubrey, 203
Snows of Kilimanjaro, The (1952), 164
Song of Bernadette, The (1943), 52, 54–55, 63, 71–80, 112, 117, 166–67, 169–72, 191, 202, 206, 239n87, 241n113
Song of the Islands (1942), 202
Song to Remember, A (1945), 88
Spellbound (1945), 10, 49, 88, 99–100, 109, 151, 177, 199
Spider's Stratagem (1970), 155
Spiral Staircase, The (1945), 11, 70, 90
Springtime in the Rockies (1942), 202, 207
Staiger, Janet, 171
Stander, Lionel, xi
Stanislavski, Konstantin, 201
Stanwyck, Barbara, 63, 103
Star Is Born, A (1937), ix–xii, 9, 22, 82
State Secret (1950), 163
Sten, Anna, 39, 46, 149, 227n44
Sterritt, David, 201
Stevens, George, 180
Stevens, K. T., 103
Stevenson, Robert (director), 5, 52, 64, 253n4, 256n70
Stevenson, Robert (writer), 49
Stewart, James, 9, 24, 82–83, 99, 101
Stinnett, Jack, 47
Story of Seabiscuit, The (1949), 135
Story of the Count of Monte Cristo, The (1961), 160
Stradling, Harry, 28–30, 42, 230n40
Strasberg, Lee, 201, 267n27
Street of Chance (1930), 6
Stromberg, Hunt, 6, 103
Studlar, Gaylyn, 4, 172
Sullavan, Margaret, 65, 69
Suspiria (1977), 155
Swedenhielms (1935), 34, **36**
Sweet Rosie O'Grady (1943), 202

Tale of Two Cities, A (1935), 7, 194
Taylor, Robert, 83
Temple, George, 115–16

Temple, Gertrude, 115–16, 125
Temple, Shirley, 3–5, 10, 18, 52–53, 79, 81, 105, 112–38, **114**, **118**, **121**, **124**, 143, 153, 157–58, 199, 203–5, 241n124, 248n3, 249n22, 252n86, 252n95, 252–53n97
Terminal Station (1953), 144, 167, 181–89, **187**, 264–65n87, 265n91
Thalberg, Irving, 6–7
That Hagen Girl (1947), 131–33
That Hamilton Woman (1941), 235n12
Thaxter, Phyllis, 66
Third Man, The (1949), 12, 109, 144, 153–55, 182
This Above All (1942), 198
This Is the Army (1943), 62
Thomson, David, 4, 183–85, 191
Thorp, Margaret, 41
Thousands Cheer (1943), **94**
Three Coins in the Fountain (1954), 188
Three Smart Girls (1936), 104
Three Smart Girls Grow Up (1939), 104
Tierney, Gene, 75, 191
Till the End of Time (1946), 11, 70, 110
Todd, Ann, 145, 203, 233n83
Tokyo Joe (1949), 162, 258n123
Toland, Gregg, 29–31, 34–35, 44, 65–66, 230n42, 231n50
Tom, Dick and Harry (1941), 85
Tone, Franchot, 93
Tracy, Spencer, 55, 93, 105
Tree Grows in Brooklyn, A (1945), 70, 125
Turner, Lana, 234n106, 261n35
Twain, Mark, 158

Umberto D. (1952), 184
Unsuspected, The (1946), 90

Valentino, Rudolph, 6, 156
Vallee, Rudy, 152
Valley of Decision, The (1945), 99–100, 109
Valli, Alida, 3–4, 12, 18, 139–40, 144–57, **147**, **150**, 162, 164–65, 200, 203, 255n44, 255n52, 256n65, 256n68
Vickers, Martha, 5, 224n16
Vidor, Charles, 13, 190
Vidor, King, 172

Vincent, Frank, 242n16

Visconti, Luchino, 155

Viva Villa! (1934), 7

Walker, Phylis. *See* Jones, Jennifer

Walker, Robert, 10, 72, 117, 120, 166, 184, 203, 241n117

Walk Softly, Stranger (1950), 153

Wallace, Richard, 136

Wallis, Hal B., 260n26

Walpurgis Night (1935), 34, **36**

Walters, Charles, 94

Wanger, Walter, 170, 231n60

Warner, Jack, 163

Waterloo Bridge (1940), 235n12

Wayne, John, 72, 134, 156, 199, 261n37

Webb, Clifton, 135

Webb, Mary, 182

Welles, Orson, 101–2, 143, 154, 242n18

Wellman, William, x–xi, 6

Werfel, Franz, 52, 72–73, 172, 239n92

Westmore, Wally, 177

We Were Strangers (1949), 170–71, 174, 266n111

What Price Hollywood? (1932), x–xi, 223n11

White Cliffs of Dover, The (1944), 86–90, 108

White Tower, The (1950), 153

Whitney, John Hay, 7, 44, 113, 225n20

Wilde, Cornel, 88

Wild Heart, The. See Gone to Earth

Williams, Esther, 150

Willson, Henry, 88, 132–33, 207

Wilson, Steve, 24

Winters, Shelley, 180

Wizard of Oz, The (1939), 115, 233n92

Woman's Face, A (1938), 231n52

Woman's Face, A (1941), 231n52

Wood, Robin, 47, 157

Wood, Sam, 58–59, 203, 238n60

Woolley, Monty, 10, 120, 201, 203

Wright, Teresa, 76, 191

Wuthering Heights (1939), 28–29, 231n50

Wyler, William, 28, 170, 172–81, 230n39, 261n35

Yank in the R. A. F., A (1941), 202

Young, Loretta, 25

Young, Robert, 68, 90, 104

Young, Roland, 24

Young in Heart, The (1938), 9, 24–25, 95

Young People (1940), 115

Zanuck, Darryl F., 73–74, 103, 160

Zavattini, Cesare, 184, 186

Zorina, Vera, 59–61, 75, 237n41, 237n52

ABOUT THE AUTHOR

Milan Hain, PhD, is assistant professor and area head of film studies at Palacký University in Olomouc, Czech Republic. His areas of interest include classical Hollywood cinema, star studies, film noir, and exile film. He is the author or coauthor of five books on cinema, including, most recently, *V tradici kvality a prestiže: David O. Selznick a výroba hvězd v Hollywoodu 40. a 50. let* (*In the Tradition of Quality and Prestige: David O. Selznick and the Production of Stars in Hollywood of the 1940s and 50s*, Casablanca, 2021). His articles have appeared, among others, in *Jewish Film and New Media*, the *Journal of Adaptation in Film and Performance*, and the *Quarterly Review of Film and Video*. In 2011 and 2012, he was a Fulbright Visiting Researcher at the University of California, Santa Barbara. Recently, he has become the recipient of the Visiting Research Fellowship at the University of Łódź, where he researches the representation of Czech and Polish identities in studio-era Hollywood. Since 2013, he has been a programmer at the annual Noir Film Festival, the only event of its kind in Central Europe. His personal website can be found at http://www.milanhain.cz/. He lives with his wife and two sons in Olomouc.